Point Park Junior College
Wood St. and Blvd. of Allies
Pittsburgh, Pa. 15222

Contributors

Ruth Benedict (EDITED BY Dr. Margaret Mead, AMERICAN MUSEUM OF NATURAL HISTORY)

J. O. Brew, HARVARD UNIVERSITY

V. Gordon Childe, UNIVERSITY OF LONDON, ENGLAND

L. S. Cressman, UNIVERSITY OF OREGON

Mary Douglas, UNIVERSITY COLLEGE, LONDON, ENGLAND

Daryll Forde, UNIVERSITY COLLEGE, LONDON, ENGLAND

James B. Griffin, UNIVERSITY OF MICHIGAN

E. Adamson Hoebel, UNIVERSITY OF MINNESOTA

Harry Hoijer, UNIVERSITY OF CALIFORNIA, LOS ANGELES

Claude Lévi-Strauss, UNIVERSITY OF PARIS, FRANCE

R. Godfrey Lienhardt, UNIVERSITY OF OXFORD, ENGLAND

David G. Mandelbaum, UNIVERSITY OF CALIFORNIA, BERKELEY

H. L. Movius, Jr., HARVARD UNIVERSITY

George Peter Murdock, YALE UNIVERSITY

Robert Redfield, UNIVERSITY OF CHICAGO

Harry L. Shapiro, AMERICAN MUSEUM OF NATURAL HISTORY

Leslie Spier, UNIVERSITY OF NEW MEXICO

Man, Culture, and Society

Edited by HARRY L. SHAPIRO

A GALAXY BOOK

New York / OXFORD UNIVERSITY PRESS

1960

© Oxford University Press, Inc., 1956
Library of Congress Catalogue Card Number: 56-5429
First Published, 1956

First Published as a Galaxy Book, with additions and corrections, 1960

Twelfth printing, 1965

IT IS CUSTOMARY for the editor of a book to delay its prospective readers by telling them something of what they are about to read. It seemed to me that the chapters of this book spoke more eloquently of the ideas they contain than I could do for them. But as its editor, charged with a certain responsibility, I owe the readers some explanation of its purpose and the authors some protection from unjustified criticism. I begin, therefore, by completely absolving my colleagues in this venture of any share in such defects as may exist in the over-all planning—but not of the content and form of their own chapters. There are limits beyond which even a willing editor should not be expected to go. Within the frame that was set for them, the authors wrote as they wished.

My original intent—I think I have kept to it throughout the vicissitudes of the book—was to present a kind of basic anthropology for the general reader and for those who were being introduced to the subject for the first time. The coverage for each chapter was consequently chosen with this in mind. In a subject as diversified as anthropology, with its enormous array of detail, one volume can hope to do little more than present salient ideas and concepts. Even certain developments like the study of personality and culture, and national character, which are currently occupying the thoughts of many anthropologists, had to be curtailed or omitted to avoid undue bulk. I have, however, comforted myself for these omissions on the score that an introductory book should confine itself to the fundamentals, just as the properly constructed curriculum begins at the beginning. This seemed to me a useful, not to say a necessary, function and one that might provide an insight into what anthropology is about.

These chapters in their original version were designed to be independent units dispersed among other scientific topics in an ambitious project covering all science. This undertaking lapsed, but the chapters on anthropology survived and, thanks to the encouragement of the Oxford University Press, are now appearing as a book. The authors with exemplary good will took back their chapters, revised, or even rewrote, them, and accepted in most cases the editor's restrained suggestions for fitting them into their new guise. Three new contributors were invited to fill in areas that the new form required.

The few instances of overlapping between chapters can be attributed to this history. In most cases they were finally allowed to remain since they either served a purpose in the concept of the chapter as such or because the repetition in another context had a certain value which it seemed desirable to preserve.

Most introductory books of this kind are written by one author. The multi-authored ones are generally highly specialized and technical compendia or treatises. Anthropology, however, has become so diversified that few of its professionals attempt any longer to do research in all its phases or even to be proficient in them. Consequently a single author in treating all the branches of the subject is bound to be dependent on secondary materials. Sometimes this method has been employed brilliantly. The fact remains, however, that the authority that comes from an expert writing in his own specialty is sacrificed in that procedure. I have hoped, in this instance, by inviting scholars to write in their own competencies and according to a predetermined plan that I might achieve authority without sacrificing structural unity.

The language used throughout was kept deliberately as nontechnical as the subject permitted. It is my hope that any reasonably educated person will be able to read the book with understanding—and perhaps with pleasure and profit.

I owe many debts incurred during the protracted preparation of this book. The various writers have borne with delays, queries from me, revisions, and other vexatious details—all with exemplary patience and cooperation. I thank them one and all. To Mr. Charles E. Pettee of the Oxford University Press I am deeply indebted—no one but he knows how much. Mr. John Begg of the Oxford University Press has been most helpful in the design and illustration of the book. I am also grateful to Miss

Leona Capeless, also of the Oxford staff, for her editorial wisdom and very helpful suggestions. And I am deeply obliged to Mrs. Jane Orttung for her help in finding suitable illustrations. To my wife I dedicate whatever labor I have put into the book. She has been a constant source of encouragement.

HARRY L. SHAPIRO

January 1956

CONTENTS

I

Human Beginnings

ABOUT A MILLION YEARS AGO—at the beginning of the Pleistocene Period—
the curtain rose on man; not on man as we know him today: big brained,
small jawed, and frequently balding, but on a creature with a small brain,
a massive mandible, and trailing in many parts of his anatomy evidences
of his recent emergence from the world of apes. This estimate of man's
antiquity is, of course, an inference drawn from an archaeological record
extending deep into the Pleistocene. It is inferred from the existence halfway through the Pleistocene of *Pithecanthropus* and his allies who had
already by that time reached a point far beyond the initial stages of
human evolution. It is suggested by the discovery in South Africa of a
variety of manlike fossils collectively known as *Australopithecinae* and
dated in the earlier part of the Pleistocene. And quite recently this
inference has been further strengthened by Dr. L. S. B. Leakey's finding
Zinjanthropus and pre-*Zinjanthropus* in the Olduvai Gorge at the very
beginning of the Pleistocene of East Africa. These earliest fossils, whose
precise relationship to man is still not generally agreed upon by the
experts, were nevertheless upright creatures with many traits suggestive
of man. If they are not man's direct ancestors, they could not have been
very different from them. And they prove that in South Africa at least a
million years ago evolution did produce a creature remarkably close to
the dividing line between man and the apes.[1] The estimate of a million

---

[1] I have not cited here the Kanam jaw as additional evidence on the antiquity of
man since some doubt still remains as to its geological age. If this fossil proves to be
of early Pleistocene age, as is now claimed for it, man would not be just appearing at
that time but would have already reached a morphologic stage close to that of recent
man. This would push his beginnings far back into the Pliocene and make it necessary, moreover, to assume that for a million years at least one line of human evolution underwent virtually no change while another, or others, were undergoing the
profound and successive modifications that the bulk of hominid fossils reveal.

years is still rather tentative. Although the recently announced date of 1,750,000 years for pre-*Zinjanthropus*, based on the potassium-argon technique, would greatly extend the time span since the first appearance of a manlike primate, it has been seriously questioned by competent authority, and until more evidence for chronological readjustments becomes available, a million years more or less seems to fit most of the data.

To our minds, conditioned by a historical perspective that represents Greece and Rome as the ancient world, a million years seem an unconscionably long time. Actually in relation to the age of our planet and to the length of time that life has existed here, man is a johnny-come-lately. In the time-honored analogy of the clock, if the twenty-four hours of the day be taken as equivalent to the lapse of time since the beginning of life on earth, then man would have to be shown as appearing only within the last minute and our own type, *Homo sapiens,* within the last few seconds of the twenty-four hours. But if man's sojourn on earth by this comparison seems short, it has been long enough to produce far-reaching changes of an order unique in evolution.

There have been a number of attempts to identify the specifically human characteristics of man. He has been set apart from the other animals by his upright posture and highly developed brain. He has been distinguished as the creature that laughs, speaks, or thinks. He has also been described as the creature that has a culture. These attributes are all true, some at least in degree, but perhaps the fundamental fact that makes most of them possible and certainly sustains all of them is the technology that has become so much a part of man that it is virtually impossible to conceive of him without it. The simple ability to use tools is perhaps not a completely exclusive faculty of man. Apes are known to use sticks or boxes to attain a goal. But no other animal has employed tools so persistently as even primitive man has done, and it is only among man's closest primate relatives that anything like this propensity appears. But man not only uses stray objects as tools—as extensions of his arms and hands—but he makes them artfully and, in the course of human evolution, with increasing skill and variety. The purposeful chipping of a crude fist axe of the Lower Paleolithic, or even of the simpler pebble tool, is already far beyond the demonstrable capacity of any animal including the apes. And no other animal except man has shown the slightest ability to build on past achievement and to develop the accumulation of technology that culture and civilization represent.

We know virtually nothing about the precise way by which this tool-using and tool-making propensity of man became an established attribute of his. But we can be sure that without it his evolution as we know it could not have occurred. For it is on the basis of this ability to make tools that culture and society are constructed. And culture in turn has provided the milieu that more and more mediates raw nature as it affects man and thereby his evolution.

We do know, however, that man through the peculiar circumstances of his evolution inherited anatomical adaptations that made it possible for him to make and use tools. He inherited intact a remarkably generalized hand to which had been added the ability of grasping objects. He acquired apparently at the very outset of his career an ability to walk on his legs, freeing his arms and hands from the responsibilities of locomotion and thus releasing them for other functions. He possessed a brain already larger than any other primate's and by inference more advanced. One cannot overstress the potentiality of these characteristics in making it possible for man to create for himself the tools and eventually the cultures which must have affected profoundly the continued evolution that transformed an ape-like hominid into modern man.

The hand that we have inherited is in certain respects a primitive organ. Compared with the hoofs, pads, and paws of various other mammals the human hand—indeed the primate hand—has retained much of its original structure with a minimum of change. It has long been agreed that it was the arboreal adaptation of the primates that provided the means of preserving this structure which in ground living animals underwent such a variety of modifications, all of them sacrificing in greater or lesser degree that basic pattern. The necessity, in moving about in the trees, for grasping, for reaching, for holding branches—in short for using the hand and foot in the most flexible manner possible—made the ancient five-fingered hand a valuable mechanism. Its adaptation for such purposes was enhanced by the acquisition of the ability of opposing the thumb to the other fingers, thus permitting a true grasp. This highly adaptable hand with its opposable thumb has in certain primates undergone some deviations through response to specialized types of locomotion, but it has on the whole remained astonishingly intact. That timing had something to do with its preservation becomes obvious when we see the quite different kind of adaptation that became necessary when other mammals took to an arboreal career at later stages in their evolution after a compromise with ground living had deprived them of some degree of its original structure. Animals that use claws often make extremely adept arborealists, but they have for better or worse lost that supreme instrument, the hand.

Among the primates the hand has been used in a variety of ways to aid locomotion. Wherever grasping is an important adjunct the opposable thumb remains intact. Among the largest primates—the simians—a form of locomotion developed whereby the body was swung from hands used rather more like hooks than as reaching and grasping organs. This type of locomotion, known as brachiation, requires less of the thumb and we find, generally speaking, that the anthropoid apes have degenerate or reduced ones. This has suggested to some students of human evolution that the hominid or human line could hardly have emerged from a well-developed form of brachiating anthropoid ape.

The human hand, although a heritage of adaptation to arboreal life, is also admirably fitted for other functions that could not have been anticipated of primitive primates living in trees. In this the hand is like a number of other parts that have appeared in the course of evolution. Although in a sense designed to serve a specific function, the hand retained and acquired so great a range of potentiality that its possessors could make use of it in another context, thereby opening new possibilities of livelihood and even of evolution. Man had in the hand the means of making, holding, and using tools, which as I have previously suggested may be regarded as the trigger for further evolution.

But the hand could scarcely have acquired these new functions until it was released from its old ones. This occurred when man's ancestors adopted a new form of locomotion. It is again necessary to turn to the arboreal world of the primates to understand how man acquired his unique posture. Man is not, of course, the only animal that appears to be erect or that can rear up on its hind limbs. The kangaroo holds its body erect much of the time and even the trained dog can raise itself to mince on its hind legs, but these postures do not entail the full extension of the legs on the trunk. Nor can they be maintained for long or without subsidiary support. The kangaroo stiffens his tail to make, along with his hind legs, a sort of tripod for support as the so-called bipedal dinosaurs also did many millions of years before. Although arboreal life allowed the primates a variety of locomotion: crawling, hopping, leaping, running, and brachiating, all of them required some adaptation to semi-erect posture. For these animals committed to a grasping hand, locomotion in the trees meant moving in a vertical direction as often as in any other. Thus, whether leaper, hopper, or crawler, the primate that climbed up a tree went up head first with the body in an upright position, with the weight of the entire body supported by the hind limbs. It is significant that the foot of the primate, although frequently very hand-like in conformation and even in its grasping ability, is always more rigidly constructed and reveals greater adaptation for supporting the weight of the body than the hand ever does. Thus some degree of specialization of the hind limbs for weight support and a semi-erect posture appeared early among the primates and remained characteristic throughout their history except for those that abandoned arboreal life and assumed a pronograde gait on the ground. When and how this primate adjustment to partially upright posture became converted into a fully erect one is still obscure.

It has been said that brachiation by suspending the body from the arms maintains it habitually in what amounts to an upright posture and thus might have served as the introductory phase of upright locomotion on the ground. There are, however, some difficulties in this hypothesis. Some accomplished brachiators like the chimpanzees do not walk fully erect but use their arms as ever ready additional supports. The gorilla, who of all the anthropoid apes is most given to ground living, also uses his arms as he lumbers about with his body in a 45 degree angle to the ground. Indeed, it is even claimed that it is precisely because the gorilla is a reformed brachiator that he must use this incompletely erect position since his over-developed arms and upper torso have shifted his center of gravity so far forward that the fully upright posture would be foreign to his anatomy. Thus those who claim that brachiation could hardly serve to pre-form the body for fully erect ground locomotion refer the transition to an earlier stage of primate evolution. Strauss has suggested a cercopithecid (Old World monkey) stage, but it might be mentioned that the living cercopithecids that did take to the ground became pronograde animals. The baboons run around quite handily, but with their bodies in a horizontal position. The truth may well be between these two views and that man's ancestors took to the ground when the simian radiation from a cercopithecid stock was taking place and some degree of brachiation had been adopted but not yet so developed as to block the use of a completely erect posture with the body at a 90 degree angle to the ground and the legs fully extended.

It is, of course, difficult to know with precision what it was that induced our primate ancestor to take to life on the ground. Whether it was his increasing size, together with an already existing ability to stand upright, that forced him gradually to give up what must have been an increasing struggle with gravity can only be inferred, or, as some have surmised, the consequence of a change in the environment that destroyed his arboreal milieu. But once on the ground and eventually fully adapted to upright locomotion, his range became enormously widened, eventually to embrace the whole world.

The third of the triad of gifts that have in part been responsible for man's evolution from its primate beginnings is a highly endowed brain. It is also the organ about whose evolution we know least. We can study its outer form and to some extent the proportions of its parts for whatever light this may shed on the nature of its evolving powers. But unfortunately the fossil evidence for this is scanty and, even if it were fuller, it would be valuable only for the lack of anything better. We cannot, therefore, assert with confidence that man's ancestors took to ground living because of their burgeoning intellectual equipment. Nor do we know very much about the role of the brain in guiding the initial stages of the emancipation of the hand. As far as the fossil evidence goes, it suggests that upright posture and some use of the hand as a tool were well established before brain volume had increased very much. Man's ancestors, of course, in common with other primates already enjoyed the use of a highly developed brain that had evolved through arboreal adaptation. But the remarkable increase in size and presumably the powers of the hominid brain seem, however, to have occurred after upright posture had been adopted. It is a reasonable hypothesis in our present state of knowledge to assume that just as arboreal life had initially stimulated the growth of the cerebrum and its cortex in the infra-human primate, that living on the ground and the use of the hands for manipulative, explorative, and creative purposes furnished an additional stimulus that later led to the enormous increase of the brain and its intellectual capacity in man. This, in turn, would have enabled the hand to perform more and more elaborate functions and thus for man himself to begin the arduous business of accumulating a culture. Here we would have what amounts to a kind of feed-back—the brain and culture mutually affecting each other, with the hand, at least in early stages, mediating the process to a large extent. We would expect, if this hypothesis is correct, that a substantial increase in brain size would follow on the acquisition of a human-like posture and the rudiments of a culture. This reconstruction would explain why we do not find the Australopithecines and other early hominids strikingly different from the anthropoid apes as far as brain size is concerned, although their skeletal structure had gone a very long way toward the erect posture characteristic of man. Up to the time of the discovery of the early African fossils, the most primitive hominid known was *Pithecanthropus,* whose brain size was roughly intermediate between the apes and *Homo sapiens* and whose posture was erect. The general assumption was that we would find in the precursors of *Pithecanthropus,* leading back to the ultimate point of departure from the primate stem a gradual transition, *pari passu* in both brain size and in adaptation to erect posture. We can now see there was nothing inevitable in this kind of transition except what our sense of symmetry might perhaps have suggested.

The fossils, now grouped together as the Australopithecines, first came to light with the discovery of an immature skull in South Africa in 1925. This child, burdened with the name of *Australopithecus africanus,* was at first identified by many students as an ape, despite Dart's and Broom's insistence that it was something more—something much closer to the origins of hominids themselves. Although *Australopithecus* had a brain slightly larger than an ape child of the same age might have had and its dental characteristics were suggestive of man's, its appearance otherwise was remarkably ape-like. The subsequent finds of *Plesianthropus* and *Paranthropus* in the same part of Africa enriched our knowledge of this group of 'ape-men' but failed to dissipate the belief of many specialists that *Australopithecus* and his relatives were merely members of a group of apes that had evolved to a stage somewhat beyond other apes in the direction of man but still one that fell far short of this status and eventually came to naught. Perhaps much of this reluctance to attribute any more significance to these fossils was the consequence of a time-honored assumption that the dawn of hominid status would be heralded primarily by a brain appreciably larger than that any of the apes possessed. The Australopithecines up to this point did not seem especially noteworthy in that respect. Eventually as more and more fossils of this now quite extensive sub-family were excavated, bones of the skeleton began to appear and now there could be no doubt that upright posture was a settled characteristic of these creatures—a fact that certain cranial features had suggested.

Finds representing this important group are still being announced and we do not yet have complete or even adequate descriptions of a number of them. But it is clear that they embrace a considerable range of types and that they shed far more light on the origins of the hominids than was at first admitted. Even if we may have to decide that the Australopithecines represent an abortive effort toward the evolution of a man, they do indicate the manner in which our own ancestors achieved a foothold on the hominid ladder. Walking erect on the ground now appears to have been established very early, and very probably precedes any striking modification of the brain. In fact, I am inclined to believe that it was precisely this shift in locomotion, coupled with its consequences for the hand, that provided one of the factors in the evolution of the hominid brain. In the light of this, it is noteworthy that crude stone tools have recently been reported in association with these fossils, greatly strengthening the claim that technology had a more significant role in the transition to hominid status than was formerly admitted.

The dating of these fossils, as well as of many another, is difficult. One of the 'booby traps' in finding one's way about in this rather complicated field is the matter of chronology. Obviously it is of prime importance to know when a particular fossil flourished in time as well as in place, since sequential arrangement must be built on both, but particularly on time. If a fossil is inaccurately dated, it can thus lead to a variety of speculative conclusions all of which are likely to be wrong. Now, dating Pleistocene fossils is especially difficult at least in the parts of the world where most of the early material is being found. The guide posts provided by glacial debris or by glacial action that aid the student in northern latitudes are absent in South Africa or Java. Moreover, the generous margins of error that the paleontologist can permit himself in the perspective of millions of years becomes too great for comfort where the corridors of time serve for only a few hundreds of thousands of years. The paleontologist who can with equanimity give or take a million years in dating something about 70 million years old cannot be quite so open handed with the Pleistocene, the whole space of which is probably no more than one million years.

The morphologist must depend on the geologist in placing a fossil in relative if not absolute time. Unfortunately some fossils are found without any evidence of their age. Occasionally a veritable fossil is found by a skilled observer who is able to preserve all the data available. But even in these fortunate instances there is much room for interpretation. Caution, therefore, should be the watchword for dates that are eccentric or run counter to the weight of evidence from other finds.

As far as determining the age of the Australopithecines is concerned, we must rely primarily on their association with faunas of known date. This line of reasoning places them at the beginning of the Pleistocene, perhaps a million years ago. In July 1959 still another early hominid was reported by L. S. B. Leakey. Discovered in an early Pleistocene layer in the Olduvai Gorge of East Africa, associated with primitive stone tools and marked by special morphological features, it may prove to be a differentiated contemporary of the Australopithecines and entitled to retain its special designation, *Zinjanthropus Boisei*. Preliminary reports emphasize its sagittal crest, enormous mastoid and supramastoid development, and strong nuchal architecture. In all these features, as in others, it deviates from the Australopithecines. Although Leakey admits the general relationship of *Zinjanthropus* with the Australopithecines farther south, he is not prepared to go as far as Robinson, for example, in classifying this fossil as a mere variant of *Paranthropus*, one of the Australopithecine types. But whatever its final position may turn out to be, *Zinjanthropus* is highly significant in confirming the new concept of human evolution.

In the year following the discovery of *Zinjanthropus*, Leakey announced new finds in the rich strata of the Olduvai site. This time, there came to light an incomplete cranium from Bed II, a more recent layer than *Zinjanthropus'*, which Leakey has called Chellean man because of its association with Chellean tools. And in addition, fragmentary bones of an adult and a juvenile were discovered in Bed I, but at a lower level than the position of *Zinjanthropus*. These later fossils, currently known as pre-*Zinjanthropus*, are of special interest here. They are obviously earlier than *Zinjanthropus* in time and according to preliminary studies rather more advanced. The fragmentary parietal bone of the skull suggests a larger brain capacity than *Zinjanthropus* possessed, and in other features a lesser degree of specialization. Altogether, Leakey seems inclined to consider pre-*Zinjanthropus* as closer to the ancestral line of *Homo* than *Zinjanthropus* and his Australopithecine relatives.

It is highly significant that in the same level as the bones of pre-*Zinjanthropus*, stone artifacts of an extremely simple form were also brought to light. That these Oldowan pebble tools were used by pre-*Zinjanthropus* still remains uncertain, but in any case they establish the antiquity of the tradition of tool making and reinforce the association of this technology with the origins of man.

Around the middle of the Pleistocene we encounter a distinct advance in another cluster of fossils which we may by analogy refer to as the Pithecanthropines. These fossils found in Java take their name from the first one to be discovered—*Pithecanthropus erectus*. When it was discovered in 1891 by Eugene Dubois, a Dutch physician in the Netherlands Colonial Service in Java, *Pithecanthropus* was especially noteworthy. It was then merely a generation since Darwin's publication of *On the Origin of Species*. The concept of a human evolution from a primate stock had only recently acquired wide acceptance and the fossil evidence to support it was just beginning to come to light, or better, to be recognized. Up to that time the only pre-*Homo sapiens* type of hominid known was Neanderthal. The impact of *Pithecanthropus* was therefore enormous. The skull cap with its heavy bone buttress above the eyes and its flattened crown was obviously more primitive than any known man's. But at the same time it had a cranial volume estimated at around 900 cc., very distinctly above any known ape's. This increased size had brought about an increase in the height of the skull vault. Associated with the cranial fragment was a beautifully preserved femur which in almost every detail of its morphology agreed with the conformation of a modern femur and therefore indicated that *Pithecanthropus* walked upright. *Pithecanthropus* thus seemed to represent something approaching the 'missing link' between man and his anthropoid ape ancestor. This view we now know is an inadequate conception of the process of human evolution. Man did not evolve out of developed anthropoid apes. But he does have a common ancestry with them. Therefore as we go back in time to this point of departure, we find the human stem different from what it is today. Similarly our collaterals, the living apes, must have been different when we trace them backward in time. The 'missing link' therefore would not be a stage halfway between living man and living apes, but a form long since extinct that was common to both.

In this view, the Pithecanthropines would represent a stage in advance of the Australopithecines of South Africa who also predate them in time. Subsequent discoveries by von Koenigswald have provided us not only with another skull very similar to the type find, but also a

number of variants: *Pithecanthropus robustus* and *Meganthropus palaeo-
javanicus*. These more rugged and massive forms suggest that *Pithecanthropus erectus* himself represents a refined product of a line of development which at the least may be a local phenomenon or at most a reflection of a widespread progression.

Closely allied to the Pithecanthropines, particularly *Pithecanthropus
erectus* is the population represented by a series of skulls, isolated fragments thereof, teeth, and miscellaneous long bones found at Chou Kou
Tien, not far from Peiping in China. The first of the discoveries *in situ* of
Sinanthropus was made almost thirty years ago by Davidson Black. For
some years virtually each season yielded more material until work in
this fruitful area was closed down altogether by war. Recently the Chinese have once more resumed excavations. As far as one can count individuals from miscellaneous fragments, 40 or more were represented in
the total assemblage of fossils before they were lost at the beginning of
World War II. These ancient skulls from Chou Kou Tien are now believed to belong to the same genus as *Pithecanthropus;* their differences
being regarded as no more than might occur between species. These
differences, however they may finally be evaluated, all place *Sinanthropus* in advance of his Javanese relative. The former had a larger
brain—about 200 cc. more on the average, a distinctly more developed
forehead, a somewhat more refined cranial morphology, a less projecting
jaw, and a dentition a little closer to our own. Like *Pithecanthropus,
Sinanthropus* was adapted to upright locomotion—but not appreciably
more.

If any further evidence of *Sinanthropus'* claim to a hominid status were
required, their way of life would be ample. These people lived in caves,
the floors of which they littered with the skeletal debris of animals they
hunted and consumed. They used fire and employed stone tools of a
primitive kind. Any additional attributes of culture can only be inferred,
but it seems likely that people as advanced as this in technology must
have also had a language. But of its nature we cannot even guess.

The paramount fact, however, is that *Sinanthropus* is a hominid and
ancestral to recent man. His close relationship to *Pithecanthropus* also
lends validity to the latter's claim to a similar ancestral dignity. Together they demonstrate that already by the mid-Pleistocene, evolution
had carried the hominids a long way from a stage comparable to the

Australopithecines. The brain which in the earlier forms seemed to lag somewhat behind the rapidly evolving lower limbs is now catching up and is already more than twice the size of that of the apes. Moreover, the effects of erect posture and expanding brain are clearly visible in the reduction of the muzzle, the shortening of the dental arch, modification of the teeth, heightening of the vault of the skull, and the gradual emergence of the brow.

From roughly this point on, the traces of human evolution broaden out geographically as well as anatomically. Sequences have been found in various parts of Africa, in Europe, in Asia, and in Java that suggest an active adaptive radiation but may only reflect the greater abundance of fossils that now become available. In Java, for example, the eleven Solo skulls discovered by Ter Haar, Oppenoorth, and von Koenigswald and dated in the upper Pleistocene form together with the Wadjak skull a progression leading to a type now embodied in the Australian aboriginal. In Africa, the Rhodesian-Saldanha skulls occupy a position comparable to, but morphologically slightly in advance of, Solo man in Java. Contemporary with these, in some cases a little later in time, we find a wide variety of middle and late Stone Age fossils: Boskop, Florisbad, Fishhoek, and Springbok. Some students have linked the modern Bushman of South Africa to the Boskop of the Middle Stone Age and have distinguished still other lines of evolution.

Europe is equally rich in fossils of the same periods and of a comparable variety. The earliest is the Heidelberg jaw now referred to the first interglacial, or approximately 450,000 years ago.[2] This is a massive jaw typically without a chin as is expected for this period and morphology. Its teeth are, however, unequivocally human. Compared, however, with *Meganthropus* (the most primitive of the Pithecanthropine series), it is distinctly smaller and more advanced.

The next well-documented fossil that appears in Europe is placed in the second interglacial (250,000 years ago). This is the Swanscombe skull which, as far as its incomplete condition permits a final opinion, seems to be an early form of *Homo sapiens*.[3] Except for its unusual thickness of bone, it can easily be placed within the range of variation

---

[2] Zeuner, *Dating the Past*, Longmans, Green & Co., New York, 1952.

[3] Clark Howell has recently suggested that Swanscombe belongs to a progressive Neanderthal phase.

normal for recent populations. In the Fontechevade skull found in France in the succeeding interglacial (approximately 125,000 years ago), we encounter another sapiens type. Its relationship, however, to the Swanscombe skull is not yet determined. In addition to these two early sapiens types, there have been other claimants to a similar position: Galley Hill, Bury St. Edmunds, et cetera, but these fossils have either been shown to be later in age than was thought at first or their geological associations are too indeterminate to yield reliable dates.

The next fossils, chronologically speaking, are attributable to the Neanderthal type and are associated principally with the final glaciation, although some of the more advanced types have been found in the period immediately preceding. From first to last a large number of them have been unearthed in various parts of Europe, North Africa, and nether Asia. Some of the better known ones, named usually after their sites, are Ehringsdorf, Steinheim, Gibraltar, La Chapelle aux Saints, Le Moustier, Monte Circeo, Saccopastore, Spy, and the Mount Carmel skulls. The so-called 'classic' Neanderthal type has a heavily constructed skull, with a large projecting horizontal ridge of bone between the eye sockets and the forehead, another bony ridge stretching horizontally across the occiput, a massive but not especially prognathic face, a mandible still lacking a chin, a cranial vault fully as large as in modern man but of a form still reminiscent of the more primitive *Pithecanthropus* and *Sinanthropus*. In the hafting of the skull to the vertebral column and in other morphological details, it is evident that these Neanderthal specimens were not as completely adapted to upright posture as might have been expected with so long a history of erect posture behind them.

Curiously, these classic Neanderthal skulls seem to be clustered at the earlier stages of the last glaciation and are thus later in time than the 'progressive' Neanderthal types like Ehringsdorf that appear in the preceding interglacial period and are morphologically far less primitive. We are thus confronted with the puzzling fact that more modern types of men and more advanced kinds of Neaderthalers are both to be found earlier than the 'classic' Neanderthal fossils. Various speculations have been advanced to account for this apparent lack of an undeviating line of evolution. Some authorities have dismissed the 'classic' Neanderthal group altogether from the ancestry of *Homo sapiens*, regarding it as a special line of evolution that eventually came to naught. Others have

argued that it is in the direct ascent to modern man and became transformed in a manner and with a rapidity not clearly set forth. A recent
effort[4] at reconciling these refractory morphological and chronological
discrepancies suggests that Swanscombe and Fontechavade belong with
the 'progressive' Neanderthalers giving rise to modern man and that the
'classic' but more primitive forms represent a group cut off from the
main line of evolution by the geographic extension of the last glaciation.
The linking, however, of Swanscombe, dated as far back as the second
interglacial, with 'progressive' Neanderthal types appearing much later
in time poses certain problems of a morphological nature. In certain
respects Swanscombe already suggests a *Homo sapiens* configuration and
lacks the features that ideally might be expected to characterize a pre-
cursor of the 'progressive' Neanderthal man.

With the end of the last glaciation, Europe and indeed other parts of
the world as well were inhabited by populations that must be classified
as *Homo sapiens*, and as far as we know by no others. Thus we can say
that beginning around 30-40,000 years ago modern man took over completely and all preceding and/or ancestral types had disappeared. It is
not yet certain, however, that this was the first appearance of *Homo
sapiens*. Although one line of interpretation claims just this, another
school of thought gives modern man a far greater antiquity. Indeed this
school is divisible into a number of sects, an extreme one carrying *Homo
sapiens* to the Lower Pleistocene, where he would be virtually a contemporary of the ape-man of South Africa and a predecessor of the
Pithecanthropine group. This opinion is based primarily on the finds at
Kanam and Kanjera in Kenya, Africa, where Leakey uncovered fragments of human crania morphologically quite modern in appearance.
In fact, the Kanam mandible possesses a distinct chin, a feature that is
absent in all other forms of early man. Although the geology as interpreted by Leakey suggests an early Pleistocene date, there are several
difficulties here that make this interpretation hard to accept at face value.
In the first place, the geology of the site is especially difficult. Caution is
not out of place when its reading creates so many discrepancies. To place
a modern type of man early in the Pleistocene must necessarily push
back man's antecedent evolution deep into the Pliocene where we have

[4] F. Clark Howell. American Journal of Physical Anthropology, new series, Vol. 9,
No. 4, 1951.

no evidence of an emerging hominid development. Moreover, Kanam and Kanjera run counter to the prevailing morphological trends of the bulk of hominid fossils. And finally, to conceive of evolution as having achieved a modern type of man 500,000 or more years ago and then to have left him to continue virtually unchanged from then on is perhaps not an impossibility but is certainly improbable.

A more moderate view of the emergence of *Homo sapiens* traces its rise from the Swanscombe skull of the Middle Pleistocene and carries it on through the Fontechevade fragments attributed to the last interglacial. This reconstruction of the course of human evolution would then be obliged to account for the widespread occurrence of Neanderthal man in the last glacial advance and the re-emergence of *Homo sapiens* immediately after as a kind of migratory seesaw with *Homo sapiens* retreating before the onset of an arctic ecology and advancing with its amelioration. It is evident from this brief summary of the fossil record of the course of hominid evolution that the recent and welcome crop of new discoveries has illuminated certain hitherto obscure aspects of the story but has at the same time created new problems that have not yet been fully resolved.

It is altogether possible, not to say likely, that in the long course of human evolution some racial differentiation had occurred quite early. How far this process had gone, when it occurred, and how much of it has survived in the living races of man are questions difficult to answer. We can be quite sure that the hominids shared with other forms of life a tendency to vary. Consequently we might expect that given the proper conditions of isolation early man must have exhibited some degree of racial differentiation. This seems the more probable when we consider the wide geographic range of the early hominids and the necessity of their living in relatively small bands, circumstances ordinarily regarded as favorable for racial differentiation. On morphological grounds, Weidenreich has proposed more systematically than I am suggesting that the modern races of man were already forming early in human evolution and pursuing in specific geographic areas somewhat independent courses. To pursue his conception of the origin of human races would take us beyond the point I am making, namely, that the tendency to differentiate is inherent and expresses itself whenever it can. The more conventional view has long been that the living races first appeared with the dominance and spread of *Homo sapiens* at the beginning of the Upper Paleolithic which in Europe may be dated at about 25,000 years ago. Although we know relatively little about the rapidity with which human races may develop, this amount of time seems far too limited to produce the degree of differentiation we find today. Until, however, more fossil evidence is available, the solution to this problem will continue to be debatable.

The process, however, by which races have emerged is less uncertain, thanks to the researches of population geneticists. Their formulations drawn from the study of natural populations of insects, birds, and animals, from experimental conditions, and from genetic theory have contributed to our understanding of the dynamics of human race differentiation. This is possible because human genetics is fundamentally identifiable in principle with the genetics of all other forms of organic life.

When we think of race, we think in terms of groups of people, of populations the members of which share a common heredity but do not necessarily possess a common genotype. This is necessarily so because no two people, with the possible exception of identical twins, are ever exactly alike genetically. Consequently if every inheritable physical difference were given racial value, we would end up with virtually as many races as there are individuals. Race, then, is a classificatory device to deal with generalized *patterns* of inherited variations occurring within a species and maintained in existence by a population. Another way of saying this would be that race is the resultant of differences in gene frequencies. Differences between populations that are not inherited should play no part in such a system, contrary to widespread notions. Religion, language, customs, manners, values, and many other characteristics commonly confused with race differences are learned attributes and acquired during an individual's lifetime through exposure to social and cultural conditioning. The only legitimate criteria of race are those that are carried in the germ plasm and passed on from parents to child through physical inheritance. Since this is so, it follows that with every mating one individual draws from the population of which he is a member another individual whose genetic composition like his own is the resultant of a long history of matings within the population. If this is a random or unstructured process, their offspring then would represent a chance combination of the genetic potentialities contained within the population. And since the offspring, generation after generation, will continue to combine in a random fashion, we may conceive of the population as the stable continuing entity and the individuals that comprise

it as merely ephemeral and chance genetic expressions that the population is capable of producing. Thus the combined genes of all the breeding members of the population form what is known as a gene pool. For
some characters the genes may actually be estimated and their frequencies expressed in proportion to the whole.

Such a population is never uniform, in part because the environment
of the individual members of the population may vary and to some degree affect the development of a trait but also because the gene pool is
never homogeneous. This variety in the gene pool may arise from mutation or from other causes, but its existence produces some degree of
heterogeneity in the components of a population—the *polymorphism* of
the zoologist. The notion that the races of man were once homogeneous
gains no support from this. In all probability human populations were
always polymorphic.

Given such a population structure, how do racial differences become
established? The answer to this depends on the interaction of several
factors. If we keep in mind that any population's gene pool tends to vary,
and as far as we know all of them have or there would be no evolution,
we may discover here the *origin* of the differences. Thus if a population
becomes separated into two or more groups that are unable to share each
other's gene pool, each one will tend to develop independent genetic
changes. And whatever accumulation of genetic change occurs in one
will remain in that population and will not be shared with the others. In
other words, the gene flow which distributes genetic modification in one
population to others by intermixture is interrupted and the initial stages
in differentiation are achieved. The degree of differentiation that now
develops becomes a function, or effect, of the rate of mutation, or genetic
change, the adaptive advantage of such changes, the size of the group,
and the elapsed time during which isolation is maintained. The factors that produce isolation are numerous. The simplest and easiest to
perceive is geographic, where groups or populations are separated by
geographic barriers that reduce physical contact and consequently the
opportunity for miscegenation. In a hunting economy where the size of
a band is strictly limited in size by the difficulty of maintaining a large
group in efficient relationship to the hunting area, populations may be
widely spaced, separated by their peripheral hunting ranges and by the
hostility engendered by territorial rights. In animal populations slight
changes in breeding habits might effectively separate varieties that ac-

tually co-inhabit the same area. In man no such mechanism is known, but more subtle cultural or social structures have been thought to serve sometimes the same purpose. For example, a caste system by restricting to its own members the mating possibilities of one section of a population creates isolation for that section. Other social institutions or structures involving selectivity in mating might bring about comparable results. This is a subject that has been little investigated. It is, however, unlikely to be very significant in race differentiation since such systems do not last long enough to be very effective. The relatively frequent social reorganization characteristic of most cultures serves to break up any embryonic, or minor, distinctions that might be initiated by selective mating systems.

Although mutation is one of the principal sources of genetic distinction between populations, it is not the only one. Structural changes in the chromosomes that carry the genes may also contribute. Still another process common in human history has been suggested as highly significant. This may express itself, for example, when a daughter colony separates itself from the mother population and migrates to another region. If the migrating group is small, it may carry only a partial representation of the full complement of genes to be found in the original population. Or if all the variety of genes are present in the migrating group, their frequency percentages may differ. Such a consequence may be due to chance or even possibly the result of some selective influence, but in any case, the new population begins its corporate existence with a different gene pool from its parental one.

It is also conceivable that a disaster striking a small group might drastically cut down its numbers and thus alter the gene pool of the survivors. Such a group, when it recovered its former numerical strength, would consequently be genetically different from its prototype. The hazards to which small primitive groups were exposed were many. Warfare, famine, and epidemic must have struck frequently and devastatingly. One has only to recall the decimation created by the plagues of Medieval Europe, when as much as one-fourth of some populations perished, to realize how effective such events may be in altering the genic composition of a group. If susceptibility to disease were correlated with the genotype of an individual, the kind and extent of the destruction could profoundly affect the gene pool by selectively weeding out certain genes.

In addition to these possibilities of *originating* genetic differences between populations by the effect of chance alone or with overtones of selection, there is another mechanism in which chance is thought to play a principal role. This is commonly known as the Sewall Wright effect or random genetic drift. In certain circumstances it is supposed that random mating might account for the loss or fixation of a mutation. If the mutation rate is low and the size of the population small, the likelihood of loss by such a random process increases.

Reference was made previously to mutation as one of the principal sources of differentiation between populations. These genetic changes appear to occur in varying frequencies for different traits, but little is known about these rates in man. Nor do we know with assurance that the rate for a particular trait is the same in all human populations or different. The survival of these mutations is, however, differential, depending on the interaction of a number of processes.

The environment, too, affects the survival of a mutation. If a gene change produces a trait that is adaptive to a particular environment giving its possessor some degree of advantage in his reproductive rate, it is likely to survive and increase in frequency. This selective process reflects the manner in which a particular group becomes adjusted or adapted to its environmental niche and eventually emerges with features distinct from its related populations in other areas. Although stress used to be placed on non-adaptive features for purposes of racial classification, it is difficult to see how one can logically overlook or minimize the adaptive ones. I suspect that this distinction between adaptive and non-adaptive racial characters arose from the *apparent* lack of relationship between some characters and the environment. This, however, is a tricky distinction since ignorance of any connection is hardly warrant for its absence, especially since little systematic work in testing these relationships has been done. It has been suggested that even where a trait appears to be neutral, it may be affected by another trait that is more clearly adaptive. Despite a necessary caution in these judgments on the existence of non-adaptive traits, it would be equally unwarranted to deny out of hand that their occurrence was impossible. Until recently, for example, the abnormal sickle shape of the red blood corpuscles, which occurs widely among African populations, was considered neutral. New evidence brought forward by Allison [5] now suggests that it is asso-

[5] A. C. Allison. British Medical Journal, Feb. 6, 1954.

ciated with areas of endemic malaria and consequently its presence, at least in the heterozygous condition, is adaptive. On the other hand, the variations in the suture patterns in the pterion region of the skull elude any adaptive explanation.

Perhaps enough has already been brought forward to indicate how complex the dynamics of race formation may be. Although the process has been considerably clarified by recent investigation, much yet remains to be determined. But if the details are still somewhat obscure, the major outlines are clearly defined by the interaction of genetic change, selection, and isolation. It is difficult to conceive of race differentiation progressing without all three. Consequently, the elimination of any one might check the process or interfere with its development. Of these three factors, only isolation appears to be susceptible of radical modification. Genetic change is an inherent attribute which we have no reason to think will cease or be effectively altered. Selection is a process that can operate directly or be mediated by culture or be directed deliberately by human agency, but it appears to be as effective now as in the past. Isolation, however, we may infer from our knowledge of man's history on the earth, is a condition which is rapidly vanishing. From the point of view of race formation in man, then, the earlier stages of his development were more suited for such differentiation than they are today. Back in early Pleistocene times the geographic spread of fossil finds indicates that man was already widely distributed, but he must have been thinly distributed for various reasons. He was a hunter or a food-gatherer which imposed on him the necessity of living in small groups within large foraging areas. His primitive culture made it difficult, if not impossible, to inhabit certain areas unsuited for a primitive economy. Geographic barriers loomed large against his technological poverty. Perhaps at no other time were human populations so small and so isolated one from another, thus providing optimum conditions for race formation.

With the agricultural revolution that the Neolithic ushered in, and with increasing tempo ever since, human aggregations in town and city have increased in size. Populations could now be settled on the land and by growing their own food be able to support themselves on a fraction of the area they formerly required. Thus communities increased steadily in number. Technology improved to permit utilizing areas formerly waste and traversing great distances with relative ease. Geographic barriers became progressively less ominous. Thus, in the last 10,000 years the earth has been filling up with the result that today hardly any populations survive in the kind of isolation most favorable for the initiation or preservation of race differences. In addition to the contacts created by mere crowding, man has also vastly increased his mobility. The massive migrations of historic and recent times, and the resulting reshuffling of genes, have led to an unprecedented gene flow. Whole new populations, the offspring of race mingling, have arisen in the modern world, creating intergrades and continuities and thus blurring the distinctions of race. It would, of course, be unwarranted to predict as some writers have that the future will witness a vast intermingling of all the present races and the elimination of all racial differences. But we can say that in our own times the tide has turned in that direction. Who knows how long or how far it will run?

In any appraisal of human biology, one factor emerges as unique. This is the effect of human culture on man's biological development. No other creature has created for himself anything like it. In a sense it is a new dimension—a new environmental niche—to which mankind while creating it must also adapt itself. We are, however, only at the threshold of a true understanding of its enormous significance.

II

The Study of Early Cultures

THE STUDY OF EARLY CULTURES is usually called archaeology in the Americas, but in Europe, it is often referred to as prehistory. Most people have some knowledge of what archaeology is and what an archaeologist does, but relatively few have a clear idea of this scientific field and the complexity of the methods used in its study.

There are various definitions which have been given to describe archaeology. Prehistory is one of them, for a great part of archaeological investigations deals with periods of human history before man learned to write and record the happenings and developments that took place in a particular society. The archaeologist studies this unrecorded history by means of surviving specimens of human manufacture called artifacts; by the evidences of structures; from cemeteries, for grave goods often accompanied a burial; and by other means which will be explained later. When data of this nature have been gathered from a number of sites in a particular area, it is possible to arrange the record of human occupation in the correct historical sequence from earliest to latest. This chronological arrangement enables the archaeologist to identify the various items of human culture, say when they first appeared, and to some degree tell what effect they had upon the rest of the cultural complex. By a comparative study of the development of human culture in different areas of the globe, the archaeologist can demonstrate that with a hunting and fishing economy certain other cultural features, such as small villages, are likely to occur. On the other hand with an agricultural economy, there is a strong tendency for more settled communities such as towns and cities to appear. The study of archaeology then reconstructs the development of human culture, in so far as it is possible to

22

do so, from the earliest appearance of man to the beginning of recorded history.

The worldwide field of archaeology is divided into smaller units which are segregated by area or by time. Because of the varied nature of the data in these different units, the archaeologist must specialize in order to achieve competence in interpreting the evidence which has been preserved.

MATERIALS OF ARCHAEOLOGY

In order to facilitate his work, the archaeologist makes various classifications of the materials left in sites. Artifacts are grouped according to the kind of material of which they are made such as stone, bone, shell, clay, wood, or some other such category. These are usually further divided to identify the particular type of stone according to the names recognized by geologists or mineralogists such as flint or steatite. Bone artifacts can be recognized as coming from a particular bone of a particular species such as the shoulder blade of a deer or the upper leg bone of a turkey. Shell artifacts can be recognized as being from an ocean or fresh water environment, from a lake or river bed, and often from a fairly specific locality.

Another essential classification of artifacts is that of grouping them according to function. Thus we speak of stone axes, knives, scrapers, projectile points, drills; bone awls, hoes, pendants, beads; or, shell beads, hoes, and scrapers. Such divisions are of only general importance in comparing prehistoric cultures. To afford a more adequate basis for the comparison of one cultural level with another, or of one site with another, in ascertaining the degree of cultural connection, it is necessary to divide further and group the artifacts by the particular shape which they have and to some degree by the skill with which they were made. Projectile points of flint were made in an astonishing number of shapes and with varying degrees of skill. Each group of prehistoric weaponmakers followed a familiar pattern when they wished to manufacture their points for the hunt or for combat. This tendency of man to produce tools following an established form enables students of human culture to identify these products according to the time and place where they were made. In a particular area as time passes, new forms and techniques will gradually develop and become fashionable, or new ideas will be introduced from the outside, and so the story of human culture changes. Progress or evolution can be read by a comparative study of the artifacts in different time strata.

As important as the artifacts found in the various sites are the evidences of structures which are preserved in different ways; the burial customs of the people; the kind of location chosen for sites; and the pattern of settlement. Sometimes the only evidences available on house structures are in the form of a post-mold pattern which reveals the ground plan of the building with the size and number of the vertical supports. Occasionally, partial burning of such a wooden structure caused sections of the roof or side wall to be preserved so that the appearance and construction of the building can be understood and reconstructed. In some areas structures of roughly shaped or well-fitted stones give an even clearer picture of the type of dwelling or ceremonial building in use in former days.

BURIALS

Archaeologists usually find human burials in the sites. These may be found in different parts of a site. There are records of a great many different burial customs from the extreme degree of care in preserving the bodies that was accorded the ancient Egyptian nobility to the attempt at total destruction of the body as in the practice of cremation. Study of burial customs is one of the most important parts of archaeological field work because many peoples throughout the world had the custom of placing burial goods with the dead. By the naïve, this is often regarded as 'proof' of a belief in life after death—the individual taking such burial offerings along with him and having some need of them. While this is undoubtedly true in some instances, actual statements of primitive peoples have given additional reasons: the burial furniture belonged to the individual; it would have been 'bad luck' for anyone else to use it. These grave finds are often the best items recovered from a site, sometimes causing commercial diggers to loot cemeteries and graves in order to sell the specimens to antique dealers.

Often times, even within the same cultural group, different burial positions for the dead or different kinds of burial were practiced. Bodies were cremated, embalmed, or dismembered and interred in the ground. The body may be extended and placed on the back or on the chest; it may be placed in a flexed (doubled-up) position on either side, on the back, or in a sitting position.

Bodies are found in special cemetery areas or in special burial mounds.

They are also found in pits beneath the floor of a house, in the village site area, or in the refuse heap where it was easy digging. They may be simply wrapped in cloth, bark, or furs, or placed in a wooden or stone slab coffin, or even laid out in state in elaborate structures such as the old world dolmens or pyramids. They were buried in caves, rock crevices, in trees on wooden platforms, in a body of water, or in a boat or on a raft that was set adrift.

One type of burial often called a bundle burial results after the flesh has decomposed or been removed. The skeletal parts are placed in a compact bundle and interred in the ground. One special group of people within an Indian tribe, the Choctaw, in the Southeast allowed their fingernails to grow long so they could better pick the decomposing flesh from the skeleton.

The dead may have been buried singly, in groups, or in extensive cemeteries. An individual pit may have been prepared or larger ones to contain many corpses. Coffins, crypts, or sarcophagi range in complexity up to such elaborate structures as the Egyptian pyramids. The practice of cremation is not a newfangled idea—it is worldwide and has been practiced for thousands of years.

When the human skeletal material is sufficiently preserved, it is the duty of the excavator to uncover it with the greatest skill in order that the physical type of the people can be studied by a physical anthropologist. A knowledge of the 'racial' or subracial group to which the culture bearers belonged will provide data toward the solution of historical problems, for it is by such evidence as well as from cultural remains that indications of tribal movements and migrations are provided.

SETTLEMENT PATTERNS

Some primitive groups consistently chose similar places for their villages, for example, picking sandy areas adjacent to a body of water, while others consistently selected places whose natural features made them easy to defend. Some settlement patterns revealed through excavation are of houses grouped in a long line along a natural feature such as a ridge. Other excavations uncover walled towns with houses grouped along streets, with special areas reserved for ceremonial or civic buildings. In related cultural groups these settlement patterns tend to be very much the same.

When all of the data is gathered the archaeologist can present a reconstruction of the cultural life of the people. This reconstruction, however, is unhappily far from complete for the evidence which is preserved represents but a very small part of the total culture of the living group. To illustrate this point, one archaeologist has called attention to the very small proportion of objects in a current mail-order catalogue that will be preserved in our own habitation levels, say, five hundred to a thousand years from now. While this serves as an excellent illustration of the perishability of many items of material culture, it should be remembered that we now have a much greater proportion of such goods than was present in prehistoric times. Some inferences in regard to general social pattern and even of religious beliefs can be made, but since most of the excavated data belong to a more practical level the archaeologist finds his sources restricted indeed. It is a wonder that from this incomplete record a connected and rational story of growth and change can be produced.

Sites and cultures are named by archaeologists to provide a 'handle' which refers to the total cultural complex found. This name may be that of the owner of the site or some named feature of the landscape. For example, one of the famous prehistoric cultures of the Ohio Valley is called 'Hopewell' after the owner of one of the large and impressive sites where this type of material was found. In Europe, 'Mousterian' was named after a type site near the town of Le Moustier.

ARCHAEOLOGICAL METHODS—FIELD WORK

Some people wonder how an archaeologist knows where to go to find evidences of former cultures. This is a relatively simple part of his work for if one is interested in doing archaeology in a particular area there are quite a number of leads to site locations. The publications and museum collections of former archaeological work will give the location of the sites excavated or merely surveyed. Historical documents often tell of former inhabitants in an area and sometimes place names will hint at occupation by an earlier people. Books and records published or preserved by other scientists or surveyors give leads to the location of sites. In Central America the native chicle gatherers have called many sites to the attention of archaeologists. In almost every area there are a few people who have collected the relics of the past and preserved them in their own collections. These people provide one of the most fertile sources of information because competent collectors usually know the exact spot where finds were made. Finally, an archaeologist should survey an area himself to obtain a first-hand knowledge of site location and the variety of artifacts obtainable by surface collecting. After sifting this information, it is possible to recognize some of the historical and cultural problems of the area and to identify some of the sites most likely to provide data to answer initial problems.

One of the first principles of archaeological work is that excavation should be done when there are definite problems of cultural importance upon which the materials from the excavation will throw light. Unless a contribution is made to cultural history, excavation even by professional archaeologists may not be regarded as justified. In all deposits resulting from human living, there is a valuable record not only in the artifacts themselves, but also in the nature of the association of the artifacts to each other and to the other deposits in the ground. The manner in which this record was deposited has the correct story which if disturbed by excavation of any kind is lost forever. When a site is dug, it is destroyed no matter whether the destroying is by commercial steam shovel, river erosion, or the archaeologist's trowel. In the last case as complete a record as possible is made of all evidences of human handiwork, for anything in the site which shows human contact has significance.

It is easy to see why the excavation of a site should be done with great care by trained men who are competent to interpret the cultural deposits and the manner in which they were laid down. Excavation techniques vary according to the type of site being excavated. A cave or a rock-shelter is quite different from a village site, which in turn presents different problems from large ceremonial structures. The ideal technique would be to remove the natural and human deposits in the same order in which they were accumulated. This ideal is rarely approached because it is almost impossible to determine that order before excavation and is often difficult after the excavation.

In excavating village sites, or large blocks within former cities, convenient-sized squares are usually accurately surveyed in a grid pattern. Such squares are then connected with a permanent landmark and are located on the detailed map of the site. All objects or features of the occupation of the site can then be accurately placed on the site map. Excavation in the village site is usually done by the skinning or peeling technique which removes successive horizontal layers until the deepest part of the occupational debris is reached. The depth of these horizontal cuts varies according to the nature of the site. If natural stratigraphy is present, the excavator should adjust his digging to recognize and take advantage of the resultant cultural groupings. By this technique it is relatively easy to recognize disturbances in the soil such as post-molds, pits, and fireplaces. In instances where either successive occupations or a long-continued one have complicated the site and caused the presence of many 'features,' it is common practice to also make a vertical cut which will often indicate when one pit or other soil disturbance has intruded upon another.

Burial mounds of moderate size have been excavated by the trench technique. This proceeds, like the vertical slicing of a cake, by removing successive slices of the mound, usually by starting at the top of the slice and working toward the bottom. In this way a vertical profile is kept, and it is rather easy to see disturbances or special features in the mound earth. Domiciliary mounds are usually excavated by a combination of trenching and peeling. A number of trenches are cut a short distance into the mound so that the structure or stratigraphy can be seen in the cross-section. Then the flat-top surface is carefully cut down horizontally to each occupation level and the evidence of the former dwellings is uncovered. In more complex groupings of buildings and rooms as in the American Southwest, Middle America, or certain areas of the Old World, the individual rooms are cleared down to the floor before the room walls are studied, mapped, and removed. Caves and rock-shelters are also adapted to the combined stripping and trenching techniques.

For rapid sampling of a considerable number of sites, the archaeologist will excavate a number of small test trenches in areas with considerable surface debris, removing the material by horizontal layers. A study of the specimens recovered from the different levels will reveal the changes in culture from the bottom to the top of the site.

RECORDING OF THE DATA

It is, of course, essential that accurate records are made of all finds and features. One of these records should be a field catalogue in which the objects found are listed and described with the location from which each was obtained and the association with other specimens, or features, such as burials or fireplaces. In this catalogue the object is assigned a field catalogue number. Special catalogues or notebooks may be used to record burials and associated artifacts, house floors, drawings of important designs, or other special features. Duplicate copies are made, and one dispatched to the institution sponsoring the excavation or to some other safe place. A written progress report of all the work should also be made in duplicate and should be a descriptive journal of the excavation. No excavation has ever been too fully recorded by these various techniques.

Photographs have come to play a very important part in the recording and interpretation of sites and their excavation. Aerial photographs have disclosed unsuspected features of sites in areas such as Ohio and England, and have been invaluable in locating sites difficult of access in Peru and Iran. Photographs must always be taken of burials, structure floors, fire basins, significant soil or debris stratification, and of important finds. Photographs of objects which were taken at the time the specimen was found in the grave sometimes become the only visual record, for the specimen may not appear in the museum for one reason or another. Good photographs serve to jog the memory of the archaeologist when he is writing his report.

PREPARATION OF THE REPORT

After the field work is over, the excavated material and the records are taken to a laboratory for all of the necessary routine work which must be done before the specimens are studied. Sometimes a part of this is done in the field. The items must be cleaned, preserved, and repaired. They are then given permanent catalogue numbers, or some of the material, once identified, may be discarded. The specimens are then classified in various ways and a description is prepared of the typical material and variants. This description will form one part of the report and, along with the illustrations of the specimens, a most valuable part indeed. A description of the site and the various features is also prepared to tell the story of the association of the objects with burials, houses, fire basins, or refuse pits. The next section of the report is the comparative statement which discusses the relationship of the site to previous work, in an effort to gather all of the information that will aid in the interpretation of the site. The summary section presents the archaeologist's considered judgment in regard to his finds. There are also at times appendices to the report which will include articles by specialists on the physical type of the skeletal material, on physiographic features, on the animal or bird remains, or on other identifications. This report, when published, furnishes other archaeologists with additional comparative material, and thus there is built up a body of data on the prehistory of various areas which is subject to continuous reinterpretation as new facts are presented. From time to time broad syntheses are attempted by experienced archaeologists to present the story of the cultural development over a large area. Such statements are valuable for they indicate the progress made and usually point out the blank spots needing additional field work.

ANALYSIS OF ARTIFACT MATERIALS

Following the excavation of the site all of the artifacts must be identified and classified. One of the obvious ways of separating related artifacts is on the basis of the materials from which they were manufactured. Such an initial sorting would set into groups the items formed of stone, bone, shell, pottery, metal, ivory, wood, and other plant material.

A division of the stone material could next be made on the basis of the manner in which it was given its completed form. Two major divisions would be into polished stone and flaked or chipped stone, for these are again easily discernible and have been of considerable importance culturally. The polished stone group can then be further divided into tools or utensils, such as the axe, adze, celt, lance, hand-knife, gouge, hoe, and bowl; or into ornaments such as beads, gorgets (a stone tablet with perforations allowing for its suspension on the chest of an individual), effigies of man or other living things, and other objects. Another refinement of the polished stone objects, after separation into the kind of tools, might be made on the basis of the type of stone which had been employed to manufacture the various specimens. Such identifications are of considerable importance because it is often possible to identify the source of particular kinds of stones which will then indicate whether a specimen was formed from local material or whether the specimen was brought from a distant spot. If the latter is the case, then it could have been carried in as a finished product or the raw material may have been imported for local shaping. Stone that can be chipped, such as flint or obsidian, has been shaped by man for hundreds of thousands of years. This is an easier process than shaping stone by polishing, and such implements can be fairly abundant on a site. A division according to the function of the implement or the use to which it was put would result in the identification of arrowheads, projectile points for spears, lances, or the throwing stick (or atlatl), celts, chisels, knives of various types, scrapers, gravers, sickles, hoes, and even effigies and eccentric forms. Each of these groups is capable of considerable subdivision, on the basis of form, size, workmanship, and the particular type of flint employed. Many archaeologists have made classifications of arrowheads and projectile points to aid in the recognition of the specific forms which are characteristic of certain cultural groups. The variety of shapes which have been produced by man to serve as the penetrating end of an arrow is almost unbelievable.

The same type of divisions, but on different bases, can be made for bone, shell, and metal implements and ornaments. In general, however, their usefulness in indicating cultural units is not as great as in the stone category. Taking all cultural items found in habitation or burial sites into consideration there is no question but that pottery is the best interpretive material for the archaeologist. For a long time in man's history, he did not know how to manufacture pottery, but once it became a part of the culture complex it reflected better than any other single item gradual changes and influences which were taking place in the social group. Pottery is easy to make and to break. Its shape, surface finish, decoration, and the materials of which it was made conform to the style of the community. Yet these vessels were handmade and thus each differed from its brother. Different craftsmen (women apparently made most of the primitive pottery) would vary considerably in their skill and in their ingenuity or inventiveness. Then too, new ideas were introduced by contact with other groups. Thus, there were these two forces of conservatism and change always at work. Usually the changes in pottery were brought about so slowly and the combination of features is so distinctive that it is possible to identify vessels, or fragments of vessels, as to the particular spot in the world where they were made and the specific time period or cultural group to which they belong. The study of ceramics is so important, and there is so much of it to study, that some archaeologists spend almost all of their time on this particular phase of archaeology.

The aim in all of this work devoted to the analysis and classification of artifacts and features of sites is to provide an objective description to facilitate the placement of the site within the cultural history of the area. That is, to what other sites is this one related? Is it older, later, or contemporary? What are the outside connections of the site? Does it seem to have developed new ideas which were then spread outward to contemporary and later groups, or was it an isolated site, or a borrower from stronger culture centers?

CULTURAL CLASSIFICATION

One of the most important phases of archaeological work is that of recognizing the presence of distinctive culture units which were in existence at a particular moment of time in a particular area. We know, as a result of our knowledge of primitive peoples who are living now and from eyewitness records of groups of primitive people who lived in the past, that the culture of such groups is likely to be very much the same. After the archaeologist has selected a site, excavated it, and analyzed and described its contents he must then present his interpretation of where the site belongs in the known cultural sequence of his own restricted area and in the more general story of cultural development in a geographic region. Just as he has classified the artifacts and features at his site on the basis of the strong resemblances of groups of specimens to each other, he now compares the significant culture units at his site with those reported, described, and illustrated in previous reports. By so doing he observes the degree of connection his cultural complex (or superimposed cultural complexes) has with other complexes. He observes in what particular features his site conforms to, or diverges from, the most closely related complex. Usually he finds that sites in the adjacent area are most closely connected on the basis of the high degree of similarity of the material, and that these closely related sites can be placed, either in a relative or absolute time scale, at approximately the same time period. One of the most intriguing phases of this part of archaeology is the search for data on the unusual artifact or custom which does not normally appear in most of the closely related sites. Such artifacts or customs are, of course, unusually important for they may be holdovers from a preceding period and shed light on the source of part of the culture. These unusual items may also represent new elements which will become much more common at a later period, thus indicating the direction in which this culture complex was growing. Or, he may find these exotic features are the result of trade or other contact with neighboring peoples or areas.

Archaeologists have recognized and named cultural units which have considerable variation in the life span or the culture content of the complex to which they refer. Thus, the Paleolithic or Old Stone Age takes in a time span of hundreds of thousands of years and includes such diverse smaller units as Abbevillian and Magdalenian. These two units are included within the Paleolithic because neither has the characteristics of the Neolithic and not because they have any very close specific connections. In general, it can be said that archaeologists recognize differing degrees of cultural connections. One of these is a term such as Magdalenian which implies a high degree of similarity in the artifact types or other features at a number of sites. Some broader cultural units can also be recognized as the grouping of Aurignacian, Solutrian, and Magdalenian into the Upper Paleolithic. These divisions of a Lower and Upper Paleolithic should be prefaced by the words European or western European for, as clearly distinguishable units, they are almost limited to that area. The various divisions are also representative of successive cultural periods, but they are identified as distinct culture units because their traits differ.

It is the duty then of the archaeologist to demonstrate in a most definite manner (if he can) the specific culture to which his materials belong and indicate the modifications of former interpretations resulting from his excavation. He must also indicate the relationship of his material to the broader cultural units to which it belongs.

THE PLEISTOCENE PERIOD IN HUMAN HISTORY

An archaeologist should know enough geology to recognize when the advice of a trained geologist is needed to interpret the association of natural features with the evidence of man's occupation. The geologists are particularly necessary in areas which were affected by the changes caused in the earth's surface during the Pleistocene Period, or Ice Age. During the last hundred years geologists have been able to recognize four major periods within the last million or so years, when, in certain areas of the northern hemisphere there were large accumulations of snow and ice, much as in present-day Greenland. As the snow and ice accumulated in depth in those areas where weather conditions were most favorable, the edges of the ice mass moved outward until great areas in northern Eurasia and North America were covered by these continental glaciers. As the ice moved, it incorporated within its mass and on its surface the loose mantle of earth, sand, and gravel, and thus acted as a scouring agent during the thousands of years of its growth. When the weather became more moderate, these great ice fields gradually diminished in size, shrinking backward from their margins and depositing the earth and stone which had been accumulated during its outward movement.

There are two major divisions of glaciers. Mountain glaciers begin above the snow line and with the continual addition of more and more snow and ice they gradually move down their valleys until they fan out over more level ground at the bottoms. Such widened ice-sheets formed from mountain glaciers are sometimes called piedmont glaciers. Mountain glaciers may be seen now in the Rocky Mountains, Alaska and the Alps.

The second major division is the continental glacier. About 2,000,000 square miles of Europe and 4,000,000 square miles of North America were glaciated. In North America three ice-sheets have been identified. The Labrador sheet was centered in the area of Labrador and spread outward from there reaching northern New Jersey and the Ohio Valley. The Keewatin ice-sheet centered in the area just west of Hudson Bay spreading south to about the line of the Missouri River. The third sheet was not a continental sheet, but a mountain glacier, or glaciers, formed in the Rocky Mountains. The great Keewatin sheet was 2000 miles in a north-south direction and some 1300 miles from east to west, while the Labrador ice concentration was even larger. In some areas the ice was well over a mile thick.

All of the rock and clay which is deposited as the result of glacial action is referred to as 'till.' All of the land formation deposited by the glaciers is usually called 'drift' in North America. Geologists have given more specific names to quite a few of the formations which have consistent shapes and composition. The most prominent features resulting from glacial action are the moraines, or hills of gravel with some sand or clay, which were deposited usually on the end of ice-sheets as terminal moraines or on their sides as lateral moraines, or between two projections of ice where they are called interlobate moraines. Kames are somewhat conical hills of sand or gravel. An 'esker' is a ridge of sand, gravel, and clay deposited by a glacial stream in an ice tunnel. A drumlin is a smooth oval hill.

During the Pleistocene Period then, there were geographical factors at work which made great changes in the environment in which man and his culture developed. In western Europe one major area of ice formation was in the Alps and another was in Scandinavia. It is in these areas that the first studies of glaciation were made. In addition to the four major ice advances and retreats (our present period may be the fourth interglacial), there were minor climatic changes accompanied by movements of the ice fronts. Even within the last few hundred years there have been significant changes in the present glacial masses in the northern areas.

It should be remembered that these climatic changes took place very gradually as can be seen by estimates of the length of time of the whole Pleistocene Period which ranges from 600,000 to 1,000,000 years. With colder conditions and the advance of the ice, those animal and plant forms adapted to warm weather were not able to survive and their places were taken by forms adapted to the colder times. Thus, there are found in Europe the skeletal remains of such animals as the elephants, rhinoceros, and a group of horses related to the zebra, all of which indicate a much warmer climate than the present. There are other remains, such as the mammoth, the reindeer, and the arctic fox, which reflect the colder period. Some animals reflect a forest environment, the beaver, the red deer, brown bear, and lynx, while steppe or prairie conditions are indicated by the horse and a certain antelope. At times under favorable conditions plant remains are preserved furnishing additional evidence of the weather conditions to which man had to adjust. Forms that are distinctive of a particular time are sometimes referred to as fossil horizon markers.

In Europe the presence of man during the early part of the Pleistocene is known from finds in the gravel deposits dating from this period. These consist primarily of flint implements of various kinds, described in the following chapter, and a few skeletal parts of early forms of man. During the last two glacial and interglacial periods, there is an increasing amount of human skeletal material and cultural data which is found in cave or rock-shelter deposits, where it is often better preserved than in the open sites, and where the conditions of deposition and association of items are usually somewhat easier to interpret. Where the deposits are deep they reveal the same sequence of animal forms as are recovered from the deposits in river terraces or the outwash plains.

Of considerable interest and importance is the study of the various animal forms which have lived with man during the various Pleistocene periods. Not only do the remains of these animals provide leads about the type of climate, but also other facts are learned for they furnished food, bone which was used by man for implements, and skins which were utilized for clothing.

During the Pleistocene many animal forms in the two northern hemispheres of America and Eurasia were very similar. This was true because their ancestors in the preceding geologic period, the Pliocene, were very much alike and because during the Pleistocene there was a land bridge between Siberia and Alaska which allowed free movement of such forms as were adapted to the environment. The size of this connecting link probably varied from time to time according to change in the level of the land and the amount of water in the sea.

One of the important indicators of the beginning of the Pleistocene is the appearance of certain animal forms. Among these are the cattle belonging to a particular group, with the bison a prominent member; the horse, Equus; true elephants; and camels. So constant is their association with the evidence of the first continental glaciation that they are regarded as marking that time period when they are found in areas which did not have the great ice-sheets.

The great amount of moisture needed to produce the great ice-sheets was drawn from the moisture on the earth and as a result the level of the oceans was lowered. The weight of the ice on the land depressed some areas, but since the last removal of the ice they have been slowly rising. This has been carefully studied in Scandinavia and in the Great Lakes area. The rise and fall of the general sea level due to the melting or forming of the glaciers is called glacial 'eustasy,' while the uplift of the earth due to the melting of the ice mass is called the 'isostatic reaction.' Throughout much of the world, beach lines and river terraces were formed during the glacial period which are now at varying distances above the present sea level or river flood plain. In some areas these old beach lines and terraces have been correlated with the glacial varve chronology or other glacial phenomena. Human occupation often took place along these beaches or terraces. In the older terrace remnants stone artifacts have been preserved.

Major streams flowing from glacial melt waters to the sea formed impressive successive terrace formations. Let us imagine this stream flowing down to the sea is able to move a given amount of clay, sand, and gravel because the slope of the river bed enables the water to move with sufficient force to do that work. If the sea level rises so that the slope is reduced then the river will not be able to carry its former load to the sea and will instead deposit the material in its valley building up its bed. It is then called an aggrading stream. If the outlet is then lowered, the stream will again cut into the valley and will carry away a part or most of the valley floor deposited in the former stage. The deposits along the valley sides that are not carried away remain as relatively horizontal remnants and are known as river terraces. In Europe, particularly, these gravelly river terraces contain stone industries which can be dated as no younger than the formation of the terrace if the implements were not introduced into the formation after it was laid down. Such production of river terraces can also be caused by changes in the volume of water in a stream, for the greater the volume the more force is available to move the stream load. During the periods of maximum glaciation so much moisture was solidified in the great ice-sheets that the rivers tended to deposit gravel throughout their valleys. Then, with the great volume of water available as the glaciers gradually melted, these valley floors were to a large extent carried downstream. In some areas such as northwest Europe both these methods of river terrace formation were in operation. Marine terrace formation has been extensively studied in Europe both in the Atlantic and Mediterranean areas. Along the east coast of North America from New Jersey to Florida there are seven coastal terraces whose formation has been correlated with the glacial stages. The highest beach is some 265 feet above sea level and is correlated with the pre-glacial period. During the first, or Nebraskan, glacial period the sea level dropped. When the first, or Aftonian, interglacial period arrived the sea level rose again and a beach 215 feet above present sea level was formed. This series of beach forming activities has continued to the present day.

CHRONOLOGY

Of the greatest importance to the archaeologist is the determination of the chronology of the area with which he is dealing. There are two end points on this ladder of human development. The top rung is the latest culture complex, which in the Americas is usually recognized by the presence of European manufactured trade items such as glass beads, iron knives, or brass. The bottom rung is represented by the earliest appearance of artifacts utilized by man to aid in his struggle for existence. It is essential that the most complete sequence of cultures be obtained so that the cultural story is a continuous one from the first to the last stage. When this is available, it is possible to record the changes in styles and in techniques that have been the result of local development and also to see the influences and materials that have come in from other areas and become a part of the local cultural growth.

The determination of the chronology or time period can be made either by means of relative or absolute chronology. The former is much more common. Relative chronology is obtained through stratigraphy, seriation, typology, and other techniques discussed later. It provides a sequence of artifacts and cultures but does not provide this time frame-work with accurate dates in terms of a year-by-year count. As a result one knows where a particular culture belongs in relation to others but the length of time it existed or how long ago is not precisely known. In contrast, there is the much more accurate dating, or absolute chronology, afforded by a year-by-year count as in dendrochronology, the record of glacial varves, or by ancient coins as in the Mediterranean area.

STRATIGRAPHY

Excavation of stratified sites, where one cultural level is found over-lying an earlier one provides one type of relative chronology. In such a case the fact that one culture is later than another is perfectly clear, but what is not known is the length of time that each existed or how long an interval of time separated them. In an attempt, perhaps, to infuse a bit of life into such relative chronologies archaeologists often assign a period of years to these culture groups or periods. The span of years is based on 'guesses' which utilize whatever evidence there is that is suggestive of a time factor. For example, some archaeologists who have excavated large shell mound sites have taken the number of burials, and by knowing the average death rate of similar groups, have used it as a figure to determine the probable size of the group which deposited the shell mound as a refuse accumulation. They have then estimated how much shell food these individuals would likely eat in a year, and then, taking the cubic content of the mound into consideration, have arrived at a possible figure for the age of the mound. Obviously, however, such estimates are not accurate for there are too many unknown factors so that the result is hardly worth the labor of calculation. Other estimates have been given on the basis of comparable cultural units where the length of time is known. The horizontal extent of a site, the depth of material present, and the areal extent of a cultural division within a geographic region give some indication of its possible length of life. The main point to remember is that in most areas of the world the archaeological sequences are placed in a time scale of years by rela-tive chronology, and this is always subject to change until there is dis-

covered a method which can date archaeological sites in the most accurate terms.

Fossil Pollen

Another method of determining relative chronology and connecting
cultural material with climatic phases is by the study of fossil pollen.
Like the study of glacial varves it is most useful for comparatively recent times. In north Europe, particularly, archaeological material has
been found in peat deposits or in other beds with well-preserved botanical remains. The most important of the various botanical sources is
tree pollen which reflects the types of trees which were in existence
during the formation of the deposits. The most valuable studies have
been made where deposits of some depth were found which provided
evidence for considerable changes in the forest flora and these in turn
reflect significant climatic changes. In some instances peat deposits with
good pollen contents have been obtained from directly on top of varved
clay beds which could be dated, or on raised beach lines which also
could be connected with a known chronology. Pollen analysis has not
been studied very much in relation to archaeology in North America.
The change in flora, already amply demonstrated, is now being correlated with radiocarbon dates.

Seriation

This technique of arriving at a relative chronology is based on the
principle of stylistic change which takes place through time in a given
class of materials. In primitive cultures those manufactures which were
easily and rapidly made and which also were sufficiently variable to reflect the style of the moment are the best for seriation. For this reason
pottery, figurines, projectile points, axes, or other items from a considerable number of sites over a fair sized area are arranged in a stylistic
or logical sequence in relation to some known end point, which is either
the end or beginning of the series. This technique was successfully employed by Professor Kroeber of the University of California to determine
the relative age of sites in the southwestern United States, Mexico, and
Peru. In this manner it would be fairly simple to arrange examples of
various automobiles in their order of production by means of their style
if one had a fairly complete series of examples from the earliest to the
latest.

TYPOLOGICAL METHOD

The crudity or excellence with which artifacts have been produced has sometimes been taken as evidence of relative age. This is sometimes justifiable and is supported by such examples as the early crude flint weapons of Europe's Old Stone Age. Such tools are, however, no cruder than relatively modern Australian types. This criterion for age is not a reliable one and should be employed with great care.

DISTRIBUTIONAL OR AGE-AREA METHOD

When culture traits are found in the same general area, those having the greatest distribution are sometimes considered to be the oldest. This assumption works best when dealing with closely related forms such as the house types in the Southwest where the small semi-subterranean house was distributed over a wider territory than the large, complex multi-roomed pueblo structure. At best, however, this method is only suggestive and needs to be verified by stratigraphy.

PATINATION OR WEATHERING

Some attempts have been made to provide a relative age for artifacts on the basis of the chemical or mechanical weathering shown by the specimen as the result of exposure to climatic conditions or long burial. These observed differences in such specimens cannot be measured by any known technique, and there are usually too many unknown factors which may have produced the changes.

ABSOLUTE CHRONOLOGY

In some areas of the world there has been achieved the arrangement of prehistoric cultures into a year by year chronology. In the southwestern United States dendrochronology and in northern Europe glacial varve chronology (both of these techniques are described later in this essay) have provided the accuracy of dating which is desired in every area. In the Maya area the archaeologists have the advantage of the Maya calendar which records the date of erection of various monuments and buildings. It is of great assistance in arranging the various sites or portions of sites with regard to the Maya calendar, and within its own system is remarkably accurate as a year by year chronology. Unfortunately this Mayan calendrical system has not been satisfactorily correlated with our present chronology, although the margin of error within a number of different correlations is rather small.

GLACIAL VARVES

This method of determining chronology was the first which produced an accounting of geological events in terms of years. The different layers or lamina observed on the floors of former glacial lakes are called 'varves' in Swedish. It was Baron Gerard de Geer, a Swedish scientist who pondered on the meaning of these sediments during the latter part of the nineteenth century and initiated the development of techniques for interpreting this geological record. De Geer and his colleagues have demonstrated that the varves were deposited on the floors of glacial lakes or other relatively quiet water bodies. The melting of the glaciers during their recession was accelerated during the summer months and the run-off spread over the lake carrying with it sand and clay particles in suspension. The heavier coarser grains would naturally sink to the bottom first while the finer material might not have reached the bottom until winter when the melting would cease. This process went on year after year. Not only can the yearly succession be observed by the change in size of the deposited material, but the coarser grains are almost always noticeably lighter than the finer sediments. By carefully studying and comparing these annual deposits from southern Scandinavia to the more central mountainous area, a chronology from the present to some 10,000 years ago has been obtained. This chronology can be connected with the deposition of moraines and other surface features which can in turn be connected with human occupation areas. This resulted in unusually accurate dating of these successive cultural periods in the Baltic and North Sea areas.

This same method has been applied in northeastern North America but with less success because the most recent varve deposits cannot yet be connected with the Christian chronology. This is due to a gap of unknown time span between the varve series in the Connecticut valley and the varve series northeast of Lake Huron. Most of the evidence of early man in North America (some 25,000 years ago) has come from the western part of the continent. Our time estimates of North American prehistory up to the radiocarbon dating were in considerable measure based on this none-too-accurate time scale in the Northeast.

DENDROCHRONOLOGY OR TREE RING CHRONOLOGY

In the southwestern United States the study of the development of the prehistoric Indian cultures has been greatly aided by dendrochronology which has permitted an arrangement of the archaeological material into the Christian calendar. This field was made possible because an astronomer, Dr. A. E. Douglass, was interested in determining the long range effects of sun spots on the weather of the earth. To do this, he utilized the annual growth rings of certain southwestern trees, particularly Western Yellow Pine, which reflect climatic variation in the width of rings and their growth pattern. This method of tree ring study is by no means a simple one and only trained individuals with considerable experience in handling, recording, and interpreting the ring sequence are competent to pass judgment on the age of prehistoric specimens.

By working backward from trees of modern or known cutting date, the inner ring pattern is compared with the outer ring pattern of older specimens taken from buildings erected some 100 to 200 years ago. From such specimens Douglass was able to pass to the wood and charcoal specimens of late prehistoric age and gradually extend the sequence until it is now possible to date archaeological sites in certain areas of the Southwest as far back as 1 A.D. with great accuracy.

SOIL PROFILES

In recent years the study of soils, called 'pedology,' has been of considerable assistance to the archaeologist even though the primary purpose of this branch of knowledge has been to benefit agriculture. Soils are formed from the native rock of a region by mechanical weathering and by the disintegration of vegetal material which with rain water produces chemical weathering. The formation of soil is most rapid in temperate regions for it is in such areas that the chemical weathering is most effective. The decomposing vegetal material is called 'humus,' and under certain conditions has an acid effect on the soil. The stages of soil formation and alteration are studied by means of vertical sections which are technically referred to as profiles. Soil analysts can recognize horizontal zones with differing characteristics which are called horizons.

Different climatic zones produce significantly different soils irrespective of the underlying rock formations from which they were derived. Because of this, it is possible to recognize the climatic conditions which were in operation when a particular soil horizon was formed. Soils formed in coniferous forest areas with relatively cool summers and ample rainfall are called podsols. This combination produces an upper, or A, horizon of acid humus forming humic acids when carried down with the rain. The acids dissolve the bases and certain other components called sesquioxides to produce the lower part of the A horizon. When the humic acids can carry off no more sesquioxides, these are deposited as a brownish or reddish or black zone which is called the B horizon. The leaching takes place in the A horizon and in its lower zones the soil often assumes a light color. Horizon C is the unaltered parent material below the B horizon. Since podsols have the bases and sesquioxides carried downward, it is an acid soil which attacks organic matter such as bone, wood, shell, and other materials deposited in a site and hastens their decomposition.

Another soil type called the brown-earths forms in areas with a warm summer and moderate rainfall. In this soil the top humus layer is sufficiently aerated which oxidizes the decaying vegetal material and the soil is thus either neutral or only slightly acid. Another soil type, largely of loess origin, is called 'chernozem,' or 'black-earth,' and is usually found in continental grassland areas such as the eastern plains of the United States or in south Russia. This soil because of the continued presence of bases is never acid. In dryer steppe condition 'chestnut' soils are produced.

A mature soil profile takes a considerable period of time to develop and it will vary according to the climatic factors. In California some of the older cultural levels have been located which underlie mature soil profiles estimated by experts to be at least 4000 years old.

Chemical Analysis of Soils for Identification of Occupied Areas

One of the results of soil study and analysis has aided archaeologists in the identification of sites. Soil chemists have provided a method for the determination of acid or base soils. Briefly, this method recognizes pure water as having a value of pH 7 in regard to its acid or base composition. Soils which provide a watery solution more acid than water have a pH value lower than 7; and soils which are less acid than water will provide a pH value greater than 7. Most soils have values between 4 and 9. Inexpensive sets can now be purchased which enable anyone to determine the pH value of his soil, and this is of use to farmers and garden growers. It helps the archaeologist interpret his site, for an acid soil will cause disintegration of perishable material much more rapidly than will a base soil. When the acidity of the soil is known, the archaeologist has a better idea than before whether a poor condition of bone implements or refuse and burials is the result of a long period in the soil or of rapid decay. In Scandinavia there are certain large areas where the soil consistently shows a base reaction. Quite a number of sites have been located by making soil collections at regular intervals in likely locations. When the soil tests show an acid reaction or pH value less than 7, it is likely the spot represents a former human habitation area which by the deposition of organic material has changed the acid-base relationship. The presence of phosphate in the soil caused by the decay of discarded bones is an excellent clue to the location of a site. It is said that the soil of an area that was formerly densely occupied may contain as much as fifty times the normal amount of phosphate. Thus within a large site it is possible to determine the areas with the maximum occupation.

Recent Aids to Archaeology from the Physical Sciences

Archaeological field work has benefited from the application of methods long in use in mineral exploration. Recently in the Valley of Mexico, the linear electrode method of detecting sub-soil irregularities was employed, and during subsequent excavation a human skeleton buried in deposits of a former glacial swamp was uncovered. By sending electrical current into the ground and using instruments to record its passage, it is possible to identify areas which are more resistant to the electrical current and thus indicate objects which might repay digging.

There has come into prominence recently a number of techniques for determining relative chronology by the study of the age changes which take place in skeletal material buried in the ground for long periods of time. It is known that the natural organic mineral and water content of bone normally decreases with the length of burial, and that in some soils mineral matter is deposited in the bone. The fluorine test has been successfully applied to mixed deposits of human and animal bone from a specific deposit to determine if they contain the same amount of fluorine and thus are, or are not, of the same relative age.

For some years the age of the earth and of its various major geological periods have been dated by means of the radioactivity method. Through research in physics it is known that there is a constant and determinable rate for the disintegration of a radioactive mineral so that such mineral, particularly the uranium family, taken from a specific geological stratum can be used to date that stratum. This method has not been available to archaeology since the whole Pleistocene Period falls outside of its scope. Very recently, however, research physicists have been studying the radioactive carbon isotope 14 which also changes in form at a constant rate. This means that with a small amount of carbonized material it is possible to give the age of sites with a very small percentage of error, enabling the archaeologist to study the rate of cultural change in terms of absolute time periods.

The method of radiocarbon dating was developed by Dr. W. F. Libby and his associates at the University of Chicago. There are now (1955) some ten radiocarbon laboratories in the United States, eight in western Europe, and one in New Zealand. This method provides dates over a span of some 30,000 years, with a statistical margin of error, and for any single specimen there may be intrinsic errors. With a fair number of samples dated from a specific zone or of a particular culture, it is usually possible to observe a clustering of dates around a limited time span. This method of dating has great value and has already provided significant time periods for both natural and human history.

Ethnobotanical Identification

One of the most promising products of the combination of the study of man and his culture with other fields of scientific investigation has been the development of ethnobotany, which deals with man's utilization of the flora of an area and the effect on the flora of man's occupation in present and past time. In many areas of the world it has been possible to identify the presence of an archaeological site by the recognition of either different kinds of plants at certain spots from the more common types of the landscape, or the greater luxuriance of the ordinary vegetation.

In Tierra del Fuego, Darwin, on his famous trip with H.M.S. *Beagle*, noticed that a bright green wild celery and scurvy grass grew commonly on the shell heaps and helped to differentiate the shell heaps from the surrounding area. Throughout the Arctic areas explorers have often commented on the change of color and greater luxuriance of plant life on habitation sites where the organic materials left by human refuse and offal provide nutritive elements for plant growth. Similar plant differences have been reported throughout most of the United States.

Another means of identifying sites is by the presence of plants which were for one reason or another of particular value to the people. In California, a botanist noticed that he only found wild tobacco in association with shell heaps. On the Plains, a particular sage plant that was utilized in medicines and ceremonies is often abundant about the village sites. In Florida, wild plants with distinct food possibilities are found only on archaeological sites. In Virginia a plant of importance for the production of fiber has been found north of its native range and consistently in association with Indian sites. This suggests that it was carried in by migrating Indians or brought in by people who recognized its value to the Indians living in the South.

In other instances, a knowledge of the direction of movement of cultural ideas can be obtained from the domesticated crops. It is quite evident that corn was not first domesticated in the United States area but it was grown by the majority of the Indian groups when the Europeans arrived. There are other plants grown north of the Rio Grande which were domesticated south of the border. At one of the famous pueblo sites in the Southwest, V. H. Jones, a prominent American ethnobotanist, has worked with the plant material used as binder in adobe (sun-dried mud) bricks to obtain information on the crop plants. This study has not only provided data on the native domesticated plants but has been of special interest because of the recognition of plant material brought in by the early Spanish missions, for this particular site lasted well into the historical period. Unfortunately this material has not been published. Another interesting identification of the native plant material consumed as food was made by Jones from an analysis of desiccated human feces from a Kentucky rock-shelter.

Another field of study from the biological sciences is that of the study of molluscs which accurately reflect changes in water temperature and in the salt content of the water. This has been particularly valuable in the Baltic-North Sea area. Here the shells preserved in deposits indicate an arctic environment during the glacial periods; from some of the interglacial levels samples are preserved which are Mediterranean species. During the minor advances and retreats of the last glaciation the Baltic Sea was alternately fresh water, ocean, fresh water, and then salty again. The presence of molluscan fauna which only exists in fresh water indicates that the first post-glacial water in the Baltic Sea was the fresh melt water from the receding glacier which overflowed into the North Sea through a gap in southern Sweden. Subsequently the level of the fresh water lake was lowered and a particular sea shell called 'Yoldia' entered with the salt water. Its name has been given to this stage. As the glacier receded the land level rose and the Baltic area again became a body of fresh water. A fresh water mollusc genus Ancylus gives its name to this second fresh water period. Still later as the land rise slowed down relative to the rise in sea water, the salt water entered and with it came the common periwinkle Litorina which gives its name to this stage.

One of the best examples of the association of archaeological cultures with natural features is in southern Finland where most of the sites of an early primitive cultural complex with rough stones and no pottery are located along the beaches of the Litorina Sea. None of them are located in areas covered by the water of this period. A later culture with cord-impressed pottery has many sites in areas which were covered by the waters of the Litorina Sea.

THE RECONSTRUCTION OF SOCIAL BEHAVIOR FROM ARCHAEOLOGICAL DATA

Reasonable inferences can be made from archaeological investigations in regard to various social customs of the living group. If a series of sites belonging to one culture are small in size with few artifacts, few burials, very little depth of debris, and with little or no evidence of structures, it is reasonable to infer that the social group represented by such remains was a small, more or less, family unit engaged in a hunting, fishing, gathering economy. On the other hand when a particular culture is characterized by large sites with extensive and deep cultural deposits, with considerable evidence of houses, large complex ceremonial buildings, and remains of stockaded palisades around the site a quite different social and economic pattern is suggested. This situation indicates a large and relatively stable group with an adequate food supply usually based on agriculture. The stockade suggests the presence of an adequate defense organization under the direction of a war leader or leaders. Presumably groups organized for defense also have a similar offensive structure. The presence of ceremonial structures implies a further assignment of special duties to civil and sacred officers. If there are large and impressive burial mounds with extensive burial accoutrements and evidence of human sacrifice the evidence for complex mortuary beliefs and ceremonies is quite clear. The famous wall paintings of the Late Paleolithic caves of southwestern Europe reflect a belief in sympathetic magic and fertility ceremonies, as well as an appreciation of true artistic endeavor.

SUMMARY

Archaeology, then, may be described as an historical discipline whose major purpose is the reconstruction of the history of man and his culture from the earliest times to the present. To aid this reconstruction the archaeologist calls to his assistance all of the data provided by other fields of knowledge so that there is available all of the pertinent information on this cultural problem. Information and deductions from physical science, natural science, social science, and art are all blended to produce the story of the development of human culture from remotest antiquity to our modern cultural level.

From our knowledge of the history of various archaeological cultures, it is possible to suggest certain axioms of cultural development.

1. Each culture group develops distinctive processes and skills which are conditioned by its particular environment.
2. When two divergent cultural traditions meet a blend is usually the result rather than the elimination of one or the other.
3. With increasing control of the food supply settlement patterns become larger and more complex, reflecting increased populations and, probably, more complex social patterns.
4. Cultures developing in isolation will normally change less rapidly than those with more extensive cultural interrelations.
5. Man appears to be a self-domesticated animal and his culture the result of his own ingenuity.
6. Early distinct cultures in a given large geographic area tend to merge into a larger whole as they become more complex, enlarge, and expand.
7. Utilization of environmental resources depends on the stage of cultural development and on no other factor.
8. While specific cultural units appear to 'die out,' the more general or broader cultural division, of which the former is but a part, continues in existence.
9. There are no static human cultures that continue without change for long periods of time.
10. The more complex and richer cultures with greater control of their environment dominate and tend to supplant the simpler cultural units.
11. On a primitive or early cultural level a marked climatic change in an area will produce a noticeable cultural change in that area.
12. The rate of change of various cultural units is not uniform within the total cultural complex. At one period art forms will reflect considerable activity while at another period the economic aspects may reveal the considerable change.

H. L. MOVIUS, JR.

III

The Old Stone Age

PREHISTORIC ARCHAEOLOGY in the Old World deals with the immense space of time between the first appearance of man and the beginnings of written record—a period of perhaps some 1,000,000 years duration at a conservative estimate. As indicated on the chart (Fig. 1), during approximately 49/50ths of this time, man was in the Old Stone Age, or Paleolithic and Mesolithic stages of cultural development. These stages cover the entire span of the Pleistocene, or Glacial, Epoch of geologic time as well as Early Post-Glacial, or Recent, time. The archaeological record of the Old Stone Age is incomplete, because it can only be studied from those imperishable objects of man's material culture that have been preserved. With the exception of a relatively few localities, mostly of the Mesolithic Period, objects of wood, skin, and other perishable materials have long since completely decomposed. Thus tools of flint, stone, and bone, as well as the remains of contemporary animals hunted by man, are in the main all that we have to go on in attempting to reconstruct life during Old Stone Age times. In general, the artifacts demonstrate a slow, gradual development from a single, all-purpose stone tool and a few rough flakes to a kit of highly varied and specialized stone and bone tools. In other words, just as during historic times, the trend was from simple to complex, from a stage of nonspecialization to a stage, or stages, of a relatively high degree of specialization.

Throughout the entire span of the Old Stone Age (including both Paleolithic and Mesolithic Periods) man was a food-gatherer, depending for his subsistence on hunting wild animals and birds and collecting wild fruits, nuts, and berries. The earliest stone implements which can be recognized as the work of man mark the beginning of this period, which

49

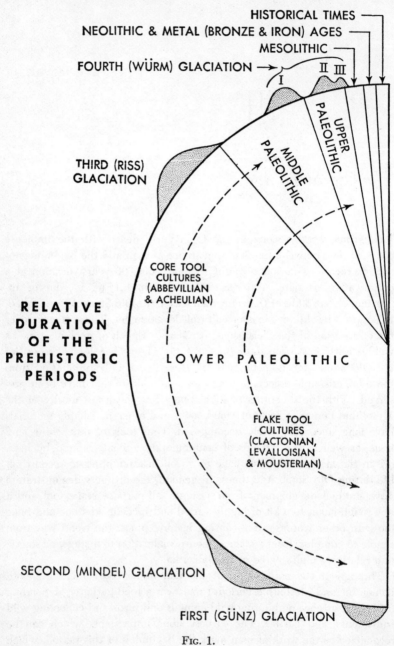

HISTORICAL TIMES

NEOLITHIC & METAL (BRONZE & IRON) AGES

MESOLITHIC

FOURTH (WÜRM) GLACIATION →

I

II III

THIRD (RISS) GLACIATION

MIDDLE PALEOLITHIC

UPPER PALEOLITHIC

CORE TOOL CULTURES (ABBEVILLIAN & ACHEULIAN)

RELATIVE DURATION OF THE PREHISTORIC PERIODS

LOWER PALEOLITHIC

FLAKE TOOL CULTURES (CLACTONIAN, LEVALLOISIAN & MOUSTERIAN)

SECOND (MINDEL) GLACIATION

FIRST (GÜNZ) GLACIATION

Fig. 1.

on the geologic time scale falls in the later part of the Lower Pleistocene. Before this, early types of hominids presumably used any object that came to hand—natural stones, or pieces of wood or bone. Scientists have long attempted to identify such tools of pre-Paleolithic times, referred to as Eoliths, the period being called the Eolithic, or 'Dawn Stone,' Age. It is almost impossible, however, to distinguish a stone which *might* have been used by Eolithic or 'Dawn' man from the millions of stones fractured or chipped by natural causes. Therefore, our study of the earliest evidence of human culture must begin with unquestionable artifacts made of stone definitely fashioned by men who recognized the fact that a better tool could be produced by chipping a stone into a chopping or cutting implement than was otherwise obtainable. In other words, the finished form of the earliest tool was first a preconceived idea in the mind of early man, who thereupon set about fashioning a given nodule of flint, or similar rock, into the desired shape.

There is no direct evidence as regards man's social organization or dress during Old Stone Age times, and, with the exception of natural caves and rock-shelters, very little is known of his habitation sites. On the basis of paintings, engravings, and sculpture of the later part of the Paleolithic Period, there is abundant and direct evidence that his basic economy was intimately associated with hunting. But there is no definite information concerning his methods of hafting his stone tools in connection with his food-gathering activities. In spite of the fragmentary nature of the evidence, however, certain facts may be deduced concerning man's material culture, and these will be referred to in this chapter.

Since many of the earliest prehistoric discoveries were first made in France, French place names have long been used to designate the various subdivisions of the Paleolithic Period. This terminology has been widely adopted, and the French stratigraphic succession has been employed as the classic basis for comparison for nearly a century. Consequently the French sequence is used here to give the foundation for the study of Old World prehistoric archaeology. Although this main outline often holds good in other parts of the world, other cultures naturally appear elsewhere, in addition to mixed industries [1] resulting from the contact of several groups possessing different cultural traditions for manufacturing stone artifacts.

It is not to be assumed that the French sequence provides the key to

---

[1] An industry is the group of stone and/or bone tools belonging to a given archaeological horizon or phase of a given culture.

the development of culture during Paleolithic times all over the Old World, nor that the cultures represented there originated in western Europe. Indeed, a great deal of additional work is needed before the origins of these cultures can be established, and the migrations of the peoples who developed them traced.

The Paleolithic Period is subdivided into three main groups, as follows: I. Lower Paleolithic; II. Middle Paleolithic; III. Upper Paleolithic.

The Lower and Upper Paleolithic groups are easily recognizable. However, the Middle Paleolithic is emphatically *not* a separate compartment, since it overlaps and dovetails into the other two subdivisions.

Each Paleolithic culture possesses one or more type tools which characterize it, while many of the other tools are common to several horizons. In designating tool types certain accepted terms are used for convenience, for example: 'points' or 'scrapers.' But, since there is absolutely no evidence concerning the actual use of most stone tools, this terminology should be taken as a description of *form* rather than of *use*. Indeed, 'points' and 'scrapers' may have been employed as perforators or knives.

TECHNOLOGY

Paleolithic man fashioned his stone tools by chipping or flaking. A direct blow on a flat surface of a stone nodule, or core, will detach a flake, leaving certain definite and unmistakable characteristics on both flake and core. These prove that the process was intentional and not due to such natural causes as heat and cold, battering by waves, or pressure in the earth. In most cases, before attempting to remove a flake, our prehistoric forebears trimmed the nodule, or core, in such a manner that it exhibited at least one flat surface from which the flaking could be executed. This flat surface, on which the blow, or blows, were delivered is called the *striking platform* (Fig. 2). On the cleavage plane of a flake, just below the point where the blow was struck (the *point of impact*), a marked swelling is produced which is known as the *bulb of percussion*. Normally, just to one side of the bulb of percussion, somewhat below the point of impact, a small flake scar is present. In French this is known as the *éraillure;* it is formed simultaneously with the flake upon which it appears. The other characteristics exhibited on the bulbar surface, or cleavage plane, of an intentionally struck flake may be defined as follows:

Ripple Marks—These are also called concentric rings, or waves, of percussion. They characterize the flake surfaces of those substances—flint, glass, obsidian, et cetera—which have a conchoidal fracture. Ripple marks are a system of small concentric rings circling the point-of-force application and comparable to the ripples caused in a pool of water when a stone is dropped into it. In other words, they radiate outward from the point of impact.

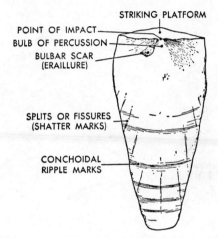

STRIKING PLATFORM

POINT OF IMPACT

BULB OF PERCUSSION

BULBAR SCAR
(ERAILLURE)

SPLITS OR FISSURES
(SHATTER MARKS)

CONCHOIDAL
RIPPLE MARKS

Fig. 2. Diagram showing the characteristics of the bulbar surface of a flint flake produced by percussion.

Shatter Marks—These are also called splits or fissures. They are lines on the flake surface which converge on the point of impact and are caused by the splitting or tearing action set up in the flint core by the blow delivered during the process of removal of the flake. In a general sort of way, these lines are perpendicular to the ripple marks, or at least to certain chords subtended by them.

If the phenomena described above are consistently displayed by a series of flaked stones from a given Pleistocene horizon, the chances are very good that one is dealing with the work of man and *not* of nature. In any case, these terms are fundamental for purposes of describing the flint-working techniques of the Old Stone Age.

Paleolithic tools were made by the following methods:

1. By striking a nodule against a fixed stone, called an anvil stone.
2. By striking a nodule with a wood or stone hammer held in the hand.
3. By striking an intermediate tool, placed at the exact point where the flake is to be detached.

The final shaping of many tools was done by secondary chipping, called *retouch*. Either light percussion or pressure flaking (Fig. 3) was employed in this process.

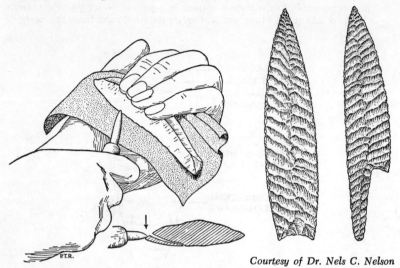

Courtesy of Dr. Nels C. Nelson

Fig. 3. Pressure flaking is a relatively evolved technique for the manufacture of stone tools. It is ordinarily used for shaping implements and for providing them with fine cutting edges.

The following four principal tool types are generally recognized:

1. *Bifacial core tools,* called hand-axes. These are core implements with two opposing cutting edges.
2. *Single-edged core implements,* called chopper and chopping-tools. These are often made on pebbles, and they may be flaked on either one (choppers) or both sides (chopping-tools) of the cutting edge.
3. *Flake tools,* which are large, elongated or oval artifacts with a plano-convex section. These are produced either by the so-called anvil technique, or by direct percussion with either a stone hammer or a baton made of wood.
4. *Blade tools,* which in a sense are very well made flakes detached from specially prepared cores. Blades are normally thin, relatively long, and parallel-sided implements, the length-breadth ratio of which is at least 2:1. They may be produced either by direct or indirect percussion.

In general, the assemblages of artifactual materials that characterize the earlier and middle portions of the Old Stone Age are characterized by core implements, as well as by an abundance of flake tools, while during later times artifacts made on blades predominate.

THE PALEOLITHIC PERIODS OF EUROPE

A. *Lower Paleolithic*

The time span of the Lower Paleolithic was enormously long, for it occupied approximately three-quarters of the Pleistocene, or Glacial, Epoch. During this period river valleys and terraces were being formed, the northern regions and mountainous areas of the globe were being subjected to the advances and retreats of the ice-sheets, and great changes were being induced in the fauna and flora of the earth, as described in Chapter 2. Early man apparently lived for the most part in the open near his water supply and near the animals he hunted, since his stone tools are found mainly in or adjacent to the valleys. If the tools are sharp and unworn, they are as old as the deposits in which they are found, but they may be heavily weathered and rolled indicating that they have been derived from even older horizons. The deposits themselves are dated geologically and paleontologically—by their stratigraphical position and physical characteristics, as well as by the bones and teeth of extinct animals which they contain. So far, as stated above, there is no definite trace of man prior to the First, or Günz, Glacial Stage; the earliest stone tools in western Europe appear in deposits of the First, or Günz/Mindel, Interglacial Stage.

The Somme Valley in the north of France and the Thames Valley in the south of England are not only particularly rich in Pleistocene deposits containing Lower Paleolithic implements, but also they furnish excellent stratigraphic sequences for the entire Pleistocene Epoch in western Europe. Neither region was actually glaciated, but their proximity to the ice-sheets in each case gave rise to periglacial conditions. On the basis of the evidence from these two regions, it has been possible to subdivide the tool-making traditions of the Lower Paleolithic in western Europe into two groups, *hand-axe traditions* and *flake traditions,* as follows:

Hand-Axe Traditions	*Flake Traditions*
1. Abbevillian	2. Clactonian
3. Acheulian	4. Levalloisian

Although the principal element characteristic of the hand-axe traditions is the bifacial tool, or *coup-de-poing* (a more or less pointed implement made on a core and worked on both upper and lower surfaces), flake tools also occur in all hand-axe levels. In some cases these are rela-

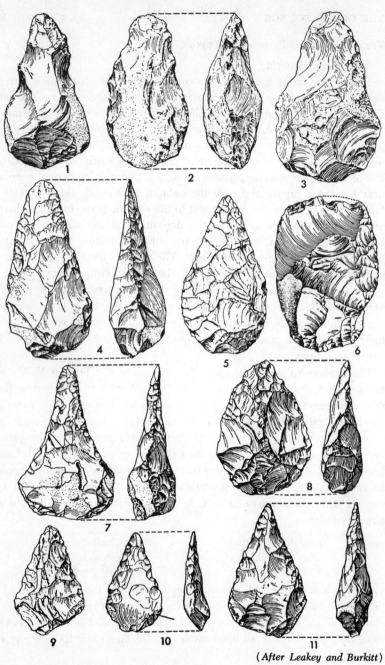

(After Leakey and Burkitt)

tively simple, consisting of the utilization of waste material resulting from the manufacture of hand-axes; in other cases very much more complex types are found. On the other hand, a few sites have produced assemblages of flakes and are devoid of hand-axes; at these localities the flake tools are generally produced by specific techniques resulting in the manufacture of definite forms.

1. ABBEVILLIAN   The Abbevillian, which apparently is the oldest tool-making tradition of the Paleolithic in western Europe, takes its name from Abbeville in the Somme Valley of northern France. It was formerly called Chellean, but some twenty years ago this name was changed because at Chelles, the former type site, Abbevillian (or Chellean) tools are not found in place. The Pleistocene deposits at Chelles are, in fact, situated on a low terrace which was formed after the Lower Pleistocene, and the many tools of Abbevillian type found there have been derived from higher ground. Abbevillian tools are only found *in situ* at a few localities on high terraces, such as the 45-meter terrace at Abbeville. The scarcity of comparable sites is due to the fact that most of the high terraces have been badly disturbed by erosion and other weathering processes.

Abbevillian tools consist mostly of hand-axes (Fig. 4, Nos. 1-3). Not only are these the oldest, but they are also the crudest types of hand-axes found in the Lower Paleolithic. Their forms vary and the flaking is generally irregular, producing sinuous cutting edges. It is probable that they were manufactured either with a stone hammer or on a stone anvil. Associated with these hand-axes, flake tools are found, but they are very crude and no definite tool forms exist. The majority are flakes resulting from the manufacture of hand-axes.

2. CLACTONIAN   The stratigraphic position of the Clactonian, named after the type site at Clacton-on-Sea, Essex (England), is most clearly shown at Swanscombe, Kent, in the Thames Valley. There it underlies

---

FIG. 4. *LOWER PALEOLITHIC BIFACIAL IMPLEMENTS*

Abbevillian (Nos. 1-3) and Acheulian (Nos. 4-11) hand-axes. Nos. 1-3, typical Abbevillian examples from Lower Pleistocene deposits in western Europe; No. 4, elongated ovate (Early/Middle Acheulian); No. 5, typical Acheulian ovate; No. 6, cleaver—note the slightly curved but long cutting edge instead of a point; No. 7, lanceolate hand-axe; No. 8, Middle Acheulian (IV) ovate showing S-twist; No. 9, sub-triangular type hand-axe of the Late Acheulian; Nos. 10 and 11, typical Micoquian (Final Acheulian) hand-axes.

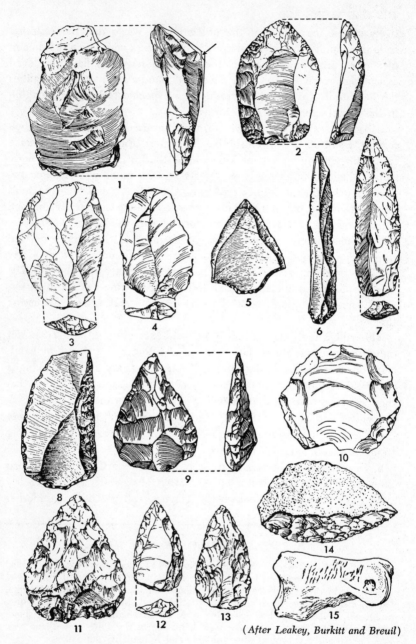

(After Leakey, Burkitt and Breuil)

58

a Second, or Mindel/Riss, Interglacial gravel horizon containing Middle Acheulian hand-axes, in addition to several derived and rolled Abbevillian types.

As stated above, the Clactonian is predominately a flake tool tradition, although core tools—very rough choppers and chopping-tools—also occur. The latter are nodules of flint either alternately worked on one end to a zig-zag, chopping-tool edge, or flaked along the upper surface of one side as choppers. The associated flakes are rough and struck from unsystematically prepared cores. They exhibit large, wide-angle (>90°), plain, striking platforms, and prominent bulbs of percussion (Fig. 5, No. 1). Actual retouching or secondary working of the edges of the flakes is found in some cases (e.g. Fig. 5, No. 2), but for the most part it is crude, and edge-chipping resulting from use is far more characteristic.

3. ACHEULIAN The Acheulian covers by far the longest time span of any of the various Paleolithic subdivisions. It begins in the Second, or Mindel/Riss, Interglacial Stage and ends toward the close of the Third, or Riss/Würm, Interglacial Stage. During this immense period of time, there was comparatively little advance in stone chipping technique.

Acheulian tools are abundantly represented in both the Somme and the Thames Valleys, but the principal stratigraphic development has been established in the 30-meter, or middle, terrace of the Somme Valley at St. Acheul, the type site, where six of the seven levels are found. The oldest Acheulian occurs in early Second Interglacial gravels of the 45-meter, or high, terrace. In general, the Acheulian may be subdivided into Lower, Middle, and Upper, although the actual sequence is somewhat more complex.

FIG. 5. *LOWER AND MIDDLE PALEOLITHIC IMPLEMENTS*

Clactonian (Nos. 1 and 2), Levalloisian (Nos. 3-10), and Mousterian (Nos. 11-15) tools; all except Nos. 9-11 and No. 15 are flakes. No. 1, flake typical of the Early Clactonian (I); No. 2, well-worked Late Clactonian (III) flake tool; Nos. 3 and 4, Early Levalloisian (I/II) flakes; No 5, Middle Levalloisian (IV) pointed flake with 'Chapeau-de-Gendarme,' or policeman's hat, type of faceted striking platform; Nos. 6 and 7, Middle Levalloisian blades; No. 8, Middle Levalloisian side-scraper; No. 9, small hand-axe of the Late Levalloisian Stage; No. 10, Middle/Late Levalloisian tortoise core (struck); No. 11, cordiform hand-axe of the Mousterian; Nos. 12 and 13, typical Mousterian points; No. 14, Mousterian side-scraper; No. 15, utilized bone from a Mousterian horizon in south-central France.

Fragments of a human skull of modern (*Homo sapiens*) type were found in a Middle Acheulian horizon at Swanscombe (Kent) in the Thames Valley. This is the only locality in western Europe where fossil human remains have ever been discovered in direct association with a Lower Paleolithic cultural horizon.

The type tool of the Acheulian is the hand-axe (Fig. 4, Nos. 4, 5, 7-11). Flake tools also occur in all levels, their numbers increasing in the Upper Acheulian. However, there is very little typological difference in the forms of the hand-axes found in the various layers. In general, there is a larger proportion of ovate forms (Fig. 4, No. 5) in the Lower Acheulian than in the other levels; the Upper Acheulian has a higher proportion of lanceolate forms (Fig. 4, No. 7)—finely chipped hand-axes with straight, or even concave, edges. Cleavers (Fig. 4, No. 6), which are bifacial tools with a squared, or slightly convex, sharp cutting edge at one extremity, are comparatively rare, although they occur in all Acheulian levels. Ovate hand-axes (Fig. 4, No. 8) with a markedly sinuous edge, known as the 'S-twist,' are especially characteristic of the Middle Acheulian. Triangular (Fig. 4, No. 9) and heart-shaped forms are found throughout, but they are rare in the earliest horizons. In general, a very gradual improvement in technique may be noted between the early and late phases of this culture.

The Micoquian, or Final Acheulian, is named after the type site of La Micoque in the Dordogne region of south-central France. Micoquian-type hand-axes (Fig. 4, Nos. 10 and 11) are characterized by very straight and finely chipped edges, and they are generally of sub-triangular or elongated form. At La Micoque, hand-axes of this type were found in association with a large number of flake tools, including points with a triangular cross-section.

Flake tools occur in all Acheulian levels, as previously stated, the side scraper being the predominant type. Many of these tools were made from trimming flakes struck off during the process of hand-axe manufacture. In general, flake tools are found in greater quantities in Upper Acheulian (Micoquian) levels.

4. LEVALLOISIAN The Levalloisian, named after a locality at Levallois, a suburb of Paris, is a flake tradition that was formerly considered to be separate and distinct from the Acheulian. But recent investigations in the demonstrably Second Interglacial gravels of the Amiens region (Somme) and the Swanscombe region (Kent) by independent workers have shown that flakes of characteristic Levalloisian type, together with tortoise cores,

occur in direct and indisputable association with Early-Middle Acheulian materials. Thus the so-called 'prepared' striking-platform/tortoise core technique (Levalloisian) first appears in the middle of the Acheulian stage of development, continues to evolve during the Upper Acheulian and Micoquian, and reaches its final expression in the Mousterian of Levalloisian facies, also called the 'Levalloiso-Mousterian.' Certainly the Levalloisian is an important innovation in that it represents an advanced technique of manufacturing flake tools by a special method of core preparation. For in the earlier assemblages the flakes had been obtained in a more-or-less haphazard fashion.

The Levalloisian technique involved the careful preparation of the nucleus or core with a view to striking off one flake tool of a desired and specific form, either round, oval, or triangular. The core was first chipped bifacially by convergent flaking in order to shape up one surface and an extremity for the removal of a symmetrical flake (Fig. 5, No. 10). Since struck cores of this type are of plano-convex section and often suggest the form of a tortoise, they are known as tortoise cores.

The upper surface of a Levalloisian flake clearly indicates this careful preparation by its pattern of more-or-less converging trimming-flake scars that were truncated when the flake was detached from the core (Fig. 5, No. 3). The striking platforms of most flakes display a series of small, roughly parallel, vertical flake scars, called facets, that were prepared on the core prior to the object's detachment. The majority of the striking platforms are at an approximate right angle to the cleavage plane—the long axis of the flake.

The use of the Levalloisian technique resulted not only in the production of more symmetrical flakes, but also in larger ones in proportion to the size of the nucleus, since a well-struck blow frequently detached almost the entire prepared convex surface of the core. The chronological development of the Levalloisian technological development may be considered under four groups, established on the basis of the stratigraphy of the Somme and Thames Valleys, as follows:

Lower—The phase, which is found in deposits of the Second Interglacial and the Third, or Riss, Glacial Stages, is characterized by heavy flakes (Fig. 5, Nos. 3 and 4) and blades struck from tortoise cores. The striking platforms are normally rather roughly faceted.

Middle—The Middle Levalloisian occurs in place in the fluvial deposits of the Third, or Riss/Würm, Interglacial Stage in the low terraces of the Somme and Thames Valleys. Elsewhere in western Europe, however, this stage is known as the Mousterian of Levalloisian facies. It is generally characterized by smaller, thinner, and better retouched flakes (Fig. 5, No. 8) than those of the Lower Levalloisian, and by the presence of numerous blades (Figs. 5, Nos. 6 and 7). The rectangular blade core appears for the first time in this horizon; another distinctive feature is the frequent 'chapeau-de-gendarme,' or policemen's hat, shape of the faceted striking platforms (Fig. 5, No. 5).

Upper—This phase is also known as the Micoquian of Levalloisian facies. It is characterized by the regular occurrence of hand-axes of triangular shape (Fig. 5, No. 9). These are associated with large, oval flakes, similar in size to those of the Lower Levalloisian, but at the same time thinner and of better workmanship.

Final—Characteristic of the Final Levalloisian, also known as the Mousterian of Levalloisian facies (as is also the case with the Middle Levalloisian), are retouched blades and triangular points, struck from carefully prepared cores. This phase occurs in two separate levels in the loess of the Fourth, or Würm, Glacial Stage, and there is no typological difference between them. Retouched tools are more common in the Final Levalloisian than in the preceding levels.

B. *Middle Paleolithic*

From a typological point of view the main criterion for subdividing the Lower and Middle Paleolithic rests on the presence or absence of hand-axes, or *bifaces* to use a term that does not imply function. Technologically, as indicated above, it is the presence or absence of flakes with faceted striking-platforms and the characteristic Levalloisian preparation of these flakes on the core prior to detachment that are of fundamental importance. However, contrary to generally accepted opinion, these two features are not necessarily related. But the situation is even more complex due to the common occurrence of the discoidal nucleus, or 'Mousterian flaking technique' at Middle Paleolithic sites. Now flakes struck from discoidal nuclei are commonly mistaken for true Levalloisian flakes, although in point of fact the two techniques have very little in common. In the main this is due to the occurrence on both the discoidal and the tortoise cores of careful trimming around the edges, as well as the scars of a series of centrally directed flakes. The fundamental difference lies in the fact that the objective of the Mousterian knapper was to obtain these centrally directed flakes rather than to prepare the core for the removal of a special type of product. Normally, the discoidal nucleus is more markedly convex (although in some instances flat or even slightly concave) than the Levalloisian form, and it may be alternately worked on the two faces, giving it a bi-pyramidal section. In both cases, once the initial series of flakes had been removed, the craftsman proceeds by selecting the base of the ridges separating the scars of two previously detached flakes as the striking-platform. A triangular flake, which resembles a Levalloisian point but with a thicker butt and of clumsy appearance, is often obtained in this manner. Also in the Mousterian there are flakes with plain, unprepared striking-platforms, frequently inclined toward the lower surface, in which case they are sometimes erroneously classed as 'Clactonian.' But as yet there is nothing to demonstrate a transitional stage between the Clactonian and the typical Mousterian.

The Middle Paleolithic may be assigned to the Third, or Riss/Würm, Interglacial Stage, and to the first major oscillation of the Fourth, or Würm, Glacial Stage, on the basis of the available geological and paleontological evidence. Mousterian man is of the Neanderthal race, but as yet no human remains have been found associated with a true Levalloisian assemblage in western Europe.

The two technological traditions—Mousterian and Levalloisian—do not occur in any consistent stratigraphic sequence. In a broad sense, however, certain regional distinctions can be made between the two traditions. For the Mousterian is found chiefly in caves and rock-shelters, whereas the Levalloisian generally occurs at open-air sites. It is in the Mousterian levels of the caves and rock-shelters of southwestern France that the earliest evidence of the use of fire and the first definite burials have been discovered in western Europe. On the other hand, the principal Levalloisian development was in northwestern France, Belgium, and southern England. True Mousterian is comparatively rare in these areas, but common elsewhere in western, southern, and central Europe. In this latter region, it is often found in association with warm fauna of Third, or Riss/Würm, Interglacial age. Most of the French Mousterian sites, however, have yielded a cold fauna of the first oscillation of the Fourth, or Würm, Glaciation.

5. MOUSTERIAN The cave of Le Moustier in the classic Dordogne region of southwestern France is the type site of the Mousterian. In the oldest Mousterian levels in France, a large number of rather small, heart-shaped hand-axes (Fig. 5, No. 11) have been found, together with typical Mousterian points (Fig. 5, Nos. 12 and 13) and side-scrapers (Fig. 5, No. 14). In the Middle Mousterian hand-axes are relatively rare, while flake tools are very abundant. At the summit of the deposits containing the Late Mousterian a very few hand-axes occur. Throughout the Mousterian a few bifacial chopping-tools, in some cases made on large flakes, are found. They appear to be more numerous in the hand-axe levels—

called Mousterian of Acheulian tradition—than they are in those containing only flake tools.

As indicated above, the Levalloisian technique predominates at many
Mousterian sites. At other localities, however, it is almost completely
absent, and the flakes were detached by the discoidal core technique and
then retouched. A possible explanation may be that in regions where
natural flint occurs in large nodules the Levalloisian technique was used
in order to obtain as large a flake as possible. Where smaller nodules
of the material were available the simpler Mousterian method is found.
Irrespective of the technique employed, however, it is a cardinal fact
that the typology of the finished artifacts covers an extraordinarily constant range.

A crude bone industry appears in the Mousterian for the first time.
This medium may have been used by Lower Paleolithic man for fashioning into tools, but open-air sites are not favorable to its preservation.
Mousterian bone tools consist of compressors and chopping-blocks, or
anvils, bearing traces of use (Fig. 5, No. 15).

More human skeletal remains have been discovered in Mousterian
levels than in those of any other Paleolithic horizon. They all belong to
men of the Neanderthal race.

C. *Upper Paleolithic*

The last of the three main groups of Old Stone Age cultures, the
Upper Paleolithic, occupies only approximately 1/10th of the time span
of the entire Paleolithic Period. Yet during this comparatively short time
prehistoric man made his greatest cultural progress. Diversified and
specialized tools made on blades replaced the hand-axes and flake tools
of the earlier cultures. Although the blade tools appeared previously, and
transitional phases may be noted, the main development of specialized
implement types made on blades began with the advent of the Upper
Paleolithic. In addition to flint and other similar rocks, bone, ivory, and
antler were extensively used. In Central Europe, south Russia, and Siberia the earliest man-made dwellings have been found—simple, semi-
subterranean pit-houses of oval or elongated shape. Of prime interest
and importance was the beginning, flowering, and decadence of Paleolithic art. The location of certain Upper Paleolithic settlements suggests
a more complex social life, including perhaps collective hunting. There
is evidence for fertility magic, private property, and possibly social
stratification. Furthermore, primitive types of early man disappeared,

and men of the *Homo sapiens*, or modern type, alone are found in Upper Paleolithic deposits.

The Upper Paleolithic comprises the Périgordian, Aurignacian, Solutrean, and Magdalenian cultures, each of which in turn is further subdivided both on the basis of stratigraphy, as well as on the basis of one or more distinctive tool types which characterize each horizon. These latter occur in addition to a number of types common to all levels—gravers, end-scrapers, points, et cetera. The graver, itself (e.g. Fig. 6, No. 4), is a very important tool, for its invention made possible the extensive working of bone and facilitated the development of art. It is possible to speculate on the probable uses of many other tools found in Upper Paleolithic deposits, and thus gain a clearer insight into the cultural and social life of man during that age. For instance, tanged points (e.g. Fig. 6, No. 22) suggest projectiles with hafted tips, needles with eyes (e.g. Fig. 7, No. 19) imply sewing of garments.

The fact that Upper Paleolithic man lived chiefly in rock-shelters and caves has furnished an absolute stratigraphical succession of his cultures; but not all of them, including their several subdivisions, are present at any one site. Moreover, articles of bone and antler, which would have perished in open-air sites, have been preserved in these protected localities. Although many open-air Upper Paleolithic sites are known, in the majority of instances they cannot be accurately dated.

In general, Upper Paleolithic art falls into two mutually related categories: *mural art* and *home art*. The former includes finger-tracings, paintings, engravings, bas-reliefs, and sculptures on the walls of caves and rock-shelters. The latter is characterized by small engravings and sculptures on stone and bone found in the occupation layers. Certain of the artistic manifestations may well have had religious significance, or they may have been connected with a belief in supernatural powers exerting an influence on daily life.

The climate of the period varied from cold-steppe, or even arctic-tundra, to north temperate, or taïga, similar to that of southern Canada of the present day. The Upper Paleolithic cultures developed during the Fourth, or Würm, Glaciation, but as yet it is impossible to make an exact correlation between the various horizons and the several well-established oscillations of the Würm Ice-Sheets.

The chronology of the first major interval of the Upper Paleolithic, which covers over one-half of the time span of the Upper Paleolithic and which was formerly called the Aurignacian, is rather complex. Ap-

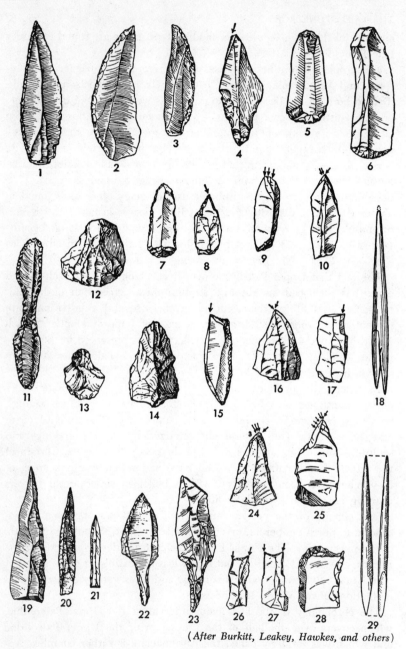

(After Burkitt, Leakey, Hawkes, and others)

66

parently two more-or-less contemporary cultural traditions—the Périgordian and the Aurignacian—were present in western Europe. The recognized sequence is as follows:

Périgordian—Lower (Châtelperronian) and Upper Aurignacian (Gravette/Font Robert-Noailles) of the original system; and
Aurignacian—Middle Aurignacian of the old classification.

Few authorities have ever agreed on the dates that should be assigned to these major divisions, or on their correlation with the various stages of the last Alpine glacial cycle. At the upper end of the sequence the final development of the Magdalenian probably took place between *c.* 10,000 and *c.* 8,000 B.C., but in suggesting that the transition from the Mousterian to the Périgordian occurred some 25,000 years ago, one does so with the full realization that this is no more than a guess-date unconfirmed by Carbon-14 measurement.

Early men of the Périgordian and Aurignacian stages of cultural development include representatives of both the white and black races. The former are represented by the Cro-Magnon and Combe-Capelle types, and the latter by the well-known negroids of Grimaldi. The animal bones from sites occupied at this time show that such forms adapted to cold conditions as the woolly mammoth, the woolly rhinoceros (both now extinct, the reindeer, the cave bear, the cave lion, and the wild horse were hunted.

6. PÉRIGORDIAN   In the Périgordian, which is named after a region in southwestern France, blades with one steeply retouched edge, or back, are typical. The Lower Périgordian is the oldest Upper Paleolithic culture, and it directly overlies the Mousterian at many rock-shelters and

---

FIG. 6. *UPPER PALEOLITHIC IMPLEMENTS*

Lower Périgordian (Nos. 1-10 and 17), Aurignacian (Nos. 11-16 and 18), and Upper Périgordian (Nos. 19-29) tools. Nos. 1-3, Châtelperronian points (Lower Périgordian); Nos. 4, 8 and 17, angle burins; Nos. 5 and 6, end-of-blade scrapers; No. 7, double side and end-of-blade scraper; No. 9, flat burin; No. 10, screw driver, or bec-de-flûte, burin; No. 11, 'strangulated,' or notched, blade; Nos. 12 and 14, steep scrapers (Aurignacian); No. 13, nose scraper; No. 15, angle burin on retouched blade; No. 16, core burin; No. 18, split-base bone point; Nos. 19-21, Gravettian points (Upper Périgordian); Nos. 22 and 23, Font Robert tanged points; No. 24, polyhedric burin; No. 25, beaked burin; Nos. 26 and 27, Noailles (small, multi-angle) burins; No. 28, end-scraper and perforator; No. 29, point with beveled base.

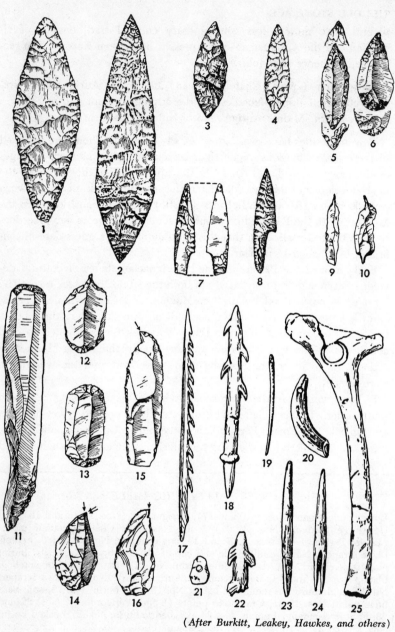

(After Burkitt, Leakey, Hawkes, and others)

caves. It is characterized by large curved points with blunted backs that are known as Châtelperron points (Fig. 6, Nos. 1-3). Most authorities believe that the straight points with blunted backs, called Gravette points (Fig. 6, Nos. 19-21) and typical of the Upper Périgordian, were developed from the Châtelperron type. In addition to Gravette points, the Upper Périgordian (Stage IV) is characterized by small human sculptures (Fig. 8, Nos. 4-6), while in the Final Périgordian (Stage V) there occur diminutive, multi-angle gravers, called Noailles burins (Fig. 6, Nos. 26 and 27) and tanged points made on blades, which are known as Font Robert points (Fig. 6, Nos. 22 and 23). All of the Aurignacian and Périgordian levels contain the usual Upper Paleolithic blade tool types—burins (Fig. 6, Nos. 4, 8-10, 15-17, 24 and 25), end-scrapers (Fig. 6, No. 28), et cetera. Notwithstanding these similarities, however, it seems apparent that more than one intrusive cultural element penetrated into western Europe at the beginning of Upper Paleolithic times.

7. AURIGNACIAN The Aurignacian is named after the type site near the village of Aurignac, in the Department of Haute-Garonne in southern France. At many sites it is found intervening between horizons referable to the Lower and Upper Périgordian, while in other instances it appears to be contemporaneous with occupations that are considered to be transitional between the two main stages of the Périgordian. The leading tool types include steep-ended scrapers (Fig. 6, Nos. 12 and 14), nose scrapers (Fig. 6, No. 13), blade artifacts with heavy marginal retouch, strangulated blades (Fig. 6, No. 11), busked gravers or burins, and split-base bone points (Fig. 6, No. 18). Bone was used extensively, mainly for javelin

---

FIG. 7. *UPPER PALEOLITHIC IMPLEMENTS*

Solutrean (Nos. 1-10) and Magdalenian (Nos. 11-25) tools. Nos. 1 and 2, bifacial, laurel-leaf points (Middle Solutrean); Nos. 3 and 4, small, bifacial, leaf-shaped points (Middle Solutrean); Nos. 5 and 6, proto-laurel-leaf points (Lower Solutrean); Nos. 7 and 8, shouldered points (Upper Solutrean); No. 9, single-ended awl, or perforator; No. 10, double-ended awl, or perforator; No. 11, end-scraper on long blade (Magdalenian); No. 12, end-scraper and awl, or perforator; No. 13, double-ended scraper; No. 14, end-scraper and angle burin; Nos. 15 and 16, parrot-beak graver (Upper Magdalenian); No. 17, harpoon with single row of lateral barbs (Magdalenian V); Nos. 18 and 22, harpoons with double rows of lateral barbs (Magdalenian VI); No. 19, bone needle; No. 20, perforated horse tooth ornament (Aurignacian or Magdalenian); No. 21, small, perforated stone ornament; No. 23, javelin point with single beveled butt; No. 24, forked-base javelin point; No. 25, baton-de-commandement, or arrow straightener.

points or *sagaies* (Fig. 6, No. 29), chisels, gouges, perforators, and 'batons-de-commandement,' or arrow straighteners (Fig. 7, No. 25). Articles of personal adornment, probably worn as necklaces, such as pierced teeth (Fig. 7, No. 20) and shells, decorated bits of bone, stone (Fig. 7, No. 21), and ivory, appear for the first time in the Aurignacian.

The oldest manifestations of art appear during the Aurignacian, and the development continues throughout Upper Périgordian times. These consist of engraved and painted profile drawings of various animals in black and red (Fig. 8, Nos. 12 and 15), as well as a number of sculptured human torsos representing the female form (Fig. 8, Nos. 4-6), referred to above. Of special interest are the painted hands (Fig. 8, No. 9), in some cases mutilated, which are found on cave walls and are attributed to the Aurignacian. Finger tracings in the layer of damp clay found on the walls of certain caves are of comparable antiquity. These describe meandering, interlacing patterns, which in some instances form drawings of a primitive sort. When one considers the economy of these naturalistic drawings, their vigor is all the more remarkable.

8. SOLUTREAN   The type site for this culture and the one after which it is named is located at Solutré, near Mâcon (Saône-et-Loire), in east-central France. It is noted for having produced the finest examples of flint workmanship of the Paleolithic, and the term Solutrean has come to be more or less synonymous with flat, regular, parallel flaking (compare Fig. 7, Nos. 1 and 2). This technique first appears in certain of the latest Upper Périgordian levels, and it reached its full development in the Middle and Upper Solutrean with their beautiful, symmetrical laurel leaf, and shouldered points. The usual Upper Paleolithic tool assemblage made on blades is also present, including gravers, end-scrapers, points, perforators, et cetera. Many of the scrapers display fine Solutrean chipping, while others are quite roughly made.

Typical of the Lower Solutrean are points retouched mainly on the upper surface, but with the bulb on the lower surface usually removed by flat retouch, and the point commonly shaped by delicate chipping on the lower face (Fig. 7, Nos. 5 and 6). These points are called either proto-laurel leaves, or proto-Solutrean points. True bifacial laurel leaves (Fig. 7, Nos. 1-4) appear in the Middle Solutrean, the earliest being rough and thick, the later ones thin, regular, and skillfully made. The Upper Solutrean is characterized by the shouldered point (Fig. 7, Nos. 7 and 8), as well as by small, beautifully made laurel leaves at many sites.

In general, the end-scrapers, side-scrapers, points, gravers, et cetera, found at Solutrean localities are indistinguishable from those of the Aurignacian and Périgordian. Especially typical of the Solutrean, however, are small, well-made perforators (Fig. 7, Nos. 9 and 10), of either single- or double-ended type.

The Solutrean has a limited distribution. It is found in very primitive form in the caves of Hungary, Poland, and elsewhere in central Europe, but the main development occurs in southwestern France and the northern coastal region of Spain. Recently Solutrean levels have been identified in southeastern Spain as well. Bone tools are present at many sites, but their importance is secondary, and there are no really characteristic types.

Examples of Solutrean art are comparatively rare. They consist of sculpture in the round and incised stone slabs. The most important finds were made at Le Roc, Charante, where several large boulders sculptured in deep relief were discovered. These portray a series of realistic animal (horses and bison) forms.

To date no skeletal remains of early man have been found which can be attributed to the Solutrean. The fauna indicates that this culture flourished under the conditions of a relatively cold climate.

9. MAGDALENIAN   The rock-shelter of La Madeleine, near Les Eyzies, Dordogne, is the type Magdalenian locality. This final period of the Upper Paleolithic is noted for the wealth of bone and antler tools, especially characteristic of Middle and Upper Magdalenian horizons, and for the remarkable works of art which it has produced.

The wide variety of bone tools include javelin points with beveled or forked bases (Fig. 7, Nos. 23 and 24), harpoons (Fig. 7, Nos. 17, 18, and 22), needles (Fig. 7, No. 19), arrow straighteners, or 'batons-de-commandement' (Fig. 7, No. 25), perforators, spear-throwers (Fig. 8, No. 1), chisels, et cetera. The usual Upper Paleolithic stone tools are also present, but they have no special characteristics with the exception of one type—the parrot-beak graver (Fig. 7, Nos. 15 and 16)—of the Late Magdalenian. In general, long and parallel-sided blade implements (Fig. 7, No. 11), and dual-purpose tools—scraper perforators (Fig. 7, No. 12), double-ended scrapers (Fig. 7, No. 13), and scraper burins (Fig. 7, No. 14)—are typical.

The various phases of the Magdalenian have been established stratigraphically and are characterized by the contained bone implements. In the Lower Magdalenian bone javelin points with flattened, conical, or

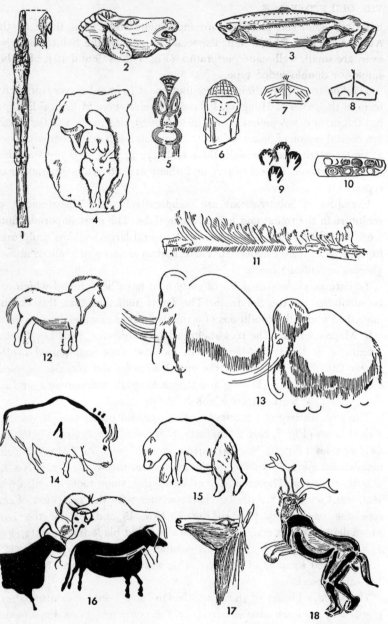

(After Burkitt)

beveled bases (Fig. 7, No. 23) are typical; in the Middle Magdalenian harpoons of bone and antler with a single row of lateral barbs appear (Fig. 7, No. 17); the Upper Magdalenian is typified by harpoons with a double row of lateral barbs (Fig. 7, Nos. 18 and 22).

The Magdalenian, by far the richest culture with regard to Upper Paleolithic art, has yielded countless fine examples of both mural and home art. Animals of the period, the usual subject matter, are portrayed in paintings, engravings, and sculptures. Human skeletal remains, all of *Homo sapiens,* modern type, have been discovered at several sites. The fauna from the various Magdalenian horizons demonstrates that cold conditions prevailed at the end of the Paleolithic.

Magdalenian Home Art—Home art [2] objects of all types are common in the Magdalenian: delicate engravings and carvings on stone, bone, antler, and ivory, as well as sculptures in the round (Fig. 8, Nos. 1-3). Many bone and antler tools, such as javelin points, harpoons, arrow straighteners, and spear-throwers (Fig. 8, No. 1) were either engraved or carved with animal likenesses of both realistic and conventionalized pattern. Tools and flat stones or bone fragments were also decorated with geometric and stylized designs (Fig. 8, No. 10). A few sculptured

[2] Also known as 'portable' art. In French the home art is known as *art mobilier.*

FIG. 8. *TYPICAL EXAMPLES OF UPPER PALEOLITHIC ART*

Home art objects (Nos. 1-6, 10 and 11) and examples of cave art (Nos. 7-9 and 12-18). No. 1, spear-thrower carved in the form of an ibex; No. 2, small sculpture in the form of a horse's head; No. 3, painter's palette carved into the form of a fish; No. 4, engraving of a female figure carrying a bison's horn from Laussel (France), known as the "Venus of Laussel'; No. 5, conventionalized engraving of a 'Venus' from Předmost (Moravia); No. 6, the so-called 'Venus of Brassempouy'; Nos. 7 and 8, typical tectiforms—possibly these represent dwellings of some type; No. 9, negative mutilated hands at Gargas (France); No. 10, highly conventionalized drawing on bone; No. 11, stylized drawing depicting a herd of reindeer (from Teyjat, France); No. 12, engraving of a horse (Phase 2) from Cantabria; No. 13, two mammoths at Font-de-Gaume (Phase 4) in the Dordogne—note the incomplete outlines; No. 14, bison partly engraved and partly painted in red (Phase 3) from Pindal, Cantabria; No. 15, engraving of a cave bear (Phase 2) from Combarelles, Dordogne District; No. 16, superpositions of paintings of different phases at Font-de-Gaume, Dordogne: the head of a rhinoceros in red outline (Phase 1) is covered by a shapeless figure in black, which in turn is covered by oxen in flat black wash (Phase 3), and lastly by a feebly polychrome bison of Phase 4; No. 17, engraving of a hind (Phase 3) from the Cave of Castillo in Santander; No. 18, the famous 'sorcerer' from the Trois Frères Cave in southern France.

human torsos have been found, as well as several engravings of masked
human figures. Sculptured objects were often elaborately engraved.

The skill and foresight of the artist frequently enabled him to arrange
his composition in such a way as to take advantage of natural contours
in the material, or to make his design fit awkward pieces. This was
often accomplished by turning the head of the animal back on its body,
or by gathering up its legs in the crouched position.

Magdalenian Mural Art—Countless Magdalenian paintings and engravings adorn the walls of caves in central and southern France and
northern Spain (Fig. 8, Nos. 11, 13, 14, and 16-18). In rock-shelters
mural art is rare, but a certain number of engravings have been found,
as well as several important examples of sculpture.

The paintings range from monochrome profiles of animals, done in
outline or solid color, sometimes with shading, to the famous poly-
chromes of Font-de-Gaume, Altamira, Niaux, et cetera, in which the
extremely lifelike figures of animals have been modeled by shading in
different colors.

Some of the engravings were lightly, others deeply, incised. Examples
of geometric patterns, called tectiforms, are fairly common; it has been
suggested that the type illustrated in Fig. 8, Nos. 7 and 8, may be an
attempt to represent dwellings of some type. Animal delineation varied
from simple outlines to the most accurate portrayal. Often the contours
and hair were indicated by delicate hatching (Fig. 8, No. 13). Occasionally engravings were carefully made and then painted. The materials used in the cave paintings were manganese and various colors of
ochre—red, yellow, et cetera.

There are many cases of superposition. Older paintings and engravings were transformed, or covered one on top of another by new paintings and engravings (Fig. 8, No. 16). The careful study of these superimposed examples of Upper Paleolithic art has led to the recognition of
a sequence of several periods of art style. The precise dating of each
of these main periods, however, has not yet been determined.

It is interesting to note that in general prehistoric man did not inhabit the caves in which he actually practiced his art. Furthermore, the
paintings and engravings are often to be found in the most inaccessible
portions of the caves. These facts tend to corroborate the theory that
the artistic manifestations of Upper Paleolithic man had some sort of
ritualistic or magical significance.

THE MESOLITHIC PERIOD IN EUROPE

During the Mesolithic Period, which lasted for 5000 or 6000 years into Early Post-Glacial or Recent time, the basic Old Stone Age economy of food-gathering—hunting, fishing, fowling, and collecting—persisted. In this regard the cultures referable to this phase are comparable with the Paleolithic cultures of the Pleistocene, or Glacial, Epoch. Indeed the Mesolithic comprises a well-defined stage during which several distinct terminal food-gathering cultures flourished in Europe, which, in point of time, fall between the Paleolithic Period on the one hand and the Neolithic, or New Stone Age, on the other. In no way, however, should these developments be regarded as forming an evolutionary link between the two periods.

In a positive sense the Mesolithic defines a stage in cultural development, basically founded on the economy of the Upper Paleolithic, but profoundly modified by the changes in environment induced by the recession of the ice-sheets at the close of the Glacial Period. It is in this sense that the term is used here, since with the coming-in of the new food-producing Neolithic civilization, bringing its associated elements— pottery, domestication of animals, agriculture, and the art of polishing stone—there is a fundamental break in the sequence. Admittedly certain elements from the earlier phase continued in use, as no new forms replaced them, but these cannot be regarded as evolutionary. Instead they represent the survival of types of implements for which there was still a need, and in place of which no innovations were introduced by the new culture.

For purposes of description the Mesolithic cultures of Europe may be considered on a geographical basis. However, since the sequences in the southern and eastern parts of Europe have not been as yet worked out in detail, only the well-established cultures of western and northern Europe will be described in the present chapter.

A. *Mesolithic Cultures of Western Europe*

With the gradual northward shifting of the climatic belts of the North Temperate Zone, induced by the recession of the last Pleistocene ice-sheets in northern Europe, as well as in the Pyrenees, Alps, and other high mountain regions, new cultural influences slowly penetrated western Europe from the Mediterranean lands of the south. In the latter area, where the Late Pleistocene climate was less rigorous than in the regions proximal to the arctic ice, fundamentally modern groups of Upper Paleolithic food-gatherers had developed a series of closely related cultures, the leading tool-types of which were small, geometric flints, known as microliths. These so-called 'microlithic cultures' have been found in the Iberian Peninsula, southern Italy, and northwestern Africa. Influences from these sources first appeared in western Europe during Early Post-Glacial time—their arrival may be regarded as marking the close of the Paleolithic and heralding the beginning of the Mesolithic Period. In western Europe the Azilian is the earliest Mesolithic culture; this was followed by the Tardenoisian. Contemporary with these, a local culture, known as the Larnian, was developed in northeastern Ireland and southwestern Scotland. A second local culture—the Asturian—also arose at this time in the northern coastal section of the Iberian Peninsula.

1. AZILIAN This culture is named after Mas d'Azil, Ariège, in southern France, where its stratigraphic position in clearly established between the Final Magdalenian, below, and the Tardenoisian, above.

The Azilian is characterized by flat harpoons with a perforated base and made of stag horn (Fig. 9, Nos. 1 and 2), and by the famous painted pebbles (Fig. 9, Nos. 6-8), both of which occur at most sites. Although hundreds of these pebbles have been found, their significance is still un-

---

FIG. 9. *MESOLITHIC IMPLEMENTS FROM WESTERN EUROPE*

Azilian (Nos. 1-8), Asturian (No. 9), Tardenoisian (Nos. 10-46), and Larnian (Nos. 47-58) tools. Nos. 1 and 2, Azilian harpoons of stag horn; Nos. 3-5, small, rounded ('thumb-nail') scrapers typical of the Azilian culture; Nos. 6-8, Azilian painted pebbles; No. 9, Asturian pick made on a pebble; Nos. 10-20, Late Tardenoisian types from Belgium—small backed blade (No. 10), triangle (No. 11), perforator (No. 12), hollow-based points (Nos. 13 and 14), evolved types of trapezes (Nos. 15-17), trapezes, or transverse arrowheads (Nos. 18-20); Nos. 21-33, 37 and 38, Middle Tardenoisian types from Belgium—truncated blades (Nos. 21 and 22), rhomboid (No. 23), lunates or crescents (Nos. 24 and 25), triangles (Nos. 26 and 27), hollow-based points (Nos. 28, 32, 33, 37 and 38), small backed blades (Nos. 29-31); No. 34, microliths mounted in a slotted haft; Nos. 35 and 36, diagrams showing method of manufacturing microliths by the so-called notch technique; Nos. 39-46, Early Tardenoisian types from Belgium—obliquely truncated (non-geometric) blades (Nos. 39-44), backed blade (No. 45), trapezoid (No. 46); Nos. 47 and 48, utilized blades of the Early Larnian culture; No. 49, Late Larnian perforator made on a flake; Nos. 50 and 51, Upper Paleolithic-type steep scrapers (Early Larnian); Nos. 52 and 53, small perforators (Early Larnian); No. 54, coarse, utilized flake (Late Larnian); Nos. 55 and 56, small, rounded ('thumb-nail') scrapers (Early Larnian); No. 57, notched, or concave, scraper (Late Larnian); No. 58, Larne pick typical of the Late Larnian culture.

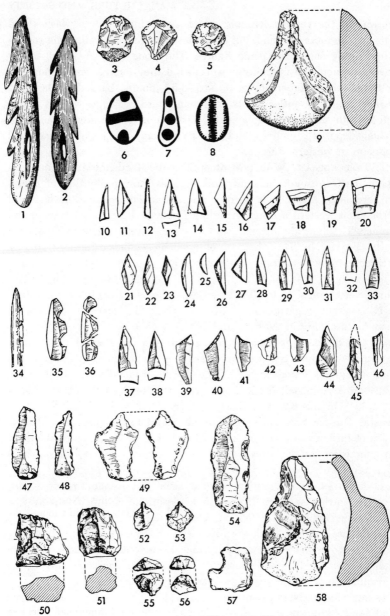

(After Obermaier, Clark, Hawkes, and Movius)

known. Of the various symbols, which are painted in red, dashes and dots are the most common, but other designs occur as well, some resembling highly conventionalized figures. The stone tools are small—many have a pronounced microlithic aspect—and they include small rounded, or thumb-nail, scrapers (Fig. 9, Nos. 3-5), points, backed blades, and burins. Bone and antler points and gouges also occur, as well as perforated teeth and other ornaments. The fauna found associated with Azilian deposits is modern, and consists of many species of animals still common in western Europe.

2. TARDENOISIAN With rare exceptions the Tardenoisian is found in open-air sites, usually on sandy soil, such as the type locality of Frère-en-Tardenois, Aisne. It is a truly microlithic culture, and it is found throughout western Europe, including England, Belgium, Germany, and France. The flints are all small, and they were usually mounted in slotted hafts (Fig. 9, No. 34). They are chipped in geometric forms: triangles, crescents, trapezoids, transverse arrowheads, and tiny backed blades and points (Fig. 9, Nos. 10-33 and 37-46). Of special interest is the microburin, very typical of the Tardenoisian and related microlithic cultures; it is generally regarded as a by-product in the process of microlith manufacture (Fig. 9, Nos. 35 and 36).

In general there is little difference between the sites of this period, except that a given type of implement may be frequent in one site and rare in others. Three stages of the Tardenoisian—Early, Middle, and Late—are recognized; these have been established on the basis of stratigraphy. On the island of Téviec, in the Gulf of Morbihan, Brittany, several Tardenoisian graves containing complete skeletons were found. Each of these graves yielded microlithic flint tools and bone implements. In some cases the skeletons were covered with stag antlers. The physical type represented was modern man in all essential respects.

3. LARNIAN The Larnian, named after the classic site at Larne, County Antrim, northern Ireland, is a Mesolithic culture relatively free of the new influences which penetrated western Europe during Early Post-Glacial times. It is likewise basically of Upper Paleolithic tradition, but the people who developed it came from southern England, where they had survived the last glaciation. In the Early Larnian many Upper Paleolithic types of implements—blades (Fig. 9, Nos. 47 and 48), steep scrapers (Fig. 9, Nos. 50 and 51), perforators (Fig. 9, Nos. 52 and 53), and points—are present. There are also a few thumbnail scrapers (Fig. 9, Nos. 55 and 56) resembling those of the Azilian. In the Late Larnian,

however, which was developed under climatic conditions somewhat milder than those of the present day, heavier implements are predominant. In some cases these were presumably used as wood-working tools. They include heavy flakes and blades (Fig. 9, No. 54), large perforators (Fig. 9, No. 49), choppers, rostrate implements, concave scrapers (Fig. 9, No. 57), and a special type of pick, known as the Larne Pick (Fig. 9, No. 58). As in the case of the contemporary Obanians of Scotland, the Late Larnians were essentially a coastal, food-gathering people, dependent in the main on the sea for their livelihood. Even after later peoples bringing progressively more advanced cultures had settled in Ireland, the descendants of these Upper Paleolithic survivors continued to live on the coast in much the same manner as their Old Stone Age ancestors had done before them.

4. ASTURIAN Overlying the Azilian occupation layers in many rockshelters and cave sites in the coastal region of northern Spain and Portugal are the remains of extensive shell middens, which contain cultural material referable to the Asturian culture. For the most part, the shells consist of oysters, cockles, and limpets (mussels come only from the later levels), and they apparently formed the principal diet of this shore-dwelling population. Asturian implements include pebble-tools in the main—rough axes and scrapers of quartzite, simple picks (Fig. 9, No. 9) for detaching shellfish from the rocks, and a few choppers. In addition, there are some bone and antler implements, but nothing else is known of the Asturian culture, which apparently flourished contemporaneously with the Late Tardenoisian.

B. *Mesolithic Cultures of Northern Europe*

As the north European ice-sheets slowly retreated toward the close of the Pleistocene Epoch, more and more land in northern Germany and Scandinavia became available for human settlement, and people of Upper Paleolithic stock gradually moved in. The changing climatic conditions under which they lived are demonstrated both by the types of wild animals represented in their occupation sites, and by the remains of vegetation (preserved in peat bogs), which indicate the growth of forests. With these developments there also occurred several important changes in the levels of land and sea, which profoundly effected the movements of peoples and the conditions under which they were forced to live. A chronology in years has been obtained covering Early Post-Glacial time in northern Europe that is based on the counting of layers of silt laid down by the melting ice. By these means three periods, based mainly on climatic factors, have been recognized, as follows:

Period I .... 8,300 to 6,800 B.C.

Period II .... 6,800 to 5,000 B.C.

Period III .... 5,000 to 2,500 B.C.

The three main groups of cultures which were present in northern Europe at this time are as follows:

Tanged Point Cultures—These were dominant in Period I, but they survived throughout the other periods.

Axe Cultures—These first appeared in Period I, but they gained in importance in Periods II and III.

Microlithic Cultures—These were in the main of Tardenoisian character (see above); they existed throughout most of the Mesolithic Period on the southern periphery of the north European area in sandy and treeless regions.

Each of these three cultural traditions persisted in modified form after the introduction of the food-producing cultures of the Neolithic Period.

5. TANGED POINT CULTURES The Tanged Point Cultures extended from Belgium to the Russian Ukraine during Period I. Traces of them are especially abundant in the ice-free region adjacent to the southern Baltic. In addition they spread northward along the Norwegian coast. The chief implement types include tanged points (Fig. 10, Nos. 1-2 and 4-6)—perhaps ultimately derived from the Font Robert Point of the Upper Aurignacian, which likewise occurs in the Upper Magdalenian—

FIG. 10. *MESOLITHIC IMPLEMENTS FROM NORTHERN EUROPE*

Implements typical of the Tanged Point cultures of Period I (Nos. 1-6) and the Axe cultures of Periods II and III (Nos. 7-21). Nos. 1 and 2, tanged points of the Lyngby culture of the Baltic region; No. 3, reindeer antler axe or pick of the Lyngby culture (Denmark); Nos. 4-6, tanged points made from blades—No. 4: Hamburg (northern Germany), No. 5: Swiderian (Poland), No. 6: Ahrensburg (northern Germany); Nos. 7-9, Maglemosean barbed bone points; No. 10, typical Maglemosean core axe of flint; Nos. 11 and 12, transverse arrowheads of the Ertebølle culture showing method of hafting; No. 13, barbless bone fish-hook of Period II (Maglemosean); No. 14, perforated antler axe of the Maglemosean culture; No. 15, flake axe from Svaerdborg (Maglemosean culture); Nos. 16 and 17, flake scrapers (Period II) of the Maglemosean culture; No. 18, perforated antler sleeve showing method of hafting a core axe (Maglemosean culture); No. 19, pecked stone axe with ground edge (Ertebølle culture); No. 20, flake axe, or tranchet, of the Ertebølle culture; No. 21, pottery vessel (late Period III) of the Ertebølle culture.

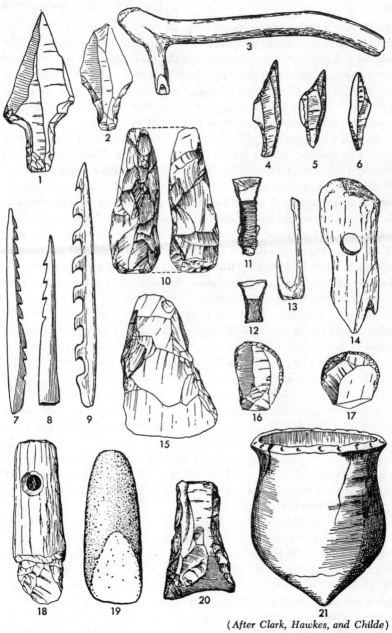

(After Clark, Hawkes, and Childe)

and reindeer antler axes or picks (Fig. 10, No. 3). There are also micro-liths, gravers, and blade scrapers—all of Upper Paleolithic tradition. The almost complete absence of axes, with the exception of a few scattered antler axes, suggests that these people did not deal extensively with wood from the trees of the sparse forests. Nevertheless, a few axes do occur, and their presence may be regarded as the first reaction to the appearance of trees following the retreat of the last ice-sheets.

6. Axe Cultures (a) *Maglemosean Culture*—Although this culture makes its first appearance late in Period I, its main development was in Period II. It extended over the North European Plain from Britain to Russia, including regions now covered by the sea. The sites were mainly on the shores of inland waters and marshy regions, and the economy was based on food-collecting—hunting forest animals and birds, fishing, and gathering wild nuts and berries. The only domestic animal was the dog. That this culture was adapted to the forest is demonstrated not only by the game hunted, but also by the fact that axes and wooden implements—handles, dugout boats, paddles, et cetera—were used. These latter have been preserved in the peat bogs.

The most important tools are bone points (in many cases barbed), which belonged to spears, fishing-spears, and leister prongs for catching birds (Fig. 10, Nos. 7-9). Flint axes, their edges formed by the intersection of two or more flake scars, are normally made from cores (Fig. 10, No. 10), although a few flake axes, or tranchets, also occur (Fig. 10, No. 15). Stone pebbles with sharpened ends likewise served as axes. Perforated antler axes (Fig. 10, No. 14), adzes, and sleeves, or sockets, for flint axes (Fig. 10, No. 18) are also common. In addition, there are burins, micro-burins of Tardenoisian type, scrapers (Fig. 10, Nos. 16 and 17), points, and simple forms of microliths. Characteristic bone implements include barbless fishhooks (Fig. 10, No. 13). Many of the flint and bone tools strongly suggest Upper Paleolithic derivation, but the axe types are of Mesolithic origin.

(b) *Ertebølle Culture*—This apparently developed from the Maglemosean during Period III, but it flourished mainly in Denmark. Elsewhere, especially in Britain, the eastern Baltic area, Scandinavia, and in the interior of Jutland, cultures of local origin and based in the main on Maglemosean tradition persisted. During this period the sea encroached upon the land, and the reduction and separation of the north European region which resulted brought part of the population to the coasts, where, associated with their occupation sites, huge middens of shells of edible molluscs accumulated. These sites closely follow the contemporary coast-line, which was well above the present one in many places.

In the Ertebølle Culture the bone point becomes rare, and flake axes or tranchets of flint (Fig. 10, No. 20) far outnumber the core axes of Maglemosean type. Stone axes smoothed by pecking or polishing (Fig. 10, No. 19) are derived from the pebble axes of Period II. Antler axes perforated for a haft are also found; in type they are similar to those of the Maglemosean. Scrapers of various types are generally made on the rounded end of long blades, but short, broad, oval scrapers are also characteristic. Gravers of Upper Paleolithic type continue. The presence of transverse arrowheads of Tardenoisean type (Fig. 10, Nos. 11 and 12) implies the use of the bow. Coarse cooking pots with rounded bases (Fig. 10, No. 21) have been found at several Ertebølle sites; presumably these were derived from contact with incoming Neolithic peoples to the south toward the end of the second millennium B.C.

THE PALEOLITHIC CULTURES OF AFRICA

The Paleolithic Period in Africa is characterized by a variety of stone tool assemblages and industries, some of which are purely local, while others are very similar to, if not identical with, certain of the Old Stone Age traditions of Europe. It is only during recent years that geological investigations in Africa have been undertaken on a really adequate basis. The results to date indicate that, owing to fluctuations in rainfall, the Pleistocene Epoch throughout most of Africa can be subdivided on the basis of a succession of Pluvial (Kageran, Kamasian, Kanjeran, and Gamblian) and Interpluvial Periods, which perhaps may eventually be correlated with the successive Glacial and Interglacial Stages of Europe. The cultural succession is well established in certain areas, however, but this does not apply as yet to the continent as a whole.

A. North Africa

At one locality in Algeria a series of very crudely worked pebble tools has been recovered in direct and undisputed association with a Lower Pleistocene (Villafranchian) mammalian assemblage. This is one of the earliest sites in the Old World to have produced implements of definite human manufacture. Lower Paleolithic hand-axes of both Abbevillian and Acheulian type associated with a variety of flake tools have been found in great numbers throughout Tunisia, Algeria, Morocco, and in the Sahara Region, which was apparently less arid during Pleistocene

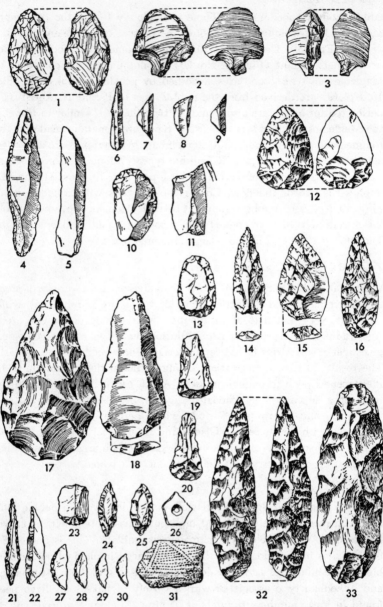

(*After Leakey, Burkitt, and Wulsin*)

times than it is at present. Most of these specimens are heavily weathered
and patinated; in some cases they occur in direct stratigraphic association
with an early fauna, similar to that of Europe. The most famous sites
where hand-axes have been discovered in this region are in the vicinity
of Casablanca in western Morocco, Palikao in western Algeria, and at
Gafsa in southern Tunisia.

Levalloisian-type flakes, or rather flakes made by the striking-platform/
tortoise core technique, have been recorded at a number of localities,
but actual stratified Levalloisian material has only been found at a few
places. The true Mousterian sites are extremely scarce in this region.
Late Levalloisian types, perhaps of Middle Paleolithic age, have been
excavated at several localities. These are associated with a fauna which
is later and contains more highly developed forms than that which ac-
companies the Lower Paleolithic. The archaeological material from these
Late Levalloisian localities demonstrates that a special development took
place in this region, known as the *Aterian* culture. The type site, where
this culture was first recognized, is near the well of Bir-el-Ater, about
forty-five miles due south of Tebessa. In all essential respects the Aterian
may be considered a North African variation of the Levalloiso-Mousterian

---

Fig. 11. *STONE AGE IMPLEMENTS FROM AFRICA*

Typical Stone Age tools from North (Nos. 1-11), East (Nos. 12 and 31),
South (Nos. 13-30) and Equatorial (Nos. 32 and 33) Africa. No. 1, example
of a S'Baïkian point; Nos. 2 and 3, typical Aterian points; Nos. 4-11, series
illustrating the Lower Capsian culture—backed blades of Châtelperronian type
(Nos. 4 and 5), small pointed blade (No. 6), triangles (Nos. 7 and 9), truncated blade (No. 8), end-scraper (No. 10), angle graver (No. 11); No. 12,
point typical of the Stillbay culture from Kenya (East Africa); No. 13, 'duck-
bill,' or oval double side- and end-scraper of the Smithfield culture (South
Africa); Nos. 14 and 15, Middle Stone Age types of points with faceted strik-
ing platforms from Glen Gray Falls (No. 14) and Fish Hoek (No. 15) in
South Africa; No. 16, bifacial, leaf-shaped point of the Stillbay culture (South
Africa); Nos. 17 and 18, typical implements of the Fauresmith culture of South
Africa—hand-axe (No. 17) and flake with faceted striking platform (No. 18);
Nos. 19 and 20, 'duck-bill' scrapers typical of the Smithfield culture (South
Africa); Nos. 21-30, series of implements illustrating the Wilton culture of
South Africa—perforator (No. 21), small backed blade (No. 22), small end-
scraper (No. 23), double crescents (Nos. 24 and 25), Ostrich egg-shell bead
(No. 26), crescents or lunates (Nos. 27-30); No. 31, pot-sherd with typical
incised ornament of the Wilton culture (Kenya, East Africa); Nos. 32 and 33,
Sangoan implements from the Belgian Congo (Equatorial Africa)—typical
elongated laurel-leaf point (No. 32), and bifacial, pick-like implement (No. 33).

culture complex of the Middle Paleolithic. It is characterized by tanged points made on flakes with prepared striking platforms and struck from tortoise cores (Fig. 11, Nos. 2 and 3), and it seems very probable that these so-called Aterian points were used as arrow or spear heads. The actual tang is formed by the removal of small flakes from the upper surface of the piece, which left flake scars on the lower surface. Bifacial leaf-shaped points (Fig. 11, No. 1), known as S'Baïkian points and believed to have been evolved locally from the Upper Acheulian, or Micoquian, triangular points of Mousterian type, side-scrapers, end-scrapers (rare), a few blades, Levallois flakes, discs, and tortoise cores complete the inventory of a normal Aterian series.

In very late Upper Paleolithic and Mesolithic times, the Aterian was succeeded by two more-or-less contemporary cultures—the *Capsian* and the *Oranian*. The distribution of the former is essentially inland and is centered around Gafsa in southern Tunisia and Tebessa in southeastern Algeria, while the latter, which was formerly called Ibero-Maurusian, occurs everywhere along the coast from northern Tunisia westward to the Atlantic seaboard of Morocco. The Capsian is characterized by backed blades, points in the Châtelperron-Gravettian tradition, scrapers, gravers, and true microlithic forms (Fig. 11, Nos. 4-11); in its earliest phases it suggests a fundamental though distant relationship to certain of the Upper Paleolithic developments in western Europe but it is much later in time. The Oranian, on the other hand, is quite distinct. In comparison with the Capsian, the flint implements are rather crude, while a larger proportion of bone tools are present. Human skeletal remains found associated with both the Capsian and the Oranian cultures show that northwest Africa was inhabited by men of essentially modern, or *Homo sapiens,* type, during Upper Paleolithic times.

B. *Egypt*

Archaeological material found in place in the Pleistocene terraces of the Nile Valley demonstrates the presence of Paleolithic man in Egypt. The 30-meter terrace contains typical Abbevillian, primitive Acheulian, and an African version of the Clactonian. In the 15-meter terrace developed Acheulian has been recorded, while the 9-meter terrace yields large flakes and cores of Levalloisian type. In the low terrace, which occurs at a height of 3 meters above the river, developed Levalloisian (originally called Mousterian) has been reported. Overlying the low terraces, a local culture, known as the *Sebilian* is found. It contains very highly evolved Levalloisian types, and, in its later phases, a definite microlithic industry. Of approximately the same age as the Sebilian are several sites in the Lower Nile drainage, the Fayum depression, and the Kharga Oasis, where an Egyptian version of the *Aterian* has been discovered.

C. *East Africa*

In Kenya, Uganda, and Tanganyika, pebble tools of crude form have been discovered. These come from beds which are apparently older than the strata containing typical Lower Paleolithic hand-axes. According to Dr. L. S. B. Leakey, who has done a great deal of very intensive work on this area, the early series, known as the *Kafuan* culture, consists of simple pebbles, roughly chipped to an edge on one side only. This apparently evolved into a culture characterized by pebbles chipped to an edge on both sides, called the *Oldowan* culture. Beds containing true Lower Paleolithic hand-axes of definite Abbevillian and Acheulian affinities in turn overlie the Oldowan. Moreover, in Uganda the same strata as those containing abundant Acheulian material have yielded typical Levalloisian flakes and cores. Dr. Leakey assigns the Kafuan to the First Pluvial Period of East Africa, which, according to his chronology, is Lower Pleistocene. On the same basis the Abbevillian and Acheulian of East Africa are Middle Pleistocene, and are contemporary with the Second, or Kamasian Pluvial, Period.

In higher geological horizons, and thought to be roughly of the same age, are found two distinct cultures—the Kenya Capsian and a sparsely represented Levalloisian. The latter is in turn followed by a special African development known as *Stillbay*. The Kenya Capsian and the Levalloisian-Stillbay (Fig. 11, No. 12) are believed to be contemporary with the Fourth, or Gamblian Pluvial, Period, which falls in the Upper Pleistocene of East Africa. Human remains of men of modern type have been discovered in association with the Upper Paleolithic of Kenya, a culture which in certain respects recalls the Capsian of northwest Africa.

D. *South Africa*

The South African sequence is well established on the basis of the terraces of the Vaal Valley, and as the result of many well-excavated cave sites. Just as in East Africa, the sequence begins in the Lower Pleistocene with a pebble culture of Kafuan type. This develops into what is known as the *Pre-Stellenbosch,* which is in all essential respects very similar to the Oldowan. The *Stellenbosch* itself is simply a South African version of the Lower Paleolithic hand-axe complexes—Abbevillian and Acheulian—of western Europe. It contains hand-axes, cleavers, crude flakes struck from Victoria West-type cores, and, in its later phases, typical Levalloisian flakes. The Stellenbosch was followed stratigraphically by the *Fauresmith,* which is characterized by evolved hand-axes (like the Micoquian of western Europe) and flakes of typical evolved Levalloisian form with faceted striking-platforms (Fig. 11, Nos. 17 and 18). Together the Stellenbosch and Fauresmith comprise the so-called Older Stone Age of South Africa, a period roughly equivalent to the Lower and Middle Paleolithic of Europe.

The South African Middle Stone Age is marked by a series of more-or-less contemporary flake tool assemblages, each of which displays many local features. These are known as Mossel Bay, Glen Gray Falls (Fig. 11, No. 14), Howieson's Poort, Fish Hoek (Fig. 11, No. 15), Bambata Cave, Stillbay (Fig. 11, No. 16), et cetera. Only one of these—Stillbay, which occurs in Kenya and Uganda—is found outside of South Africa. Collectively these suggest on the basis of the shape of the implements and the technique of their manufacture, a combination of Levalloisian and Upper Paleolithic influences, together with bifacially flaked points in the case of Stillbay (e.g. Fig. 11, No. 16). From a geological point of view, they all seem to belong to the Upper Pleistocene.

The *Smithfield* of the Orange Free State and the Transvaal falls into the Late Stone Age group of South African cultures. The tools of this industry, usually found on the surface, are made of indurated shale. There are many types of scrapers (Fig. 11, Nos. 13, 19 and 20), perforators, discs, bored stones, et cetera. The *Wilton,* also of the Late Stone Age group, is a typical microlithic culture in which geometric forms prevail (Fig. 11, Nos. 21-30). Associated with this culture, which also occurs in East Africa, pottery (Fig. 11, No. 31) is normally found.

Surface sites abound in South Africa, but in recent years the stratigraphic succession of most of the above industries has been firmly established, especially in the Pleistocene diamond-bearing gravels of the valley of the Vaal River.

There are many paintings in rock-shelters and engravings on stones in open-air sites which are undoubtedly prehistoric. It is probable that the oldest of these belong to the Late Stone Age; nevertheless, the same styles of art persisted until well into historic times.

E. *Equatorial Africa (Congo)*

Prior to 1930 the only stone tools reported from the Congo were surface finds of bifacially chipped core axes and points, called *Sangoan* (formerly Tumbian). In recent years, however, tools of Lower Paleolithic type have been found in Pleistocene deposits at various sites throughout the area.

The Sangoan is characterized by adzes and picks made on bifacially flaked cores (Fig. 11, No. 33), hand-axes of developed Acheulean type, the tranchet type of axe, large side-scrapers, and many elongated bifacially flaked points (Fig. 11, No. 32). Small Levallois flakes and tortoise cores also occur. In the Congo, the Levallois technique appears to have survived until the end of the Stone Age. Although the exact chronological position of the Sangoan has not as yet been established, it definitely appears to have first developed during Upper Pleistocene times, and to have persisted well into the Neolithic Period in Equatorial Africa.

THE PALEOLITHIC CULTURES OF ASIA

Recent work on the prehistoric archaeology of Asia indicates that during the Paleolithic Period this vast region was divided into two major culture provinces, each of which has yielded a distinctive cultural sequence. The first of these provinces is in the south and east, the second is in the west.

The southern and eastern province includes China, Burma, northern India and Pakistan, Malaya, and Java, where the characteristic implement types include choppers and chopping-tools. None of the well-known Paleolithic assemblages of Europe and western Asia seem to be represented.

The western area includes Palestine, Syria, Turkey, Mesopotamia, and peninsular India. Here we find a succession of Old Stone Age developments which very closely parallels that of Europe. Hand-axes of Abbevillian and Acheulian type, Levallois flakes in profusion, Mousterian and Aurignacian types [3] are all found in this area, which in prehistoric times seems to have been an eastern extension of the still larger culture province which included Europe and North Africa, as well as the Near East.

No convincing relationship has yet been established between the Paleolithic sequences of these two major regions of Asia. There are several intermediate areas, however, in which the two fundamental traditions seem to have met and to a certain degree overlapped. In Pakistan and

[3] No true Mousterian or Aurignacian tools have as yet been found in India.

northwestern India there have been found not only hand-axes and Levallois flakes of 'Western' type, but also choppers and chopping-tools, like those of China and Burma. Furthermore, in Siberia and the Ordos regions of northern China implements occur which show the influence of the 'Eastern' chopping-tool tradition, together with blades, gravers, and microlithic forms, similar to those of western Asia and Europe.

The people responsible for the Paleolithic cultures of southern and eastern Asia were as racially distinct as the stone tools which they manufactured. In China and Java the skeletal remains of Peking man (*Sinanthropus*) and Java man (*Pithecanthropus*) cannot be related on the basis of present evidence to any of the fossil human material from the Pleistocene deposits of Europe and western Asia. On the other hand, in the Middle East we have the remains of Neanderthal and modern man (*Homo sapiens*), just as in Europe.

With regard to southern and eastern Asia as a whole, the Paleolithic sequences of the several regions under discussion may be summarized as follows:

Burma—Recent work in the terrace gravels of the Irrawaddy Valley of Upper Burma has led to the recognition of a new Lower Paleolithic culture—the *Anyathian*—in which hand-axes are absent. Throughout, the Anyathian is characterized by single-edged core implements: choppers, chopping-tools, and hand-adzes, as well as by large, crude, flake implements (Fig. 12, Nos. 1-5). The Early Anyathian is found in the second terrace deposits of the ancestral Irrawaddy River, which are of Middle Pleistocene age; the Late Anyathian, found *in situ* in the fourth terrace, is Upper Pleistocene in date.

India and Pakistan—During Paleolithic times this vast region appears to have been a marginal area lying between the two great culture prov-

---

Fig. 12. *PALEOLITHIC IMPLEMENTS FROM SOUTHERN AND EASTERN ASIA*

Implements typical of the Lower Paleolithic assemblages from Burma (Nos. 1-5), Pakistan (Nos. 6-8) and Northern China (Nos. 9-13), Nos. 1 and 3, Anyathian choppers from Burma; No. 2, hand-adze of the Anyathian (Burma); No. 4, Anyathian chopping-tool from Burma; No. 5, large flake implement of the Anyathian (Burma); No. 6, chopper made on a pebble typical of the Soanian of Pakistan; No. 7, Soanian hand-adze made on a pebble (Pakistan); No. 8, pointed pebble-tool of the Soanian (Pakistan); implements of quartz from the *Sinanthropus* deposits at Choukoutien, Northern China—point (No. 9), side-scrapers (Nos. 10 and 11), and end-scrapers (Nos. 12 and 13).

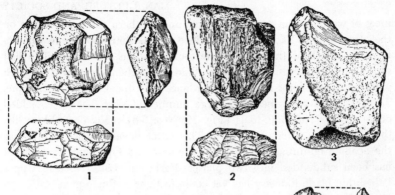

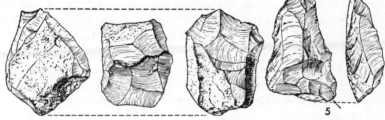

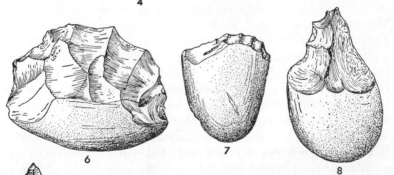

(*After Paterson, de Terra, Pei, Teilhard de Chardin, and Movius*)

inces of western Asia on the one hand, and southern and eastern Asia on the other. In the East Punjab Province of Pakistan implements characteristic of each of these two basic tool traditions are found. The first series includes hand-axes of Abbevillian and Acheulian type, associated with flakes and cores made in accordance with the Levallois technique. To the second series belong a large number of sites that have yielded choppers and chopping-tools (Fig. 12, Nos. 6-8) made on pebbles like those of Burma, China, and Java. This latter development is known as the Soanian culture; both on stratigraphical and typological grounds it has been subdivided into two phases—Early and Late. No true Upper Paleolithic blade industry has yet come to light in this region. Although Lower Paleolithic types of implements abound in central and southern India, information on them is based almost entirely on surface collections, since no thorough work has yet been done in this vast region.

China—Our knowledge of early man in China is based mainly on the evidence secured at the important site of Choukoutien, a small limestone hill located some thirty-one miles southwest of Peiping. This hill contains an enormously rich series of fissure-deposits. Associated with the remains of Peking man (*Sinanthropus*) at the important 'Locality 1' site, a large series of choppers and chopping-tools made on pebbles has been found. This site has also yielded smaller types of implements, consisting of many types of scrapers and points made on quartz flakes (Fig. 12, Nos. 9-13). Large hearths occur throughout the deposit demonstrating that Peking man was familiar with the making and use of fire. The Lower Paleolithic artifacts made by Peking man, collectively known as the *Choukoutienian,* belong to the same basic chopper and chopping-tool tradition as the Soanian of Pakistan, northwest India and the Anyathian of Burma. In this connection, it is interesting to note that the so-called Java Ape-man, regarded as Peking man's first cousin, also seems to have manufactured implements that belong to the same tradition. Both of these primitive types of early man lived during Middle Pleistocene times.

Java—In addition to the now-famous discoveries of the Ape-man of Java (*Pithecanthropus*), as well as other finds of very primitive early types of hominids, the former presence of early man in this island is demonstrated by the discovery of a large number of crude stone implements of Lower Paleolithic type during the years 1935 to 1940. After the locality where these were first found, they are called *Patjitanian.* Although a few bifacial tools resembling crude hand-axes occur in the

Patjitanian, the main types of implements consist of choppers and chopping-tools that can scarcely be distinguished from those associated with the Early Anyathian, the Early Soanian, or the Choukoutien of Burma, Pakistan, northern India, and China respectively. This evidence indicates that Java must be included in the larger culture province of southern and eastern Asia which existed in southern and eastern Asia during Middle Pleistocene times.

Malaya—In the Pleistocene tin-gravels of Perak, northern Malaya, a large series of Lower Paleolithic implements made of quartzite was discovered in 1938. These implements, which have been referred to as the *Tampanian*, since they were first found at a place called Kota Tampan, are almost indistinguishable from those found at Patjitan in south-central Java and mentioned above.

The actual dating and relative chronology of the Paleolithic cultures of Asia involves many problems, and more archaeological research is needed before it will be possible to reach final conclusions. In the western province, however, the sequence of the various horizons is well established by the stratigraphy of the Mt. Carmel caves, just south of Haifa, in Palestine. This sequence reveals that a development very similar to that of western Europe took place in the Near East during Paleolithic times. Therefore, it may be assumed, at least until further evidence is forthcoming, that the Abbevillo-Acheulian, Levalloiso-Mousterian, and the Aurignacian cultures of Palestine are roughly contemporary with their European counterparts. In the Near East, however, the Solutrean and Magdalenian cultures of western Europe are absent, and present evidence indicates that the Aurignacian continued to develop throughout Upper Paleolithic times.

In southern and eastern Asia there is also stratigraphy to guide us, as previously stated, and by means of the abundant geological and paleontological evidence the relative dates of the Paleolithic cultures of Pakistan, northwestern India, China, Burma, Malaya, and Java have been established. In general, the oldest cultures are found associated with river terraces of Middle Pleistocene age, while the later artifacts are Upper Pleistocene in date. As yet, however, there is not sufficient evidence to make direct correlations between southern and eastern Asia and Europe.

IV

The New Stone Age

ABOUT 18,000 YEARS AGO the last Ice Age is conventionally considered to have ended; the Old World and the New began at last to assume the form familiar from our atlases today. Consequently human societies had to adapt themselves to quite novel conditions. But they had ample time; for the change-over from Pleistocene to (geologically) Recent conditions was not abrupt but a very slow process occupying several thousands of years. The glaciers in high latitudes did not vanish overnight, but took nearly 12,000 years to melt away. The changes in climate, vegetation, and distribution of land and sea were equally gradual and varied greatly in intensity in the several parts of our globe. The most general result was an universal rise in sea level when the enormous quantities of water, previously locked up in glaciers, flowed back to the oceans. One of the incidental consequences was the separation of Britain from the continent of Europe. But this general rise in sea level was no more sudden than the melting of the glaciers that caused it. Moreover it was offset by a rising of the land in areas that had been thickly covered with ice. The weight of the ice on the mountains of Scandinavia and Scotland had actually depressed the earth's crust there. So, when the weight was removed, the crust rebounded. The rate of the rebound was at first faster than the general rise of sea level and accordingly delayed the separation of Britain from the Continent and converted the Baltic into a brackish lagoon (the Ancylus Lake). It went on after the rise of sea level had caught up with it so that round the coasts of Scotland and Scandinavia beaches formed when the sea had reached its maximum height are now fifty or more feet above the present shore.

The changes in climate were also gradual and discontinuous. In gen-

94

eral of course, the weather in temperate latitudes became warmer, in the Mediterranean and subtropical zones drier. In northern Europe between 9000 and 6000 years ago the mean annual temperature was higher than today, but the climate of Britain, Denmark, and Sweden was more continental with sharper winters, but longer and warmer summers. For the next two thousand years the climate remained warmer but was nearly as damp as today, while thereafter drier conditions returned without a serious fall in the temperature for some 1500 years. It was only about 2600 years ago that the British and Danish climates deteriorated to their present notoriously damp and chilly level. In the Mediterranean area, on the contrary, and still more in North Africa, Asia Minor, and Iran the rainfall must have been diminishing all this time, but this desiccation may have been interrupted, like the deterioration of climate in northern Europe.

The climatic changes were followed by changes in plant and wild animal life. In the temperate zone of Europe forests invaded both the large tracts of steppe and tundra, that had fringed the river glaciers and ice-sheets, and also the northerly plains and mountains that had actually been covered with ice. Forest trees appeared everywhere in the same order, first birches, then pines, then oaks, and other deciduous trees. Further south, on the contrary, forests withered from drought, and prairies gradually turned into deserts—both processes being accelerated by the destructive activities of men. On the other hand, the regime whereby some great rivers—the Nile, the Tigris and Euphrates, the Indus and the Yellow River—regularly overflow their banks every year was now established, and the annual floods converted considerable tracts of incipient desert into swamps or potential gardens. Incidentally the silt brought down by these floods has actually built up considerable areas of dry land, e.g. part of the Nile Delta, in 'recent' geological times.

The first attempts of human societies to adjust themselves to these novel conditions resulted in the creation of what archaeologists call 'Mesolithic' cultures. Economically such do not differ essentially from the Paleolithic cultures from which they were derived. That is to say, the basis of life—the food supply—was still obtained exclusively by gathering, hunting, or catching what nature kindly supplied. Judging by the best known Mesolithic cultures—outside Europe such are really known only in North Africa and Palestine so far—more importance was now attached to gathering, i.e. collecting nuts, berries, roots, snails, shellfish, and so on, than in the Paleolithic. At least in northern Europe where conditions were very propitious, fishing too was intensively developed.

One result seems to have been that Mesolithic communities appear less nomadic than the Paleolithic; they tended to camp regularly for part at least of each year where a good supply of that sort of food could be confidently expected every season. In most European camps at least we find the bones of dogs, still very wolfish or jackal-like. Presumably ancestral dogs had already begun to attach themselves to men and even to help in the hunt in return for the offal that huntsmen would cast away. In Europe the dog would have been particularly useful in the new sort of chase imposed by the post-glacial landscape. For when forests invaded the tundras, the large herds of gregarious beasts that Paleolithic tribes had pursued so profitably vanished. Mesolithic groups had to pursue red and roe deer, wild oxen, wild pig, and other solitary game among the thickets, and in this pursuit the dog could easily make himself useful as he still does.

Another feature common to most Mesolithic societies is that they made considerable use of very minute implements of flints, termed microliths, that despite their small size are usually beautifully trimmed often to neat geometrical shapes. No one knows exactly how these were used, still less why their makers took such pains over shaping them. But their makers were of normal stature, not pygmies, and some were killed by arrows armed with microliths as heads. Of course not all Mesolithic tools are abnormally small and not all microliths are Mesolithic.

Far the most important advance in human control over external nature achieved during the Mesolithic stage, at least in Europe, was the creation of an effective kit of carpenter's tools. Such were obviously needed since forest was a dominating factor in the Mesolithic landscape throughout the temperate zone after trees had spread over the steppes and tundras. Yet by no means all Mesolithic societies devised utensils for dealing effectively with these encumbrances or utilizing the timber they would provide. The Azilians, for instance, of western Europe, lineal descendants of the reindeer-hunters termed Magdalenians, lacked carpenter's tools. For the same reason the principal groups who made microliths, the Tardenoisians, kept to sandy soils, windswept coasts, and treeless uplands. But tribes who hunted and fished beside the rivers and meres of the great North European Plain while it stretched, still uninterrupted by any substantial expanse of sea, from the Urals in the U.S.S.R.

to the Pennines in England, did develop a kit of adzes and chisels, and eventually axes and even gouges.

The earliest were made of bone or antler and may have developed out of wedges. The Indians of British Columbia used to split planks off the great trees of the Pacific coasts with the aid of wedges of bucks' antler. Wedges of reindeer's antler had apparently been used by Paleolithic hunters in southeastern Europe where trees survived during the Ice Age; the edges were sharpened by grinding and polishing. In the northern forests their Mesolithic successors seem to have got the idea of inserting a flint to form a sharper edge which could then be used for chopping and attaching the implement to a wooden handle to form an adze. East of the Baltic where flint was scarce, the blades of adzes and chisels had to be made of fine-grained rocks. In such a material, however, a really durable and trenchant edge could best be obtained by grinding and pol-ishing—the process already applied to bone and antler. So, by transfer-ring to stone a technique originally devised for bone, the ground stone adze-blade, or 'celt,' was created. A most potent instrument of production was thereby placed at man's disposal.

It is worth noting that at first these heavy wood-working tools were all mounted as adzes. So, today native carpenters throughout the Pacific use the adze in preference to the axe. With this equipment the hunter-fishers of northern Europe did produce some novel inventions, some of which have been preserved in peat bogs. These include the oldest extant paddles—other and earlier societies had been able to cross even straits, but neither their 'barques' nor their propellants survive. For transport over the snows a sledge was invented; a runner was unearthed in a Fin-nish bog. Eventually a local breed of wolfish dog was trained to draw these earliest vehicles.

There is at present no evidence to show whether other societies in the Mesolithic stage created independently or possessed such efficient car-penters' tools. The polished stone celt—axe- or adze-blade—used to be regarded as the criterion of the higher, Neolithic, stage, which is here defined by food-production. Nevertheless many recent 'savages' including not only many Red Indians but also some Australian aboriginal tribes used polished stone celts; indeed the economy of modern savages is gen-erally more like that of European Mesolithic groups than that of their Paleolithic precursors. It just happens that owing to the extent of peat in northern Europe and the preservation in it of implements made of per-ishable material, the culture of the hunter-fishers on the great North

European Plain is far better known than that of any contemporary society elsewhere.

These Mesolithic North Europeans certainly developed a very efficient equipment for exploiting their territory's natural wealth in game, wild fowl, and fish, and utilized well available raw materials. Even during the pine-wood phase those living east of the Baltic had devised a type of bone arrowhead for slaying fur-bearing animals with minimum damage to the pelts. All fished with spears, harpoons, hook-and-line, and nets. Some had noticed the electrical property of amber—when rubbed with fur, it will attract dry leaves—and valued it as a magic substance.

Later, when the land bridges across the North Sea were submerged and the Baltic depression was filled with warm salt water, coastal tribes settled down all the year round where oyster banks offered a permanent and abundant supply of nourishment; near the Danish coasts—the land has risen since then—immense shell-mounds still survive to mark the sites of their encampments. By 4000 B.C. such sedentary folk had already discovered the art of converting clay into pottery and developed large and serviceable but rough vessels.

The characteristic fishing tackle, hunting weapons, transport devices, and even pot forms and techniques developed during the Mesolithic stage on the North European Plain, being well adapted to the exploitation of that environment, survived there for centuries. They recur beyond the Urals on the Plain's Siberian extension and to a remarkable degree even in the Woodland Zone of North America as far as Massachusetts. But meanwhile other societies, less easily situated but presented with ampler opportunities, had taken the revolutionary steps that mark the transition to a new economy and a higher cultural grade.

What the archaeologists call the Neolithic Stage and ethnographers term barbarism is characterized by 'food-production'—the cultivation of edible plants or the breeding of animals for food or the combination of both activities in mixed farming. Food-production constituted a real economic and technical revolution. Firstly, it put society potentially in control of its own food supply. Paleolithic and Mesolithic societies, like contemporary savages, had to rely entirely on what nature obligingly provided in the way of plant, animal, fish, or insect food. The supply was always limited, and the human population was limited by it. But, at least in theory, cultivators can augment the food supply by simply tilling more land, and so can provide for the support of a growing population. The herdsman has only to abstain from eating lamb and veal and to clear fresh pasture to obtain a like result—again of course in theory. Secondly, plant-cultivation and stockbreeding for the first time put men in control of sources of energy other than human muscle-power. The latter was the only force, apart from fire heat used in cooking and for hardening spears, available to earlier societies, unless perhaps the harnessing of dogs to pull sleighs by Mesolithic hunter-fishers in the north precedes the Neolithic revolution in time; sails certainly come later. But plants and animals are, to borrow a phrase from Leslie A. White, 'biochemical mechanisms,' and by breeding or cultivating them men make these mechanisms work for them.

Naturally the Neolithic revolution—the transition from pure hunting and collecting to farming—was really a complicated process actually spread over many centuries and perhaps millennia. It is unprofitable to speculate how the transition was effected; we have no direct archaeological evidence at all. We do not even know whether cultivation or stockbreeding came first. Many barbarian tribes today cultivate some plants but breed no animals for food, and to that extent the first alternative may seem the more likely. But the archaeological record from Europe, Hither Asia, and even China has so far revealed no trace of pure cultivators preceding the mixed farmers typical of the Neolithic in the Old World. This typical Neolithic economy was based on the cultivation of cereals—at first only wheat and barley—and on breeding horned cattle, sheep, goats, and pigs, or at least one of these species.

These cultivated cereals are derived from annual grasses that grow wild in rather dry and elevated steppe country. Possible cradles are Syria-Palestine with Iran and Cyrenaica, Abyssinia, and western China. So cereal cultivation cannot have originated independently in temperate Europe, upper Asia, or the tropics. Wild sheep again occur in North Africa, Hither Asia, Iran, and central Asia and could only be domesticated there. Beyond this we are not justified in making any assertion as to where the farming began, though recent discoveries do point rather explicitly to the hill countries of and bordering the Fertile Crescent as the cradle of wheat and barley cultivation.

The simple phrases, 'cultivation of cereals' and 'stockbreeding,' denote a number of quite complicated operations and a variety of alternative techniques. For the cultivation of cereals the ground should in the first instance be prepared for the seed by breaking up the surface. That is now done with a plow drawn by a tractor, horses, mules, or oxen. But the tractor is a very modern device, and it is more than doubtful whether any sort of plow was used by truly Neolithic societies. Two other devices are current among modern barbarians—the digging-stick or dibble in the Americas and the Pacific, the hoe in Africa. The first leaves no trace on the archaeological record; the use of hoes has been inferred for Neolithic Europe from objects supposed by some archaeologists to be stone hoe-blades or antler hoes and established for Egypt by representations of wooden hoes in later pictures. Today cultivation by either method is usually done by women and in small plots that may be interrupted by tree stumps or rocks rather than in fields. The term 'agriculture' should therefore be reserved for plow cultivation and is applicable only to the latest Neolithic farmers, if to any.

After sowing, the seed needs water if it is to grow. The source of the water divides cultivation into two contrasted branches—irrigation- and dry-farming respectively. The requisite water may be provided by a river or stream that naturally floods the plots by overflowing its banks at a convenient season. The Nile does this most obligingly every year; many rivers in Asia do so too but seldom so opportunely or reliably. Alternatively the life-giving fluid may be led to the plots by artificial channels from springs as well as rivers, but at least in the latter case it would be necessary to lift the water from the bed. Still irrigation cultivation has one great advantage; it not only waters the grain, but also renews the soils since the waters are usually charged with silt containing just those chemicals withdrawn from the earth by the crop. In really arid regions like Egypt, southern Iraq, Iran, and central Asia, as in Arizona and New Mexico, corn-growing has always had to depend on irrigation.

Elsewhere, even in north Syria and the Mediterranean basin as well as in the temperate latitudes of Europe and America, rain may be relied upon to water the crop. But then the farmer will be in for trouble. The elements withdrawn from the soil are not automatically replaced. So the soil soon becomes exhausted, and the yield declines. When this happens to a plot, some African tribes like the Lango today just abandon that plot and clear another patch of virgin soil. Then, when all handy plots have been in turn cropped to exhaustion, the whole group packs up, deserts the hamlet, and starts the cycle afresh somewhere else. This easy but extravagant mode of exploitation must once have been general. It was demonstrably practised by the Neolithic Danubians in central Europe and probably by other Neolithic Europeans too. Plainly such farmers were nearly as nomadic as Paleolithic hunters, perhaps even more so. Their migratory habits will explain the spread of their Neolithic techniques and economy over enormous areas and into territories where, in default of domesticable plants and animals, such practices could not arise spontaneously.

A slightly less wasteful method, slash-and-burn cultivation, is applicable in wooded or scrub country. When the cultivated plot will bear no more, it is allowed to return to bush for a few years, then cleared again, the scrub being burned on the plot. The ashes act as a fertilizer. On grass lands you may let the exhausted plot return to grass and serve as pasture, if you have domestic stock, and the droppings will manure it for you. In north Syria, Asia Minor, and the east Mediterranean where perennial supplies of drinking water for man and beast were obviously restricted and the cultivable land itself did not seem unlimited, one or other of these primitive 'rotations' must have been adopted very early; Neolithic settlements were really permanent hamlets or villages, occupied so long and reconstructed on the same site so often that their ruins now rise above the plains as mounds or *tells*. In temperate Europe, where the water supply is abundant and where to the first sparse population of Neolithic farmers the land itself seemed unlimited, such evidences of permanent habitation are lacking.

Thrift is compulsory for any farmer. His one crop must feed the family for the whole year and in addition provide seed for the next sowing. In practice it cannot have been too difficult on average land to produce more than was needed for domestic consumption. This excess of foodstuffs accruing to the household and the whole community is the basis of what economists call the social surplus. Naturally it is easier to produce a social surplus under a Neolithic economy than by hunting and collecting; for the storage of grain is very much easier than that of berries, grubs, fish, or meat. But provision for storing the crop was necessary. Granaries or silos are conspicuous features in any Neolithic settlement. The Neolithic Danubians erected regular barns, raised above the ground on posts. In Egypt straw-lined pits served as silos, and in Mesopotamia large jars were manufactured to hold the grain.

Special implements were needed for harvesting the grain and converting it into flour. The oldest surviving reaping appliances are straight pieces of wood or bone armed with a short row of serrated flints. But even in Neolithic times a genuine angular curved sickle of wood or an animal's jawbone, still edged with flints, came into use. Grain could be pounded with pestle and mortar, but in the Old World it was more usually ground either with a bun-shaped stone on a saucerlike slab or with a sausage-shaped rubber on a flat slab. The latter was eventually ground down to the form of a saddle. The resultant 'saddle quern' remained the standard form of mill until the rotary quern was invented somewhere near the east Mediterranean about 600 B.C. (Till then, of course, and indeed much later each household ground its own flour every day in such hand-mills, as some of us today grind our coffee.)

In addition to cereals many Neolithic communities also cultivated beans or other leguminous plants and also flax—perhaps at first for its seeds rather than its fibres. Some in Hither Asia, the Mediterranean basin, and the Balkans began also to cultivate fruit trees, olives, figs, date-palms, and vines. Even in temperate Europe the native apple eventually may have been deliberately cultivated, as wild apples were demonstrably collected and dried in Neolithic times. Orchard husbandry must have exercised a stabilizing influence upon its practitioners. A *corn* plot is planted to yield a single crop; an orchard, once the trees mature, will bear fruit for many years. Its owners will not desert it willingly, while a corn-grower may lightheartedly leave his plot once the harvest has been gathered.

Stockbreeding did not involve so much fresh equipment as cultivation, but had more striking social repercussions. A herd of cattle or a flock of sheep represents capital more conspicuously than does seed *corn* or even fruit trees. If exploited primarily to provide milk (or even blood) and not treated just as a handy reserve of game to provide flesh, it will manifestly increase and multiply itself. Being easily moveable, livestock can conveniently be exchanged or stolen. Perhaps even in Neolithic times as in early historical periods, cows (or sheep or pigs) served as media for exchange, standards of wealth, and prizes for war. Cattle raiding indeed must have been an economic inducement to warfare; on the other hand, land, whether for hunting grounds or for tillage, is seldom acquired by savage or barbarous tribes through hostilities owing to superstitious inhibitions. In Neolithic Europe anyhow, as more and more emphasis came to be laid on stockbreeding (in the temperate zone this would in fact be more productive than plot cultivation), weapons of war become increasingly prominent in the archaeological record. At the same time herding is traditionally a man's job, whereas plot cultivation with digging stick or hoe is normally entrusted to females. So pastoralism enhances the economic importance of the males and should favor a patriarchal organization of society. On the contrary where the cultivation of plots contributes the major portion to the food supply, the community's dependence on the produce of female labors is compatible with matriarchy. Finally pastoralism does not necessarily involve the degree of nomadism made familiar by the Biblical account of the Hebrew patriarchs. Cattle herders in Neolithic Europe, as in contemporary Africa, normally kept to one small territory; indeed the most sedentary community known in Neolithic Britain, the villagers of Skara Brae in Orkney, lived almost exclusively on the produce of flocks and herds. At worst, cattle breeding may involve a sort of annual migration termed transhumance, whereby a considerable part of the community leave the village for a season and escort the beasts to summer pastures.

We should expect that, at first, plants would be cultivated and livestock bred just to supplement the wild fruits, fish, and game provided by nature. Food-production should in fact have contributed less to society's food supply than food-gathering. Now a few very early Neolithic settlements in the Near East—in Iran, in the Fayum, and on the edge of the Nile Delta—do in fact seem to illustrate just this sort of economy. But in the most familiar Neolithic sites of Europe—the Swiss lake-dwellings, the English 'camps,' the great stone tombs of Denmark—farming is predominant; hunting, fishing, and collecting seem to have supplied only supplements and variety to menus—as indeed they still do, only more so. Indeed the earliest lake-villages in Switzerland seem more 'Neolithic' than those, still Neolithic, that immediately succeed them; for in the food refuse from the latter the proportion of game to domestic animals is higher than in the earlier villages. This observation confirms the inference already drawn that the Neolithic economy was introduced into Europe after having been developed in a different environment. The nomadism imposed on plot-cultivators as explained above now helps us to understand how the introduction may have been effected. Of course not only would such cultivators have to move on to new land as their plots become exhausted, their younger sons would have to open up fresh territory if an expanding population were to be accommodated. On the other hand the economy evolved in an arid climate would not work in temperate latitudes without modification, and its adjustment often looks like degradation.

In addition to actively co-operating with nature to increase the supplies of food, all Neolithic societies went on to manufacture substances that do not occur ready-made in nature. Thus all but the very oldest, like a few Mesolithic groups, made pottery; of course the preparation and storage of vegetable foods and milk imperatively demand water-tight containers. In converting clay that when moist is completely plastic, and that will disintegrate with an excess of moisture, into rigid and impervious earthenware, men—or rather women—were controlling a startling chemical transformation, a veritable transubstantiation.

Secondly all Neolithic societies that have left adequate evidence manufactured textile fabrics by spinning and weaving. The raw material—flax or wool—had to be cultivated or bred. (Most wild sheep carry mainly hair; woolly fleeces result from selective breeding. How far woolly sheep were available in the Stone Age is uncertain; they were probably unknown in Egypt but may have been bred already in Asia.) Then the fibers had to be converted into serviceable threads by spinning; for that only a spindle was needed. But the threads had to be woven together on a loom and that is quite a complicated mechanism comprising a rigid frame with at least two moveable parts. Being made entirely of wood, no Neolithic loom survives. After 3000 B.C. three distinct types are already traceable—one horizontal, attested for Egypt, and two vertical, current respectively in Hither Asia and temperate Europe. In pre-Columbian America on the contrary no such elaborate apparatus seems to have been known. Nets certainly and baskets probably were known to Mesolithic communities, and both techniques were generally familiar in the Neolithic Stage.

The dwellings of Neolithic farmers were generally—but not always—more substantial and commodious than those usually occupied by hunters and fishers whether today or in the remote Old Stone Age. Yet caves, when available, were still used as shelters and dwellings—in fact they are today. The Neolithic peasants, termed Danubians and inhabiting the löss lands of Central Europe, lived in very long, rectangular, gabled houses like the long houses of the Iroquois which doubtless accommodated the same sort of social group. The reed huts of barbarians in the marsh lands of Egypt and lower Mesopotamia were not beyond the powers of Paleolithic savages. But even the earliest farming village yet known (Jarmo in Iraq, occupied about 4500 B.C.) consists of substantial and commodious dwellings comprising several rooms. In the Near East, adobe was the favorite material for the walls; in Europe, split saplings or a screen of intertwined withies plastered with clay and dung (wattle-and-daub) sustained by posts. The roofs must normally have been of thatch. Apart from the Danubians' lodges which would house several natural families, a clan in fact, under one roof, many dwellings comprised two rooms, the main living room and kitchen generally measuring well over 100 square feet.

These dwellings must have been quite well furnished, but the fitments being mostly of wood have generally perished. But in Orkney where there were no trees, wooden articles had to be translated into durable stone. Hence, we know that late Neolithic houses in Europe were provided with fixed beds, that might be covered with canopies, very modern-looking dressers of at least two tiers of shelves, and various wall-cupboards or keeping places. Model stools and couches from the Near East bear similar testimony. Some light and warmth was provided by an open-fire, generally placed near the center of the room. Of course it served for cooking too, but for this purpose it was often supplemented by a clay baking oven such as are still used by peasants in the Balkans and Hither Asia. In cold climates, like south Russia, these ovens grew into regular stoves that, like their modern counterparts, surely served for heating as well as culinary purposes. Drains under the house floor usually carried off moisture, but there can have been no chimney to let out the smoke, only a hole in the roof, or more probably a gap under the eaves.

Only in Europe have whole Neolithic villages been uncovered. These comprised from eight to fifty houses, and such must have been the normal size for Neolithic communities. Until improved agricultural techniques had increased the yield per acre and indeed until wheeled carts had been invented, it would be inconvenient for more households to live together. For they must live close enough to the plots on the produce of which they depended, to be able to transport without undue labor to the common center the bulky grain which was their staple diet. So the number of persons who could comfortably inhabit a single hamlet was limited by the produce of the few plots in say four square miles that could be cultivated simultaneously under the rural economy already described. As soon as that limit was reached, the younger sons (or daughters) must hive off from the parental roof and found a new hamlet on virgin soil if they wanted to set up house on their own.

In such a community each household would normally provide its own equipment. In particular its female members not only ground the flour, prepared and cooked the food, spun the yarn, wove textile fabrics and made clothes therefrom, but also manufactured the domestic pots. On the other hand, there were public works in which the whole group must have co-operated. Streets—cobbled, paved, or corduroyed—for instance, are well attested. Some late Neolithic villages at least are defended by moats and palisades. On the Alpine lakes whole villages were built on piles along the shelving shore.

It is the essence of the Neolithic economy that each village or hamlet could be self-sufficing: both its food and the materials for the manufacture of essential tools and appliances could be obtained locally. Hence Neolithic communities tended to be rather isolated. In their isolation they had time to develop idiosyncrasies. On the one hand they could discover and exploit opportunities peculiar to their home land. On the other hand they developed seemingly arbitrary shapes for common tools, designs for decorating pots and weapons, rites for funerals, and so on. So archaeology reveals no single Neolithic civilization or culture—in the sense that we can speak today of an American or even a Western civilization—but an enormous number of cultures each distinguished by its own peculiar balance in farming, forms of tools, weapons, and ornaments, burial practices, artistic styles, and so on.

Yet the ideal of Neolithic self-sufficiency was never fully realized. Indeed even in the Old Stone Age the transportation of marine shells hundreds of miles from the coast revealed some interchanges between distinct communities. Among Neolithic societies interchanges were more frequent and more extensive. Mediterranean shells have been found in Neolithic villages and graves all over the Danube basin and beyond its northern watershed far down the Oder, Elbe, and Rhine. In Hither Asia shells and semiprecious stones were just as widely distributed. Moreover for the manufacture of axeheads, querns, and similar appliances specially suitable stones were often fetched from quite a long way. Indeed even in the Neolithic Stage small communities seem to have specialized in mining flint or quarrying choice rocks and in manufacturing from their winnings commodities for the market. Eventually a few people may have begun to supplement their livelihood by peddling the products to remoter groups. Both intercommunal specialization and trade in these senses are detectable in Neolithic times, but neither miners, axe-grinders, nor hucksters are likely to have been 'full-time specialists'; that is, their industrial or commercial activities would always have been combined with, and generally subsidiary to, the prime job of getting their own food by farming, hunting, or fishing. So our flint-miners, axe-manufacturers, and peddlers, attested in the New Stone Age, need not have lived, and probably did not live, on the social surplus (the food above domestic requirements produced by farmers, hunters, or fishermen) as industrial workers, clerks, professional men, and many others do today and had begun to do already in the prehistoric Bronze Stage.

Still, as we have said, there was already a social surplus. It must have been exceedingly small. From fully excavated villages like Skara Brae (Orkney) and Köln-Lindental (on the Rhine) we get the impression that it was pretty evenly distributed in early Neolithic times. Land and live-stock would be owned communally by large kinship groups. Co-opera-tion within the group would be organized as it is in a family. The vil-lage of Skara Brae could be regarded as a single house divided into seven tenements just as well as an aggregation of seven one-roomed houses. No chief would be needed to order about members of such groups, and, as far as early Neolithic times are concerned, there is no convincing archaeological evidence for chieftainship.

If plant cultivation preceded, and was for a time more important than stockbreeding, and if, as today, the plots were hoed by the women, the female section of the society would have made the principal contribu-tions to its food supply and might therefore be expected to have enjoyed a degree of authority. Confirmation for this assumption is considered by some to be provided by the observation that nearly all early Neo-lithic societies were accustomed to model or carve little statuettes of a female personage; they may represent a 'mother goddess' or a 'virgin,' and were almost certainly used in magic rites or religious ceremonies. In the later Neolithic of Europe such female figurines tend to disap-pear. Their place is sometimes taken by phalli or other male symbols. Now, at the same time stockbreeding, combined with hunting, had be-come relatively more prominent in the European economy. Since pas-toralism is associated with patriarchal organization, the contemporary disappearance of female figurines may reflect the diminution of that sex's status.

Again weapons of war, as contrasted with hunters' tools, are not con-spicuous in early Neolithic graves or settlements, and the latter were normally undefended. Later Neolithic villages, on the contrary, are often girt with defensive works; stone battle-axes and flint daggers figure prominently among later Neolithic relics in Europe. That coincides with the increased emphasis on stockbreeding, and, as we have suggested, cattle-raiding offered a motive for warfare. Moreover the still predatory methods of exploiting the soil might well have led to a competition for cultivable land keen enough to overcome superstitious scruples against annexing other people's territory.

In any case warfare, adequately attested for Late Neolithic Europe, would give opportunities for the rise of chieftains; it might result in the stratification of society. Under any Neolithic regime a man should be able to produce more than his keep. It would therefore be worth while retaining captives, taken in wars or raids, as slaves or reducing whole communities to a servile or tributary status. Late Neolithic developments might therefore result in the concentration of the social surplus in the hands of a small ruling or slaveholding class or of individual chiefs. That would prepare the way for a new economic order realized in the Bronze Age.

That farmers should be as much preoccupied with magic ceremonies to promote fertility as hunters is not surprising. The female figurines just mentioned were doubtless connected with such rites. The earth, in which the seed is planted and from which the new corn springs, is conceived as a great mother. But the dead too are implanted in mother earth. Surely their ghosts or spirits will be potent agents in the fertility process. In any case Neolithic farmers paid even more attention to the ritual burial of their deceased kinsmen than hunters and fishers. The body was normally doubled up when it was buried—the position of the embryo in the womb. Ample provision of food and drink and personal possessions—ornaments, weapons, and some tools—accompany the corpse. In northern and western Europe in late Neolithic times monumental tombs were constructed with enormous labor wherein the dead of many generations might 'sleep with their fathers.' The most imposing are termed megalithic (from the Greek μεγας great and λιθος stone) because they are built of extravagantly large stones any one of which may weigh up to eighty-six tons! Other tombs of the same plan and function built of small stones laid in rough courses without mortar and roofed by corbelling imply even greater ingenuity and scarcely less physical toil. Both megalithic and corbelled tombs were usually covered by a huge barrow that may contain as much stone as a modern parish church, and every stage in tomb building was accompanied by elaborate rites and ceremonies. Finally chambers of the same plan might be quarried out of the rock where it was suitable.

Collective tombs of the foregoing kinds are most densely distributed along the Atlantic coasts of Europe from southern Spain to Scotland and then across the North Sea to Holland, Denmark, and southern Sweden. In all areas the agreements in tomb plans seem too close to be fortuitous. Yet the grave goods, always poor, differ conspicuously in most provinces. Only one specialized type of collective tomb (the Paris cist) found in the

Paris basin, Brittany, Westphalia, and Sweden regularly yields such a similar assemblage of relics as to be attributable to a single culture that might have been diffused by an actual migration of people. For the rest, unless one admits independent invention at a number of adjacent points, the ideas of religion embodied in such collective tombs would seem to have been adopted by several communities, already culturally distinct, and to have been diffused by 'missionaries.'

It has been suggested that such 'missionaries' were really prospectors who set out from somewhere in the eastern Mediterranean and traveled westward by sea searching for gold, copper, tin, amber, and other commodities. As such prospectors would have been Bronze Age while the tomb furniture in the British Isles and northern Europe is classically Neolithic, considerable degradation of culture has to be postulated on this hypothesis. (That Bronze Age in Egypt or Greece is contemporary with Neolithic in Britain and Denmark is in fact almost certain.) But no early tomb in the east Mediterranean is really very like the northwest European family vaults; Egyptian tombs for instance were designed to hold the body of a single pharaoh or noble, not for a whole clan or lineage. Only the late 'tholos tombs' of Mycenaean Greece, built after 1550 B.C., have really significant parallels farther west. But the Spanish and Portuguese tombs that really are strikingly like Mycenaean tholoi have been shown by recent excavations to be late developments of the funerary architecture of the Peninsula. The demonstrably older megalithic tombs which yield a Neolithic furniture find no really close analogies in the east Mediterranean. So, even diffusionists today are disinclined to look beyond the Iberian Peninsula for the starting point of the 'megalithic cult' and are even toying with the idea of an occidental origin for the tholos tombs of Mycenae!

Megalithic tombs then seem to document a potent ancestor cult in Neolithic Europe and dramatically illustrate the force of religion among Neolithic societies and its role in promoting sustained social co-operation.

Naturally there is no one artistic style common to all the diverse cultures classifiable as Neolithic. And what survives of Neolithic art is much less attractive to modern taste than the famous creations of reindeer-hunters in France and Spain. No such realistic magic paintings are assignable to Neolithic societies. Such representations as survive are highly conventionalized. They do not attempt to reproduce the sensuous detail of the object as seen, but rather to suggest the object by abbreviated symbolism. Aesthetically this may be a regression, but intellectually it may indicate an advance—a new power of conceiving and expressing an abstract, general idea, transcending but embracing the concrete, individually different objects actually presented to the senses. It may then be the visual counterpart of more abstract forms of linguistic symbolism and so of more comprehensive reasoning.

Neolithic art is principally represented by geometric patterns mostly preserved on pots. We should class them as mere decoration, but we know from modern barbarians that apparently geometric decoration is really symbolic and charged with magic potency.

In conclusion, it may be well to repeat that the Neolithic Stage, though usually called an Age, does not represent a definite period of time. It began in Hither Asia perhaps 7000 years ago, but in Denmark probably no more than 4500. In Australia it never began at all. It survived in the Americas, except in Peru, till the advent of Europeans; in the Pacific to the nineteenth century; in parts of New Guinea till today. But in the Near East it gave place to a new technological stage, the Bronze Age, over 5000 years ago, in the Mediterranean basin not much later, in Denmark by 1500 B.C., even in north Russia about 1000 B.C. Any Bronze Age culture depended for its very existence on trade, and the great Bronze Age civilizations of the Near East actually drew supplies from an enormously wide area. Some features of Neolithic culture in barbarian Europe may therefore be really distant echoes of Oriental civilization. We have tried to discount this, but may not have succeeded altogether.

V

The Metal Ages: Copper, Bronze, and Iron

TOWARD THE END of that era of prehistory known as the Neolithic, or New Stone Age, man became aware of special properties in some of the hard materials of the earth's surface. He learned how to mine metallic ores, how to get the metals from the ores, and how to work the metals when they had been extracted. The effect of this new knowledge was tremendous and far-reaching.

At the end of the Paleolithic Period, the Old Stone Age, there had been a great change in the affairs of mankind. It was brought about by the discovery that both animals and plants could be domesticated. Villages and towns became possible through a large controlled food supply and the development of trade and transport. Until then most of the energies of the people had been spent in trapping or tracking wild beasts for food or in searching for berries, wild greens, and edible roots. Cultivated fields and tame herds of cattle and sheep gave the householders in the hamlets leisure time such as man had never known before. The new freedom to sit, to think, to experiment, and to exchange ideas produced many valuable inventions, such as pottery, and vastly improved techniques for making tools and other utensils. The advanced civilization described in the previous section of this book and called Neolithic by students of prehistory was thus made possible.

The discovery of metals and their uses was the next step of major importance. It, too, added to man's ability to cope with the problems of existence. His power to subdue and adapt the forces of nature and to reap its bounty was greatly enhanced. He was also better able to hold his own against his own kind, both in defense and attack. Metal plows and axes and hoes meant an increase in the size and number of his fields.

111

Lumbering and carpentry tools and hardware improved his houses and public buildings. Metal spears and daggers and armor made him more effective in war and enabled him to build up great empires which, in spite of their many faults, served further to develop human culture.

Remains of these developments have been dug from the ground by archaeologists, laboriously and with great care. Only a small part of the evidence, however, has as yet come to light and our knowledge is still very limited. We know more about these times, indeed, than we do about earlier eras. Populations were greater; towns and the houses in them were larger; and men of the Metal Ages had more things to leave behind them than did their predecessors. Yet many of the details are still unknown, large areas on the map of the world are still a blank, and our picture of the course of events, even in the best known regions, needs extensive revision, clarification, and proof. The young archaeologist will find a fertile field awaiting him in the study of man's life and achievements during the Bronze Age and the Iron Age.

Before beginning such a study, however, the student should examine thoroughly the seemingly simple questions, 'What is archaeology?' 'How do archaeologists handle their finds and reach their conclusions?' Answers to these questions will not only help the student to decide whether or not he wishes to enter the field of archaeology but will also lead him to an understanding of the picture of the Metal Ages which archaeologists are now able to present. He must learn at the outset that the picture is as good as the evidence behind it and as reliable as the wisdom of the archaeologist's interpretation. For the archaeologist has two sets of duties; he must dig up the evidence; and he must work out the story of the past on the basis of his finds and the finds of other excavators.

The first part of his job lies outdoors, on the ancient sites. He must learn how to excavate, how to preserve fragile specimens, how to make maps and take pictures, and countless other things. He must, in fact, be a 'jack-of-all-trades.' He must learn also to deal with men: his laborers, his scientific assistants, government officials, landowners, and local scientists and collectors. The labor and difficulties involved in all this are repaid by the thrill of discovery and by the satisfaction of gaining knowledge held by no other man.

One must not be led into this field, however, simply by the romance of discovery. Such moments are but pinpoints of time in the midst of months of hard work and knotty problems. Those who come to archaeology merely for its romance are doomed to discouragement and disappointment.

For the second part of the job, and by far the longest part, lies indoors, in libraries and museums, at the drafting table and at one's study desk. The specimens and notes, the photographs and drawings obtained in the field must be arranged and rearranged, studied and restudied for months on end. They must be compared in museums and libraries with the findings of other investigators. Every last drop of information must be wrung from them and checked against the knowledge we already have. This, too, has its romance, but it is the solitary and anonymous romance of Sherlock Holmes. One works largely alone with occasional talks and arguments with the few scientific colleagues who are working on similar problems. Most of these contacts, however, must be by mail.

And then, when the evidence has all been sifted, when the comparisons have all been made, and the study pushed forward as far as possible, a report must be prepared for publication. For unless a report is published the work is of little or no value.

It will immediately be seen that what the archaeologist does with the material he finds, his interpretation of it, is fully as important as are the finds themselves. Our knowledge of the period in which he is working comes from his reports. We know the Bronze Age and the Iron Age through the writings of men like Childe and Hencken. The methods by which they handle their evidence, make their presentations, and reach their conclusions must be understood just as thoroughly as the methods by which they excavate. A bronze sword from the Danube in a case in the British Museum tells us little, by itself. We must know the part it played in the history of the Bronze Age and thereby in the history of mankind. The ground plan of an Iron Age Villanovan village in Italy is an interesting thing to study but it means little to us unless we know the details of the life that went on in it, the ideas that were held and developed there, the hopes and fears, aims and ambitions of its inhabitants. The information which we have on these points, and the accuracy and validity of that information depend in large measure on the efficiency of the methods of analysis and study employed by the archaeologists who present it to us. Therefore a knowledge of these methods is necessary before we can begin to understand what we already know of the Metal Ages or of any other period in which we are interested.

The main difficulty in our problem is that we never have *all* of the information. When Hencken digs up a Late Iron Age crannog (lake dwelling) in Ireland he gets only part of the goods possessed by those lake dwellers. When his excavation is completed he has in hand only a limited number of the tools and ornaments, only fragments of some of the other traits of the culture: the ground plan of a house without its superstructure; the bones of an ox without its flesh, hide, or color; a piece of the prow of a boat; the counters of a game; a segment of the rim of a bucket; part of the skull of a man who might have been friend or foe, dear relative, or Norse invader. In fact, his finds are simply those few things or bits of things which have not decayed with the passage of time. And he is particularly fortunate in the crannog for the juices of the Irish bog have preserved much that is usually not recovered, pieces of cloth and leather, wooden implements, and wooden carvings. In a Hallstatt Iron Age hamlet in Moravia not even this much remains. The so-called 'open site' on the hill or in the plain usually provides the excavator with only the 'imperishable' objects of the culture, those made of metal and stone, pottery and glass, and sometimes bone. The metal itself is often rusted and corroded beyond recognition, the houses merely a pattern of post-holes in the ground surrounding a hard-packed earthen floor with perhaps an open hearth.

And all of this does not reveal, of itself, the language of the people who made and used these things, nor their religion, their form of government, their economic system, their social organization, and the race to which they belonged. These are the things we wish to know. How then does the archaeologist set about filling this gap?

He begins by classifying his finds on the basis of the materials of which they are made, their form and shape. This is called typology and is an important part of all studies. As a result he discovers that he has a number of different kinds of swords, of safety-pins (fibulae), beads, house-types, et cetera.

These different types of objects must now be placed in their proper position in time. One of the primary aims of archaeological research is dating. The chapters in this book dealing with earlier times describe dating techniques which use our knowledge of geology and botany; glacial geology, varved clays, changes in sea level, pollen-analysis, et cetera. These aids have only a limited application to the problems of the Bronze and Iron Ages which from a geological point of view had their existence in recent times after the earth had for the most part achieved its present form.

Fortunately, however, the problems of the times with which we are concerned in this chapter gain assistance from a source not available for the Paleolithic and Neolithic eras. Written records extend back into our periods, well back in some places, particularly in the Middle East and around the shores of the Mediterranean. In the regions of northern and central Europe and for the remainder of the world this aid is either lacking or where written records do occur they are so rare and of such limited nature that they provide little of the kind of information we need. A poetically romantic account of a boar hunt and a collection of mutually contradictory king lists fail to give us the kind of information we need and wish. Consequently, even though the Late Iron Age (Early Christian) in Ireland, for instance, can be classified as a historic period, we must turn to archaeology for our knowledge of it. And the archaeologist, in order to obtain this knowledge, must rely largely on his established techniques of stratigraphy and typology.

Stratigraphy is the most accurate and reliable method we have of determining sequence. When the foundations of a house or a village are found built on top of, or set down into, another set, the former is obviously later than the latter. Stratigraphy in trash piles, from which so much of our information comes about the sequence of types of tools, vessels, and weapons, is sometimes more complicated because the refuse can be, and on occasion has been, moved from its original position during the course of the growth of the town. With care, however, this situation can often be deciphered.

Having arranged his finds typologically, then, and having found out from his notes where the different types occur in the stratigraphy of his excavations, the archaeologist has the beginnings of a local sequence. In some cases he knows which types came first in his site or region, which ones were intermediate, and which ones were the latest. Now he must compare his sequences with those of other regions, near by if possible, where more work has been done and where the dating (chronology) has been more thoroughly worked out. Certain types for which he has no local sequence, which run throughout his deposits or which are isolated finds, must also be fixed in time by this method of comparative typology.

By these methods then, typological arrangements compared stratum by stratum, site by site, river valley by river valley, and region by region, tying up wherever possible in the upper levels with known chronology through written records, a history of the Copper, Bronze, and Iron Ages can be written. And sequential classifications of a different kind can be made up, sequences of cultures rather than sequences of objects. So from types I, II, and III of bronze swords at a given site and types A, B, and C of decorated pottery we pass by analysis and interpretation to 'cultural' groupings. Thus we get Montelius' classification of Bronze Age periods I, II, III, and IV, in France; Hallstatt Iron Age periods I and II in central Europe followed by La Tène periods I, II, and III; the Iron Age in Cyprus beginning at 1100 B.C. with Geometric periods I, II, and III followed by Archaic I and II, Classic I and II, Hellenistic, and finally Roman. There are many other cultural classifications of this kind. They differ from each other in several ways and it is important for the serious student to understand these differences. Each classification is affected by the nature of the evidence upon which it is based and by the experience and point of view of the man who makes it. For all of these classifications, of whatever kind, are man-made and they are made not by the early people we are studying but by modern scientists as an aid in those studies. And this is proper scientific procedure. Classifications are a way of handling the mass of materials we dig up, which otherwise would be chaos. They are tools of analysis and study just as shovels, trowels, and whisk brooms are tools of excavation. They are arbitrarily selected by the archaeologist who picks out a particular kind of classification for a specific job just as he picks out a particular kind of knife to clear the earth from around a gilded belt buckle in an Iberian walled town in Spain. The nature of his problem and of his evidence determines the nature of his classification. And, if he is wise, when his problem changes, when his evidence becomes more complete, he will *change his classification*. We have pointed out earlier that the archaeologist has in hand only a part, often a very small part, of the culture he is studying. For this reason his classifications are not 'historic reality' but are, in fact, simplifications of the actual cultures which once existed. As we gain more knowledge of an area we are able to draw a better, more detailed picture of the ancient life. Therefore, it will be seen that the kind of classification we use in presenting the picture varies with the increase of our knowledge. The more evidence we get the closer our picture comes to reality and the less simplified the classification.

From these various sequences of cultures, deduced by archaeologists from the evidence they have dug up and arranged by them into what they consider to be the proper order of development, an over-all picture of the Metal Ages of the world has been welded together. It is presented as three major periods, the Copper Age (Eneolithic), the Bronze Age, and the Iron Age.

We will now examine some of the results of researches into these periods. It must be remembered as we do so that the evidence is far from complete, that we know much more about some parts of the world than we do about others, and that men's opinions differ, still, on most of the conclusions.

Although gold and silver were known and used well back in the Neolithic, it is with the development of the use of copper that we begin the Metal Ages. For it is not the mere presence of metal nor its occasional appearance as precious ornaments which we consider to be important. The great changes in man's way of life which metal helped to bring about came with its industrial use.

Copper first appears in sites in Mesopotamia and Egypt. A spear point was found in the Al Ubaid III period at Ur of the Chaldees and further finds suggest that copper implements came into use in Mesopotamia between 4000 and 3500 B.C. The first tools were probably made from native copper, cold-hammered. It is not possible yet to say when the smelting of copper began. Lauriston Ward believes that it was probably during the Jemdet Nasr period, shortly before 3000 B.C. In Egypt a pin and two beads have been found in the Badarian period, just after 4000 B.C. In the Middle Predynastic period at about 3500 to 3400 a few flat implements appear, axes, and daggers. So we may conclude that copper implements were in use in limited numbers in these two early centers of cultural development during the 4th millennium B.C.

Then, just before 3000 B.C., there was a great burst of metallurgical activity in both Egypt and Mesopotamia. Implements and ornaments of copper occur in great numbers in the sites and we are certain that both smelting and closed mold casting had become widely known techniques.

The next important step was the invention of bronze, an alloy of copper and tin. Many believe that the discovery of the valuable results of mixing these two minerals was made in the mountainous regions of Asia Minor and Armenia, but this is far from proved to everyone's satisfaction. Experimental alloys and some good bronze appear in the Early Dynastic period in Egypt close to 3000 B.C.

Wherever the invention occurred, it is certain that it was exploited effectively in Mesopotamia and Syria and spread to Troy and the Aegean and eventually, but much later—probably not very much before 2000 B.C.—to the Danube and subsequently to northern Europe. It is found in India by at least 2500, reached China by 1500, and Siberia later still. Parts of Siberia never received bronze, according to present archaeological record. It must be remembered that these dates are neither absolute nor certain. They are merely the best we can do with the evidence at hand at the moment. For instance, the difference of 1000 years between India and China may very well be greatly reduced with further excavation. The program of carefully planned systematic archaeological exploration of China is just beginning and offers a fertile field for important discoveries.

To continue to trace the pathway of bronze, it worked slowly westward on both sides of the Mediterranean until by at least 2000 B.C. its manufacture was a standard practice along both shores, to Spain on the north and to Morocco on the south.

In the New World there was an apparently independent development of metallurgy along similar lines. Americanists are convinced that it had no connection with Old World metal industries. There are some European scientists who believe otherwise, but they have not as yet succeeded in proving their claims.

The center of high development of metallurgy was in the Andean region in South America, in Peru and Bolivia. Gold work, including tiny beads and lacy filigree, was outstanding, but the copper and bronze development was also remarkable. Dating in Peru is much less well established than in parts of the eastern hemisphere, but copper seems to have been in use by early in the first millennium A.D., at least. It is found in sites of the Tiahuanaco I period in the Lake Titicaca region in the highlands and in the Middle Chimu period of the Peruvian coast. Tin and bronze appear in Tiahuanaco II and Late Chimu. The Inca, the late prehistoric empire which was encountered by the Spanish invaders, had many techniques including hammering, embossing, welding, casting, and soldering. Copper and bronze and all these processes were known in the Quimbaya area of Colombia but cannot as yet be well dated there. In Mexico copper, on a large scale at least, and bronze working was late, chiefly developed by the Aztecs who controlled much of the country when the Spaniards came. North of Mexico metallurgy never passed beyond the stage of cold-hammering native copper in prehistoric times. Large deposits of native copper occur in the Great Lakes region and it is also found in many other widely separated areas from the Coppermine River, where it was obtained by the Eskimos, to Nova Scotia and to Arizona.

Before considering the broad effects of these discoveries on human cultures it will be helpful to look briefly at the techniques themselves.

For they reveal, in their complexities, the progress that man had made since the days of the Paleolithic hunters in the caves of the Dordogne.

Copper occurs in a native state as a pure metal in many parts of the world. It also comes in various ores where it is mixed with rocks and other metals. One of the commonest of these is malachite, a copper carbonate, which is often ground up for use as a green paint as well as being used as a source of metallic copper. Another copper carbonate of striking color, blue rather than green, which is also often used for paint is azurite. Other important ores are two oxides of copper, cuprite and melaconite. In addition there are many sulphides of copper. The sulphide ores are our chief sources of the metal in modern times, but they occur mainly in deep veins, are less easy to find, and it is much harder to get the copper out of them, so they were not much used by the early peoples.

Copper occurs in almost every ore-bearing area. Native copper occurs in large masses in a few regions but it is widely found in the form of small masses and nodules. There are many deposits throughout Asia, and the mountainous regions of the Near East where the development of bronze is generally believed to have taken place were well supplied with it. In Europe it is again very common, but the best sources are in Cyprus, Hungary, and Spain. The largest African deposits are in the Katanga region of the Belgian Congo, but it has not been proved that they were worked before the Middle Ages.

The first copper used by man was almost certainly small lumps of native copper picked up on the surface of the ground and used for paint and ornaments. Even when we come to the early industrial uses of the Bronze Age we must remember that the primitive metal workers did not need the great, concentrated deposits which are necessary to make modern commercial mining of copper pay. They could and did utilize surface nodules and small deposits, many of which it is believed they used up completely.

Tin deposits are much more rarely met with. Tin is usually found in the form of cassiterite, a heavy dark sand which does not even look metallic. Small or moderate deposits occur in Armenia, Syria, northwest Persia, and Bengal. So we see that the second as well as the first metal of which bronze is made was found in the mountains of the Near East. Large deposits occur in the Malay Peninsula in southeast Asia and in China. The principal European sources are Bohemia, Spain, and the British Isles where the traffic from the mainland to the tin mines in Cornwall was so important in bringing the cultures of central and northwestern Europe and of the Mediterranean to the islands. In Africa the notable deposits are in northern Nigeria and Transvaal where there are old mines, although the age is uncertain.

The earliest method of working copper is shown by the archaeological finds to be that called cold-hammering. Neolithic peoples were expert stoneworkers as their tools and weapons show. Able workmen would have often tried different stones from the ones their fathers had taught them to use. Such experimenting would show that when pieces of native copper are hammered they do not chip like flint and chalcedony but flatten out into many shapes. Some enterprising flint-knapper saw the possibilities in this and was able to convince enough other people of its value to start the Copper Age on its way.

The next step was to learn how to get the metal from copper ores, which were much more common than the deposits of native copper. There are many theories as to how this came about. All of them have to do with accidents, native copper being caught and melted in accidental fires or getting into the hearth or the campfire. This is a quite probable explanation, for the clay floor of the hearth would keep the metal clean. Primitive copper smelting furnaces are still simply holes in the ground.

Smelting is not so simple, however, as the melting of native copper. For instance, when malachite (copper carbonate) is smelted at a low temperature, such as would have been the case in the early experiments, the first result is to drive out the carbon, but the residue is still a copper oxide. Charcoal must then be added to provide more carbon which combines with the rest of the oxygen in carbon dioxide and carbon monoxide, leaving, finally, pure copper. The metal was allowed to run out into small trenches where it cooled into ingots of standard size for storage, transport, and trade. An added refinement was the addition of a substance, such as limestone, which is now called a flux. This made the metal running out of the furnace more liquid and also served to seal off the top of it in the trenches to prevent reoxidation.

It is immediately apparent that the invention of the smelting process was a considerable step toward man's mastery of nature and toward the scientific achievements of high civilization. It is generally considered to have been a great advance for it is believed that smelting opened up a supply of copper large enough to affect human cultures seriously in the regions where it was practiced. At first, however, the copper so obtained was probably worked by the same old method of cold-hammering.

It is reasonable to believe, however, that it was not long before some-one realized that the melted copper would flow into other shapes and that the sizes and outlines of these shapes could be controlled. In other words certain copper objects could be made simply by running the molten copper from the smelter into molds of the proper size and shape instead of laboriously hammering them out of the ingots. Also, many kinds of implements and ornaments which could not be made easily by hammering could be made by the new method, which is now called *open mold* casting. The first molds were merely prepared holes in the ground, like those for the ingots, but soon molds of clay and stone were used. The invention of the open mold may have come before the invention of smelting but most people believe that it did not. This is one of the many important parts of our story which has still to be checked and proved.

The next step is quite logical—the *closed mold,* made of two or more pieces. This permitted the metal worker to cast his copper in shapes that did not have to be flat, or flat on at least one side. He could now make full use of the fluid nature of melted copper. He could give up the old shapes which were merely copies of stone models and develop in place of them new and truly metallic shapes. To this he quickly added the trick of casting a core inside the mold, thereby making hollow sockets at the butt ends of his axes and spearheads so that they could be more easily and quickly mounted (hafted) on the handles and spears.

With the closed mold we approach bronze. As will be seen, the closed mold needed bronze, or at least it needed an alloy, and bronze proved to be the most practical. Most copper ore contains other metals, espe-cially nickel, lead, antimony, arsenic, and occasionally tin. The presence of these metals has three valuable effects on the casting process and its products:

(1) A copper object that contains tin or arsenic is considerably harder than pure copper and makes a better cutting edge;

(2) When metals with a lower melting point are present in the copper ore the melting point for the whole is lowered. This is a great convenience and was especially so for the early Bronze Age metal workers with their primitive furnaces. The melting point of copper is about 1083° Centi-grade, of antimony 630°, of lead 327°, and of tin 232°. Obviously tin in particular is a very desirable companion for copper;

(3) The greatest advantage of all is in casting. Because of the generation and escape of gases which cause explosions and cracking of the molds, it is very hard to cast copper in a closed mold. For certain physical reasons the presence of other metals in the mold with the copper re-moves or greatly cuts down this difficulty.

The experience of early workers with the closed mold would show that some copper ores produced a metal that cast better and made harder implements than others. This led to experiment until the reasons were found out. Then the other metals or their ores were intentionally melted with the copper, in controlled quantities, and the process of alloying had been invented. It will be seen from the list of effects above why tin turned out to be the best metal for the alloy. The most practical percentage for successful casting is 10 to 12 per cent tin with 90 to 88 per cent copper. For the fine mirrors of the Bronze Age a much higher per cent of tin was used. For the hardest edge on axes, knives, and spearpoints the percentage of tin was decreased by 2 to 3 per cent since this made the product less brittle.

With bronze man gained many advantages. The new metal was better for most purposes than the stone, bone, wood, and shell tools which had formerly formed his kit. It meant that he could do numerous things more easily and more quickly, from the major tasks of plowing his fields, felling trees, and building houses to the simpler and more personal chores of shaving and carving his meat. The group which had hard metal weapons had a striking advantage over the 'barbarians' who hadn't them, the advantage of the 'new weapon' still pursued by our military strategists.

The results are to be seen in the archaeological sites. Many of the tools and vessels that had previously been of other materials are now of bronze. Improvements and artistic variations in these objects arose rapidly and there was a striking increase in the number of purely ornamental pieces for personal adornment. The early archaeological attempts to present this situation followed the lead given by Montelius in France, already referred to above. He defined four periods with different types of objects for each period. They differed in size, shape, tangs, barbs, sockets, blades, and ornamentation, depending on the nature of the implement or vessel.

As more excavations were made throughout the Old World and similar sequences were worked out in neighboring and distant regions it was found that the development of the Bronze Age cultures did not all follow the same pattern, just as the steps were not contemporaneous in the various areas. Some types were earlier in some places and some were earlier in others. Influences passed forward and backward although it was obvious that the main trend was outward from the Near East and the eastern Mediterranean. The details of the four periods of Montelius in France did not fit elsewhere. Sometimes the variation was small, in other cases it was considerable. When more became known in France it was obvious that the early classification did not even always fit within the borders of the country for which it was designed. Following the theory of proper and most useful procedure in archaeology which we outlined in the early part of the chapter, it is obvious that a new type of classification is needed to handle all this increase in information and to present a more practical and more real picture.

An attempt to design one has been made by Professor V. Gordon Childe. He builds his new classification on the basis of the use to which the metal objects were put. He makes three major stages: when they were used

(1) For weapons and ornaments only,
(2) For tools in the various crafts and skilled trades which were developing rapidly,
(3) Finally, in agriculture and rough work.

This, under present circumstances, seems a more intelligent and useful approach. But we must realize that the reason it is so lies in the fact that Childe has much more evidence before him than did Montelius. For, while we continually change our classifications when more evidence appears, we must not, as some students do, criticize the old-timers who did not have our knowledge. Their classifications form the academic basis for our modern work and they served a useful purpose in their time. Those whom we should criticize adversely are the archaeologists who fight to hold on to the old classifications when their day is done and they have become obsolete and useless or, as is often actually the case, misleading in the light of present knowledge.

With a modern scientific point of view Childe knows and, as a good scientist should, admits that his new classification is not the final word on the subject. In discussing it he writes: '. . . in my recent attempt at subdividing the Bronze Stage into three modes by the use of metal . . . I could not prove that the second was always preceded by the first and always preceded the third. Probably several parallel series will have to be admitted and the correlation will raise delicate problems.' In other words, the same thing will eventually happen to this new classification as has happened to the old ones. It will wear out and its usefulness will fade as succeeding archaeologists add their bit to archaeological knowledge. Then some of them will make new schemes to hold the new facts.

Now we come to the final aim of archaeology. What is the meaning of all this? What was the Bronze Age? Obviously it was much more than a collection of implements, ornaments, dishes, houses, and town plans. The reader must pause here and realize that even the terms Copper Age, Bronze Age, and Iron Age are merely labels made and applied by archaeologists. The development of industries around these metals was of great importance in the history of mankind but we must not let the labels overemphasize the part played by the metals in relation to the whole culture of the times. Men of the Bronze Age were not all miners and metallurgists nor were the men of the Iron Age all blacksmiths! It is now time to look at the entire mass of evidence that archaeologists have collected and see how good a picture we can deduce of the Bronze Age and its meaning in our history.

The full meaning of the Bronze Age can only be indicated here in brief outline. There is time and space to touch only some of the high spots. V. Gordon Childe has written two books of a general nature on the history of man, *Man Makes Himself* and *What Happened in History*. In these books are long and detailed chapters dealing with the Copper, Bronze, and Iron Ages. They should be read by those who wish to follow these periods farther.

The changes which were brought about by the great discoveries and inventions between 4000 and 3000 B.C. have been called by Childe the *urban revolution*. Previously men had been relatively independent of each other and self-sufficient in small family groups. The new inventions, however, brought people together at the tail end of the Neolithic Age into larger co-operative groups. The new trades and techniques demanded specialists, and when a man specialized in mining, for instance, or metal working, other people had to provide food and clothing and the other necessities and luxuries of the times for him and his family.

And the picture as we see it now contained many more specialized and co-operative trades and activities than just mining and metallurgy. There was irrigation, developed then, which demanded the co-operation of sizable communities both in digging the irrigation ditches and in administering the division and use of the water so obtained. There was the great development of trade in order to get the raw materials to the specialists and, afterward, to circulate the manufactured articles. This led directly to the development of money to make the trade easy and also to the invention of a system of records in order to keep track of the transactions. The records were at first largely kept by priests because the wealth brought into being by the new industries and trade was mostly in the hands of the officials of the temples as trustees of the gods. These records later developed into systems of writing and it became possible to correspond about the transactions as well as to keep records of them.

Another far-reaching advance was the conversion of animals to the purposes of industry and trade. The Neolithic peoples had used them for meat and for milk, but the demands of trade produced the beast of burden. From the horse's back it was an easy step to place a larger load on poles (the travois) dragged along by the horse or ox; and again, to place a heavier load than that on a sledge pulled by the beast; and finally to the wheeled cart which would permit an even heavier load at increased speed. Archaeologists have uncovered evidence of the use of horses and camels for these purposes, including riding as well as packing, in Copper Age levels in Persia, Egypt, and Turkestan. The pack animal and the cart gave rise to further groups of specialists; caravan men, carters, and charioteers to operate the beasts. It also brought into being new classes of men and buildings in the centers and along the routes to care for the animals and the men who drove them. Furthermore, although the pack animals might sometimes be able to graze at night and the packers might get some game along the way, in general both men and beasts had to be fed at the termini and en route.

The discovery that animals could be used for power as well as for food was soon turned to other purposes than transport, the most important of which was to pull a plow and thereby to help provide the expansion in farming which was necessary in order to feed the increasing number of specialists who did not produce food. Many people think this discovery came first and that the use of animals for transport followed after. It is a nice point to explore. How soon after all this the power in the animals was used to lift water in the irrigation ditches and to thresh grain and to run treadmills is not known as yet, but it need not have been very long.

Another type of power was brought under control as part of the *urban revolution,* the power in the winds. This, too, was tied up with trade and transport, but on water rather than on land. Pictures of boats with sails occur on Egyptian vases dated before 3000 B.C. And with the sail came still another group of specialists, the sailors. Instead of a man building a raft or owning a canoe for use whenever he or his family wished to cross a body of water or catch some fish, we now see men spending their active lives on the water, carrying other men and goods from port to port and up the rivers. They, too, had to be fed, except for such fish as they had time to catch, with food produced by others.

The wheel brought about another industry besides freighting and charioteering. It was soon discovered that it could be adapted to pottery making. A potter could shape a pot much more quickly and also more precisely if his clay was on a revolving base. The invention of the potter's wheel brought an end to pot-making as a housewife's task in the Near East. Commercial potteries came into being, ceramic factories where a few men could make the vessels, needed over a considerable region, to be sold or traded for. And so another group of specialists was born, also needing to be fed.

The natural result of this specialization of industrial and transport workers was that the people left on the land were also transformed into specialists. Instead of groups of people scattered about the earth's surface, each group gathering or raising or making all the things it needed, the men and women who were still on the land became almost purely farmers, to raise food for those other specialists, man and beast. The Neolithic pattern of life had been broken.

The other specialists lived in towns or cities. And that is why Childe calls this epoch the *urban revolution*. No longer do we see only isolated farms and ranches, or small hamlets and villages of farm houses gathered together in the center of their fields for protection. Now also there are cities, in which live the nonproducers of food. Even some of the farmers moved into the cities, going out at dawn to work their fields and returning at dusk to their houses in the town. For they too had more leisure. They no longer had to make all their household goods and tools but could buy them, and also meat, with the profits from the excess of grain and fruit and vegetables they raised to feed the others. Therefore, except for the busy times of plowing, planting, and harvesting, they had time on their hands. Residence in the large towns and cities offered them more ways of spending that time and also it meant that some of their sons could perhaps learn one of the new trades as apprentices to a copper worker or in a bronze foundry or a pottery. Who knows, a son of the house, or at least a son's son, might even raise himself by this means to wealth and an important position in the great city. For special trades and great wealth and power brought social stratification and some classes were held in higher esteem than others.

So we find towns and cities growing up with the coming of the times which for convenience we call the Copper Age. The movement seems to have got really under way in the Near East; at Ras Shamra and Byblos on the Syrian coast of the Mediterranean, Sialk in western Persia, Tepe Gawra and Nineveh beyond the Tigris, and Anau in Russian Turkestan. There are surely others still to be found to help fill the great gaps which still exist, as you can see, in our knowledge. And some of the sites now famous for their later periods probably hold records of these beginnings in their depths.

The early phase in the Near East was followed by the Halafian, named for Tel-Halaf on the river Khabur and that in turn by the al'Ubaid period, named for a site in Mesopotamia near Ur. At the same time things were stirring and large towns were developing on the Egyptian oases and in the fertile lands of the Nile delta. But the early periods there are still mostly unknown, a challenge to future archaeologists.

The Copper Age towns, by the processes of cultural development, invention, diffusion (trade), and migration, gradually grew up to be Bronze Age cities, and new ones were built, as well. In Mesopotamia, on the agriculturally rich Tigris-Euphrates delta came the Sumerian cities, growing out of Copper Age settlements at Sumer, Ur, Layash, Erech, and Eridu. The Sumerian culture soon spread upstream to the north as far as the Khabur on the Euphrates and to the vicinity of Baghdad on the Tigris. Archaeologists divide it into two phases, named for important sites, Uruk followed by Jemdet Nasr.

These were paralleled in great part by cultures along the Nile in Egypt as the dynasties developed and their hieroglyphs and an entirely distinct form of script (hieratic) kept pace with the writing of the Sumerians and Babylonians in Mesopotamia. Fortunately the Bronze Age cities of Egypt are much better known than their Copper Age predecessors.

At the same time Bronze Age cities were growing up in another fertile region, in India in the Indus valley and its tributaries in the Punjab. Carts and the potter's wheel and other techniques as well as bronze-making were known. Some of these were identical with the Mesopotamian techniques and actual evidence of trade between the Indus and the Tigris-Euphrates has been found. The best-known sites in the Indus are Mohenjo-daro and Harappa but many more await the archaeologist.

As the Bronze Age continued to develop in the region which we are more and more convinced was its homeland, and the kingdoms of Ur and Babylon came into being and waxed strong, its influence spread farther and farther afield. From Egypt and the Syrian coast it spread to Cyprus where there are tremendous deposits of copper; to Troy and other cities in Asia Minor; to the Greek islands and mainland where the Minoan-Mycenaean Bronze Age cultures set the stage for the Classic Mediterranean civilizations from which so many of our own traits have come down directly through the ages. The great structures which have been uncovered by archaeologists at Knossos, Phaestos, and other Minoan cities in Crete are combination palaces, factories, and warehouses as were the temples of Sumer and Babylon.

From the Aegean the Bronze Age spread westward through Malta and Sicily and northward through Italy to central, western, and northern Europe. Trade routes, by land and sea, carried the new products to the ends of Europe where they were exchanged for Danish amber, Cornwall's tin, and Irish gold. And along the amber routes and the tin routes went ideas as well as bronze castings, jewels, and fancy faïence beads. The ideas passed both ways, south to north, and north to south, as did the trade, to the mutual benefit of all. But there is no doubt that the south had the more to offer in the realm of ideas, both as to quantity and quality. So, although the Mediterranean gained a certain amount of knowledge from the north along with the tin, amber, and furs the balance of ideas and inventions was in favor of the south, and we say that the Bronze Age spread to the Illyrian (eastern) and the Celtic (western) provinces of central Europe, to Gaul and Britain, to Germany and Scandinavia.

The growth of all these cities made a great change in the lives of the people over and above the new industries practiced in them. Large numbers of people were now collected in close quarters and new forms of social organization, governmental and economic, had to be worked out to handle the situation. Also, the old superstitions and their accompanying ceremonies became more complex and more important when there were greater numbers of people to take part in them. Since these were all developing rather rapidly together it is natural that the new political and economic systems got entangled with the new and expanding systems which were being built around the old superstitions. The result was a series of totalitarian city-states, ambitious to become widespread kingdoms, operating on the basis of economic imperialism through and with the support of highly organized religions.

Monumental temples were built to house this new force in the affairs of men. In themselves they were an example of the new-born co-operative ideal, because hundreds, even thousands, of men had to work together, according to plan, to get them up. They were of stone, brick, or wood, or combinations of these materials, depending on the locality. Here are some more specialized crafts, not mentioned above: quarry men and stone masons, brick manufacturers and bricklayers, woodsmen and carpenters. We also see further evidence of the advances of trade and of the transport industry. Pine timbers in the Mesopotamian temples had to be brought from the Persian mountains or from Syria.

When built, the temples or palaces housed the kings and the priests and all their works and wealth; images of the gods, goods and merchandise, factories and workshops, scribes, bankers (money-changers), slaves, and soldiers. For business of this kind called for professional soldiers, mercenary standing armies. And one of the results of the business was captives, from the defeated cities and the tribal territories which were 'liberated' from their old way of life. A system of slavery solved two pressing problems. It provided a use for the captives and it relieved what must have been an acute labor shortage.

The commerce which flowed in and out of the temples needed not only the trade routes we have mentioned but also standardized weights and measures, harbors, canals (not only for irrigation, but, as at Ur, for boats), and specialized commercial agents at the shipping points and harbors and at the termini of the caravan routes.

The old barter systems were not good enough for such active and complicated trading, so money economy was invented and great wealth accumulated within the cities and great estates outside of them. Trade and work had to be regulated and this was done by various methods. For instance, Hammurabi in Babylon fixed maximum prices for certain commodities and maximum wages for specific work (Childe points out that no minimum wages were mentioned). He also established formal legal rules which have become known as the Code of Hammurabi. And then, to administer these rules and regulations a civil service was set up.

With the increase of leisure and wealth and the emphasis placed upon crafts, artistic development flourished. There was much scope for art in architecture and pottery-making. Painting on pots and on walls became a fine art and sculpture and music also found favor with the leaders, who were at the same time civic and religious.

The exact sciences began to come into their own. Weights and measures have already been mentioned. In addition in commerce, architecture, and among the crafts there was a need for arithmetic and geometry. And time began to be important to everybody. So in these early cities were laid the foundations of our modern science. Sundials and water clocks on the hourglass principle were invented. A lunar calendar was established by the Sumerians and the Egyptians produced a solar calendar which, with refinements, is the one we use today.

From this condensed account it can be seen that the Copper and Bronze Ages were indeed revolutionary, that we still have a very great deal to learn about them, and that, since they played such an important part in the background of our own culture, all that we can learn about them is important.

We now come to the Iron Age. Iron is the other metal of supreme industrial importance in history. Perhaps it is now losing its supremacy to the fissionable materials necessary for the production of atomic power but until now, at least, it has led the field. We do not need to list its properties or the many uses to which it can be put. In the Iron Age, however, its structural and engineering advantages were not utilized. Then it meant almost entirely one thing: a wonderful material for tools and weapons, better in most respects than bronze and very much better than stone, bone, wood, or shell.

Another great advantage was that it could be found almost everywhere. The earth's surface is 4 to 5 per cent iron. Earthly iron is almost never found pure except in some cases, in certain basalt rocks for example, where it occurs in such small particles as to be of no practical use. There is a heavenly source of iron, however, which is much purer, as might be expected. The meteorites which occasionally drop on the earth from the sky consist largely of iron and mankind early made use of this source. But they are rare and the main sources are the iron ores. The commonest of these are certain iron oxides, haematite, limonite, and magnetite and a carbonate of iron, siderite or spathic iron.

To obtain metallic iron from the ores it is necessary to get rid of the oxygen or carbonic acid with which it is combined and also the silica and other rocks mixed in the ore. To do this, the ore must be heated in a charcoal fire. Then the carbon in the charcoal combines with the oxygen in the ore (if it is an oxide ore) and passes off as carbon dioxide, while the silica combines with part of the iron and runs off as slag leaving the rest of the iron in a spongy mass, not melted but in metallic form, although the mass still contains some silica. The slag (ferrous silicate with variations depending on the other rocks in the ore) actually plays an important part in the process, for in liquid condition it forms a scum over the iron and prevents reoxidizing by contact with the air. A limestone flux, as in the case of copper, can be substituted to do this and then, the slag being no longer needed in the process, much more of the iron can be saved. The spongy mass is then hammered or heated and hammered, heated and hammered repeatedly in an operation now called 'puddling' until more of the silica is worked out and the iron has become a solid mass of metal.

There are three main forms of metallic iron. When treated as described in the last paragraph it has hardly any carbon in it, is relatively soft and malleable, therefore easily worked, and is called *wrought iron*. If the heat in the furnace is hot enough, however, instead of forming a spongy mass the iron melts and flows off. This iron has more carbon in it. If the amount of carbon is high the result is *cast iron*, hard but brittle. If the quantity of carbon is small, more than in wrought iron but still not much over 1 per cent, the result is steel which can be of varying degrees of hardness and toughness or brittleness.

As we have shown, the history of the invention and spread of bronze is still uncertain. The history of iron is much more so. A generally accepted theory is that the working of iron was invented in Asia Minor near the Black Sea at an unknown date. Apparently it was known in the Near East by approximately 3000 B.C., about as early as bronze. But iron objects are very rare in sites of that era. The surprising thing about it is that we do not find serious references to it in the records of the Near East until fifteen hundred years later. And many more centuries pass by before it becomes generally used. This is a puzzling situation and it gives rise to three particular questions for which archaeologists want answers but which cannot be answered at present:

(1) Were all iron objects in the Near East before 1500 B.C., or so, made of meteoric iron or were some of them made of iron taken from ore?
(2) If they were all made of meteoric iron, why did it take man in the Near East so long to learn how to smelt iron ores while he knew how to smelt copper, lead, and several other ores?
(3) If, on the other hand, some of the early iron objects were of iron from smelted ores, why was the general use of iron delayed for 1500 to 2000 years when it had so many advantages over copper and bronze?

This is a fair sample of many problems that are still unsolved in archaeology. A great deal of the important information we wish from the past is still to be found out. The possibilities for future archaeologists are endless and this is one of the most interesting of them, because it plays such a great part in man's development and because we are sure that the answer awaits us in the ground, if we can find it and read it properly.

Let us see how far we can go, briefly, in answering these questions. The first possibility which occurs to the archaeologist's inquiring and skeptical mind (and archaeologists must ever be skeptical) is that our dating is wrong and that the sites we date at 3000 B.C. should be much nearer to 1500 B.C. This would go a long way toward solving the problem, but, without going into the evidence here, it can be stated that the chronology of the periods under discussion in the Near East is one of the best we have. In fact some students will think the date of 3000 B.C. which I have given for the beginning of the general use of bronze is too conservative and that it should be earlier.

Turning now to the actual questions listed above, the second provides the most suggestive answers. We have seen that it is more difficult to smelt iron than copper. The melting point of iron is 1530° Centigrade, about 500° above that of copper or gold. Furthermore, this was no 'native' iron, like native copper, that could be obtained merely by heating. It might well have taken a long time for the development of the chemistry of iron to the point where its smelting could be mastered. Also, it has been suggested that the spongy mass which is wrought iron as it comes from the smelting might not have been recognized for some time as a useful metal.

The first question presents a different sort of problem, one of mineral theory and analysis. Were all the earlier finds made of meteoric iron? Mining engineers insist that meteoric iron always has at least 5 per cent nickel in it. Iron beads from Predynastic El Gerzah and an early iron dagger from Ur do have nickel, the latter 10.9 per cent. On the other hand, pieces of iron found between blocks of stone in the Fourth Dynasty Great Pyramid in Egypt show on analysis only traces of nickel, not nearly enough to satisfy the generally accepted definition of meteoric iron. In this case, however, the date of the iron is questioned. There are those who claim that the iron was not in the pyramid when it was built but was dropped there, perhaps broken from the tools they used, by Arabs removing stones for the walls of their own buildings. This could have happened in fairly recent times. There are, however, two finds to which early dates are assigned which keep the problem alive. Iron beads from Abydos show only traces of nickel and a dagger from Tell Asmar, with an assigned date of 2800 B.C., has no nickel at all. These are not sufficient to prove the point, but they do support the possibility that iron other than meteoric may be very early.

We are now left with the third question, if iron smelting was indeed known at about 3000 B.C. why was it not followed up for one thousand or fifteen hundred years after that? This must be left unanswered until we have more information on the other two. The problem must be thoroughly investigated both by excavation and by mineral analysis.

Leaving the early examples we shall now outline briefly the development of iron as an important part of man's material culture. The records of Amenhotep III (1411-1373 B.C.) contain a letter promising to send him some iron. Tut-ankh-amen (1350 B.C.) had a dagger and miniature tools of iron. An iron spear is mentioned in an inscription of Tylath-Pileser I (1125-1000 B.C.). Many weapons and tools were found in the palace of Ashurnasirpal III (883-859 B.C.) but these may have belonged a century or so later because Sargon II (722-705 B.C.) used the palace for a storehouse. Certainly by the time of Sargon II iron was coming into its own in Mesopotamia for a hoard of 175 tons was found in *his* palace, including bars, grappling hooks, mattocks, chains, and so on.

The most common account of the history of iron is that it began with the Hittites in the Near East and spread out from them in all directions until by 1000 B.C. it was in general use in western Asia, Egypt, and southeastern and central Europe. This was the 'civilized world' of its time and the Iron Age can be considered to have been well on its way by then. The date of 1000 B.C. may, however, be a few centuries too early for some of the regions mentioned. Archaeology goes in cycles, like so many other things. There are times when experts have a tendency to push dates back while at other times the majority is in favor of pulling them forward. At present we are on the conservative tack, moving dates up, although the turning-point in the cycle seems to have been reached in the New World, at least. Present interpretation indicates that central Europe and the western half of southern Europe were still in the Bronze Age at 1000 B.C.

In the newly opened European Bronze and Iron Age room in the Peabody Museum at Harvard, Hencken presents the Italian Iron Age as beginning with the founding of Greek colonies in southern Italy at 750 B.C., and through the following fifty years. Proto-Corinthian pottery found at Cumae (near Naples), Tarentum, and Locri and at Syracuse and Megara in Sicily fixes the date in relation to the historically established Greek sequence. Further to the north in Italy, in Etruria, the beginning Iron

Age date is a quarter of a century later, fixed by the same tie-up (cross-dating technique) with Late Geometric Greek pottery. There, Villanovan period I began at 725 B.C. Its chief town was Tarquinia (the modern Corneto). The Villanovan towns later became the great Etruscan cities of central Italy.

Farther to the west the advent of the Iron Age as a strong cultural factor was somewhat later, during the seventh century B.C. It was touched off by the founding of Cadiz and other towns in southern Spain by the Phoenicians from the coasts of Palestine and Lebanon at the eastern end of the Mediterranean. They were great traders who roamed the Mediterranean Sea after the collapse of the Bronze Age Minoan-Mycenaean civilization of Crete and Greece. They were apparently attracted to Spain by its known wealth in gold, silver, copper, and tin and they introduced the local Iberians and Ligurians to the advantages of the Iron Age.

In central Europe, Hencken believes that the safest date at present for the inauguration of actual Iron Age culture is 650 B.C. The first phase is called Hallstatt A or Hallstatt I, named for a famous cemetery site in the Austrian Alps. It is a continuation of the local Urnfield and Tumulus Bronze Age cultures with the addition of Iron Age traits from the Villanovan (Benacci II period) and other Italian cultures by which it is dated.

The reader must realize that these dates do not represent the first appearance of iron objects in Italy, Spain, and central Europe. They are, rather, the points in time when it is believed that there had been a sufficient change in the general nature of the local cultures to justify a change in label from Bronze Age to Iron Age. Most of those changes arose as the result of influences spreading out from the eastern Mediterranean.

Recent finds in France and Germany illustrate the spread of wealth out from the Mediterranean at this time. At Vix, in France, a late sixth-century Hallstatt tomb has revealed spectacular Greek bronzes. This is the largest Greek Iron Age find yet made and demonstrates the great wealth of the Celtic ruling families in France and also their close connection with the Greek world. At Heuneberg in southern Germany, a considerable amount of black-figured Greek pottery has been found in the course of excavation of a sixth-century fortress. Again the wealth and influences extending from the Mediterranean northward and westward is strikingly illustrated.

On the other side of the Near East, India and the Far East are still practically virgin fields as regards iron. A questionable date of the fifth

century B.C. has been advanced for China. In India there is a tradition of
early iron working. It appears in megalithic graves. Huge forged columns
up to forty-two feet in height with a weight of ten tons are found in the
north. But there is no archaeological or historical evidence as yet to show
iron in India before the beginning of the Christian era.

In North Africa iron was introduced by the Phoenicians and the Car-
thaginians. At some time in its history iron spread widely through Negro
Africa and the work of Negro blacksmiths is famous. The development
of iron working among the Negroes is so great that there are those who
think that it may have begun in Africa, where old mines do exist. But
as yet there is no reliable archaeological evidence for iron working there
before the camel was brought to northwest Africa some centuries after
the birth of Christ. The camel is believed to have brought about extensive trade across the Sahara Desert and iron probably reached Negro
Africa after this had occurred.

Although bronze was well developed in parts of the New World and
the use of native copper was widespread, nothing has as yet come to
light to justify an American Iron Age. A little meteoric iron was used—
cold-hammered. Non-meteoric iron seems to have been post-Columbian,
presumably introduced by the invading Europeans.

The meaning of the Iron Age in terms of man and cultures can be
simplified (though we must be ever on our guard against too great sim-
plification) to the statement that it saved the civilizations of the col-
lapsing Late Bronze Age empires. These great empires, the Egyptian,
Minoan, Mycenaean, Hittite, and Babylonian, built up through the con-
solidation of the city-state of the Early Bronze Age, were being thoroughly undermined by the sterility of their own economy and the increasing numbers of 'barbarians' that they had hired as mercenary soldiers.
The tribute they collected is described by Childe as 'not the production
of fresh wealth' but merely 'the theft of wealth from those who had produced it.' Ruinous wars with each other, invasions of 'barbarians,' and
rebellions of both subjects and barbarian mercenaries finished them off,
every one of them, by about 1200 B.C. As archaeologists and historians
read the record, a dark age followed. But civilization was saved and a
new prosperity with different leadership arose through the introduction
of new wealth, widely available, in the form of the new metal—iron—
ever so much cheaper and more plentiful than bronze.

New empires and trading groups arose. We have already seen the activity of the Phoenician cities in spreading the knowledge of iron. They

suffered least in the general Bronze Age collapse and because of that fact were able to expand their trade and influence widely as the great empires fell to pieces. There was an important change in the nature of the Phoenician expansion in comparison with the pattern of the Bronze Age empires. The Bronze Age despots captured towns and districts and held them by means of military garrisons for the purpose of extracting tribute. The newly established Phoenician cities of the Iron Age were colonies in a more modern sense. They did not pay tribute to the homeland. The latter obtained such profit as it got from the colonies through trade, the establishment of new markets, the receipt of new commodities in exchange, and the provision of outlets for surplus population. Carthage was one of the Phoenician colonies, yet history records it as an independent republic. This is a far cry from the position of the tributary cities under the heel of Sargon.

The mainland Greeks had been badly disorganized by the Bronze Age debacle. But the habit of urban life is not easily given up. Although losing ground for the time being to the Phoenicians, they began to recover by about 1000 B.C. and subsequently built up a strong Iron Age civilization on the remnants of the Minoan-Mycenaean culture, much of which was neither destroyed nor forgotten.

In the Near East the small kingdoms of Palestine, Lydea, and Phrygia were built on the wreckage of the Bronze Age. These were merged by the Assyrians into a new empire extending from the Mediterranean to beyond the Tigris. This in turn, after a considerable amount of backing and filling, was taken over by the Persians. Thus in 500 B.C. the Persian Darius controlled an empire extending from the Aegean to the Indus, brutally wrought, but permitting through its unity the rapid spread of the ideas of the Iron Age.

Toward the north, in central Italy and as far up as the present Bologna, Iron Age culture was organized by an immigrant group from Asia Minor, the Etruscans. The knowledge they possessed, both miltary and industrial, had been acquired as mercenaries and subjects under Bronze Age empires. The brutality of their miltary methods was tempered by their knowledge and teaching of the new industrial techniques. Their rule, however vicious, stopped the rot of the Bronze Age collapse in Italy and welded the remnants into an active and progressive Iron Age community out of which, by rebellion, came Rome.

Farther to the north, emancipated 'barbarians'—the Celts in the west and the Scyths on the Eurasiatic steppes—prepared the way for the first real developments outside of the 'ancient world' of the Aegean, Egypt, the Near East, and India. The Classical civilizations of Greece and Rome have, particularly through their literature, overshadowed this northern progress in our knowledge up to now. But excavation is beginning at last to reveal its importance. We owe a great debt to Celt and Scyth as well as to Greek and Roman.

The details of the development of civilization through the Iron Age are too extensive to list here so only a general statement will be made. Cheap iron tools ended the situation Childe describes as the 'state monopoly and great household stores' of the palace-temples. Types of industries increased in number and workshops became larger, employing more men. With these increases the amount of trading also grew.

The invention of true alphabets brought the possibility of literacy to all—not just the priests, officials, and clerks, as formerly. Stamped coins of standard, guaranteed value replaced the bars of silver which were awkward to handle and easy to manipulate for purposes of fraud. This development was necessary and important. For with the appearance of cheap goods frequent purchases were made by small farmers and artisans, as well as by wealthy traders and large landholders. The new coins provided not only a better medium of exchange for important sales but also small change for the minor transactions of the marketplace.

With the introduction of the cheap iron plow, extensive cultivation of the land spread widely, as far north as southern England. Cities increased in size with many acres of parks and gardens. The populations of the largest ran into the hundreds of thousands.

Political changes were varied and uneven. In Asia the Bronze Age traditions of monarchy continued; but in the west, particularly in Athens, governments of definitely republican character were built up. Universal suffrage was unknown and slavery continued but the ruling class operated upon a truly democratic basis. The new ruling classes were broadened to include craftsmen and merchants as well as priests and great landholders. Their governments produced public works and free dramatic performances, and they generally devoted at least part of their efforts to the benefit of the populace rather than merely of their own treasuries.

The developments in social organization, philosophy, science, and religion were numerous and rapid after the Iron Age got under way. The 'natural philosophers' laid the foundations for the theory of organic evolution and the theory of music. The study of mathematics made great strides forward, particularly in Greece where the mathematicians of the Iron Age developed the theorem of Pythagoras and learned to solve quadratic equations. Astronomers in Mesopotamia and Greece learned to predict eclipses. Medicine was greatly freed from magic (or, at least, from demons) and the work of Hippocrates is still well known today. Growing knowledge of how men think, of how our brains work, culminated in the logical systems of Aristotle. Religion became more of an individual matter as in the Greek mystical cults; monotheism (the theory of a single god) arose and the teachings of the Jewish prophets, Buddha, Lao-tse, and Confucius formed the basis for many of our important modern religions.

It must be realized and remembered, however, that the benefits of all this were not applied to a very great extent to people as a whole but were restricted largely to members of the ruling classes.

The Iron Age reached its peak in the great Classical civilizations of Greece, Rome, China, and India which are now quite well known through the researches of historians and archaeologists.

L. S. CRESSMAN

VI

Man in the New World

POPULATION OF THE NEW WORLD [*]

THE DISCOVERER of the New World was neither the Norse raider nor the Genoese mariner, Christopher Columbus. The first man to set foot on the shores of America was some adventurous Asiatic ancestor of the American Indians. He first saw the hazy Alaskan landscape on the horizon some fifteen or twenty thousand years ago, when the people of western Europe were adapting their ways of life to the changing environment caused by the retreat of the last Pleistocene glaciers.

How do we know that the American Indians came from Asia? Is it not possible that the Indians originated in the New World, as we know that man did in the Old? The answer to these questions is that there are no animals, living or fossil, in the New World closely related to man and, therefore, he could not have evolved there. Now we know that the American Indian is like the peoples of Asia in skin color, hair color and

[*] The discussion in a single chapter of a subject so vast as the Populations and Cultures of the New World requires that the writer must be selective. I have chosen to treat the subject more in terms of how the 'culture worked.' In the simpler stages of culture, there is obviously a closer relation of a population to the ecology than in the more advanced stages when the cultural development frees man to a marked extent from the earlier environmental imperatives. This concept has been important in organizing the thinking and selection of materials to be discussed here. Subject matter was deliberately chosen from cultures of different complexities rather than from a single culture. The listing and discussion of the various stages of cultural development which are well recognized by archaeologists were avoided for one can hardly justify the inclusion of a sequence from one area and not include other areas equally well known. Also, it seemed important to include certain well-recognized theoretical premises which define the conceptual framework within which the anthropologist works. The selection of these has also influenced the subject matter covered as well as the method of discussion.

form, body build, and other racial features; he is not like the European whites or the Negro. Since man did not originate in America, the Asiatics could not have migrated from there to Asia. Therefore, the American Indians must have come from an Asiatic homeland to the New World.

Antiquity of Man in the New World and Migrations

The earliest migrants into the New World in all likelihood came into Alaska from Siberia some fifteen to twenty thousand years ago during the latter part of, or after, the last Ice Age. The dating of these first settlements is based on the discovery of human remains associated with extinct species of the horse, camel, bison, mammoth, dire wolf, and other animals, and association with geological features such as terraces or glacial moraines which can be dated. Suggestions have been made that man might have crossed to Alaska during the last Ice Age and lingered for a time in the favorable environment there. Most archaeologists, however, hold that man did not occupy the main American continent until post-glacial times.

How did man reach the New World? We know from recent investigations that he did not come by the Aleutian Islands, so he must have crossed Bering Strait from Siberia. The Strait is about sixty miles wide at the narrowest point, with two islands lying near midway. The shoreline of the opposite continent can be seen on a clear day from Cape Prince of Wales in Alaska or East Cape in Siberia. At times during the last Ice Age the Strait was closed by a lowering of the sea level, as a result of the great amount of water held in the glacial ice. The lowered sea level exposed a land bridge to connect the two continents. The earliest migrants could have crossed on this bridge while hunting the animals who also used it, or while seeking new lands, or they might have come by boats of some kind when the Strait was open; in some cases they might even have crossed on ice farther north.

The land bridge method of entry would have brought the ancestors of the Indian into Alaska into a large area of not less than two hundred thousand square miles, with a favorable climate and probably rich in game. It has been stated that these pioneers could not have pushed immediately into the interior of the continent, for it was covered with a vast ice-sheet. This ice barrier disappeared as the ice receded with increasing temperature about twenty to twenty-three thousand years ago. A clear route was then opened up the Yukon River into the Mackenzie River drainage, and southward into the Great Plains lying east of the Rocky Mountains.

Recent studies of pollen profiles in the area where the ice barrier was supposed to have been in western Canada tend to show that there was no ice barrier in the last part of the last period of glaciation. If this is so, then any theory that the earliest immigrants were held up in Alaska by such an obstruction has to be given up. This would mean that the migrants who might have crossed a late Ice Age land bridge could have moved down into the interior of the continent as they wished.

The dates suggested above for the time of migration into the New World will probably have to be changed to more recent ones in the light of the dates indicated for the end of the Ice Age by radiocarbon (C14) dating. There is still some question in the minds of competent scholars that these dates are correct. If they should eventually prove to be right, then the end of the Ice Age should probably be put about thirteen thousand years ago and man could have crossed a land bridge probably as recently as fifteen thousand years ago.

The Indians who arrived first and their descendants gradually pushed south until they could go no farther, for they had reached the extreme limits of South America. The lines of migration are only partially known. The major stream with a number of 'fronts' branching off probably moved down the North American continent east of the Rocky Mountains. Another current flowed southward between the Rocky and Cascade Mountains; it pushed westward to the Pacific Coast and south toward Mexico, and it occupied California. The lure of new lands and the pressure of peoples behind carried explorers through Mexico and down through Central America along the Isthmus of Panama into South America into what is now Colombia. Here they possibly split into two main streams, one moving south through the corridor between the Andes Mountains and the Pacific, and the other following the drainage of the great rivers toward the Atlantic to the east. It is possible that any eastward route was blocked by the jungle and that the migrants into the east and south passed through the Highland corridor to reach the other areas.

In North America the Indians gradually occupied all available country. The later arriving groups found the northerly regions more habitable with the changed post-glacial climate; they moved across southern Canada and into the northeastern United States. These are the Algonkian-speaking peoples. The Eskimo, probably of a northeastern Siberian origin, crossed later and spread along the Arctic Coast as far east and south as Greenland and the St. Lawrence River. These routes are the suggested lines of major movements of population throughout North, Central and South America.

Earliest Population Types

It is impossible to give any definitive statement of the physical appearance of the earliest populations because we do not have enough skeletal material from that time. There are a few skulls and fragmentary skeletal material which are recognized by many archaeologists as coming from a time when now extinct Ice Age animals lived, but there is no unanimity of opinion on most of them. Furthermore, no one is justified in defining a population type on the basis of one or two skulls, for we have no way of knowing where the single specimen comes from on the scale of variation to which it has to be related. Skeletal material comes from caves in the Lagoa Santa region of the highlands of eastern Brazil and one skull, the Confins Skull, was recovered in 1935. This skull is said to be generally similar to those found approximately 100 years ago in caves in the same region by T. W. Lund, but unlike those of the modern Indian. The skull is long, cranial index 69.1, rather low in the vault, with a somewhat sloping forehead, quite broad face, prominent cheek bones, and a slightly projecting face. There is nothing particularly primitive about it and in view of the time at which *Homo sapiens* or modern man appeared in the Old World, there is no reason to expect anything but 'modern' types in the New. The fact that earlier population types differ from contemporary is to be expected in view of natural and social selection, that is, adaptation, hybridization, extinction of small groups, marriage within larger population groups such as a village consisting of two subgroups called moieties, required cross-cousin marriage, mating with women from enemy groups defeated in war, et cetera.

At Punin in Ecuador a skull was found in 1923 which is generally assumed to be of the same age as extinct animals found in the same bed but not directly associated with it. This is generally similar to the Lagoa Santa type of skull.

In 1945 near the village of Tepexpan in the Valley of Mexico, a skeleton was found at a level which also contained the remains of mammoths. There is no unanimous agreement that this body is of the same age as the mammoth remains, for some archaeologists believe that it may represent an intrusive burial. Dr. De Terra, one of the discoverers, believes it is to be assigned the same age as the mammoths and thinks it is about eleven thousand to twelve thousand years old. The skull shows no 'primitive' characteristics. In contrast with most of the other 'early' skulls, this one is round, cranial index 80.

In 1953, Mr. Keith Glasscock discovered some fossilized human bones at the bottom of a sand 'blow-out' on the Scharbauer farm near Midland, Texas. These fragments together with artifacts found at the same site aroused sufficient interest in their significance to encourage a careful scientific investigation of the site and the surrounding area. The results of this study were published in 1955 and indicate that Midland was the seat of a population older than Folsom man. Tentative analyses suggest a date before the last Wisconsin advance, perhaps considerably before 10,000 years ago, but according to Antevs not as far back as 20,000. The skull itself is a long, narrow-vaulted one similar in certain respects to other early types found in Texas.

Other skulls and skeletal fragments have been reported from Florida, Kansas, Minnesota, Wisconsin, Wyoming, New Mexico, and Arizona. All of these have been dated relatively, that is, by association with fossil remains or geological beds in which they were interred. However, there is disagreement among archaeologists about the age of practically every one of these. Perfectly good authorities take opposite points of view and the conclusion anyone draws to a large extent depends on the subjective evaluation he makes of the evidence. The writer is inclined to think that most of the claims to antiquity are valid. As pointed out above there is no reason to expect that the earliest occupants of the New World would show any marked degree of primitiveness, nor since in the instances of finds mentioned, which are often separated by perhaps one to two thousand years in time, should we expect to find too close correspondence in physical types. It is generally expected that the early populations were long headed. This is generally the case with the specimens reported but the cranial index ranges all the way from 69 for Confins man to 80 for Tepexpan. The features of the skull vary too, from narrow faces to broad ones, correlated to some extent at least with cranial index. At least now we know enough about our problem that we do not throw out a skull as having little antiquity just because it looks very much like a modern Indian specimen. The test is this: Is it associated with an extinct fauna, or is the geological bed in which it is entombed of an age which clearly indicates a certain antiquity, and is the entombment natural and of the same time as the deposition of the bed? The use of the fluorine method of determining relative age of bones should help the archaeologist in the future to make more exact determinations of the period to which the specimen belongs than has been the case in the past.[1]

CULTURAL CHARACTERISTICS OF THE NEW WORLD

The Earliest Cultures

The earliest immigrants to the New World were hunters of game and gatherers of seeds, roots, and wild fruit. They probably moved in groups consisting of a number of families; they sought good hunting and pleasant places to live. In an unpopulated continent they were free to wander almost at will. They left few traces. Like most hunting peoples, they were almost continually on the move. As their population increased and as hunting became more intensive, game animals became more scarce. Some were killed by hunters; others moved out of the area in which they were not safe. Naturally the hunters had to seek out places where game was plentiful. Hence, the remains they have left of their camp sites are scattered and it is seldom that one site ever covers a long period of time.

In some areas such as the Great Basin lying between the Rocky and the Cascade Mountains and the adjacent region to the south we find that the early hunters, who were also gatherers in this area, occupied certain sites, mostly caves, over long periods of time. Ventana Cave in western Arizona, Bat Cave in New Mexico, the Whitewater Draw in southeastern Arizona (an open site), Danger Cave in the western shoreline of Great Salt Lake near Wendover, sites in Nevada, Fort Rock Cave, and others in Oregon, all preserve long records of occupation after an initial use dating in some cases back to probably not less than ten thousand years ago and perhaps even more. In South America the main source of information on the early hunters comes from the extreme southern tip of Patagonia in two caves, Palli Aike and Fell's caves. The archaeologist has much better opportunities for getting evidence of a long time development of culture from these cave localities than from the open sites. East of the Rocky Mountains where the emphasis for sustenance was on hunting, we would expect more mobile populations than in the western region where a considerable reliance was placed on gathering activities as a source for food. There is every reason to believe that the caves served as a kind of operating base to which the hunting parties returned. As the evidence shows, the caves were places where

[1] See Chapter 2 for discussion of methods of dating.

families lived for all the housekeeping equipment is found in the debris.

The archaeologist has a less difficult task to piece together the story of early cultures where long occupation occurs as in the caves than where short periods of use are to be found as in open sites. Unless he can get a site that shows differences of culture appearing in order from bottom to top, he has difficulty in determining which culture is older when they are found in widely separated places. Furthermore, usually as a result of disintegration of all perishable materials in open sites from the moisture from precipitation, about all the archaeologist finds is stone and perhaps some bone. But often this latter disintegrates very quickly. Hunting camps are not likely to give a very good representation of the kinds of household equipment in use at a more permanent home site.

As a result of the work of the last few years we can, however, describe certain early cultures. The best known of these is the Folsom. It was named for an ancient site in northeastern New Mexico, where the American Museum of Natural History and the Colorado Museum of Natural History in 1926 found a special type of stone projectile point which was used in hunting an extinct species of bison. This Folsom point, as it is called, is about three inches long and has a long flake taken out on each side from the concave base almost to the point. It is widest about three-quarters of the distance from the base to the point. The general type of point is now called 'fluted' and the specific one 'Folsom fluted.' Points like this are found east of the Rocky Mountains from Canada southward along the High Plains. Some sites have been reported from Pennsylvania, Virginia, and North Carolina. None has any depth. No generally accepted Folsom sites have so far been found west of the Rocky Mountains, with the exception of Sandia Cave north of Albuquerque, New Mexico. This location, however, is south and west of the Rocky Mountains in an area where movement westward was fairly easy. The significance of the Folsom points from Borax Lake, about 100 miles north of San Francisco, is not clear. Folsom points have been found widely scattered, but a point or two does not make a culture.

Another type of fluted blade, the Clovis fluted, is found in sites ranging across southern Arizona and New Mexico to western Texas and Colorado. These points are usually larger than the Folsom fluted but they vary considerably from as much as five to two-and-a-half inches in length. While in over-all shape they are like the Folsom fluted, they have only short flakes removed from the convex base. These have been found in association with mammoth, horse, and camel.

Recent work near Clovis, New Mexico, has indicated that the Clovis fluted is earlier than the Folsom. While in general the areas occupied by the two types of points are separate, there is an overlapping border and in this at Blackwater Draw, near Clovis, the stratified depths put the Clovis type as the earlier. Since the Folsom fluted is associated with hunting of the Pleistocene bison, we expect to find it somewhat later than the Clovis fluted and also in a deposit representing a different kind of environment.

It was thought at first that the makers of the Folsom points were the earliest immigrants into this continent and brought this type of weapon with them. A few years ago Mr. C. T. Hurst made the suggestion that the Folsom point originated in the south and was carried north as the hunters moved slowly in that direction with the bison herds as the climate changed following the Pleistocene. The suggestion that the Folsom fluted point is a specialized development from the Clovis fluted is now beginning to have wider acceptance.

The name Llano Culture has been suggested for the complex which is represented by the Clovis fluted points, from the Spanish word *Llano,* meaning 'plain' or 'level ground.'

A date of 9883 ± 350 years is given by radiocarbon analysis for the Folsom site near Lubbock, Texas. This is the only fluted blade industry site dated as of now. The Clovis fluted should be older than ten thousand years.

Between the Rocky Mountains and the Cascades from central Oregon to Mexico there were other people living roughly at the same time as the fluted blade people; their way of life differed considerably from the hunters of the Plains. Their weapon points were much more like the modern arrowheads with which we are familiar, only larger. They are barbed and notched, some leaf-shaped, and sometimes like the fluted shape but without the fluting. In addition to hunting, these people were gatherers of roots, seeds, nuts and used grinding stones to prepare their food for eating. An upper stone, mano, was held in the hand and worked circularly or back and forth upon a lower one, metate, usually a crude rock or slab. In the caves in the dry area between the mountain ranges, there are fairly deep deposits of refuse these people left behind. Also, along the shore of lakes now dry we find their tools. C-14 dates for Gypsum Cave in Nevada give about eight thousand five hundred years ago, and for Fort Rock Cave, Oregon, nine thousand.

Sandia Cave, north of Albuquerque, New Mexico, the home site of another early people, reveals a type of stone point lying beneath the Folsom which means that its makers lived there before those who left the Folsom Points. These points are leaf-shaped, with a shoulder on one side and a square or concave base. They are called Sandia points. So far, this is the only Sandia site that has been found though isolated Sandia points occur elsewhere from Texas to Oregon. On the basis of this limited evidence, it is rather difficult to say that the Sandia points were earlier everywhere than the Folsom.

In 1952 artifacts were found associated with a mammoth in the Valley of Mexico not far from Mexico City. The tools are not distinctive but are probably of the same age as the Clovis fluted or somewhat earlier. Some pre-agricultural fishing and hunting sites have been found along the coast line in Peru. A cave in Chile has provided remains of a hunting culture, together with bones of extinct mammals, and dated by C-14 at over eight thousand five hundred years ago.

No indications of the house types, costumes, or religious beliefs of these earliest people have come down to us; their weapons, tools, in some cases sandals and baskets have been preserved. They used scrapers, knives, projectile points, and hammers of stone, and made some objects of bone. Perishable objects like basketry, if any, have rotted away in the open sites and so have not been preserved. These early ancestors of the modern Indians used the spear thrower instead of the bow and arrow.

The spear thrower is usually called 'atlatl,' a word derived from the Aztec language (Nahuatl). The thrower was a stick from eighteen inches to two feet long, with a grip for the hand on one end, and a hook or point on the other pointing forward toward the grip. The base of the spear was placed against the hook of the atlatl, steadied by the fingers of the throwing hand, and then thrown like a spear. The spear thrower, by lengthening the thrower's arm, provided greater leverage. It was better than just an arm but not as effective as the bow. Caves excavated in Oregon and Nevada show that the spear thrower was gradually replaced by the bow, although in the southeastern United States, Mexico, and Peru it continued in use until the arrival of the Spaniards in the sixteenth century.

Hunting and Gathering in Recent Times

The Indians of North America at the time of Columbus' discovery formed two main groups, according to the methods of securing food. Agricultural groups lived east of a line drawn from the mouth of the

Colorado River to the western part of the Great Lakes and down the St. Lawrence River; hunting and gathering tribes, for the most part, occupied the territory west and north of that line. Along the Pacific Coast were groups depending largely on fish, molluscs, sea mammals, and some land animals.

While these non-agricultural groups formed important, interesting societies, we cannot discuss them in detail here. It will be sufficient to point out that the economic life centered largely around the major type of food animal or source available in the area; bison in the Plains, fish and particularly the salmon in the Pacific Northwest, seal, walrus, and fish in the Arctic, and caribou in interior Canada. In California and parts of the arid region to the east, wild seeds were the main source of food supplemented by small rodents and occasionally antelope, deer, or mountain sheep.

In South America the main non-agricultural area was in the extreme south where the guanaco, a variety of small camel and a descendant from a large North American variety, was hunted. Along the coast, fishing was a mainstay.

No hunting and gathering society has ever developed a large population or a complex civilization. Complex civilization develops only when sedentary life, that is, life in a fixed place, is possible. This again is dependent on agriculture, the domestication of plants and animals.

The Development of Sedentary Life and Its Significance

A kind of semi-sedentary life did develop along the Pacific Northwest Coast, where the ocean supplied vast quantities of food and the regular fish-runs up the rivers gave a certain economic security. But these settlements were usually only partly sedentary because the seasonal search for food—game in the mountains and berries during their seasons—would frequently take the whole group, or various parts of it, to different areas of natural abundance.

Advances in the arts and crafts and increase in population were brought about chiefly by the domestication of plants. The main crop in the New World was maize, or corn, and it was intensively cultivated from the southern part of the United States to northern Chile. In South America the concentration on maize was limited to the area west of the Andean divide. East of the Andes there was a vast area from Venezuela to Argentina in which manioc, a root plant from which tapioca is made, was the main domesticated plant. Some maize was grown, however, in spite of not very favorable conditions.

In the northeastern part of the United States, maize was an important crop but was not as intensively cultivated as in the areas to the south. In the north Atlantic states it was grown with beans and squash, together making a diet generously supplemented with game. In the Gulf states game was less important as it was in the Southwest. In the Southeast sweet potatoes, melons, and gourds replaced the northern plants. In the Southwest the Pueblo peoples raised melons, beans, squash, and sunflowers in addition to maize, and added other plants to these after the coming of the Spaniards in the sixteenth century.

The earliest record of agriculture, as a basic economy, that we have is found in the area of later intensive cultivation; it is associated with small village populations in Mexico, Central America, and the Andes. In Mexico these cultures are sometimes called the 'Middle Cultures' because they came between the late high cultures and the earlier hunting and gathering type. However, the term 'archaic' is also used to designate this early culture. We do not know when agriculture began, but these Middle Cultures go back to the beginning of the Christian era and undoubtedly considerably earlier.

In many places, such as Guatemala, Honduras, southern Mexico, and much of Brazil, farming required clearing fields of brush and forest before planting. After four or five years of use the soil would no longer be as fertile as before, and would have to lie fallow (unplanted) for several years. This meant that other areas would have to be cleared in order to produce crops. When a village increased beyond the size that could be supported by the land available, a part of the population moved to a new locality and started again the process of land clearing. So, after a period of time, there would be scattered villages of related people throughout a large area.

In an agricultural society of this nature, religious ceremonies are usually held at various times during the year to make sure that the seeds will grow, that there will be good harvests, and to celebrate the gathering of the crops. Centers for religious purposes would be established; the people from the different villages would come to these centers at appropriate times for the ceremonies. The community would need priests, caretakers, and other functionaries not only during the ceremonies but also during the intervening periods. In this way it would seem that the start was given for the imposing religious centers that developed in the cities in Central America and, in a simpler form, in the southeastern United States.

The course of development of communities was often quite different. In some places in the Andean area and the American Southwest, where the inhabitants practiced irrigation and fertilization of the soil, or where the fields were constantly replenished by fresh soil brought down by rivers, intensive agriculture became possible.

When man engages in intensive agriculture, he is freed to a marked extent from dependence on nature. Both men and women work in the fields in intensive agriculture although often at different kinds of work. As their skill increases, a surplus of food beyond that needed for survival is produced. Then, as the food supply becomes greater, the population usually increases. A surplus of food also means that some classes can live without having to work in the fields; therefore, skills and crafts can develop because men and women can give their time to becoming specialists.

So in Central America and the Andes, where intensive agriculture was practiced, there were specialists in metallurgy, war, religion, statecraft, architecture, and weaving. These special crafts were developed only because those engaged in agriculture produced enough food for all.

Agriculture was developed in America quite independently of Europe or Asia, and there were probably different centers for different plants. Maize was domesticated from a wild variety but just where is uncertain. All we can be sure of is that it was somewhere in the area of intensive agriculture between Mexico and Peru. Bat Cave in New Mexico gives us our earliest dated form of domesticated maize, starting 2500 B.C. with a primitive form and showing an evolutionary sequence continuing to the top where we have essentially modern corn. The date of its domestication farther south must have been still earlier. Wheat was the great cereal crop of the western part of the Old World and millet of northern China, while rice was the chief cereal of southeastern Asia. Had the Indians brought a knowledge of agriculture with them, the chances are that they would have sought a wild seed similar to that in use in Asia, but this is not the case. The entire technique of maize cultivation is different from that of millet or wheat since the latter two are sowed and permitted to grow to harvest. Maize is planted in hills or holes and must be cultivated during growth to secure a crop. The similarity of methods of maize culture throughout the entire maize-growing area strongly suggests that it spread throughout the entire agricultural region from the one central point of development. Local species were gradually evolved to fit special environments, ranging from the Andean highlands to the northern area of the St. Lawrence River with its short growing season.

The only mammals domesticated in the New World were the dog, the guinea pig, the llama, and the alpaca. The two latter animals are small relatives of the camel and live in the Andes. The Americas lacked animals suitable for domestication. The meat of the llama was eaten but usually in connection with religious ceremonies. The llama and the alpaca were used largely as pack animals and for their wool. The turkey, bees, and perhaps the duck were also domesticated.

The American Indians have contributed enormously to our food supplies. Corn, white potato, sweet potato, bean, both kidney and lima, squash, melon, tomato, pumpkin, and pineapple were all native to the Americas. Corn made it possible for the New England colonists to survive. They took over almost all the details of corn raising, even to husking bees, from the Indians. We have continued to raise corn in much the same way, apart from the use of modern equipment.

In the New World, as in the Old, the earlier stages of agricultural society did not necessarily produce advanced civilizations, but only the seed from which they grew. Agricultural villages of the earlier stages were self-sufficient economically. But unless trade with other villages introduced new wares and new ideas, the earlier villages continued to remain provincial. As trade developed and new wares came to the attention of the people, new ideas developed. Along with them were introduced different ways of living. These tended to break down the isolation or provincialism of the village; they stimulated thought and ideas and made the whole related area interdependent, the beginning of One World.

This happened particularly in Central America and in the Andean area. At first there were many scattered, independent groups of agricultural peoples often mutually hostile. Then, as trade developed, their contacts increased and their frontiers were pushed back. Trade brought interdependence of communities and the extension of common features of living. On this basis political action then built up extensive power; and economic, religious, and political organization built rich civilizations.

Arts and Crafts

The arts and crafts did not develop uniformly throughout the hunting and gathering regions or the agricultural regions of North America.

Leather work was particularly well developed among the Plains Indians and those in the northeastern part of the United States. The skins of the bison, deer, elk, wolf, fox, and other animals were all used as articles of clothing for daily use as well as for ceremonial purposes. The men killed the animals and the women prepared the meat and the hides. Sometimes parts of the costumes were decorated with dyed porcupine quills or paint. Later, beads in geometric patterns served as adornments. Men's shields and buffalo robes were painted by the men with symbols which were supposed to confer supernatural power, and also with pictures of the owner's exploits in war and the hunt. The conical tents of the Plains Indians—the *tipis,* or *tepees*—were made of bison hide and when properly furnished with furs and hides were very comfortable.

The most efficient skin clothing was made by the Eskimo of the Arctic coast-line. The skins of seals were tanned and sewed together to form clothing so warm and efficient that Arctic explorers now use it in preference to our own products. American soldiers in the far north also use some articles of Eskimo clothing, especially the parka, or loose-fitting, shirt-like outer garment with a hood to pull over the head. While the costume looks bulky, it is extremely efficient and in some cases tastefully decorated by sewing pieces of different skins into it to make a colorful pattern. The Eskimo made a waterproof coat of seal intestines, and this he wore in his skin canoe, or kayak. Even if the kayak were turned over in the water the paddler would be quite dry when the craft was righted.

Bark was used in the birch forest areas of Canada for canoes and household articles and other utensils. This material was often decorated with carvings and porcupine quill ornamentation.

Wood carving was highly developed along the coast of the Pacific Northwest. The totem poles which displayed the family crest of the owner are the outstanding examples of the work. There were large houses of heavy cedar slabs, split with elk-horn wedges and cut with stone tools; a powerful chief's house was decorated with many carvings. Storage boxes, canoes, household utensils, and above all the masks used in dances gave the artist an opportunity to exercise his skill. The introduction of steel tools by white traders greatly stimulated the development of the art of wood carving by the northwestern artists.

Basketry was widely made and was probably universal, although with the development of pottery it tended to have a secondary value. Perhaps this is the reason why in some areas of high culture we hear little of basketry and much about pottery. Basketry falls into three main classes:

plaited, twined, and coiled; each is found in the New World. Plaited baskets are made by interlacing the fibers as in a mat. Twined basketry is made with a series of warps radiating from the center of the bottom, with two weft rows passing over and under them and crossing over between warps thus reversing the order on the surface. Coiled basketry is built up with a coil starting from a bottom center and then as each layer is laid on the preceding one in a continuous spiral, it is sewed fast to the underlying coil by a splint which is inserted through holes punched with a bone awl.

A good deal of beautiful basketry, both coiled and twined, was produced in California. Especially fine pieces were made by the Pomo Indians in the Clear Lake district north of San Francisco Bay. In this area exquisitely beautiful patterns were applied to both coiled and twined baskets by using different colored bird feathers. In a culture otherwise very simple, we thus have an example of superb skill in a single craft.

The natives of the Canadian Northwest Coast, southern Alaska, and the western Aleutian Islands also made beautiful twined basketry. The coast Indians used split spruce roots to secure a very fine material and their baskets were expertly made. The best baskets of Attu Island, in the Aleutians, are made from a fine grass; the workmanship on some is so expert that the baskets seem to be made of fine linen.

The Pima Indians of the Arizona desert also made beautiful baskets. They have been extraordinarily successful in their decoration by which they skillfully modify the lines, usually in black on a white background, to give the impression that they curve when they are straight, as all lines must be on a basket unless the design is painted.

The Indians of the southeastern states used strips of cane for their basket work; bark of other small bushes and trees were also used. Storage and carrying baskets and a wide variety of special types made for winnowing and sifting grain and flour and for other special uses show highly developed skill. Nests of baskets were also made, with a series of progressively smaller pieces in a large basket. Decorative patterns in geometric designs were produced by dyeing the strips of cane, usually black or red, before starting the basket. When these were woven into the basket, the designs appeared on both surfaces but in alternating spaces.

It is difficult to determine the antiquity of basketry techniques because of the highly perishable nature of baskets. Nevertheless, we know from specimens found with sandals in Fort Rock Cave, Oregon, that they go back nine thousand years and possibly were among the crafts brought into the New World by the earliest immigrants.

Cotton was cultivated in the area of intensive agriculture and provided the weaving material for most of the garments. It appeared in the American Southwest before A.D. 800. In the Andes and in Mexico, cotton was quilted and in Mexico it was soaked in brine to harden it for use as armor. This was so effective against arrows that the Spaniards came to use it instead of their heavy metal armor.

Wool was used in the Andes and to a limited extent along the southern Peruvian coast. It was secured from the llama for ordinary coarse garments, but the vicuna furnished the finest type which was used for the clothing of the ruling classes. In Peru we find the finest and most varied weaving in the New World. The highest development was reached along the south coast when both cotton and wool were used. In Alaska the Chilkat blanket was woven from the wool of the mountain goat. To give added body and strength, cedar bark was twisted into the wool as it was spun. Some coast Salish tribes of western Canada wove blankets from mountain goats' wool and adulterants, and from hair of white dogs with which adulterants were also mixed to increase the material.

It has usually been thought that the origin of pottery in the New World was to be found in Meso-America and attributed to a single invention. However, even though recent studies tend to show a distribution of pottery on the archaic time level from the Valley of Mexico to Peru in which there are certain elements of style of pot and techniques of decoration in common, we are not justified in assuming from this alone a single point of origin. There is also the possibility of independent invention of pottery-making among the late Basketmakers of the American Southwest. Strong evidence also exists now for the introduction from Asia of the basic type of pottery known as the Woodland in the northeastern United States.

Whatever the points and times of origin, pottery has provided in human history an important technological development as well as an important vehicle for the development of aesthetic expression. The basketmaker is limited in the type of art forms which may be created, since basketry is either woven or sewn and either form results in a series of rectilinear patterns since all lines must of necessity be straight. The most skilled weavers have learned to create the illusion of curvature but it is still illusion. Painting cannot be used on basketry with any success because of the rough surface.

Pottery provided the pot-maker with a product which could be modeled to a great variety of shapes, a smooth surface which could have the texture modified to produce designs or painted to express the aesthetic patterns of the people. In addition to these were the opportunities for the demonstration of skill in technical processes of construction and firing.

Once the basic techniques of pottery-making were mastered, regional differentiation quickly took place. Local styles both in shape and decoration are readily recognized. Pottery was something that could be traded and the distribution of sherds found by the archaeologist shows that some styles were more popular than others. Two or three examples will illustrate the point. In the Southwest a very attractive black-on-red ware called St. John's polychrome is very widely distributed from its point of origin in New Mexico. In Meso-America a fine orange ware was widely distributed and a glossy black ware known as plumbate was popular and widely traded from Central America, its point of origin.

Archaeologists who work in areas where pottery was made and used rely heavily on the changes in ceramic types as the basis for their chronological sequences and cultural relationships of their sites with those from other areas. Pottery does not disintegrate, although in the tropics color may be leached off and the sherds show not only the method of manufacture but the change in styles of pots as well as the change in the art styles as reflected in this craft.

In North America pottery is found in Alaska and probably is part of a continuous extension with the widespread Woodland type, although there is still a gap in the distribution in Canada. This pottery is thought to have derived from Asia and have been carried to the New World by migrating peoples. The Woodland pottery is not painted but depends for its decoration on a modification of the surface texture by the use of a cord wrapped paddle, punctation, comb scoring, and other devices. To the south of the area occupied by the Woodland, where the culture is referred to as the Mississippi Pattern, we find that both surface texture modification and painting occurred as decorative devices. In addition there was a great variety of different shaped pieces. Various kinds of animals served as models for the potter to add to the variety of more conventional forms. In the Southwest there are three generally recognized areas of pottery styles; the Puebloan or Anasazi in the Colorado

Plateau and the Rio Grande, the Hohokam in the Salt River region of Arizona, and the Mogollon in southern and southwestern New Mexico. The Anasazi was in the main characterized by two main styles: a black-on-white, and a black-on-red. The Hohokam relied on a red or buff base with the designs in a contrasting red or brown color. Mogollon pottery was usually red with the use of a burnished black interior sometimes extending as a band partway down the outer surface. There also occurs a red-on-white type and, with the extension of Anasazi influence in classic Pueblo times, the stimulus was given that produced the beautiful Mimbres ware.

I have not gone into the details of variation in styles for obvious reasons, nor have I discussed the utility wares of the areas as separated from the painted styles used for household purposes other than cooking and for ceremonial activities.

Pottery, but of a fairly simple kind, extended westward across California and up into Nevada. West of the Rocky Mountains and north of the southwestern periphery true pottery does not occur, although some half dozen sherds were excavated by the writer in a cave in southeastern Oregon but so far it has been impossible to relate them to the ware of any other region.

Mexico saw a high regional development in pottery as did the other areas of high civilization. In the areas dominated by the great religious centers, as we would expect, there is a close connection between the fine pottery and the ceremonial activities. In the Nayarit part of the major Tarascan area of western Mexico, a great deal of attention was paid to the production of realistic works, dancing groups, family scenes, pets, and other objects and activities of daily life. Of course, the customary range of pots was also made. However, the realistic products of these people give one the impression that they had a certain gaiety and got a lot of fun out of the ordinary things of life. Here alone is this emphasis developed.

Polychrome ware is found throughout nuclear America. In Mexico perhaps its highest development was reached in the Puebla-Mixteca area where complicated designs were produced with fine clarity and control of the color and line work. A distinctive feature of the Zapotec area is the use of burial urns, or more correctly, urns used with burials in which the figure of some deity is represented in the conventional masked form. The color of the pieces is usually a dark grey.

Mayan pottery often uses both surface modification and painting in combination. Black, orange, and red pigments are effectively used in design patterns. Elements of ceremonial action or ritual designs in the Mayan style occur here as do characteristic, ritualistic, and symbolic designs in the Aztec, Zapotec, and other areas.

Peruvian pottery has been quite justifiably placed in a very high position of esteem. Here as elsewhere there are both regional differentiations and changes within each region through time. The Chimu pottery of the north coast is distinguished for the great skill shown in modeling by its makers. Characteristic features are pieces probably representing portrait modeling, representation of daily life scenes again in modeled form, stirrup spouted jars, et cetera. The high quality of this pottery declined from its former excellence in the period before the conquest.

Along the south coast the Nazca pottery is noted for the great skill in decoration in polychrome style with strong and vivid colors. The dominating design pattern is the conventionalized puma or feline design although, of course, many others are found. The design pattern shifted its incidence during the process of the development of the culture.

In the Highland area a series of styles developed with a high quality of art expressed in the Inca period in color techniques, design patterns, and shapes of the pots and jars.

Metallurgy, the process of removing metal from ore by the use of heat, and the reworking of the raw metal into various products, had been developed in the area from the Andes to Central Mexico. Copper, silver, gold, platinum, and tin were used. Bronze, usually a mixture of tin and copper, was made in the Andean region at the time of the conquest. Other metals were mixed with copper and the process of fusing them into an alloy was known. From South America it is thought that at least some of the metal-working techniques spread north to Mexico.

Metal was used mostly for ornamental and ceremonial objects; only a little of it served to make tools or weapons. All the great stone monuments and architectural masterpieces of Mexico, the Maya area, and South America were built with stone tools. What the future might have held for the Americas had there been no Spanish conquest we cannot say, but it is interesting to note that in the Old World the Bronze Age is one of the great stages in human progress.

Architecture, if we mean by the term substantial structures of stone, was limited primarily to the Andean-Mexican area, with some extension into the Pueblo area of our American Southwest. The Pacific Northwest produced impressive timbered houses. The southeastern area of North

America developed a ceremonial town center for religious purposes by building earth pyramids to support timber and thatch sanctuaries or temples. Masonry, either with or without mortar, was limited to the Pueblos and to the peoples further southward, including the Incas.

The builder's skill outside of the present boundaries of the United States found expression almost entirely in designing temples, forts, tombs, and palaces for the nobles. In the Maya area and in Mexico, magnificent temples were built upon pyramids whose sides were faced with stucco-covered rock. Imposing stairways led to these temples; in some cases, the balustrades bore great stone sculptures of the god worshipped in the temple.

The temples were grouped with other public buildings and palaces in the center of the town and completely dominated the area. When Spanish soldiers saw the impressive massing of buildings with their color and ornamentation against the blue skys of Mexico and Yucatan, they could not hold back their admiration. One of a group of soldiers strolling in Mexico City wrote that not even his home city of Seville could boast of anything comparable to it.

In the Andean region, buildings were without mortar. The architects depended upon heavy, perfectly cut and fitted stones for stability. Or the stones were cut into irregular patterns, and these were fitted together accurately—a style called *polygonal*. In some cases the stones were held together with copper clamps for greater security. Andean architecture, despite its supreme excellence in stone fitting and its use of massive cut rock for building purposes, never approximated the variety or magnificence of the achievements in Central America.

In contrast with the elaborate religious, state, and palace buildings in Central and South America, the houses of the ordinary person were unimpressive affairs. The development of excellence in architecture seems to have closely followed upon the elaboration of systems of religious thought and development of a wealthy class in both the Old World and the New. Apart from religious buildings, the best architectural achievements in the New World are to be found in the Pueblo area of the Southwest. At Mesa Verde in southwestern Colorado and at Pueblo Bonito in the Chaco Canyon of north central New Mexico, extraordinarily beautiful buildings and groupings of them were made. These were dwellings for humans and not for gods. It is of some interest that pueblos of this kind are still used as dwellings, while the imposing temples farther south have been abandoned and lie in ruins.

Writing

Writing, which is so important for communication of thought and development of scientific knowledge, made little progress in the New World. All over the continents there are paintings and carvings on rocks and cliffs that were probably intended to record some event or to recall some experience in the mind of the painter or carver. None of these approximate writing. The only place where writing did develop was in Mexico and Guatemala. The Aztecs and the Maya had manuscripts written on long, narrow sheets of paper, folded to make books. The Spanish priests destroyed all of these they could lay their hands on because they were mostly about religious rituals and the native religion they meant to stamp out. Deciphering these books is difficult. So far only the dates in the calendar system and some place names can be read in the Maya writing. We have a better knowledge of Aztec picture writing because the Spanish authorities in governing the conquered colonies used the native method of writing to compute tax lists, et cetera. These were often copies in Roman characters into both Nahuatl (the language of much of the conquered area) and Spanish.

No writing existed in the Andean region. Records were kept here by officials, such as tax collectors and census takers, by means of the quipu, a series of colored cords with knots to indicate numerical values. The colors of the cords had different meanings and could be interpreted by the trained officer.

Religion

Religious activities and beliefs varied extensively throughout the New World. One may naturally expect some differentiation between the religious expressions of people in a hunting and gathering economy, in an agricultural type, and those in a complex civilization even though the economic base is still agricultural. In this last case there may well be a distinction between the official ceremonial rituals carried out by the priesthood and the beliefs of the peasants, though it is more likely to be one of degree rather than of kind.

A large part of the northern part of North America was characterized in its religious activities by the quest for a supernatural guardian or helper, usually spoken of as a Guardian Spirit. Over a large part of the Plains area the Guardian Spirit was a pretty distinct object or being, while in the western area or the Pacific Northwest the concept was somewhat less definitely conceptualized. The Power Quest is the name frequently applied to the experience in this area although there were very frequently quite specific objects which became the source of power and thus corresponded to the Guardian Spirit.

Adolescent boys and sometimes girls had to go through the experience of securing a 'vision' and the success or failure of the quest was the proof of or lack of evidence of supernatural interest and assistance. The experience, when successfully carried out, was the positive proof or validation of the achievement of adulthood. Likewise when almost any kind of act beyond the ordinary day-to-day activities was planned, the individual tried to secure a vision as a proof of supernatural aid and success in the effort. A raid for horses, a war raid against an enemy party had to be validated by a 'vision' before anyone could secure the followers he needed.

Various methods were in use to secure a vision but most of them required the individual to expose himself to a lonely and dangerous vigil in some isolated spot. Here with fasting, prayer, and sometimes by sacrifice of a part of his body such as a finger joint, he sought the aid of the supernatural beings. In the area where four was the ritual number, it usually required four days to secure the vision. In the Pacific Northwest the seeker for aid usually went at night to the mountains or forest where he swam in the mountain streams or piled rocks into cairns, experiences which were sometimes accompanied by dreams in which a particular animal or object appeared to the dreamer and became his particular guardian. Sometimes power seems to have been derived from the sheer activity by which the individual had to go unarmed in an area dangerous because of wild beasts and possibly human enemies. It became a demonstration of the courage and the quality expected in adulthood.

Among the tribes of the Pacific Northwest Coast of Canada spirits were a property right and were inherited as any other form of property according to strict rules governed by kinship organization.

The property minded Yurok of northwestern California made a contract with the supernatural beings and both members were bound by its terms.

Among the agricultural pueblo dwellers of the Southwest, religious activity was communal in contrast to the individualistic character of that just described. The religious performances here were in the hands of various clans and the performances were carried out according to certain periods of the solar year. The main concern of the religion of these people was the promotion of the success of their crops. Much of the activity was concerned with production of rain so essential to farming in the dry country. The concept of fertility looms large in their thinking. In this communal activity we see the development of a somewhat more complex stage where certain specially prepared ministrants are responsible for the performance of the religious rituals which in turn benefit the whole community. However, the individuals of the community are not without their responsibility, for violation of the taboos which are imposed during the periods of religious dances may interfere with the success of the very performances. The religious rituals in this area are carried out after proper preparation in the plazas of the pueblos with the non-participants looking on and participating vicariously perhaps. The performances are ritual dances which are still very close to the people.

In the areas of high cultures in nuclear America we find a great elaboration of religious belief and ritual. There is quite clearly here (1) an official calendar of ritual performances of a very complex nature, and (2) the simpler level of belief and practice of the peasant peoples. The culture of this area was based on agriculture of a very efficient kind. It had to be to support the large populations and the classes of people engaged in the construction of the temples and public buildings and in public and administrative services. All our evidence indicates that the peasant religion was little different from what we infer it to have been all during the archaic period when it was a very simple nature religion concerned mainly with the success of agriculture at a simple level and essentially magical in nature. One of the basic concepts of this early religion must have been that of the renewal of life, reproduction and fertility, as expressed in the plants on which life depended. While the concepts went through amplification, redefinition, and refinement with the development of the priesthood and the division of labor derived from the richer economy, nevertheless these ideas are but the branches of the tree whose roots are to be found in the archaic fertility rituals and beliefs.

While differences of emphasis existed in the different regions of Mexico the period which we know best is the Aztec or last. The Aztecs had established their political authority over a vast area from the Gulf of Mexico to the Tarascan frontier in the west and to the Isthmus of Tehuantepec in the south. Consequently we would expect to find some of the concepts of the Aztecs gaining a foothold among the conquered peoples. To illustrate our point we shall briefly discuss certain of the Aztec beliefs and practices.

At the risk of oversimplifying our material, it may be said that the Aztec religion conceived of the world as a battlefield of pairs of conflicting forces. Day, presided over by the sun, was in conflict with the darkness of night. Each night the sun died or was sacrificed for man to overcome darkness and restore the life-giving light. Each morning the sun was reborn to make life again possible. This dichotomizing of life or dualistic principle made a world of sharp contrasts. The world was black and white, not shades of grey. Aztec architecture reflects, at least to this writer, the same sharpness of definition. Its angularity, precision, and organization seem to express in the stones of their temple structures this same military-like discipline and austerity.

There were many gods: the sun, the god of rain, the war god, and many others. The gods, like humans, had to be fed and gods were fed by sacrifices offered by specially trained servers, the priests. The favor of the gods could thus be secured. In Toltec times, several centuries before the Aztecs came into power, the idea of sacrifice had been amplified by the priests and the concepts defined concerning what kinds of offerings were best calculated to secure the favor of the gods. The Aztec priests developed these ideas still further. The sun had to be fed the life-giving qualities of man, and these resided in the heart. So human sacrifice came to hold an extremely important part in the Aztec religion. The sun was fed by the heart offered from the sacrificial victim. Human lives were offered also to the other gods as the most valuable sacrifice that could be made.

The performance of the official religion was carried out in the temple plazas and in front of the sanctuaries of the temple on top of the pyramid as well as within the sanctuaries. Many of these performances were highly dramatic in nature with each step of the ritual leading irresistibly to the sacrifice at the platform at the head of the long stairway of the temple. The common people did not participate in these rituals, but they were, of course, aware of them. This was an activity for trained and specially prepared people whose actions were carried out for the benefit of the whole people.

Not all rituals were of the same importance, nor were all social in nature. For example, a business man going on a trip to another area on business might offer a slave as a sacrifice to insure the success of his project. However, while this was an individual act, it was within the framework of the community's demands, for it was a priest who made the sacrifice and it was valuable in terms of the established system of values of the community.

The sacrificial victim became a god and the priests and the individuals who made the offering ceremonially ate parts of the body of the victim that they might share in his sacredness, a truly sacramental concept.

The temples were built on platforms made of rubble or adobe sometimes quite small at first. When a new god was introduced to replace an earlier one, he was usually honored with a temple built over that of the god whom he displaced. The earlier pyramid and temple were not destroyed, but simply served as a base over which a greater building was erected. By Aztec times, religious belief decreed that at the end of every fifty-two year cycle, the old life should be destroyed, at least symbolically, and a new cycle started. This meant that all fires had to be extinguished, all household pottery, et cetera, be destroyed, and all the temples had to be enlarged or renewed. The priests kindled fire anew and then it was distributed to the people. New articles for household use were made. New temples were built over the earlier ones. The excavations by the Mexican archaeologists have clearly demonstrated the sequence of temple building.

The calendar system of the Aztecs was closely related to the religious performances throughout the year. The rituals intended to influence nature and benefit the community by their effects on the crops had to be performed at stated times in the cycle of the year and so the calendar served both as a guide and a prescription for the performance of rituals on which the community welfare depended. Warfare, too, was integrated into the system of beliefs centering on religion. Some acts of war were for the sole purpose of taking prisoners to offer in sacrifice. Even where conquest was the object, it was preferable to take the enemy prisoner to offer later in sacrifice, rather than kill him in battle.

This brief description of some aspects of Aztec religion serves two purposes: first, to give a brief factual introduction to it, and second, to show how a system of values with certain dominating or integrating concepts organizes the fabric of a people's life.

In the Maya area, we find again the great dependence of religion on agriculture, especially maize as the central concept. Here, too, we have the distinction between the official religion and that of the peasants, the close association with architectural achievements, and with the calendar to guide the ritual performances. Here, too, as in the Mexican area proper, the temples and associated wares, such as ceremonial pottery, provided the medium for the great development in the sculptor's and painter's art. Life among the Mayas depended upon the success of the farmers' efforts, as to be sure was the case among the Aztecs. Here, however, we find in some way a much more genial civilization developed. The development of the hieroglyphic system of writing with the calendar provided both a stimulus and a challenge to the artist in stone. The use of feathers and floral designs provided a freedom outside the conventionalized forms of masks and other ritual objects. In the temples on their platforms at Palenque and Piedras Negras the art of the sculptor reached perhaps its highest stage in the New World, and here it was in the service of religion. With Toltec influence entering northern Yucatan in the thirteenth century we find the introduction of Mexican religious ideas, carried on and developed by the refugees and their descendants from the great center of Tula when it was destroyed by the Chichimecs some two centuries earlier. At Chichen Itza we find not only architectural features of Toltec origin but human sacrifice on a scale entirely foreign to the limited practice of the Mayas. Contemporaneously at Uxmal approximately 100 kilometers distant we find no Toltec influence, but the whole atmosphere is Maya, with its emphasis on worship of the beings so useful to agriculture, and the architectural achievements reaching a stage of development unequaled in the New World. The balanced architecture with its religious symbolism and the superb Palace of the Governor indicate a well-defined value system and an almost unique capacity to express it in architectural form.

In Peru the official religion remained much closer to the original form of a nature religion than was the case with the Aztecs. However, the development of a class society and an autocratic state carried with it the necessity for appropriate elaboration of the religious concepts to explain and justify the socio-political system. By Inca times, the Inca who was the head of the state, was supposed to be descended from the sun. The sun was worshipped and the descendant of the sun shared the sacredness of his source. Human sacrifices were exceedingly rare from a comparative point of view. The llama was the chief sacrificial animal. There was a priesthood to perform the official rituals for the state. Throughout the year there were elaborate ceremonies, month by month, in which the Inca symbolically took part in person or through his priestly representative, thus indicating the concern of the entire state in the rituals. These were to insure a bountiful harvest and the harvests were followed by elaborate ceremonies of thanksgiving. In these planting and harvest rituals, there was wide participation by the people.

Religion does not appear to have assumed the same importance in the whole complex life of the Peruvians as was the case for the Mayas and Mexicans. Among the northern peoples, as has been pointed out elsewhere, their concept of life was determined by a vast number of supernatural beings or forces whose favor needed to be won or hostility averted and consequently the elaborate series of rituals and religious concepts developed to insure the well-being of the community. In Peru, on the other hand, the thinking was oriented much more toward a strong political and economic organization in which the welfare of the state was dependent to a large degree on the people themselves with religion playing an essential but minor role.

Political Organization

The only real political state to develop in the New World was that of the Incas of Peru. The Aztecs never went beyond the idea of a loose unity of conquered tribes based upon the lust for power and tribute. So when the Spanish attacked them, it was easy enough to win over allies from subject peoples who hated their conquerors.

The Incas, on the other hand, developed a very successful form of government and extended their state along the Andes and the coast from northern Chile well into Ecuador. If we can say the Inca state had but one dominant idea in its organization, it was to produce an efficient economic life and social security for all. The rulers progressively extended their power and incorporated conquered peoples into the Inca realm as full-fledged members. They explained their wars as an effort to carry the benefits of Inca civilization to the less fortunate who lacked it, a common justification for powerful aggressor states in all ages.

The Inca government extended the use of the Quechua language, the language of the ruling group, throughout the state. Roads were built to speed communication and aid in the administration. Careful censuses of the population were made and vital statistics were kept. Taxes were paid in the form of labor on the state fields or in some other activity, such as the army. Storage houses for food were maintained throughout the country so that in time of need, supplies could be sent from public warehouses to relieve local shortages. The Inca state, organized to provide economic security for its people eventually overreached itself, by extending its boundaries beyond its capacity for control, and the Spaniards found ready allies in disaffected peoples to bring to an end the Inca power.

RETROSPECT AND SUMMARY

In this brief survey of New World peoples and cultures, we have tried to present it in terms of functional developments and adaptation to habitats. In our discussion, we have had to choose from the vast body of information that describes the life of the New World peoples. We have tried to pick out those elements which seem most significant to us, though another author might well have chosen other topics for discussion. Not all subjects have been discussed with the same degree of fullness for not all are of the same importance. Pottery was discussed at some length because of its usefulness to the archaeologist and because of its significance in the technological and aesthetic developments of the life of a people. Religion, likewise, was discussed at length to illustrate the individual type of activity, the communal expression, and finally the complex type of an official religion with an organized priesthood associated with a class system. In addition, religion is of great importance in understanding a culture, for this can be done only if we can see the value systems which define the life of the people, their beliefs, and the resulting actions. Religion with its definition of the world and man's part in it becomes of extreme importance in this task.

Some inferences should be drawn from our discussion and made more explicit. It is clear that the simpler the culture of a people, the more closely are they a part of the ecological pattern of which their life is a part. With the improvements of economy from food-gathering to food-producing, men arrive at a position where they are able to exploit the environment to a greater extent. A necessity for any complex culture is an adequate food supply to produce an economic surplus which in turn makes possible a high degree of division of labor with development in the crafts and arts. The story in the New World is like that in the Old where, from a relatively undifferentiated base of simple economies, centers developed for one reason or another in which change occurred fairly rapidly according to different preferred patterns and regional differentiation in culture followed. Then trade occurred both in material objects and ideas and some of the regionalism broke down but not completely. If out of this regionalism warring rivalries arose then, unless they were halted, the development of the civilization tends to collapse as is shown by the Maya record. If a single power came to the fore as the Aztecs or the Incas, the patterns of this dominating group tended to establish a uniformity and the regional differences became less marked. Through the years the culture changed by innovation and diffusion to the distant areas from the more advanced centers.

A further point needs emphasis, namely, that no culture ever develops all its parts with the same degree of efficiency. Our discussion has illustrated this important general point about cultures, a point that is true of ours as it was true of those we have discussed.

One question which we should like to answer, but cannot and probably never shall, is what were the forces that brought about the development of the complex cultures or civilizations as some prefer to call them from the simple farming type. Economic efficiency, political organization, highly developed skills and knowledge are reflections of the development, not an explanation of how it took place. The archaeologist deals with mostly the bare bones of history, not the pulsing life of the living organism. He never digs up the ideas, the hopes, and aspirations of a people. In the story of development it is without doubt the ideas which make the difference but these unfortunately are probably forever beyond the reach of the archaeologists' tools.

By the study of living societies representing as closely as possible those whose fragmentary remains he digs up, the archaeologist tries to clothe the bare bones with flesh and create again the living society and the people in it whose life, long since gone, he is now attempting to understand.

E. ADAMSON HOEBEL

VII

The Nature of Culture

WHAT IS CULTURE?

HUMAN BEINGS are unique among all the creatures of the animal kingdom in their capacity to create and sustain culture. Each society of men
possesses its own distinctive culture, so that the members of one society
behave differently in some significant respects from the members of
every other society. We observe, for instance, that the Andaman Islander
from the Indian Ocean weeps with ceremonial copiousness when he
greets a friend or relative after a long absence; a Frenchman kisses his
comrade on both cheeks; while we content ourselves with seizing his
right hand to agitate it with a pumping motion.

The situation is the same in each of these instances, as is the social
function of the behavior; namely, to emphasize and reconstitute the special bond that exists between the two persons. But the cultures of the
Andaman Islander, Frenchman, and American call for and produce different modes of action.

This is but a single instance of a culture pattern. However, culture is
more than a collection of mere isolated bits of behavior. It is the integrated sum total of learned behavior traits which are manifest and
shared by the members of a society.*

The factor of learned behavior is of crucial importance. It is essential
to the concept of culture that instincts, innate reflexes, and any other
biologically inherited forms of behavior be ruled out. Culture is, therefore, wholly the result of social invention, and it may be thought of as
social heritage for it is transmitted by precept to each new generation.
What is more, its continuity is safeguarded by punishment of those mem-

* For another definition of culture with somewhat different emphases see Chapter 11.

bers of a society who refuse to follow the patterns for behavior that are laid down for them in the culture.

Social life as such and cultural processes must not be confused. Many animals in addition to man experience social life and even possess social organization. The complex structure of ant society reveals an intriguing division of labor among queen, workers, fighters, and drones. The ingenious exploitation of captive aphids as food resources by some species of ants adds an auxiliary population to their social organization. Yet for all its complexity the social organization of ant society rests not in culture but upon instinct. There is no transmission, so far as we can tell, of behavior through learning. A set of ant eggs, properly incubated without the presence of any adult ants, will produce a host of ants, who on maturity will re-enact in every detail all of the behavior of the myriad generations of the species before them.

Would the same occur if a collection of human babies were cut off from all adult supervision, care, and training? Assuming that they could survive, which they could not, we would not expect them to manifest any of the special traits of behavior that characterized their parents. They would be devoid of language, complicated tools, utensils, fire, arts, religion, government, and all the other features of life that distinguish man among the animals. They would eat and drink, and they would mate as adults, and they would presumably find themselves shelter, for these would be direct responses to basic biological drives. Their behavior would be instinctive and, in large measure, random. But what they would eat and how they would eat would not be according to the specialized tastes and palates of men as we know them now. Nor would their mating conform to the limiting and channeling rules that give to each human society its present sexual characteristics. Left solely to their own instinctive devices, the children of men would appear as undeveloped brutes, although it is probable that they would soon standardize this behavior as they learned from each other what one or another had discovered. A rudimentary culture would soon take shape. The specific responses to the generalized drives of instinct would quickly become the specific patterns of culture.

The human capacity for culture is a consequence of man's complex and plastic nervous system. It enables man to make adjustments in behavior without going through a biological modification of his organism. As of this moment it is the end product of the whole process of inorganic and organic evolution which has moved in the direction of increasing complexity of the organism, including the nervous system. Only in man has the nervous system reached the stage of complexity and adaptability to make possible the creation *and* sustenance of culture through complex ratiocination, possession of a protracted span of memory for details, and the use of verbal symbols: language.

It would be an error born of self-adulation were we to think that no traces of the culture-creating capacity occur below the level of man. Our near relatives in the primate family are capable of inventing new forms of behavior in the solution of some of the simpler problems that are posed to them by experimental animal psychologists. They apparently can also reason on very elementary levels. The famous experiments of Wolfgang Köhler first demonstrated the ingenuity and intelligence of chimpanzees in joining sticks, piling boxes, and undoing locks in order to gain their goals—usually bananas. Further, it is now thoroughly established that chimpanzees can and do learn from each other the new discoveries and inventions of one of their numbers. The transmission of the discovery spreads by imitation. A new and learned pattern of behavior is temporarily shared by the society of chimpanzees. It is an element of nascent culture.

Yet neither the chimpanzees, nor any other sub-human primates, are capable of more than the most rudimentary discoveries and inventions. What is more important, they are handicapped by their limited memory spans. Unless constantly re-directed by their human masters, they soon drop and forget their new activities which pass away as fads. The accumulation of inventions to build up a permanent body of culture materials is beyond their capacity. Of even more crucial significance, however, is the inability of all sub-human forms to develop speech. The bulk of culture is phrased in thought—sub-vocal speech—and transmitted by word of mouth. It is often said with only slight exaggeration that culture exists in and through communication. The lack of developed communication bars all speechless animals from real culture forever.

In the natural world, culture is a distinct type of phenomenon, which represents the highest level of evolutionary emergence. In the terminology of Herbert Spencer and A. L. Kroeber it is *superorganic*. It rests upon and emerges from the psychic organic mechanism of men, but it is not *in* the organic structure of men. The culture that is acquired by any individual is existent before his birth and persists after his death. Individuals and groups are the carriers and creators of culture, but culture has a quality of anonymity in that it is super-individual.

The levels of natural phenomena and their respective sciences.[1]

LEVEL OF PHENOMENA	TYPE OF PHENOMENA	HIERARCHY OF SCIENCES
IV. Superorganic	Culture	Anthropology, Sociology, Social Psychology, Political Science, Economics (History)
III. Psychic Organic	Sentient animals with highly developed nervous systems	Psychology and Neurology
		Physical Anthropology
II. Vital Organic	Protozoa, metazoa (plants and animals)	Organic Chemistry, Zoology, Biology, Anatomy, Physiology
		Biophysics
I. Inorganic	Earth and cosmic matter	Physical Chemistry, Physics, Geology, Astronomy

The relation of culture to society is often left ambiguous, although it is not difficult to distinguish the two. A society may be any animal aggregation, which holds together as an interacting group, and among the members of which exists an awareness of belonging together—the 'consciousness of kind.' A wild horse herd under the leadership of a dominant stallion is a society. So is the flock of barnyard pigeons wheeling in flight, and organized in nesting pairs.

A human society is also an animal aggregation with just these qualities. In the case of human beings, however, almost all social interrelations are dominated by existing culture. We do not know of any groups of cultureless men. Therefore, a human society is more than a mere aggregation expressing instinctive behavior. A human society is a permanently organized population acting in accordance with its culture. Human society = population + culture.

In its fullest sense, culture is a series of integrated patterns for behavior developed from mass habits. However a group of people may have arrived at their mass habits, and that is a subject for later chapters, habits once established tend to project themselves into future behavior. The habitual way sets the pattern for future action.

Statistically, a mass habit may be called a behavior norm. A norm would be that type of behavior which occurs with the greatest frequency (the mode) among the variable forms, or it may be that type which is

[1] Adopted and modified from Herbert Spencer, *The Principles of Sociology* (1878), vol. 1, pp. 2-16; A. L. Kroeber, 'The Superorganic,' *Amer. Anthrop.*, vol. 19, 1917, pp. 163-213.

closest to the average (the mean) among the variables, or it may represent the mid-point (the median) between the extreme poles of the range of variation.

In social life the norms, which are culture patterns, take on a compulsive, or normative, aspect. Norms as such consist merely of what is done. The normative consists in an additional element of *ought to be*. Patterns *of* behavior become patterns *for* behavior. 'The folkways,' wrote William Graham Sumner, 'are the "right" ways.' Deviations are frowned upon and socially discouraged. Conformity is nourished and rewarded. Each new individual as he is born into or enters the group is put through the process of child training or indoctrination now called *encultration*. Throughout life the deterrent, negative sanctions of society (scorn, ridicule, ostracism, deprivation, and punishment) serve to discourage and check deviation, and the positive sanctions of approbation (rewards and prestige) serve to induce conformity to the norms. Individuals are shaped more less uniformly to the common mold. A modicum of standardization is the common lot.

Not all norms apply to all of the members of a society. Culture does not spread itself evenly over the social loaf. Those norms which do apply to all members of the society and from which there is no permissible deviation are called *universals*. An example would be the prohibition of incest. All persons must refrain from sexual relations with brother, sister, parent, child in most societies. Universals are relatively rare within any given culture.

Much more numerous are the norms that are known as *alternatives*: the patterns that exist where several different norms apply to the same situation. A permissible range of choice and leeway is available. Neckties may be called for, but the choice may be between black, white, or colored four-in-hands or bows. Meat should be cooked, but the individual may choose between baking, boiling, roasting, broiling, rare, medium, well-done, seasoned, or unseasoned.

No society is wholly homogeneous. Differentiation based on sex and age is universal. There are distinct patterns of behavior for male and female, youth and adult, some of which are biologically founded and others not. Social differentiation between married and single persons is world-wide, and all societies have their religious specialists. This means that there are internal sub-groupings in every society. Each of these groups has its own behavior characteristics that are applicable only to its members. Such norms are known as *specialties*.

The specialties of one group may be known to the other members of the society and yet not be used by them, because they are not patterns for their behavior. Many American adult men know the Boy Scout salute, having once been Scouts, but they do not use it as a form of greeting once they have left scouting behind. In a complex society, however, most specialties remain unknown to most of the people. This may be because the specialties require unique aptitudes or a rigorous course of training undertaken only by a few. Or, it may be that the specialties are the secret and hidden knowledge of a few, kept within their closed circle for the benefits that may be derived from secretiveness. The result is that no individual can ever acquire or manifest in himself all of the elements of his society's culture. It means, also, that no anthropologist, even the most assiduous, can ever make note of, to say nothing of record, all of the aspects of any culture, even the simplest known to man.

This, then, provides the answer to the oft-asked question, 'How can one speak of American culture when there are such divergencies in the cultures of New York City and the Kentucky Highlanders? Between the Italians of Lower Manhattan and the Scandinavians of Minnesota?' The universals and alternatives shared by most Americans are the common binding and integrating elements of American culture and society. The specialties of the different regional groups and socio-economic classes are merely differentiating elements. Even within a quite homogeneous society, however, specialties will occur in connection with subgroup organization. Men have one set of functions to perform, women another. Married men behave differently from the unmarried, fathers from the childless. Uninitiated adolescents have different norms from those who have passed through to manhood. Medicine men have patterns not available to the laymen.

The cohesiveness of a society is in part an effect of the relative proportion of universals and alternatives to specialties.

To return to our consideration of norms and the normative aspect of norms, note should be taken of the difference between standards for behavior and real behavior. There are always some gaps between what a people say they do, or what they think they ought to do, and what they really do. We must not forget the old admonition, 'What you do speaks so loudly that I cannot hear what you say.' There is an inevitable conflict between the standards or ideals set up in a culture for control of behavior of persons as members of the social group and errant individual impulses. Cultural standards are selected and tested, on the whole, in

terms of group benefit and group well-being. They call for the channeling and suppression of many possible lines of satisfaction of individual
impulses.

Since every person is at one and the same time an individual and a
group member, he wrestles constantly with the conflict of individual self-
interest as against his obligations to the group interests. Thus it is that
the members of a society, when thinking and acting as members of the
group, express the cultural standards of the group. But when acting in
response to dominant individual desires, they may be found consistently
to contravene those group standards. They may create in their culture
customary norms for violating the cultural standards.

An outstanding example is found in the behavior of the Trobriand
Islanders with respect to incest. Clan incest is forbidden and believed to
be supernaturally punished through the infliction of loathsome diseases
and possibly death. Trobrianders in all seriousness 'show horror at the
idea of violating the rules of exogamy . . . when judging the conduct of
others or expressing an opinion about conduct in general.' Yet to commit clan incest is the great game played by the Trobriand Islanders. It
is a custom that gratifies individual desires in defiance of their most
highly valued standards. What is most striking is the occurrence of a
highly developed body of customary techniques for thwarting the automatic effects of supernatural reaction. The natives possess a system of
magic spells and rites performed over water, herbs, and stones, which
when properly carried out is said to be completely efficient in undoing
the painful supernatural results of clan incest. So strong is the acceptance
of such actual behavior, that even when the incestuous activities of a
pair are known, there is no social reaction beyond lascivious scandal
mongering, unless someone for motives of personal antagonism undertakes to denounce the incestors publicly. Then and only then does the
body politic become upset, for this act stimulates a public defense of
the group standards. Then is the time for the incestor to commit suicide,
blaming the public denouncer for his death—an onus that causes the
public benefactor considerable discomfort.

The Comanche Indians of the Plains provide us with another example
of such a social incongruity. Their ideal pattern of marriage is one in
which a brother bestows his sister upon a man of his, not her, choosing.
The groom is usually an older man. The girl is supposed to accept the
match and learn to love and respect her husband. All Comanches sagely
aver that this is the very best kind of marriage and most satisfactory in

its results. Yet it was the regular thing in the old days for a young wife to abscond by joining an enterprising young brave on the war path. The members of the war party never objected to her presence, but aided the couple in their escape. Here was a customary pattern of group assistance in the violation of Comanche cultural standards and tribal law. For law it was, since the offended husband was forced by public opinion to prosecute the male absconder for damages and physically to punish his wife, unless the wife-stealer was powerful enough to protect her.

In these examples we see the existence of 'pretend rules': standards that are honored in spoken word, but breeched in customary behavior. Dry Oklahoma gives us a contemporary American example of what was a national exemplification of a similar situation in the days of federal prohibition of alcoholic beverages.

This sets the difference between *real culture,* what people actually do, and *ideal culture,* what they say (and believe) they should do. In awareness of this disparity no well-trained modern anthropologist is willing to take a people's word as full evidence of their real culture. He must observe their activity for himself. He insists on getting down to cases.

There is yet another aspect to this phase of culture that may be phrased in terms of *overt* and *covert* behavior. Overt behavior is that which is manifest in motor activity. It is externalized through movement and muscular action that may be directly observed. Covert behavior is that which goes on internally—thinking, dreaming, and the activity of the internal glands and organs.

The registry of sensory impressions in conscious awareness, is definitely influenced and often determined by culture. The sharp vision of the Indians on the plains is not the result of any superiority in actual visual acuity. It stems from their learned ability to read meaning in the way an animal or rider moves, the kind of dust he raises, and the lay of the land.

The moralistic story of the countryman and the cricket is a case in point. Walking down a busy city street one day, the countryman seized his city-bred friend by the arm, crying, 'Listen to the chirp of the cricket!'

The urbanite heard nothing until the bucolic friend led him to a crack in the face of a building where a cricket was proclaiming his presence unheard by the passing throngs.

'How can you hear such a little sound in the midsts of all this noise?' the city man wondered.

'Watch!' his friend replied as he tossed a dime upon the sidewalk. Whereupon a dozen people turned at the faint click of the coin. 'It depends on the things you are taught to be interested in.'

The covert culture of a people forces them to perceive some facts and to fail to perceive others. Trobriand Islanders cannot recognize any physiological similarity between father and sons. We look for and often see similarities that are doubtful at best. We feel that similarities should exist. Trobrianders feel that there should be no similarities, because theirs is a matrilineal society in which the mother's brother rather than the father has the important social position with respect to boys, and in denial of the father's significance the Trobrianders hold to a belief in spirit conception of offspring. To recognize filial similarities might insinuate the falsity of the spirit conception doctrine and work to undermine a sacred Trobriand institution. It would be a subversive implication that the father was biologically connected with his sons' creation. The power of the covert culture is sufficient to blank out the Trobriand perceptive sense at this point.

We are familiar with this phenomenon in our own social life. We know how difficult it is for us to see those facts which would be upsetting to our deep-set beliefs.

Covert culture controls perception, because it sets attitudes and beliefs. These may be translated into overt action, but not necessarily so, or directly. There may be conflicts of standards in the covert culture which permit only one of the standards to be translated into action. Attitudes, too, may be verbalized into overt expression without attaining realization in full behavior.

Anthropologists also make a distinction between *material* and *non-material* culture. Material culture is always the direct product of overt action. It consists of tangible goods: the artifacts and paraphernalia a people possess as products of technology. Non-material culture consists of behavior per se, both overt and covert. Strictly speaking, material culture is really not culture at all. It is the product of culturally determined activity. Behind every artifact are the patterns of culture that give form to the idea for the artifact and the techniques of shaping and using it.

The study of material culture can contribute a good deal toward our knowledge of actual culture, but it is impossible to learn more than a little about the lives of a people from their material culture alone. Archaeology, which deals in a scientific manner with the recovery and study of the objects of material culture buried in the earth, is always limited in the results it can produce. The use and meaning of any object depends almost wholly upon non-material behavior patterns, and the objects derive their true significance from such patterns. A pointed stick may be a dibble, a weapon, a scepter, a stake, or a phallic symbol. This can be determined only through contact with the living culture.

Thus when the archaeologist uncovers a prehistoric culture, it is not really the culture that he unearths but merely the surviving products of that culture, tangible remnants of the intangible reality. The actual culture became extinct when the society that carried it passed out of existence. No culture can exist divorced from living beings.

A culture consists of elements or single traits, but the significance of a culture is less in its inventory of traits than the manner of integration of the traits. It is theoretically possible for two societies to possess identical inventories of culture elements, and yet so to arrange the relationships of these elements to each other that the complexes within the two cultures and the total forms of the two cultures will be quite unlike. By simple analogy, a mason may take two identical piles of bricks and equal quantities of mortar. Yet according to the manner in which he lays his bricks, he may produce a fireplace or a garden wall.

The configuration of a culture is its delineated contours as shaped by the interrelation of all of its parts. It presumes internal integration of all of its parts. It presumes internal integration in accordance with some basic and dominant principles or value systems underlying the whole scheme. These are the *existential postulates* set by the culture: propositions about the nature of things; and *normative postulates:* propositions about the desirability and undesirability of things. A clear and unambiguous configuration reflects the attainment of a high degree of integration through the selection of the numerous elements of the culture in terms of their consonance with the basic postulates.

In the anthropologists' discussion of the configuration of culture the Pueblo Indians of the American Southwest have been shown to possess a culture that stresses restraint and orderliness in behavior, avoidance of emotional excess and display in personal experience and ritual, rigorous suppression of individual initiative and innovation, with quiet co-operation in group endeavor. Pueblo culture presents to the individual the philosophy of a well-ordered universe in which man is but one harmonious part of a delicate balance involving all nature forces. As long as each man plays his ordained roles in the traditional manner, all people will prosper. The rain gods will provide the precious water, the gods of plants and fertility will mature adequate crops, the dancing gods will favor the village. All functions necessary to the good life and survival of the pueblo will be fulfilled. The failure of any person to perform his roles in the traditional and proper way is believed to upset the balance and bring down disaster upon the whole society. This is a cultural code that rests upon a maize-growing subsistence economy as practiced by a sedentary people, who build stone and adobe, multi-storied communal houses in a desert environment.

As a contrasting example we may briefly draw the outlines of configuration for the culture of the people of the island of Alor in Indonesia. Like the Pueblo Indians, the people of Alor are settled gardeners. But in their lives the dynamic principle of culture, which is of outstanding significance, is the continuing exchange of wealth. Striving for personal dominance over fellow tribesmen by means of financial activity, the making and collecting of loans is the chief adult activity, especially of men. It is apparently the consequence of notable individual insecurity caused by the peculiar and unsatisfactory relationships within the family as they affect the growing child. Money, which in Alor consists of pigs, Javanese bronze vessels, and gongs, is lent out as capital on which interest must be paid, so that the debtor is bound by tight bonds of obligation to the creditor. Marriage and death, in particular, call for extensive consumption of pigs in feasts, along with tremendous exchanges and payments in vessels and gongs. The burdens imposed on the participants are immense, for they must usually go into heavy debt to meet the demands of the occasion. Except as it stimulates the growing of pigs, all this heavy economic activity bears little or no relation to economic production or utilitarian needs.

War, until suppressed by the Dutch, did not rest on any military interest as such. Rather, it was expressed as a long, drawn out series of feuds marked by cowardly assaults on men and women, and carried out by trickery and stealth.

Illness is marked by a complete collapse of the will to live and an obsessive conviction of hopelessness.

The culture of Alor emphasizes non-utilitarian striving to best one's fellowmen, pushing the ego, to which it denies serenity and security, on to its final collapse in the illness that ultimately brings surcease in death.

In the Pueblos and Alor we have two kinds of culture configurations, which are reasonably clear-cut. This is not always the case, however, for many cultures do not attain concise integration in accord with a consistent set of basic principles. The nomadic buffalo-hunting Indians of the western American Plains had one line of integration of behavior traits that emphasized extravagant sensation seeking. One of the highlights of life was to bring oneself through fasting, thirsting, autosuggestion, and, perhaps, self-torture to the phantasy state in which sensational visions would be encountered. Upon these visions, which were interpreted as supernatural visitations through which medicine power was bestowed, depended the successful outcome of any man's career. The purpose of the vision quest was to bring power and glory to the individual. Armed with such powers he could perform reckless deeds in battle. Armed with a record of such deeds, he could boastfully glorify himself, challenging other men to match their records of performance against his. This was but the central core of a whole series of culture traits glorifying rampant individualism and stimulating extreme sensate behavior.

Yet this is not *the* configuration of Plains culture, for equally strong, if not so spectacular, is another web of traits based on a contradictory set of basic principles. The first complex may be called the 'egotistical warrior' line. The second would be the 'considerate peace chief' line. This emphasized gentleness, generosity, reasonableness, and wisdom. Such virtues called for self-restraint, consideration of others, and a disposition to check the too quarrelsome assertiveness of the aggressive individualism called forth by the other line in the culture. Some men in the Plains tribes followed either one line or the other throughout their lives. In others, the incompatibilities of the two patterns set up an internal conflict for both individual and society. The restrained peace chief concept had its counterpart in important religious ceremonies such as the extremely pious and sober ritual of the Medicine Arrow Renewal of the Cheyenne Indians. For this, all male members of the tribe, except murderers and their close kin, had to be present. When the sacred arrows were unwrapped from their protecting bundle not a cry or sound was permitted to disturb the holy atmosphere. Patroling soldiers clubbed any yelping dog into stunned silence or death.

Consistency in a culture is not, therefore, wholly to be expected. It is probably true, as Sumner maintained, and there is a strain towards consistency in the folkways of any culture: that contradictory elements tend to cancel one or the other out, or else to attain a synthesis in a new form. On the other hand, it is too much to expect a completion of this process in all aspects of any culture. Inconsistencies arise and persist because, in the first place, cultures are never consciously planned or directed in their general growth. In the second place, most cultural traits are acquired through borrowing. Not many human beings are originators. The sources of borrowing for any culture are diverse and unlike. While there is always a certain amount of selection (people do not borrow blindly), new elements may be taken up even though inconsistent with elements or principles already within the culture, because they appear to be desirable in themselves. Finally, there are almost always alternative possibilities among the answers to the problems that culture undertakes to solve. It may be a matter of simple accident that the first solution hit upon and adopted is not wholly consistent with pre-existing forms in the culture. Nevertheless, it may find its way into the cultural whole because it serves a need or interest satisfactorily. If it produces a conflict within the culture, that is a matter to be suffered.

Our discussion of the configuration of culture has indicated that the behavior of each individual is strongly influenced by the patterns of the culture with which he lives. The character of each individual is unique, for one individual's experiences never match those of another, nor is it probable that the constitutional components of any two persons are exactly identical. But the patterns and configurations of the cultures of different societies produce distinctive personality types that are generally characteristic of the members of those societies. In the personality and culture studies that have developed so fruitfully in recent years culturally determined personality configurations have come to be known as national (or tribal) character, ideal personality type, modal personality, and basic personality.

The ideal personality type is the abstract image of the 'good' man or the 'good' woman that is reflected from the moral standards set in the culture. Much psychopathology is the product of an unmastered conflict within the individual who is unable to assimilate the standards of the cultural ideal to the impulses of the self. It is the Freudian conflict of the super-ego and the id.

The basic personality structure is differently conceived. It exists not as an abstract image but rather as a modal core of attitudes produced in the average individual as a result of the patterns of childtraining characteristic of his culture. How is the infant fed, handled, bathed? What are adult reactions to infant defecation and urination? Does the child receive consistent loving attention? Or is it harshly rejected, or teased, or abused? How and in what ways does it suffer deprivation or enjoy gratification of its wants? In so far as the answers to these questions are found in consistent patterns of adult behavior, so will the basic personality structures of the children take form. The basic personality structure tends to persist throughout the life of the individual, coloring adult behavior and completing the cycle by influencing the configuration of adult culture. Thus the grown-up Alorese is 'anxious, suspicious, mistrustful, lacking in confidence, with no interest in the outer world. There is no capacity to idealize the parental image or deity. The personality is devoid of enterprise, is filled with repressed hatred and free floating aggression over which constant vigilance must be exercised. The personality is devoid of high aspirations and has no basis for the internalization of discipline.' [2] Such is the effect of Alorese infant and childhood experience on the personality of the grown-up native of Alor.

In like manner, each culture puts *its* mark upon the individual who develops under its influence, whose personality is a blend resulting from his unique physical and nervous constitution, the patterns of his culture, and his individual experience in contact with the physical world and other people. Each man is a common type, molded by culture and society, and yet possessed of individuality that culture cannot submerge.

[2] A. Kardiner and associates, *The Psychological Frontiers of Society*, Columbia University Press, New York, 1945, p. 170.

RUTH BENEDICT

VIII

The Growth of Culture *

ALL BOOKS with such titles as *Progress,* or *The History of Civilization,* or *The Growth of the United States,* or *Modern Finance,* or *Modern Warfare* are books about some aspect of the growth of culture. When we talk about such subjects, they are parts of this great story, whether we are speaking about ancient Greece or contemporary Iowa. Even when we read about how the Romans destroyed Greece or the Goths destroyed Rome, we are learning about cultural growth. For destruction and growth go on together. As culture grows, it also destroys, and as it destroys, new growths appear.

The history of the human race is a wonderful story of progress. Archaeologists tell us that for thousands of years men made the same flint tools by striking stones together, took shelter in caves, and tied a skin around themselves for warmth. Only a few families could live near one another, for each grown man had to stalk wild animals to get food for his women and children. He could only accept nature's supplies as he found them; he knew no way to increase them. It was thousands of years later that his descendants discovered that plants could be sown and tended and harvested or that animals could be domesticated.

The human race is unique among all animal species because of the progress it has made from that day to this. Man alone has constantly enriched his way of life by invention and by complex learning. The fabulous growth of culture is his great achievement, and no other mammal has made this kind of progress. When we examine the growth of culture

° This article was completed by Dr. Ruth Benedict just before her death in 1948. A few editorial changes have been made by Dr. Benedict's literary executor, Dr. Margaret Mead.

in human history, we are examining the basis for man's pre-eminence. Members of the human race have a right to just one great boast: that they have an endless capacity to invent and learn. They can learn not merely as other mammals do, from imitation and from individual experience, but from experience passed down to a present generation from thousands of forebears now dead and gone.

The growth of culture in human history has created for the human race a man-made environment quite unlike the environment nature provided. Man took the wild grasses and developed them into wheat and barley and corn, which were productive enough to sustain his great cities. Even primitive people with no writing and no schools terraced mountains to make rice or corn fields and irrigated them by diverting water in regions where rainfall was not adequate.

Primitive tribes have invented tools and learned how to make pottery and baskets. They have fashioned elaborate traps and fish-weirs to make the food quest easier. They have made musical instruments to please their senses and lavished their craftsmanship on beautiful objects. Everywhere, also, among all races of men, they have expanded their world of known and seen human contacts to include also spirits and gods whom they call upon for help.

HUMAN BEGINNINGS

This long story of man's creativeness in the growth of culture begins far back with the first appearance of the human species. To us today Stone Age man seems culturally poverty-stricken because we have gone so far beyond him. But he had begun the distinctively human process of making inventions and transmitting them by teaching to his descendants. By the middle of the Stone Age, for instance, he had domesticated fire. No one will ever know what happened to make some men or women first put to domestic use that terrifying and destructive force. And what were the circumstances which led them to make water boil over a fire? They could hardly have seen in nature any boiling water. And how did they discover that they could kindle fire at will by rubbing two pieces of wood together? At any rate at least by the middle of the Stone Age in Europe man had not only learned these things; he had made them a part of his transmitted culture. He had learned ways of making and keeping fire and he could use it to warm himself when he was cold, and to cook and preserve his food. It was a complex invention which foreshadowed man's continuing career as a great inventor.

Perhaps even more significant was the gradual invention of language. It involved arranging things in the environment in different categories or classes; it involved creating verbs to show how these things could act and be acted on. Originally it involved something else too: the long, slow development of the muscles used in articulation. Early Stone Age man had less specialized tongue muscles and his speech was certainly hampered by this fact. We cannot know when human speech first became a complex set of symbols; it was certainly a long slow process. Today, however, there is no primitive tribe, no matter how poor in material culture, which has not a complicated language and a vocabulary of words with fine shades of meaning.

Stone Age man was remarkable for his skill in making implements out of flint. By striking brittle stone he could fashion tools and weapons. Stone Age man in different areas and periods made different tools. Their shape was so standardized that experts can name the period and area from which most worked flints in a modern museum come. Although their stability over centuries reminds us of the distinctive nest a robin or a crow inevitably builds this distinctiveness depends on learning, not instinct. The human race, even at that early date, had to transmit even this basic industry by teaching each generation what man could learn by experience. When he had learned, he could transmit the new technique.

Stone Age man had begun the process of creating man-made cultural environments. Because nothing is left of his works except those made of durable materials, we do not know what he had invented in social organization, in rules of marriage, or in religion and folklore. It may have been much; it may have been surprisingly little. We do know that with his handling of fire, language, and flint implements he had adopted unique human methods of invention and learning. From that day to this, man has followed this path.

OBSTACLES TO THE ADOPTION OF NEW TRAITS

The growth of culture has not been as continuous and as purposeful, however, as we often imagine when we talk of progress. Our ideas of progress are themselves cultural inventions of restless modern man avid for improvements. In the modern world in one generation we adopt and learn to manipulate the automobile or the aeroplane or the telephone or the radio or the techniques of mass factory production. We do not pray: 'Oh Lord, keep us as our fathers were.' Even in finance or art, we invent freely, with our eyes on the future rather than on the past. We even create new religious cults by the dozen. It is easy, therefore, for us to picture human progress as if man had always reached out for a new idea or a new invention and had adopted it whenever he saw it.

History is full of examples of apparently simple discoveries that were not made even when they would be surpassingly useful in that culture. Necessity is not necessarily the mother of invention. Men in most of Europe and Asia had adopted the wheel during the Bronze Age. It was used for chariots, as a pulley wheel for raising weights, and as a potter's wheel for making clay vessels. But in the two Americas it was not known except as a toy in any pre-Columbian civilization. Even in Peru, where immense temples were built with blocks of stone that weighed up to ten tons, these huge weights were excavated, transported, and placed in buildings without any use of wheels.

The invention of the zero is another seemingly simple discovery which was not made even by classic Greek mathematicians or Roman engineers. Only by the use of some symbol for nothingness can the symbol 1 be used so that it can have the value either of 1 or 10 or 100 or 1000. It makes it possible to use a small number of symbols to represent such different values as 129 and 921. Without such inventions figures cannot be added or subtracted by writing them one above another, and multiplication and division are even more difficult. The Romans had to try to divide CCCLVIII by XXIV and the difficulty was immense. It was not the Egyptians or the Greeks or the Romans who first invented the zero, but the Maya Indians of Yucatán. It is known that they had a zero sign and positional values of numbers by the time of the birth of Christ. Quite independently the Hindus made these inventions in India some five to seven centuries later. Only gradually was it adopted in medieval Europe, where it was known as Arabic notation because it was introduced there by the Arabs.

Necessity is not only not the inevitable mother of invention; it is not possible to assume that a people will adopt new inventions or accept discoveries others make. The technique of making bronze was established in Europe and Asia a couple of thousand years before iron ores were worked, and even after ways of forging and tempering iron were known, bronze remained for centuries the favorite metal. It was prettier though not nearly so good for tools. Yet iron ores are abundant and not difficult to extract, and tools of iron can be readily made at little outdoor primitive forges, as they are among African tribes today.

Primitive tribes in the modern world often continued to practice some

old and back-breaking custom even when they were in contact with some
other primitive peoples who had admirably solved that particuar technological problem. The Chukchee, a reindeer herding tribe of eastern
Siberia, carried on trade with Eskimo tribes who built themselves snow
huts. These houses are dome-shaped; blocks of firm snow are cut out with
knives and slanted inward until the final block at the top seals the dome.
A single man can build one for himself in half-an-hour for a shelter, and
large interconnecting ones are built for short-term winter dwellings.
They can be heated with blubber lamps and can keep the inmates warm
in Arctic winters. The Chukchee, however, stuck to their great skin tents,
inside which they set up a smaller skin sleeping tent. Every morning the
frost had to be beaten out of the skins, for the moisture from the breath
and from perspiration froze, and, if left in, would make the skins crack.
This daily beating of the tent covering was exhausting physical labor; in
addition, the great bundle was heavy and cumbersome to transport, and
erecting the tents on a new site was laborious. But the Chukchee never
adopted the snow house of the Eskimo, no matter what difficulties they
had with skin tents in the Arctic.

There was another side to this picture. The Chukchee were reindeer
herders. They became rich through breeding and rearing these animals
and they harnessed them to their sleds. The Eskimos, however, did not
adopt reindeer herding. On the American continent, where the barren-
ground caribou were available in large numbers and apparently might
have been domesticated as the Siberian reindeer were, no domestication
at all took place. The trait was not borrowed by American Eskimos or
Indians, even though many other cultural inventions diffused across
Bering Strait.

Even in modern western civilization, where we pride ourselves on our
efficiency, each nation excludes some existing inventions. One might suppose that in great civilizations where counting and measurement are as
important as they are in Europe and the United States, all nations would
adopt systems with convenient units. The metric system, in which the
integer is multiplied first by 10, then by 100 and 1000, can be applied
to measurements of volume, of length, and of weight, and can be used
to count money. In France the decimal system is used for every kind of
counting and measuring. In the United States we use it to reckon money,
but not volume, length, or weight. In England it is not even used in
reckoning money and no measurements of length or weight or volume
are reckoned by metric systems.

The growth of culture, therefore, has not had the kind of history an armchair student would imagine. It cannot be reconstructed logically and by deduction. Sometimes some obvious and simple thing was not discovered or accepted at all even when there was great logical need for it. Sometimes very complicated things were invented in the simplest primitive societies. This is true not merely in technology. It is true in social organization, in legal systems, in religion, and in folk philosophy. To understand the growth of culture in all these aspects, it is necessary to describe more fully how partial all men become to the special man-made environment they have created by their own cultural inventions and arrangements.

The habits of any culture fit the people who learn to use them like well-worn gloves. This fit goes very deep, for their ideas of right and wrong, their selection of human desires and passions, are part and parcel of their whole version of culture. They can react to another people's way of conducting life with a supreme lack of interest or at least of comprehension. Among civilized peoples this often appears in their depreciation of 'foreign ways'; it is easy to develop a blind spot where another people's cherished customs are concerned. Among primitive peoples this lack of interest in 'progress' has been proverbial. And for good reason. Every primitive tribe has its own elaborate cultural arrangements which ensure its survival, either technologically, or in their forms of social organization, or by ceremonies and offerings to the gods. Even though they may be eager for some things the white man brings—perhaps guns, perhaps beads, or whiskey, or empty tin cans out of which to make a knife— they do not generally look on the white man's culture as a solution of life's problems which is 'better' than the one they have. They may be culturally uninterested even in laborsaving devices. Often the value they put on time is extremely low and 'wisdom' is far more valued than efficiency. Our cultural system and theirs are oriented around different ideals.

Some primitive cultures have not been able to accommodate themselves to contact with the white man. Their whole way of living, when they were brought into contact with modern civilization, has fallen down like a house of cards. The Indians of the United States have most of them become simply men without a cultural country. They are unable to locate anything in the white man's way of life which is sufficiently congenial to their old culture. When the white man first came, the Plains tribes had a short-lived cultural upsurge when they enthusiastically incorporated the horse into their way of life, and the Northwest Coast Indians had a veritable renaissance of wood carving when they got metal. But closer contact laid bare the great gap between white and Indian values. The Indian cultures could not survive the white man's interference with their tribal war paths and the buffalo herds and salmon fisheries on which they depended. Acquaintance with the strange white customs of working for wages and paying for land and conducting private enterprise broke down their old social arrangements without putting anything intelligible in their place. The white man, for his part, was equally unable to see the cultural values which the Indian tribes cherished and which were being broken down and lost forever. Each side was blind to cultural ideals which to the other were the most real things in the universe.

In all such cases of contact between western civilization and other cultures, the white man is usually sure that he is of superior intelligence because he has the knives, the guns, the cigarettes, the metal skillets that the simpler people do not have. He judges that the others would have these things, along with reading, writing, and arithmetic, if they were not stupid. Actually careful observations and tests have shown that the matter is not so simple. Neither the intelligence nor the senses of primitive people need be inferior even when their manner of life is very simple. In western civilization we are heirs of inventions that have been made all over the face of the earth. All we have and know are items of our social inheritance. We were simply born into it by the accident of our birth. It is highly unlikely that any one of us has invented one single process. Just so, an American Indian was an heir of *his* culture. It was rather more likely than in the complex western civilization that he had individually had an opportunity to make some contribution to tribal ways or that he had had a chance to take leadership in some activities important to his people. His ways of life satisfied him because they solved human problems in ways he had been reared to understand. It had not crossed his mind to want the things the Europeans wanted. He had used his brains on a different set of activities that were more congenial.

No one has ever developed an objective scale of values according to which all different cultural goals may be graded as better or worse. Western civilization, for instance, is organized to extend its power widely over the earth. A valid case, however, can be made for the value of a cultural goal which has no place for conquest or financial domination. Every people value most the drives and emotions to which they are accustomed, and they usually condemn people who lack them. They are right in valuing their own way of life, but their depreciations of other cultures are often based on misunderstandings.

INTERNAL GROWTH OF CULTURE

Because all peoples defend their own way of life, it is easy to understand that one way in which cultures have grown richer and more complex has been by elaborating and multiplying their own most cherished customs. They carry further and further their favorite customs. Simple trading habits may be worked up into great tribal ceremonies. The potlatches of the Northwest Coast Indians were such ceremonies, in which chiefs tried to defeat other chiefs by giving them so many blankets and other goods that they would be unable to return the interest on them. Such tribes took the main theme of their cultural life from the situation of the creditor and the debtor, and they elaborated their ceremonies around this theme till their potlaches became systems of intricate cultural complexity.

In other tribes the most cherished observances are hospitable entertainments of the gods. In the Southwest pueblo of Zuñi, the spirits are thought to be happiest when they are given the opportunity to come to the world of the living and dance. Therefore men put on spirit masks and impersonate them. These Indians 'dance' their corn, too, to make it happy, and put on elaborate welcoming rites for the carcass of a deer after the hunt. They greet and honor even little pine branches they cut for their ceremonies. Since the sun, and spirits of rain, and spirits of animals, and spirits of enemies, and spirits of curing all have to be honored, Zuñi has a staggering mass of ceremonial addressed to this end. Both on the Northwest Coast and in Southwest pueblos, the local process of cultural growth has been, just as in other parts of the world, a kind of industrious weaving of a more and more complex cocoon. But the threads of this cocoon are still old, chosen, and simple habits, even when they are fashioned into such complex observances. They are valued in their congeniality.

Cultures tend to develop in this way, and it is therefore possible to understand the different lines along which, for instance, eastern civilizations like China and India have developed as contrasted to western civilizations. Unless one is to the manner born, the elaborations of another culture often seem superfluous. But the whole history of the growth of culture is full of superfluities to which people of that tribe or nation have displayed deep attachment and loyalty.

GROWTH OF CULTURE THROUGH DIFFUSION

Besides this kind of internal elaboration of preferred traits cultures have grown mightily by borrowing techniques and ideas from one another. This borrowing is technically called the diffusion of cultural traits.

Western civilization itself is based on inventions which have been borrowed from every part of the world. Many of them were made by people of simple culture who did not share in western traditions. The alphabet was invented by Semitic peoples in the area north of the Red Sea and carried by Phoenicians to Greece and Rome. Over centuries it spread throughout Europe and into India. Paper—and gunpowder too— are old inventions made in China. The true arch, with its keystone, was a great architectural invention made in Babylonia thirty centuries before Christ; but ancient Greek architecture is not based on it. The great monuments and temples of Peru and Central America were built without any knowledge of it. Gradually, however, the Babylonian invention was adopted in ancient Etruria and in Rome, and became basic in Gothic cathedrals. Modified into a dome, it is used in modern public buildings.

Man has constantly enriched his food supply by introducing grains and fruits which were originally domesticated on the opposite side of the globe. Coffee was brought into cultivation in Abyssinia, but today we associate it particularly with Brazil and Java. Potatoes are roots first tended and harvested by South American Indians, and Bolivian Indians cultivated 240 varieties. But we call our white potatoes 'Irish.' Bananas come to us today from Central America, but wild varieties were first brought into cultivation in south Asia, and Polynesian peoples had carried them over immense areas of the Pacific before European navigators made their voyages of discovery. The banana in the New World is post-Columbian; it was borrowed from the Old World. Maize, an American Indian crop, is today a staple of many primitive tribes of Africa, and tobacco, also an American Indian crop, has been adopted in all parts of the world.

The diffusion of cultural traits from one people to another has constantly enriched human ways of life. Every little tribe is indebted to its neighbors for various inventions which the latter have borrowed farther

afield and which they themselves modified after they copied it and perhaps improved.

RECASTING OF BORROWED TRAITS

Whatever traits tribes borrow from one another, they are likely to re-
cast them to make them congenial to their own way of life. Sometimes
this recasting has been drastic, sometimes not so drastic. But as a student
follows any one cultural trait through tribe after tribe, he finds strange
new meanings and uses given to it, or strange new combinations into
which it has entered. The wheel, when it was invented in the Old World,
spread rapidly in the period around 3000 B.C. into Assyria and Iran and
India, and later into Egypt. These were regions of the world where pottery was at that time very important and when the wheel spread into
Egypt, it was as a potter's wheel. Not until much later was it used as a
chariot wheel. However, when after 200 B.C. the wheel was borrowed by
peoples of northen Europe, they used it for wheeled vehicles for nearly
a thousand years before they utilized it in pottery making. Tribes and
nations could not put the wheel to use in a horse-drawn, wheeled chariot
unless they had domesticated animals that could be trained to the har-
ness, and they could not use it for pottery unless they had pottery industry and cared about making it more rapidly. So the wheel became
a part of quite different arts of life as it diffused over the world.

New meanings are given to borrowed traits as they pass from area to
area. This is just as conspicuous in traits of social organization, political
arrangements, and religious practices as it is in traits of material culture.
A religious ceremony, for instance, may be shared by all tribes over a
great area. All may erect the same kind of house or enclosure on sacred
ground, have the same kinds of torture or trance communication or order
of march, and use the same insignia for officers and the same type of
prayers. All these characteristics may have been spread from tribe to
tribe in the area. Nevertheless, in spite of all these diffused traits, a widespread ceremony like the Sun Dance of the Plains Indians has been re-
cast in tribe after tribe. In one tribe the whole ceremony is put on by
someone who has had a vision of the Thundergod and desires to honor
this spirit which has honored him; in another it is vowed by one man
who proposes to avenge the death of a relative on the war path; in
another it is a way of giving thanks for escape from danger or disease;
in another it is a ceremony for the initiation of priests or shamans. These
different meanings of the ceremony, of course, led to changes in the rites

themselves and eventually the whole ceremony in one tribe comes to have its own special character, which it does not share with any other tribe.

This recasting of borrowed traits occurs in the same way in social organization and folklore and in any other field of life. A good example is the varied meaning of cannibalistic practices. Cannibalism did not occur in all parts of the world, but where it did it had the most contrasted meanings. It was used in some tribes as a way of ensuring the birth of children; only young children were eaten and only the immediate family participated; afterwards they believed that a child would be born again to the family. In other tribes, the hearts only of brave enemies were eaten; it was done in order to increase the bravery of the eaters. Sometimes cannibalism was a lusty enjoyment of good food; sometimes it was a proof that a man could face anything in the world if he could dare to swallow a portion of human flesh. Each tribe and area had taken this piece of behavior and used it in its own special way.

It is the same with adolescent ceremonies, with kinship systems, and with the institutions of kingship. People borrow, and, when they have adopted the trait, it has already become something else from the thing they borrowed. The process of diffusion has therefore not only allowed people all over the world to share in each others' creations and inventions; it has also increased the rich variety of human cultures.

EVOLUTION

The history of man from the Stone Age to the present is a wonderful story of cultural growth. The social inheritance of man has been enriched by multitudinous inventions and arts. In spite of terrible periods of devastation and destruction, the human race has built for itself a cultural environment which is capable of almost infinite richness.

Although a large part of the history of any given culture is due to accident, an evolutionary process may be traced. The growth of culture has not been haphazard. That is, certain earlier inventions, whether of tools or of institutions or of ideas, have been necessary before other inventions could take place. In primitive tribes courts which administered tribal justice could not evolve until there was some organization of the tribal state. Kingdoms could not arise till certain political inventions had been made which brought many neighboring communities into mutual relations with one another. Standing armies in the service of chiefs required a preceding elaborate division of labor and the existence of centralized power.

Evolution can be well illustrated in two fields, the technological and the political. In technology, modern man has built upon the unplanned discoveries of the human race which began with man-made flint tools and the utilization of fire and later the invention of agriculture and herding. Modern man, however, has not left his inventions to chance. At long last, with the modern growth of scientific knowledge, man has arrived at the point where he consciously invents. That is, he sets up for himself a problem he wants to solve and tries all sorts of experiments and combinations until he solves it. He tests and retests till he is sure his solution works.

We are so used to this kind of problem-solving that it is hard for us to realize that most cultural advances have been chance discoveries rather than conscious invention. These discoveries, made without benefit of a previously imagined goal, thus were, strictly speaking, accidental. Even today primitive tribes are found sometimes in regions that have no agriculture but who have nevertheless dumped their garbage near their homes until seeds have sprouted in the enriched earth close to their houses. They had not planned to fertilize these patches and plant seed within easy reach of their camp fires. When they saw what had happened they did not think about their discovery and go straightway and plant new plots. But they picked the seeds and vegetables which sprouted on their dump heaps, and found them handy. They had accidentally stumbled upon an experience out of which the practice of agriculture could grow—probably the same experience which men stumbled upon in the New Stone Age when the human race first began systematically to exploit the possibilities of purposeful cultivation and planting of the soil.

The great upward curve of progress in technology of which man can rightly boast, therefore, is an evolution from unplanned discovery to planned invention. Man has learned purposefully to set his goal and then to check and recheck the experiments that he sets up to achieve that goal. Methods of curing diseases are a good example of this change. During most of the history of the human race, men accepted their traditional curing practices on faith. To treat eye troubles some peoples chose plants which had an 'eye' on their fruit or blossom; 'like,' they said, 'cured like.' Some of these plants were actually beneficial, but others, we know by chemical analysis, could even cause blindness. Nevertheless the dangerous plant was used. Some tribes had cure-alls for the most unrelated human ailments. It might be 'baking,' which meant putting the sick person over a bed of buried hot stones and keeping him warm for days or weeks. This was good for certain aches and pains, but they used it also for broken bones without trying to reset them. Starving or bleeding might be their cure-all, but neither of these were good cures for tuberculosis. Nevertheless they did not experiment and they continued to use their cure-alls. In the practice of medicine we have come a long way.

In man's technological progress, therefore, it required tens of centuries to arrive at the idea of scientific planning and checking. Man made his latest great step forward when he said, 'Just what is it I want to do?' and then tested his results to see if he had attained his object. In this way he discovered that planning could unlock the previously unknown.

A second great evolution in human culture is man's increasing ability to live together in large numbers. In early times and among the simpler societies only a few hundred people, or at most, on special occasions, a few thousands could be organized into a community. Man had to make inventions in social organization and in distribution of goods and in the political field before large organized states were possible. As man made more and more of these inventions, he was able to live in larger communities and to achieve law and order over larger and larger areas. Trade and ceremonies brought people together peacefully, and ideas circulated. Men were stimulated to think and build and create.

The growth of greater human communities is, therefore, in spite of all the devastation these large groups have often visited upon one another, one of the major themes of human progress. It has changed the human topography of the modern world. In earlier times small communities of a few hundred souls might be the only 'in-group' these people knew; all the rest were 'out-groups.' An in-group is a group of people with loyalties and rights and obligations which they hold in common. Out-groups are all other communities. The primitive in-group might be an economically self-sufficient community within which each person was necessary to the livelihood and well-being of the tribe. Out-group people were annoyances or out-and-out enemies. Everywhere such tribes had one system of ethics to regulate their dealings with in-group members, and a different and often opposite one for out-group people. Stealing, for instance, was very frequently unknown within the in-group, but it was a virtue if a man stole from an out-group. Generosity was often a prime virtue within the tribe, but it did not extend to out-group people.

The advantages of extending the in-group to include millions of people who can profit by mutual security and mutual trade in material goods and mutual exchange of ideas is too obvious to need comment. Mankind has gone far in this kind of progress. We can project this upward curve into the future and recognize that some day mankind will organize the whole world so that he can reap the maximum benefits of security and commerce and exchange of ideas. We have not done it yet. We keep the old primitive contrast between in-group and out-group ethics in our distinction between killing a man of one's own country—which is murder and a major crime—and killing an enemy in war—which is a duty for which we honor the successful soldier. We keep the primitive contrast, too, in our hair-trigger suspiciousness of other sovereign nations—just as they keep them about us. We set up mechanisms of law and order within each nation, but, just as in primitive times, there are no such lawful mechanisms binding sovereign nations together. There is temporary alliance, but essentially there is still the old anarchy that has been traditional in the relations of out-groups to one another. In this world which has grown so small because of modern technological inventions in commerce and finance and armament and communication and transportation, it is just as necessary today to organize the world community for the secure enrichment of human life as it was in earlier times to organize a dozen little in-groups scattered a few miles from each other along a river course.

IX

Language and Writing

LANGUAGE IS SO MUCH A PART of our daily activities that some of us may come to look upon it as a more or less automatic and natural act like breathing or winking. Of course, if we give the matter any thought at all, we must realize that there is nothing automatic about language. Children must be taught their native tongue and the necessary training takes a long time. Language is not something that is inherited; it is an art that can be passed on from one generation to the next only by intensive education.

It is difficult to realize the enormously important role that language plays in our social behavior. What would a society without language be like? It would of course have no writing or other means of communication by words, for all these are ultimately dependent on spoken speech. Our means of learning would therefore be greatly restricted. We should be obliged, like the animals, to learn by doing or by observing the actions of others. All of history would disappear, for without language there would be no way of re-creating past experiences and communicating them to others. We should have no means of expressing our thoughts and ideas to others or of sharing in the mental processes of our fellow-men. Indeed, it is very likely that we should not think at all. Many psychologists maintain that thought itself requires the use of language, that the process of thinking is really talking things over with ourselves.

A society lacking language would be incapable of engaging in any but the simplest of co-operative enterprises. An individual or group of individuals would have no way of planning such activities, of explaining them to others, or of directing the actions of the participants in co-operative enterprises toward the common goal. Each individual would be to a large extent dependent on his own strength and ability since he would lack the means of securing the help of others.

Most important, a society lacking language would have no means of assuring the continuity of behavior and learning necessary to the creation of culture. Human society, without culture, would be reduced to the level of present-day ape societies. Apes have a bodily structure very like our own. Like humans, they learn readily from experience and by observing and imitating the actions of others. A number of experimenters have shown that apes not only learn to use tools but also invent them. Despite, however, the fact that individual apes learn easily and, as individuals, show remarkable progress in the acquisition of knowledge, apes as a species have never developed a culture.

There are two reasons for this. Lacking language, the apes have no way of continuing in word and thought their separate experiences in the use of tools and techniques. When an ape has disposed of a problem the knowledge he has derived from that experience remains static. He may remember it when and if another problem of the same sort arises, but he does not in between times mull over his knowledge and devise means of applying it to further problems. Man does. His overt experiences with practical problems are, like those of the ape, separate and distinct. But because man possesses language, he can continue his problem-solving activities beyond the actual physical experience and so develop, in thought and discussion, new applications of his knowledge and improved means of solving problems. In short, by reason of language, man's experiences are continuous, not discontinuous as among apes, and so show far more rapid development.

Secondly, man's possession of language enables him to share the experiences and thoughts of his fellows and to re-create his personal experiences for their benefit. An ape's knowledge, acquired through experience and observation, is his alone, except in so far as he can demonstrate it in physical activity so that it may be acquired by another ape. No matter how skillful an ape may become in the use of tools and techniques, his offspring will be obliged to begin their learning as he began his, by experience and observation. The learned ape cannot communicate his knowledge and so enable his successors to build upon it. Culture among men reveals progress. Each generation takes over, by word of mouth and tradition, the accumulated knowledge of their predecessors, add their own contributions as drawn from their experiences and observations, and pass the whole on to succeeding generations. This cumulative aspect, which differentiates human cultures from the kind of knowledge current in animal societies, is made possible by language.

THE ANTIQUITY OF LANGUAGE

Studies of the skeletal and cultural remains of ancient man have shown that the first human beings came into being about one million years ago. Man's early cultures were very simple and crude and we know only a portion of their material remains, the tools and implements made of materials tough enough to withstand the passage of time. It is highly significant, however, that these early traces of man's cultures reveal a cultural continuity through time. As we study the several chronological phases of culture in any given area of the world, there is revealed a slow but steady advance both in the number of tools made and in the complexity of their manufacture. The men of successive generations did not begin anew each generation to fashion their cultures but built upon the techniques which had been discovered in the past and transmitted to them by their ancestors.

The fact that the history of man's cultures shows a continuous and cumulative development extending from their earliest beginnings to the present means of course that man has possessed language as long as he has possessed culture. Language must be as old as the oldest of man's cultural artifacts; it began when culture began and has developed continuously ever since.

This inference as to the age of language is amply borne out by other observations which may be made on modern languages. First, it is clear that all human societies have possessed a language for as long as we have known them; there is no group of men anywhere, today or in the past, who lack this important aspect of culture. Secondly, we may also observe that modern languages are very numerous and exceedingly diverse. The precise number of distinct languages spoken today cannot even be estimated, but we know that there are several thousand. Some of these are historically related to one another; that is, they are clearly derived from a single earlier tongue. Languages so derived are said to belong to the same linguistic family or stock, and there are hundreds of such stocks in the world today. Most of these stocks show no resemblance whatsoever to each other, because, as we may almost certainly assume, all traces of common origin have long since disappeared.

The universality of language and the amazing diversity of modern idioms can only mean that language is very old. Studies of languages known for centuries through the medium of written records reveal that languages change with relative slowness. Thus, though English and German have certainly been separate languages for well over 2000 years, they still retain many obvious similarities in both vocabulary and grammar which point clearly to their common origin. The enormous diversity of modern languages, then, must have taken a very long time to achieve.

A third and final evidence as to the antiquity of language is found in the fact that known languages, ancient or modern, cannot be classed in terms of their level of development. There are neither primitive languages nor highly developed ones, if we take into account only their structural features.

Thus, all the languages we know possess a well-defined system of distinctive speech sounds. These are finite in number, are carefully distinguished from one another, and are put together to form words, phrases, and sentences in accordance with definite rules. In this respect, there is no real difference between the languages of people who possess very simple and crude cultures and those of the highly civilized peoples of Europe and America.

Similarly, all human groups, regardless of the crudity of their culture, have a vocabulary sufficiently detailed and comprehensive to meet every need likely to arise. Languages vary, of course, in the size of their vocabularies, but this variation is cultural, not linguistic. The language of a people having a relatively simple or undeveloped culture may have a smaller vocabulary than one belonging to a group with a relatively complex and highly developed culture. It is notable, however, that the vocabulary of any group, however simple its culture, appears to be indefinitely expansible. As new cultural items are invented or borrowed, the vocabulary increases or changes to meet the new requirements imposed upon it.

Finally, all languages possess a definite and clear-cut system of grammar. Grammar may briefly be defined as the meaningful arrangement of sounds or combinations of sounds to produce words, phrases, and sentences. Well-defined rules governing such arrangements are found in all languages, whether they are spoken by the pre-literate Pygmies of the Congo forest or the culturally advanced groups of modern Europe.

The basic similarities mean, of course, that language has so long been a human possession as to have developed to about the same level among peoples the world over. There remain today no traces of an earlier and cruder stage of linguistic development.

The Origin of Language

Spoken languages obviously leave no trace in the ancient deposits which mark the history of man's cultures. Written records of human languages began only a few thousand years ago; before that time no human group possessed the technique of writing. It is evident, then, that we have no direct evidence as to the origin of language or of the long period of history that elapsed between its beginnings and the first written records. The problem of the origin of language will never therefore be solved in the sense that we shall know directly the circumstances under which language arose or be able to trace in terms of specific historical events the course of its development.

Many theories have been advanced as to the origin of language. Most of these, however, are based on two central hypotheses: the interjectional and the sound imitative or onomatopoeic theory of the origin of language.

Interjectional theories maintain, in general, that interjections or involuntary cries, because these are a good deal alike in all modern tongues, form the earliest stratum of words used by man. All other forms, it follows, must have been derived from these in one or other manner. Sound imitative theories look to words like *bow wow, meow, choo choo,* or *ding dong,* and similar attempts by men to imitate animal cries and noises as marking the beginnings of language. From such imitations of sounds encountered in his environment, man formed the hundreds of languages we now find spoken.

Both hypotheses fail to solve our problem, however, largely because they fail to account for true linguistic forms. Neither involuntary cries nor sound imitative words are as such true linguistic forms. An involuntary cry is really part of an individual's response to strong stimuli. The involuntary ejaculation of surprise is not the same as the conventional word written *Oh!* because the former represents part of the response itself and does not, like the conventional *Oh!,* symbolize the response of surprise. True linguistic symbols, such as words, are all conventional and arbitrary, and their meanings must be learned by speakers. No one learns an involuntary cry; a baby may cry out long before it learns to speak.

Sound imitative words must similarly not be confused with attempts to reproduce sounds characteristic of man's environment. A word like *ding dong,* for example, is a conventionalized representation of the sound of a bell, not necessarily self-evident to anyone except a speaker of English who has learned to associate the sound *ding dong* with the ringing of bells. To understand how languages came into being we must know how man came to establish his arbitrary or conventional habits of associating speech sounds with experience. This is not explained by the sound imitative hypothesis which points out merely that men sometimes name things and actions by the noises they make and that on occasion such names become truly a part of language.

It follows, then, that a useful theory of linguistic origins must be based on a more careful analysis and study of modern tongues. Such studies, as we have suggested, reveal that the elements of speech, such as words, phrases, and sentences, are arbitrary symbols. By this we mean symbols which are themselves no part of the reality or experience symbolized. Thus, for example, the particular succession of sounds which make up the word *horse* have no necessary relation to the class of animals symbolized by it. There is, in short, nothing horse-like about the word *horse;* it is simply that speakers of English have learned to associate the sounds written *horse* with a given class of animal, just as they have learned to associate the forms *dog* and *cat* with wholly different groups of animals.

The fact that linguistic symbols are nearly all arbitrary in nature emphasizes the social aspect of language. Languages are always associated with groups of individuals; they never belong exclusively to a single individual. An individual acquires his language from the group with which he lives. If he deviates widely in speech from other members of the group, he runs the risk of being misunderstood or of not being understood at all. *Horse* is not just a word peculiar to an individual speaker of English, it is a word used and understood in much the same way by all English-speaking peoples.

Languages function in human societies primarily as a means of communication and co-operation. By means of language an individual is able not only to re-create his own personal experiences and so share them with others, but he is also able to co-ordinate his labors with those of others. A group of men can thus work together in a task too heavy or too complex to be undertaken by any one of them singly. To exemplify this point, let us imagine that a man, hunting alone, manages to kill an animal too large for him to handle. He leaves the dead animal and returns to his encampment or village. There he tells the others what he has done and secures their assistance. They return to his kill with him and assist him to skin the game, cut up the meat, and carry it back to camp.

During the whole of this procedure, one individual may take charge, indicating in words the task each is to perform, so that the separate acts of each man will assist rather than obstruct the total performance.

Contrast the action we have just described with a similar incident among, let us say, a pack of wolves. Here, too, we have a social group albeit one composed of animals who lack language. When one of the wolves makes a kill alone, he will eat as much as he can; he will not be concerned or able to inform the pack of his feat. But should the other wolves come upon him as he makes the kill or while he is eating the carcass, they will certainly join him uninvited. Each wolf will get as much as he can and if there is not enough to go around, the weaker wolves will get none at all. The actions of the wolves in disposing of the meat will be separate and individual, with no co-ordination or co-operation whatsoever.

It is probable that the ancient animals from whom man evolved lived in groups very similar to those of present-day animals. Their behavior was only in a small degree co-ordinated. Each worked for himself alone, with the exception that the very young had to be cared for by an adult. On occasion, however, necessity must have enforced some degree of co-operation and co-ordinated effort. Man's primitive ancestor was not a formidable animal in comparison with many others who shared his environment. He must often have had to defend himself against stronger predatory animals and he probably discovered very early that such defense was more effective if undertaken in co-operation with his fellows. When such co-operative enterprises increased in frequency, the habit pattern built up may easily have led to co-operation under other circumstances, such as, for example, the hunting of large animals for food. Even wolves hunt together and, while so doing, correlate their efforts, at least to some degree.

The development of co-operative labor did not alone bring about language, however. Many insect groups are effectively co-operative without language. But co-operation among insects is evidently on a different basis than among men. Unlike the social insects men are not born to a given role in their social groups. Men must learn to adapt their behavior to the roles provided by the society, and language provides a vital tool to this kind of learning.

How and in what way man's animal ancestors came to employ language as an aid in co-operative labor we shall never know. We may safely assume, however, that man's primitive ancestor could and did

make noises and perhaps the noises which accompanied the tasks undertaken together came slowly to symbolize the several actions and ends
involved in such tasks. In any case, it appears to be fairly certain that
language arose as a result of men learning to work together toward a
common end. For whatever reasons, man's primitive ancestors were
obliged to acquire such learning, and so they, alone of the animals,
stumbled upon the tool, language, which more than any other makes
co-operative and co-ordinated activity effective.

THE STRUCTURE OF LANGUAGE

Languages, like many other cultural phenomena, cannot be observed
or studied directly. Just as we can describe a method of making baskets
only by observing the actions of individuals who are weaving them, so
can we describe a language only by observing the speech behavior of
those who use the language.

Individual acts of speech are called utterances. These are complete
in themselves and consist of a flow of speech sounds uninterrupted by
the speech of another individual. Some utterances may be quite short,
like *Oh!*, *Come!*, *Who?*, or *John*. Others are longer: *John runs, I see a
man*, or *The man we saw yesterday is dead*. Still others may be very
long, examples of these are found in speeches, lectures, or sermons. A
first step in studying a language is then to collect utterances, as many
as possible, from native speakers of the language.

Once this has been done, it soon becomes obvious that utterances
differ not only in length but also in structure. Some of them consist of
a single unit which cannot be interrupted without considerable change
in meaning. If, for example, we say *John runs?*, it is evident that the
forms *John* and *runs* are interdependent. To stop after we have said
John is like playing an unresolved chord on the piano; the listener awaits
impatiently the completion of the utterance. We can of course say *John?
Runs?* but here we create a new meaning, quite different from that of
John runs?

Utterances consisting of a single unit are called constructions and the
interdependent parts of this unit are said to be united grammatically to
one another. An utterance like *John? Runs?*, on the other hand, is made
up of two units which are not held together grammatically but only follow one another without interruption.

Grammarians express the difference we have illustrated by comparing
John runs? with *John? Runs?* by saying that *John runs?* consists of one

sentence while *John?* *Runs?* is two sentences. A sentence, then, is an utterance the parts of which are united grammatically into a construction and which is not itself a part of some larger construction. All utterances, it is clear, must contain at least one sentence.

Sentences, like utterances, vary in length and complexity. Thus, all of the following are sentences, though from first to last they increase both in length and complexity. *John, John runs, Poor John runs fast, Poor John runs very fast, Poor John, the boy next door, is decidedly the best runner of the group.* These examples reveal that sentences may be divided into still smaller units called phrases and words. A word may be defined as the smallest portion of a sentence which can be pronounced alone and still retain meaning. All of the forms written separately in the examples cited above are words, since all of them, pronounced alone, have meaning to a speaker of English. Phrases consist of two or more words, not a sentence, which compose a construction. It is obvious that some combinations may function sometimes as sentences and at other times as phrases. Thus, the combination *Poor John,* taken alone, is a sentence, but as part of *Poor John runs fast,* it functions as a phrase.

All sentences, it is clear, must possess at least one word. Longer sentences may contain two or more phrases, but the limits of sentence length depend so much upon individual or social preferences as to defy accurate definition.

The total stock of words possessed by a language is called its vocabulary or dictionary. Languages differ as to the size of their vocabularies. In general the size of a vocabulary is directly related to the culture of a speech community. If the culture is complex, as among most English-speaking peoples, the vocabulary may be very large and contain numerous highly technical sub-divisions. In a simple and relatively uniform culture, such as that of the Polar Eskimo, the vocabulary will be correspondingly smaller and contain fewer technical aspects. It should not be assumed, however, that so-called primitive peoples have very small vocabularies. We frequently hear, for example, of very primitive folk whose languages possess at most only a few hundred words. This is obvious nonsense for even the simplest culture requires a far greater number of words merely to enumerate the many objects and acts dealt with in the course of every-day occupations.

When we examine the vocabulary of a language and compare the words it contains with one another we soon discover that words, like sentences and utterances, also vary in size and complexity. Take for example English pairs like *dog, dogs; work, worker; black, blackish; combine, recombine; do, undo. Dogs* is obviously derived from *dog* by the addition of *-s, worker* from *work* by adding *-er, blackish* from *black* by adding *-ish, recombine* from *combine* by adding *re-,* and *undo* from *do* by adding *un-.* Each of the added elements conveys meaning: *-s* denotes the plural, *-er* means 'one who,' *-ish* means 'something like' (that is, a blackish object is one which is colored something like one which is black), *re-* means 'to do something again' (in this case, to combine again), and *un-* conveys a negative or opposite meaning (to undo a knot is the opposite or negative of 'doing' or tying a knot). These added elements are not words, however, because they are never spoken alone but always in combination with some other form (either a whole word or part of a word). Some words may contain more than one such element, each adding a measure of meaning to the completed word. Thus, the word *ungentlemanly* is formed by adding *un-* (not) to *gentlemanly. Gentlemanly,* in turn, consists of *gentleman* plus the ending *-ly,* meaning 'in such and such a way or manner.' Finally, *gentleman* is itself composed of *gentle* plus *man* though the meaning of the combination is no longer the same as the sum of the meanings of its two constituent parts.

Words and parts of words like *dog, -s, work, -er, combine, re-, black, -ish, do,* and *un-* are called simple linguistic forms or morphemes. Some morphemes, like *dog* and *work,* may be pronounced alone; these are called free morphemes. Others, like *-ish* and *un-,* are never pronounced alone and are therefore called bound morphemes. Combinations containing more than one morpheme, such as *dogs* or *worker,* are complex linguistic forms. Complex linguistic forms also include phrases, sentences, and utterances, however. Words having more than one morpheme are usually described as derived words or derivations.

Languages differ greatly in word structure. In some of them, Chinese is a good example, most words have but one morpheme; derivations are extremely rare. In others, like English, there may be many single morpheme words plus a large number of words having two or three morphemes and a smaller number having more than three morphemes. Languages like Navaho or Eskimo are found at the opposite extreme in so far as word structure is concerned for here we may find large numbers of so-called polysynthetic words possessing as many as eight or ten or even more morphemes.

When morphemes are combined to form words and when words are combined into phrases and sentences, these combinations always follow

definite rules of arrangement. Some morphemes, like *re-* and *un-* always
precede the forms with which they are combined and so are called pre-
fixes. Others, like *-er* and *-s,* follow the elements to which they are attached, these are suffixes. Rules of arrangement having to do with the
structure of words in a language make up its morphology, one branch
of grammar, which we may define as the meaningful arrangement of
linguistic forms. The second branch of grammar is called syntax and
has to do with the meaningful arrangement of words to form phrases
and sentences.

Languages differ widely in grammar. In English sentences of the type
he runs, for example, the verb *runs* has an ending *-s* because the pronoun is singular and third person. With pronouns like *I, you, we,* and
they, we use *run,* not *runs.* Similarly, we say *a man runs* but *men run.*
Grammarians express this rule of grammar by saying that third person
forms of present tense verbs must agree in number with the pronoun or
noun which precedes them. If the noun or pronoun is singular, the verb
is also (as in *he runs, a man runs*) but when the noun or pronoun is
plural, so also is the verb (*they run, men run*).

In German, however, the matter of grammatical agreement between
pronoun and verb in the present tense is more complicated. Here, very
often, we find a different verb form for every pronoun as in *ich laufe*
'I run,' *du läufst* 'you run,' *er läuft* 'he runs,' and *wir laufen* 'we run.'

Similar differences occur in English and German nouns. In English,
the definite article *the* is used before almost any noun, as in *the man,
the woman,* and *the maiden.* The German definite article, however, is
different in each of these cases: *der Mann* 'the (masculine gender) man,'
die Frau 'the (femine gender) woman,' and *das Mädschen* 'the (neuter
gender) maiden.'

A final step in understanding linguistic structure is to compare morphemes with one another. Such comparison reveals that morphemes are
composed of distinctive sounds called phonemes. Thus in English it is
obvious that the morphemes *cat* and *pat* are alike except for the initial
phoneme, that *cat* and *cot* differ only in their medial phoneme, and that
cat and *cap* are distinguished by their final phonemes. *Cat,* then is composed of three phonemes and any change in any one of them will change
cat to some other English morpheme or to an English-like nonsense word
(for example *cet*).

The same thing is true of all other languages, that is, in all languages morphemes are built up of one or more phonemes. Languages vary greatly, however, in the complexity of their morphemes and in the kinds of phonemes they may employ. In some languages, morphemes may be very simple, in others the average morpheme may include a relatively large number of phonemes. Similarly, the kinds of phonemes employed, even in languages closely related may be quite different in pronunciation. Thus the German phoneme written *ch* (as in *buch* 'book,' or *lachen* 'to laugh') is quite unknown in English; our closest sound is *h*, a very weak imitation of the harsher German *ch*.

The number of phonemes employed in a language is usually quite small, rarely exceeding thirty. These are of course used over and over again to produce a great variety of morphemes. The following English morphemes illustrate this point; the eighteen morphemes listed employ only six phonemes: *man, map, mat, mass, nan, pan, tam, sam, pat, pap, gnat* (pronounced *nat*), *sap, tap, sat, nap, pass, tan, tat.*

It may be noted, however, that not all the possible combinations of the six phonemes are actually employed in English. Thus combinations like *san, tas,* and *nam* have no meaning in English; they are English-like nonsense words. Other combinations, like *psa, pnt, nmt,* or *psn,* however, are not at all like English words; indeed, all of them involve habits of pronunciation so different from those employed by a speaker of English that he would regard the forms as wholly unpronounceable.

It is clear, then, that the phonemes of a language must be combined according to definite rules. Each language has such rules of combination which are observed strictly by those who speak the language as a mother tongue, and which may differ markedly from the rules characteristic of other languages.

Linguistic Change

From what has been said about linguistic structure we might easily get the idea that the habits of speech characteristic of a given community always remain the same. This is not true, however. All languages are in reality undergoing constant change. We may demonstrate this in two ways: by studying the history of a single language or by comparing and classifying the many languages now spoken.

The history of a language can only be studied directly if the community which speaks it has possessed writing for a considerable period of time. The first written records in English, for example, appear about

A.D. 900 and continue in a more or less unbroken stream to the present day. Examination of these records reveals that from A.D. 900 to the present, a period of little more than 1000 years, English has changed radically in pronunciation, grammar, and vocabulary.

This change may be illustrated by comparing the word *acre* with two of its earlier forms, *acer* and *aecer*. *Acer* belongs to the Middle English period (about 1100-1500) while *aecer* is an Old English or Anglo-Saxon word (900-1100). The principal phonetic difference between *acre, acer,* and *aecer* is in the pronunciation of the initial vowel. In Middle English *acer,* the vowel *a* was pronounced somewhat as the *o* of *sot* while Old English *ae* has a pronunciation similar to that of the *a* in *man.*

The three words also differ in grammar and meaning. Old English *aecer* belongs to a category called 'strong nouns' and had several distinctive case forms, much like the strong nouns of modern German. These are distributed as follows:

	SINGULAR	PLURAL
Nominative	*aecer*	*aeceras*
Dative	*aecere*	*aecerum*
Genitive	*aeceres*	*aecera*

During the Middle English period the noun endings became more and more alike until today modern English *acre* has but one major variant, the plural *acres.*

Old English *aecer* referred primarily to a cultivated field; thus, in the Anglo-Saxon Bible, the passage describing Jesus and his disciples going on the Sabbath into a field of ripened wheat uses the form *aeceras* to mean a field on which a crop is growing. Later the term was also used to mean a measure of land. The Middle English *acer* came gradually to mean a field small enough to be plowed by a man with a yoke of oxen in a single day. Later in the Middle English period the term was a more accurate measure of land size though its application was still restricted to cultivated or cultivatable land. *Acre* now has a still more precise meaning (160 square rods or 1/640 of a square mile) and though it is most often used as a unit of measure for land it may apply to cultivated farm lands, wild land (such as forests or mountain areas), or to the land occupied by a city (as in the phrase, 'acres of houses, factories, and other habitations').

Since, however, only a few languages have been written for a considerable period it is not always possible to demonstrate linguistic change directly. In such cases we must resort to indirect evidences of change. These are found in the fact that all modern speech communities exhibit geographical differences in pronunciation, grammar, and vocabulary. English, for example, is not the same everywhere that it is spoken. The English of England has a number of major dialects as we go from one part of the island to another and all of them differ from the English spoken in Canada, the United States, Australia, and South Africa. In the United States, too, English is not everywhere the same; differences in pronunciation and vocabulary are found between the English spoken in New York and that of New England, the south, the midwest, and the far west. This can only mean that English has changed and furthermore that change has taken different directions in different regions of the English-speaking world. What was once one more or less uniform language has divided into a large number of mutually distinct dialects.

THE CLASSIFICATION OF LANGUAGES

The discovery that languages change led to a method of classifying languages. English, as we have seen, does not really refer to only one language but to a whole group of languages or dialects broadly alike but differing in many details of pronunciation, grammar, and vocabulary. Linguists express this by saying that the modern English languages are descendants of a single common ancestral English and so belong to a single 'family' of languages. Each of the modern idioms is the ancestral English plus those changes in pronunciation, grammar, and vocabulary peculiar to the area in which it is spoken. Actually, of course, this statement is not precisely accurate historically for we know that the older forms of English were also dialectically divided. Some of the modern dialects may have developed from one dialect of the early period, others from quite a different one.

The modern dialects of English do not of course differ very greatly from one another. Much more marked differences are found between English, German, Dutch, Swedish, Danish, and Norwegian. Most of these are mutually unintelligible; that is, a native speaker of English cannot, without special instruction, either speak or understand the other languages. Despite this, however, it is evident that these languages do have many features in common; they are not so markedly different as, for example, Chinese is from English. To illustrate this let us compare the words from one to ten in English, German, and Swedish by putting these in parallel columns as follows:

ENGLISH	GERMAN	SWEDISH
one	ein	en
two	zwei	två
three	drei	tre
four	vier	fyra
five	fünf	fem
six	sechs	sex
seven	sieben	sju
eight	acht	åtta
nine	neun	nio
ten	zehn	tio

Here, it is evident, there are both differences and similarities. The differences are often marked but in only a few cases are the words unrecognizably different. Many other examples would reveal that these differences and similarities pervade the entire vocabularies of the three languages. The similarities are indeed so marked and so frequent that they cannot be due wholly to chance nor to mutual borrowings. Indeed, the latter possibility is largely ruled out by the fact that the three languages have for centuries been spoken in quite separate areas.

It follows, then, that these languages resemble each other because, like the separate dialects of English, they are descendants of a common earlier tongue. We have no record of this early ancestral language; as far back as our records go, the three languages are recognizably distinct. But, on the basis of the numerous and far-reaching similarities which today exist between these languages we can and do class them together as members of the same linguistic stock or family.

A linguistic stock, then, is a group of modern and ancient tongues between which there exist a large number of similarities and systematic differences in pronunciation, grammar, and vocabulary, too great to be explained by chance or borrowing. The member languages of such a stock are said to be derived from a single ancestral form, usually called the prototype language of the group. Thus, the languages of the Germanic stock, such as English, German, Dutch, Swedish, Norwegian, Danish, and a number of less important idioms, are modern descendants of a theoretical or assumed language called Proto-Germanic. We have no records of Proto-Germanic for our written records do not go back far enough in time.

In a few rare instances, however, we may verify an historical classification of this type. Thus, for example, we note that French, Spanish, Italian, Roumanian, and a number of other languages exhibit the same kind of similarities and systematic differences found in the Germanic group. They are for that reason classed as members of the Romance stock and are said to to be derived from a language called Proto-Romanic.

But here we have historical records which confirm, in part at least, the inferences drawn from our comparison of the modern languages. These reveal that Latin, once spoken only in the city of Rome and its environs, was spread throughout much of southern and western Europe by the developing Roman Empire. When first established, these outlying colonies spoke much the same language as Rome. Each of the colonies and Rome, however, modified their Latin in the course of time and since they were more or less isolated from one another these changes were largely independent of each other. As time went on, the changes became progressively greater until today the modern Romance tongues are not only different from Latin but also differ markedly from each other. Such resemblances as still exist between the Romance languages are due to the fact that all of them are connected by a continuous tradition to Latin. Spanish, Italian, French, Portuguese, Roumanian, and the other Romance languages are, then, modern versions of Latin, each characteristic of the population of a particular region in Europe.

How Languages Change

When we compare the several stages in the history of a given language we may note not only that the language changes in pronunciation, grammar, and vocabulary but also that changes take place in accordance with three major processes. Some of the words of modern English, for example, are direct descendants of Old English words having the same or similar meanings. Thus, modern English *cow, house, mouse,* and *louse* are directly derived by change of vowel from Old English *cū, hūs, mūs,* and *lūs,* where the vowel *ū* had approximately the sound of the vowel of *soothe.* Similarly, *why, bride, mice,* and *fire* come from Old English *hwȳ, brȳd, mȳs,* and *fȳr* (*ȳ* pronounced as in German *grün* 'green' or French *rue* 'street'), while *stone, boat, bone,* and *go* are derived from Old English *stān, bāt, bān,* and *gān* (*ā* pronounced somewhat as in *calm*). A goodly portion of our modern English vocabulary, then, existed in Old English as well, the modern forms as we have seen differing from those of the early period in pronunciation, grammar, and meaning.

We also find, however, that Old English possessed a number of forms no longer used in modern English, forms which have been replaced by modern words of different origin. Similarly, there are large numbers of words which have been added to the English vocabulary since the Old English period; words which had no counterparts at all in the earlier language. Words of this type illustrate the two remaining processes of change: analogic change and borrowing.

Analogic change takes place when the speakers of a language create new words by combining older materials on the pattern of already existing forms. In Old English, for example, the plural of *cū* 'cow' was *cȳ*. As we have seen, Old English *cȳ*, had it persisted to modern times, would have given some such form as *kye*, a word we mark with an asterisk to denote that it does not actually exist. But while we do not use *kye* as the plural of *cow*, we have a form *cows* which has this meaning. *Cows* is made up of two elements; *cow-* from Old English *cū* and *-s* from Old English *-as* (compare Old English *stān* 'stone'; *stān-as* 'stone-s'). The combination *cū-as* never existed in Old English; it was created much later on the analogy of *stone, stones; book, books;* and other similar singular-plural alternates. In brief, *cows,* though it is made up of two linguistic elements (*cow* and *-s*) which go back to Old English, is a new creation made by combining two forms not hitherto joined. Modern English has lost *cȳ* but has added *cows*.

Analogic forms are very numerous and mark every stage in the history of language. Also numerous in English and in other language are words taken over by one speech community from another; so-called borrowed forms. Take note, for example, of the following Biblical passage in Old English, its literal translation, and its form in modern English.

Se Haeland for on reste-daeg ofer aeceras; sothlice his leorning-chihtas hyngrede . . .

The / Healing one / fared / on / rest-day / over / (the)acres; / soothly / his / learning-knights / hungered / . . .

Jesus went on the Sabbath day through the corn; and his disciples were a hungered . . .

Note in particular the Old English words *Haeland, reste-daeg,* and *leorning-chihtas,* replaced in the modern English text by *Jesus, Sabbath,* and *disciples. Haeland* is derived from *haelan* 'to make well, to make whole' by adding *-end* to the stem *hael-. Hael-* is today found in the phrase *hale and hearty* (*hale* in the sense of healthy is no longer freely used) and in the word *heal* and its derivatives. The ending *-end,* which in Old English made the noun 'the healing one' from the verb *haelan* 'to heal, make whole,' no longer is used in modern English. It survives un-recognized, however, in such words as *fiend* and *friend* from Old English *feond* 'one who hates' and *freond* 'one who loves.' *Haeland* too has been lost and replaced, in this Biblical sense at least, by the proper name *Jesus.*

Reste-daeg is of course an obvious compound, the elements of which still exist in modern English. But the compound does not; we may say *day of rest,* but we oftener use *Sabbath,* borrowed ultimately from the Hebrew *Shabbath,* or *Sunday* from quite a different Old English word *sunnan-daeg* 'sun's day.' Similarly, *leorning-chihtas* 'learning-knights' has been replaced by *disciples,* borrowed from the Old French *disciple,* ultimately from Latin *discipulus.* Here are exemplified three instances in which Old English words have been replaced in modern English by words borrowed from other languages. In addition of course there are a large number of modern English borrowings for things, sections, and concepts which were not expressed in Old English. Professor Jespersen, an authority on the English language, estimates that nearly two-thirds of our modern English vocabulary is made up of words borrowed from the Scandinavian languages, French, Latin, Greek, and other sources.

PHONETIC CORRESPONDENCES

The method we have described for the classification of languages is called by linguists the comparative method. It results, as we have seen, in a division of the world's languages into historically distinct groups, called linguistic stocks or families. Within any stock there are certain words common to most or all of the languages of that stock and these words are presumed to have existed in the prototype languages as well. Thus, for example, we find that French *coeur* (earlier *cor* and *cuer*) 'heart' is paralleled in the Romance stock by such forms as Italian *cuore,* Provençal *cor,* Spanish *corazon* (from Old Spanish *cuer*), and Portuguese *coração* (from Old Portuguese *cor*). From these similarities we may infer that Proto-Romanic had a word pronounced something like *cor* which also meant 'heart,' an inference which is borne out when we actually find in Latin the form *cor* 'heart.'

When the words common to most or all the language of a given stock are examined we find that their similarities and systematic differences in sound can be summarized in a series of descriptive statements called phonetic correspondences. Such statements deal with sounds or phonemes rather than words. Properly constructed, a statement of phonetic correspondences between two or more languages will concisely describe all the phonemic differences and identities that exist between them.

A good example of a phonetic correspondence, and one which also illustrates how such descriptive statements are formulated, is found when we compare the Germanic languages with Latin and Greek and their modern descendants. The oldest known Germanic language, Gothic, had, among others, the consonants *f*, as in *fadar* 'father,' *þ* (pronounced as the *th* of thick), as in *þreis* 'three,' and *h*, as *haírto* 'heart.' These correspond to Latin *p*, as in *pater* 'father,' *t*, as in *tres* 'three,' and *k*, as in *cor* 'heart.' Initially, then, we may proceed on the hypothesis that Latin *p*, *t*, and *k* (written *c*) correspond always to Gothic *f*, *þ*, and *h*, respectively.

This hypothesis is not entirely valid, however. First, we discover that Gothic *speiwan* 'spew' corresponds to Latin *spuere*. Gothic *gasts* 'guest' to Latin *hostis* 'enemy,' and Gothic *fisks* 'fish' to Latin *piscis*. Here it is evident that a Gothic *p*, *t*, and *k* correspond to Latin *p*, *t*, and *k*. Further examples of a like nature disclose that whenever Latin *p*, *t*, and *k* are preceded by an *s* (as in *spuere*, *hostis*, and *piscis*) the corresponding sounds in Gothic are not *f*, *þ*, and *h* but *p*, *t*, and *k*.

Were we to develop this rule still further, other exceptional instances might be found until ultimately our statement of correspondences could be so formed as to cover all or nearly all of the forms in which the sounds in question occur.

Phonetic correspondences, properly stated, give the ultimate proof of relationship between languages of the same stock or family. For such relationship is never to be demonstrated by random similarities; any two languages, related or not, will reveal some unsystematic resemblances. It is only when two or more languages can be connected by regular sound correspondences, demonstrably linking forms in terms of systematic identities and divergencies in sound feature, that we may legitimately conclude that they have a common historical origin.

Why Languages Change

Many reasons have been advanced to account for linguistic change. Most of these, however, scarcely bear repetition for they are in general based upon incomplete or premature analysis. Indeed it may well be said that linguists even today know too little of linguistic change to be able to account for it.

One reason why we know so little about the actual circumstances under which languages change is that we have so far been concerned primarily with the results of change and not enough with the functional relation between language and other aspects of man's cultures. Languages are obviously and clearly related to cultures through vocabulary; as a culture increases in complexity so does the vocabulary of the language which is associated with it. English, which is associated with a highly complex series of cultures, has a far larger and more complicated vocabulary today than it had in the Old English period, when the culture of its speakers was considerably simpler than it is today. Furthermore, we can show that English changed more rapidly during the Middle and modern English period than in the Old English period. Very possibly, then, the series of extremely rapid changes which marked the shift from Old English to modern English were, directly and indirectly, associated with the accompanying shift from the relatively simple rural and isolated culture of the speakers of Old English to the highly industrialized world culture of the speakers of modern English.

It is also significant that some European languages have changed much less than English. An outstanding example is found in Lithuanian, which has changed so little that it today retains scores of older traits which have long since disappeared from English. The significance of this lies in the fact that Lithuania has also been less affected by cultural changes than the English-speaking regions of the world. It has remained very largely a rural and isolated region, participating much less in modern world cultures than the English-speaking areas.

These facts suggest that linguistic change is part and parcel of cultural change taken as a whole. The difficulty in demonstrating this hypothesis lies in the nature of language itself. For though there is an obvious relation between vocabulary and culture, the precise effect of vocabulary changes upon the sounds and grammatical processes of language is far from being clear. Is it true, for example, that large and rapidly accumulating additions to the vocabulary of a language actually results in sound changes and changes in grammatical structure? And if this is so, precisely how are such results brought about? We do not possess the data with which to answer these questions and until we can acquire such data it would appear that the factors responsible for linguistic change must remain unknown.

LANGUAGE AND WRITING

Most of us have learned so well to translate spoken words to writing and writing back into speech that we think of writing itself as a form of language. This, of course, is not so; writing, like the phonograph, is only an external device by means of which we made a more or less permanent record of speech. Many languages even today remain unwritten and the fact that a language may be written does not in itself change it in any important particular.

Writing, then, is an item of culture quite distinct from language and has a different origin and history. To begin with, writing is far more recent than language. As we have seen, man probably acquired language about one million years ago, at the same time that he acquired the first rudiments of culture. Writing, however, does not appear anywhere until the Bronze Age and even then is found in only a very few societies. For a long time the knowledge of writing was limited only to a few individuals in the societies which knew the technique; the bulk of the people neither wrote nor read. It is only since the invention of printing that such knowledge became truly widespread.

Writing was probably invented at least three times in world history. One occurrence took place somewhere in the Near East, probably among the Bronze Age Egyptians. This writing eventually spread to Europe and much of Asia in many different systems as each of the groups who took it over adapted it to the requirements of their own language. Chinese writing may well represent a second invention, taking place very soon after that of the Near East. Some scholars, however, hold that Chinese writing may be derived from some one of the earlier Near Eastern forms. Today, the Chinese system of writing is employed by only a few other groups found in the immediate environs of China.

A third invention of writing occurred somewhat later among the Maya Indians of Guatemala. Maya writing spread northward to the Aztecs of Mexico who did not, however, take over the complete Maya system but only a somewhat modified version of it. Knowledge of Maya writing died with much of the rest of their early culture; the few surviving documents cannot today be read. Aztec writing has also gone out of use though we still preserve and can read many of the older Aztec records.

PICTURES AND WRITING

There can be little doubt that writing developed from the technique of drawing pictures. All the earlier forms of writing suggest this, for all of them include characters which either are themselves pictures or are clearly derived from pictures.

Drawing and painting, incidentally, are very old techniques. As early

as the Middle Paleolithic (Old Stone Age) man made crude drawings;
a little later in the same period there developed in Europe at least a
highly competent art, expressed not only in drawings and paintings but
also in sculptures, modelings, and engravings.

Pictures are not themselves a form of writing, however, though they
may serve occasionally as reminders or memoranda of past events. In
some societies pictures were specifically used, not only as memoranda,
but also as a means of communication between one group and another.

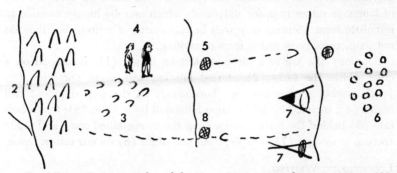

From Ernest T. Denig, Tribes of the Upper Missouri, *Washington, 1930, p. 603.*
Courtesy of Bureau of American Ethnology, Smithsonian Institution.

FIG. 1. 'Picture Writing.'

Since such pictures served as means of communication rather than art
forms and were often drawn hastily, they soon became highly conventionalized and abbreviated. The objects pictured were not drawn in detail but symbolized by some arbitrarily chosen mark. Thus, for example,
a horse might be indicated by a horseshoe-like mark, a buffalo with a
small circular mark, and a camp or stopping place by a shaded circle
(See Figure 1). Such symbols were then arranged to describe an event
or depict a narrative.

In Figure 1 a drawing of this sort is illustrated. Note the crudity and
bareness of the pictorial style; the draughtsman was clearly not concerned with accurate or realistic representation. All he really wanted to
do was to communicate as briefly as possible the experience encountered
by his group.

Such narrative drawings are often described as a kind of writing, called
pictographic writing, or picture writing. This, however, is not quite accurate. Narrative drawings are not tied to particular words, phrases, or sen-

tences; they may be interpreted by a variety of speech forms. Thus, item
(1) of Figure 1 need not be interpreted 'we are in a camp of 13 lodges';
any statement similar in meaning will do as well. Narrative drawings in
brief may be described or interpreted in words but they do not stand
for or symbolize any specific word or combination of words.

True writing, on the other hand, is distinctly tied to particular words
or word combinations. The written form *horse,* for example, can only be
read as the word *horse,* no form of similar meaning will do. A true writing, then, does not exist until the symbols used stand for specific items
of language rather than for statements which may be highly variable in
linguistic form. Pictures may well be the source of writing but they do
not as pictures represent a form of writing.

Reading: 'We are in a camp of thirteen lodges (1); encamped on a
creek above the forks (2); started hunting with eight horsemen (3)
(each symbol ɔ represents one horseman); on the way slept out two
nights (4); traveled in the direction indicated by – – – ɔ (5); found buffalo (6) behind the second creek from the camp; killed some and made
travois, or sledges (7); and slept but one night (8) on our return home.'

LOGOGRAPHIC WRITING

We do not know just how the transition from narrative pictures to
true writing took place; the earliest forms of writing on record have
already made the change. It is probable, however, that it came about
through the rebus method. A rebus, or a picture puzzle, consists of drawings meant to be interpreted in terms of the names of the objects represented rather than in terms of the objects themselves. A very simple
rebus is composed of a picture of a mill plus a stone or cement walk and
a key. Taking each picture as the symbol of a syllable, we see that the
three together stand for the name *Milwaukee.*

Narrative pictures become true writing, when the pictures no longer
serve to remind the beholder of some event but stand as symbols for the
name of the object represented. As long as the Plains Indians interpreted
the picture ∧ as a dwelling, encampment, or some similar notion however it might be expressed in words, it remained a narrative drawing.
Had they begun to interpret ∧ as a symbol standing for the word *tipi*
and never any other word, then they would have possessed a true writing.

When pictures begin to symbolize the name of the object represented
we speak of them as characters associated directly with a linguistic form.
The reader reacts to a character just as he reacts to the speech form rep-

resented by it. Words were probably the first linguistic forms symbolized in this way. A writing which so symbolizes words is called logographic and the symbols, each of which symbolizes a particular word, are logograms. Many of the characters used in the early Egyptian and Maya writing, as well as many of those employed today in Chinese writing, are logograms.

Pictures which become logograms are soon rigidly conventionalized; that is, they are always drawn in the same way and they are always associated with the same meaning. When this happens, the character may change without regard for the original picture from which it was derived. Examples may be found by contrasting early and modern Chinese characters. Thus *fire* was originally depicted as flames moving upward (a); the modern character (b) is not so expressive. The same is true of the old and new characters for *water* (c and d): (representing water flowing).

(a)   (b)   (c)   (d)

FIG. 2. The pictorial origin of Chinese ideograms is evident in their early stages of development. Conventionalization has obscured this in the recent characters.

The main difficulty with a logograph is to find a way of representing words the meanings of which are not easily pictured. This problem may be solved in a variety of ways. The Egyptians, for example, used the picture of a tadpole to represent the word meaning 100,000, presumably because tadpoles always occur in great numbers. In Chinese writing, many techniques are used. Thus, the character picturing the meaning woman (wife) is combined with that for child to express the meaning good or happy, presumably, because one who has a wife and child is happy. Similarly, the character for sun and that for moon combined symbolized the word meaning bright, a common characteristic of these two heavenly bodies.

The most common device, however, is to use a character for a word the meaning of which is easily picturable to stand also for words similarly pronounced. Thus, if English were written in logograms, we might symbolize the word *pear* by the picture of the fruit and use this picture also to symbolize the word *pare*. In Egyptian a conventionalized goose is used not only for that word but also for son, identical in pronunciation with goose. And in Chinese the word *wan* 'scorpion' is represented by the same character as the similarly pronounced word *wan* meaning 10,000.

This technique may of course lead to ambiguities; the reader may be uncertain sometimes as to which words is to be read. The Chinese solve this problem by adding a character, called a determinant, to the base character, called a phonetic, to distinguish the symbols for identically pronounced forms. Thus, the meaning of the word *fang* 'square' is easily pictured and its character then becomes the phonetic for *fang* 'district,' *fang* 'spin,' *fang* 'ask,' *fang* 'kettle,' and *fang* 'board,' all of which are similarly pronounced. The last five words are distinguished in writing by different determinants. So, *fang* 'district' is written with the character for *fang* 'square' plus that for the word meaning 'earth,' and the combined characters are read 'that word which sounds like *fang* "square" but has reference to earth.' Similarly, the character for *fang* 'spin' is that for 'square' plus that for 'silk,' *fang* 'ask' is 'square' plus 'talk,' *fang* 'kettle' is 'square' plus 'metal,' and *fang* 'board' is 'square' plus 'wood.'

It is obvious, however, that logographic writing is cumbersome; it usually requires a large number of different characters. In modern Chinees writing, for example, all symbols can only be reduced to 214 basic constituents. These and all their commonly used combinations must be memorized by one who wishes to read and write Chinese fluently.

SYLLABARIES

It is clear, of course, that no system of writing can be strictly logographic in the sense that each word is represented by a wholly distinctive character. Even Chinese writing, which employs logograms exclusively, uses only 214 basic characters which, combined in various ways, furnish enough logograms adequately to write the language without ambiguity. In so doing, it is evident that a phonetic factor is recognized: words similarly pronounced but different in meaning are represented by characters wholly or in part the same.

In Chinese writing this principle could be applied to words because of the fact that most Chinese words are uniformly one syllable in length. But in languages in which words vary in length, the principle must be applied to syllables rather than words. Thus, if English used a single character to represent not only the word *sun* but also the first syllable of *sundry,* this character would be associated directly with a phonetic form (the syllable *sun-* regardless of its meaning) rather than a linguistic form (a series of sounds plus their meaning). Such characters, like the phonetic characters of Chinese writing, take on a constant phonographic (sound representative) value and may be called phonograms.

When phonograms are used they seem most often to be symbols of syllables rather than whole words, as in Chinese writing, or single sounds as in alphabetic writing. Each phonogram in a system of syllabic writing or syllabary denotes one syllable.

Syllabaries are widespread in both ancient and modern speech communities. The ancient languages of Mesopotamia (Iraq), such as Babylonia and Sumerian, were written largely by means of a syllabary though logograms were also used. These peoples wrote on clay tablets with a stylus having a wedge-shaped end. Because the characters were different combinations of wedge-shaped impressions, the writing is called cuneiform, from the Latin word *cuneus* 'wedge.' Old Persian and the Greek of Cyprus were also written in syllabic characters. Today we find the most important syllabaries in Japan (the Japanese use two syllabaries as well as Chinese logograms) and India. Recent systems of writing, devised by missionaries for non-literate peoples, often take form as syllabaries, and among the Cherokee we find syllabary invented by Sequoyah to write his language. (See Fig. 1, Ch. XI.)

Syllabaries are, of course, far simpler than logographic systems if only because they require fewer characters. This is clearly evidenced by Japanese writing, which employs both techniques. Japanese logograms are quite as complicated and require as many characters as Chinese writing but the Japanese syllabary, quite as efficient as the logographic system, needs only 65 characters.

ALPHABETIC WRITING

Only once in human history has an alphabetic system of writing developed from the syllabary. This important event took place around 1800 B.C. when a Semitic-speaking peoples, probably living on the Sinai Peninsula, took over an Egyptian syllabary of some 24 characters and transformed these into consonant symbols. We do not know precisely who these people were but we do know that the system of writing they initiated spread rapidly to all the other Semitic-speaking peoples of the same region. Two distinct styles of writing emerged: the South Semitic which today is used, in somewhat modified form, by the Ethiopians and

the North Semitic (Phoenician, Hebrew, and Aramean) which is today
the basis of the modern writing of Hebrew, Syrian, and Arabic. The
North Semitic style, in its Phoenician and Aramean varieties, spread also
to Asia and Europe giving rise to the modern Indian writing and ultimately to the several alphabets used during the historical period and
today among the Europeans.

The Egyptian syllabary from which our alphabets sprang consisted of
24 hieroglyphic (the older logograms; literally a hieroglyph is a sacred
mark or carving) and hieratic (later abbreviated hieroglyphs) characters. These stood for syllables having only a consonant and a vowel. In
using them, however, the Egyptians paid attention only to the consonant
ignoring the fact that a given consonant might be followed by any one
of several vowels. Any ambiguities resulting were removed by the use
of determinants and logograms.

When these characters were taken over by the Semites, they used them
only for the consonants in their languages; the vowels were simply not
represented. It was up to the reader to add the vowels from the context
in which the word was used. This of course would be impossible in
English or other European languages but it did work in the Semitic languages by reason of the fact that if the consonants belonging to a word
are written and indication is made of where the vowels fit in, the reader
can easily guess the vowels which are to be supplied. Semitic writing is
then alphabetic in that each character symbolizes a single sound but it
is incompletely formed, since it does not clearly symbolize all the distinctive sounds of the language being written.

The Greeks learned the Semitic alphabet from the Phoenicians. We
know this not only because the fact is recorded but also because the
Greek word *alpha* means only the first letter in the alphabet and is probably borrowed from Semitic *aleph* 'head of an ox,' descriptive of the picture from which the characters *alpha, aleph,* and our modern *A* were
ultimately derived. Similarly, Greek *beta, gamma,* and the names for
many other characters are derived from Semitic words having a meaning
referring back to the older pictures from which the characters developed.

Unlike the Semitic language, Greek cannot be written adequately without vowel signs. In taking over the Semitic alphabet, which had symbols
for consonants unknown to Greek, the Greeks used these superfluous
characters to represent vowels. Semitic *aleph,* originally a consonant, became in Greek the character for the vowel *alpha,* Semitic *O,* a guttural
consonant became the Greek vowel *O,* and the ambiguous *I-J* of Semitic

became the vowel *I* in Greek. With these and other changes the Greeks made over the Semitic alphabet to suit the writing of their language, so devising a fairly good phonemic writing in which nearly every distinctive sound of Greek was represented by a single character.

From the Greeks this now relatively complete alphabet spread in two directions: through the Etruscans to Rome and north to the Bulgars, Serbs, and Russians. Rome in turn gave the alphabet to most of the rest of the peoples of Europe. In each of these groups to which the alphabet spread innovations arose as the people fitted the borrowed characters to the peculiarities of their own speech. The details of the spread of the alphabet and its many forms are far too complex to describe here; indeed, we have still to learn many of these historical details.

Today, however, man possesses wholly the techniques necessary to record, as accurately and efficiently as possible, any and all of the languages he speaks. This invention, the complex product of many peoples at different periods of time, is one of man's most useful and productive possessions. Without it, there could be no wide-spread communication, historical records, or education in the modern sense of the word. It is not surprising, then, that many scientists date the beginnings of true civiliza' tion from the invention of writing.

X

Inventions and Human Society

LIKE ALL ANIMALS man has had to adapt himself to his environment. In lesser part this has been physiological adaptation, in much larger measure a change of habits to meet new conditions. This great capacity for adaptations, directed by intelligence—inventing new devices and procedures—sets man apart from other animals.

Tool-nimble fingers, a flexible memory, ability to see and solve problems has made it possible for man to manipulate his environment. Man's life has not been wholly shaped by environment: on the contrary, he has selected from its resources and reshaped it to his desires. Where in simpler societies he was more or less a victim of his surroundings, through the ages he has increasingly created methods and contrivances to change its nature—planted groves, irrigated arid lands, brought materials from afar, air-conditioned his home.

Each device or idea that entered into this adaptation or modification was a specific invention. Inventions are not in mechanical devices alone, for we may legitimately speak of the invention of an idea. Indeed, the machine itself is part of the physical world, so much steel or wood: the essence of invention lies in a new idea.

The development of all civilizations has been the accumulation of mechanisms and ideas. In simpler societies of primitive peoples and in the ancient past their number was few; in the great civilizations accumulation and elaboration proceeded with ever-increasing speed.

All tools—the product of invention—are essentially extensions of the body: a crowbar lends greater leverage to the hands alone; a rifle gives striking power at a distance. As such, many tools depend on man's bodily structure; even their ultimate derivatives, automatic power machinery,

224

had their inception in these bodily-determined forms. The rotary motions of a twirled spindle or a screw depend on the outward rotation at the wrist of the two bones of the forearm. Since the world over the majority of people are right-handed, these twists are overwhelmingly clockwise, that is right-handed, as in screws and most machinery. A left-handed individual does not invent a parallel device; he is forced to make his bodily movements conform to the established pattern. With the right-handedness of machine parts standardized, it is taken for granted as part of our thought habits that substitute parts or added appliances will be of the same kind. Again, typewriter and piano keys are fitted to our ability to move the fingers individually. But the position of letters on a standard typewriter keyboard bears little relation to the relative strength of the fingers, the most frequent letters of written English being allotted to the weaker digits of the left hand. This arbitrary arrangement of keys was a matter of chance on the part of the inventors of the first practical typewriter in mid-nineteenth century. The convention they established has had to be learned by all typists; hence a reversal of relations has come about: bodily structure is ruled by a culturally determined factor. Both the invention of tools and their conventions of use show at the same time the great flexibility of human physique and mind and their channeling into cultural molds.

Invention has other roots than adaptation or exploiting environment. Sheer novelty, display of ingenuity, variations of a perfectly learned technique, purposeful improvement, aesthetic expression, and other inner urges are equally sources. Further, the new construct is as often as not the result of chance variation or combination.

Inventiveness is not confined by mental superiority to certain races as against others. Every trait of human life (culture) was invented, and all peoples have their culture. The Eskimo, like the Yankee, displays ingenuity in solving his problems; where they differ is in the Yankee's richer experience with mechanical devices and in the demands of his society for such contrivances. Again, smaller communities, where each man must attend his every need, lack the specialization of labor of larger groups whereby skill in craftsmanship is attained and attention given to particular problems. On the whole inventiveness is a rare trait: few of us invent anything quite new and at best make only minor modifications in what we have. A class of men dedicated to producing novelties—our inventors—is a specific feature of our civilization and of very recent date.

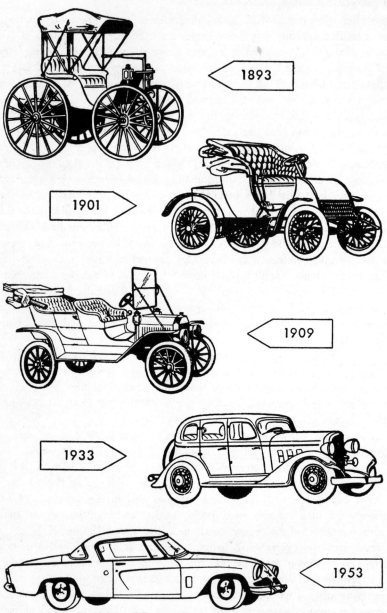

1893

1901

1909

1933

1953

Courtesy of Mr. Philip Van Doren Stern and the Viking Press, New York.
Adapted from A Pictorial History of the Automobile.

Certain primary inventions have profoundly affected the course of civilization. Some solved problems of physical need, others regulated conduct or served aesthetic and intellectual ends. Among those deserving special consideration are developments in clothing, housing, pottery, basketry, cloth-weaving, the wheel, and time-reckoning.

Little is known of the origin of the great inventions that have given direction to civilizations. Their roots are lost in dim antiquity and the record is obscure. But more significant for the understanding of cultural development is the fact that, strictly speaking, there were no 'first origins.' As the typewriter, for example, was a new combination of the alphabet, moveable type, lever action, familiarity with metals—and only as a new combination a 'new invention'—every invention was a development out of pre-existing knowledge of devices and materials.

The social consequences of inventions have been very great. In our own day, for instance, the automobile markedly changed the character of American life. Yet the automobile as a 'new invention' is no more than the adaptation of a powerful, compact, power plant to the age-old cart. (See Fig. 1.) Its impact on our social life has been great, providing convenient flexible transport, freedom of settlement and movement, and annihilation of time. It brought a move toward suburban and country living, arresting to a considerable extent the tendency for families to concentrate in large cities; factories were free to locate away from railroads and rivers; motor transport became a successful competitor of railroads as well as providing a feeder system for them; mechanization gave speed and impact to our army; ease of travel not only speeded up the tempo of business but provided pleasure and a fuller acquaintance with our country to the many. Good roads extending into the remotest sections destroyed isolation. A whole series of new industries arose—manufacture of automobiles and their accessory parts, garages, gas stations—and a new craft of repairmen. It has been said that the automobile turned us into a nation of mechanics—true in the sense that knowledge of mechanical devices and some ability to work with them is common to most men. As a consequence of these changes, there is more uniformity of custom,

---

Fig. 1. Inventions are frequently new combinations of older elements or the application of new devices to older mechanisms. The earliest automobiles (see top figure) clearly reveal their origin from a horse-drawn vehicle equipped with an engine. The subsequent developments illustrate the effect of the new principle on the design of the vehicle.

habit, and outlook over the country, and at the same time an interdependence and mutual interest in all sections. On the reverse side must be reckoned new dangers to life and limb, new fire hazards, and greater mobility for criminal activity. But good or bad, the changes in our social life effected by this invention have been profound.

It is difficult for us to envisage comparable effects of inventions in the past. Yet the case of the wheel and cart is clear: it provided transport utilizing the draft power of animals and effected a greater mobility of life. Pottery and the potter's wheel, basketry, and cloth-weaving changed the nature of domestic life and ultimately led to the development of great industries. Clothing made possible life in any climate at will and gave an outlet for the expression of social and aesthetic values. The social consequences of the other great inventions were comparable. What must be considered is that relative to the simplicity of life in earlier communities even the first forms of these inventions markedly changed daily habits, social relations, and modes of thought.

CLOTHING

The impulses toward clothing the body are compounded of protection against the weather, gratification of display and adornment, indications of social distinction, and a sense of shame. It is uncertain which one can be credited with first bringing clothing into being, but once clothing was in use these impulses have dominated in varying degrees. Man's hairlessness would seem to have called for some covering from earliest times, yet it is far from certain clothing was in use even by Paleolithic times. By the Neolithic Period, however, clothing may have been in general use, but we have every reason to believe that factors other than natural protection were at work to stimulate the use of apparel even then.

Complete covering is a characteristic of modern civilization, but this is exceptional. Among most peoples clothing for constant wear is quite scanty, extra garments being worn only when needed. Constant covering is usually confined to wrapping the loins or covering the private parts, but not always.

Clothing is often enough so ill-adapted to climatic needs that protection cannot be claimed as the prime or universal impulse. Clothing is so much a matter of habit that we who are fully clad fail to understand that the unclad are quite inured to climatic extremes. The Indians of the Nevada deserts, men and women, went completely naked for the most part in spite of sub-zero weather and excessive heat. Nor where clothing is worn for protection is it always well adapted for that purpose.

With the exception of the Arctic regions, where complete covering is worn, paradoxically full-body clothing is, in general, characteristic of temperate and hot climates. It is prevalent through a wide central area of the Old World from Japan, China, and Mongolia to western Europe. In parts of this area full covering would seem to be dictated as protection against extremes of cold and heat—as in north China, mountainous Balkans, northwestern Europe, the deserts of Arabia and North Africa— but it seems evident that in earlier times the inhabitants of these districts were relatively unclad. In general full-body clothing for the purpose of protection develops in regions of extreme dry cold or heat and is absent in hot moist regions (as tropical Africa). Where the human body can physiologically adapt itself to lesser extremes, even with some discomfort, the amount of clothing appears to bear little relation to climatic circumstances. Full clothing in the continuous zone of the central Old World argues, however, for the imitation and spread of a habit rather than repeated protective adaptations invented in each adverse region. The common lack of correspondence between full clothing and extreme climates is evidence against protection as a prime consideration in the use of clothing and suggests that other impulses were commonly dominant.

Adornment, display, and social distinction are obvious even where clothing is simple and scant. One nearly universal distinction is between men's and women's costume. Yet the marked distinctiveness of men's suits and women's dresses among ourselves is not common: we may be said to underline sex. But even where covering is minimal distinctions are made in clothing for the sexes, and these slight differences bulk large in the minds of the users. Other social distinctions are symbolized in attire: special costumes for soldiers, priests, the wealthy, slaves. While the infinite gradations of social position are markedly shown among ourselves by differences in cloth, its cut and color, and the manner dress is worn, parallel though minor differences appear in the quality and adornment of primitive clothing. Everywhere even minute differences in dress, posture, and bearing unconsciously give stamp to the social relations between individuals.

Dress is most commonly a vehicle for display and self-adornment. In most primitive communities exaggerated display in dress is characteristic of men, not women. Among ourselves (but only in recent generations) this has been reversed, a soberness of color, cut, and tendency to uniformity marking men's attire in contrast to women's.

Fashion is a concept most often associated with clothing alone, but erroneously, for there is just as much of fashion displayed in the realm of ideas, economic views, and even in science. In small primitive groups a new fashion may come from the imitation of the dress of a neighboring people. On the whole such communities are static, little interested in the foreign and in novelty. In larger communities such as ours social specialization calls constantly, not only for new appropriate symbols of dress, but for new forms and ornament for prestige sake and for sheer novelty. The new fashion spreads by imitation, wanes in its turn before the next novelty, and thus fashions have a fictitious appearance of being cyclic. Fashions are ordinarily but variations, while the fundamental contours, materials, and symbolic values of the dress remain constant, short of a complete cultural change.

Concealment may not have been an original factor in the development of clothing, but, rather, a derived attitude: concealment actually emphasizes sex and is reinforced by embarrassment and shame of nakedness among the habitually clothed. Where little or no clothing is worn, as in the tropics, or is stripped off, as inside an Eskimo igloo, exposure is a matter of course and evokes no particular response. Strikingly, the parts of the body which must be hidden at all costs (not always the sex organs) varies among peoples habituated to concealment.

The kinds of costuming that have developed in the various regions are obviously dictated by cultural considerations. In each area a specific type of dress has come to prevail and has been imitated throughout that region. Polynesia is characterized everywhere by loin 'cloths' of beaten bark (tapa), often added as an upper garment, with less common use of aprons or skirts of pendant fibers. Plains Indian men wear a poncho-like shirt, breechclout, long leggings, and moccasins, all of skin; their women a skin dress hanging to mid-calf, short leggings, and moccasins. While there are tribal, local, and individual differences the fundamental pattern is uniform.

Full-body clothing (of fur or skin) is characteristic of the Arctic and sub-Arctic. Further, this is tailored to fit the body—provided with sleeves and legs. Dress of woven cloth is characteristic of southern civilizations—ancient America from Chile to our Southwest and in the Old World from the Mediterranean to China. This was not tailored: in both regions squares of cloth were utilized just as they came from the loom, without cutting. Pueblo Indian dress, for instance, was a square wrapped around the waist by men, folded vertically around the body by women. In Mediterranean lands were the familiar uncut, draped cloth garments of classical Greece, Rome, and Egypt. This use of the uncut product of the loom as clothing in the central areas of Old and New Worlds was a parallel and independent invention. The parallel went farther. It has been shown that in North America full body clothing of skin, tailored to the limbs, spread southward into the Plains area; the use of cloth squares, for ponchos for instance, spread northward to the same region; here in the Plains a combination was made of the two—full-body clothing of skin, somewhat tailored, partially made over to the shape patterns of woven cloth. In Asia a similar combination was made: tailored skin clothing of northern Europe and Siberia coalesced in central and eastern Asia with the uncut cloth squares whose manufacture had spread from the south, giving the tailored cloth garments of Chinese men and women, for example: trousers for both, shirts and coats with sleeves. Here, in contrast to the New World, the form concept of the north prevailed but new material was substituted. In both cases invention, as usual, was essentially a recombination of things already familiar.

HOUSES AND THE ARCH

Man lives in more varied climates than any other species, partly because of the adaptability of his physique, more by reason of cultural factors, the devices he created: clothing and shelter. It must be assumed that the earliest humans, lacking a thick covering of body hair, sought and constructed simple shelters. Paleolithic men are known to have used caverns and undoubtedly made shelters in the open. From Neolithic times onward true houses have been built.

Houses are adapted to the environment, but their kind is not dictated by it. Eskimo snow houses and Central African structures of light palm thatch make use of available materials. But only Eskimos on the central Arctic shore make houses of snow; other Eskimos east and west, with quite as much snow, build of driftwood timbers and sod in the same domed shape. Quite different adaptations exist side-by-side, as in the mud-walled houses and thatched dwellings of the western Sudan. In general houses are more substantial where climate is rigorous, but there are striking exceptions. Indians of Nevada made use of a mere ring of brush even through sub-zero winters, and in central Canada the crude Indian houses are more deficient for shelter progressively north to the Arctic.

Even though shelter is the primary impulse, houses from earliest times on show convention of materials, form, and style—a definite architecture, no matter how simple. Among the items setting off the culture of one area from another is a style of building peculiar to it: the flat-roofed adobe (clay) rectangular buildings throughout the Mediterranean, the skin-covered conical Plains Indian tipi, our gable-roofed frame house and brick or stone, flat-roofed buildings. In each area specialization and elaboration of houses generally appears near its center, simpler or cruder copies near the margins (large decorated tipis in the central Plains, small crude ones at its peripheries).

Principles of house construction vary greatly. In contrast to our frame-house construction, the coastal Indians of Alaska set huge split planks upright, edge to edge, for the walls, without inner framework, resting the gable roof on their upper ends. The Hausa (northern Nigeria) first make a conical roof on the ground, lift it bodily onto supporting posts, and build a cylindrical wall of thatch around these.

Houses of early times and among primitive peoples are small, usually one-room domiciles. The small size and often roving nature of these communities inhibited large constructions. Only after large communities appeared in the ancient worlds of the Mediterranean, Mesopotamia, India, China, and in Middle America, was monumental construction attempted.

A limitation to building larger structures lay in structural principles: houses with flat roofs were limited in size by the length of their roof timbers. Greater span could be had only by introducing interior columns or walls to support series of short beams. The great architectural monuments of ancient Egypt and Greece are impressive in their massiveness or grace of line, but were hampered in development by the continued use of beam and column alone.

A new principle came with the invention of the arch, known in Sumeria six thousand or more years ago. It had its rudimentary beginnings in the tombs of still earlier date in which great slabs were leaned together to meet at the apex or with corbelled stone roofs, where the stones of the walls protruded, one above another, to meet finally at the top. The true arch is formed of wedge-shaped stones set in an arc above the opening. It can carry a disproportionally heavy superstructure, since the load is thrust sideways toward the walls by the wedging of the stones. The walls must be massive to bear the sideways thrust, but this is obviated when arches are placed side by side (as in the Roman aqueducts), each arch countering the thrust of its neighbors.

First developed in ancient Mesopotamia, the principle of the arch spread slowly westward through the Mediterranean world and eastward to India. Early uses were primarily for short spans in the interior of buildings and for bridging low places. Its use to arch over doorways, supporting upper walls, at the hands of the Etruscans (sixth to four centuries B.C.) brought recognition of its utility for embellishing the faces of buildings. The cultural heirs of the Etruscans, the classical Romans, so extended this use for triumphal gateways, aqueducts, arcades—sometimes tier above tier of arches—that it became the pattern of Roman architecture. Like other fundamental inventions of early days such uses spread only slowly from this center.

For many centuries it made no impress on the lesser-developed peoples of western and northern Europe. When in the twelfth century, western Europeans (particularly in northern France) adopted the arch, they gave it a new form, pointed at the apex (Gothic arch). In this they were influenced by their older house construction of crooked timbers meeting at the ridge. The new 'invention' was, as usual, a recombination of older elements.

Eastward also the arch took on new form. The Byzantine world, which, continuing in the Graeco-Roman tradition, had long made use of the round (Roman) arch, developed a form with incurving sides about the time of the Mohammedan Arab expansion in the seventh century. Arabic-speaking peoples ultimately carried this form west through North Africa into Spain. As Mohammedan influence penetrated, the Byzantine arch (and the Byzantine dome) spread to the Balkans, even beyond to south Germany and Russia, and eastward, by the sixteenth century, to India.

The arch itself was capable of expansion by inventiveness. Its span is normally in a flat plane, but given depth it becomes a vaulted ceiling. One of the earliest uses of the round (barrel) vault was in the Cloaca Maxima, the great sewer of Rome. A further elaboration lay in the crossing of vaults whose lines of intersection (groins) produce effects of great beauty. High pointed arches and intersecting vaults became the dominant theme in cathedral building in the Renaissance, a type ultimately carried in college and church building over the world.

A second noteworthy development was the dome; structurally this is a series of arches intersecting at their apexes. The fully developed dome seems to have been an invention of classical Rome, and, like the arch, was imitated in all lands under Roman influence. Romanesque architecture, with round arch and dome, reached into the New World with the settling of the Spaniards (as in the Mission architecture of southern California). In Byzantine incurved form it reached eastward as far as central Asia and India.

The arch and dome were invented independently elsewhere, but these few beginnings never went beyond rudimentary forms and were never applied to architectural purposes beyond the simplest. The Maya of Yucatan made use of corbeled arches, anchored by massive walls, but were limited to narrow vaulted rooms. Domed structures appeared early in Mesopotamia. The central Eskimo also achieved a small domed house of snow blocks, but their culture presented no need for other use. Arch and dome as principles of construction remained Old World devices until recent times; they spread over the area of the higher civilizations, developing new forms and purposes which, in their turn, spread over much the same regions. They became basic elements in our engineering.

POTTERY AND THE POTTER'S WHEEL

Simple as molding a vessel of clay may seem, pottery manufacture may have had but few independent beginnings. It is by no means a universal art, for it is absent among natives of peripheral regions of Old and New Worlds—Australia, Polynesia, much of Siberia, and the northern and southern extremities of the Americas. Its fundamental types are few (only two in the Americas, for example), which, with their restricted areas of occurrence, suggests spread by imitation rather than repeated invention.

A factor inhibiting its invention was common use of other containers. Often these were less fragile, more easily transported, and quite as serviceable (for cooking, for example). California Indians used baskets for all domestic purposes, Plains Indians skin receptacles, Australians folded bark vessels. Cooking in these was usually by dropping in hot stones, replacing them as they cooled—a reasonably efficient method. Pottery, which can be set directly on the fire, is a convenience, not a necessity. Yet this may well have allowed preparation of a wider variety of foods and thus changed eating habits.

Pottery-making peoples utilize the wares for many purposes other than cooking—for storage of foodstuffs and other articles, even as 'coffins.' This exemplifies the tendency in each culture area to specialize in one craft—basketry, pottery, wood or skin working—and to use it almost to the exclusion of others. Technical skills acquired in that craft and habitual familiarity with it tend to inhibit other developments.

Two levels of pottery development are distinguishable in time and area of occurrence. Vessels shaped by the hand alone appeared in the Old World in the Neolithic Period and in the Americas at some unknown but early date. Modeling by hand is still in vogue among outlying primitive groups of the Old World and was the only method known in the New. Over a more restricted, centrally located region of the Old World (China-Egypt-Europe) this was superseded in the Bronze Age by pottery spun on a wheel.

Hand-shaped pottery is commonly wide-mouthed and globular, but remarkably symmetrical and smooth. Shaping with the hands inside and out means avoiding constricted necks but does encourage surface modeling. Spinning on a horizontal wheel, with fingers lightly forming the walls, encourages graceful incurving forms (like Greek vases), with small necks more common. Wheel-made pottery is not more perfect but is produced in quantity more swiftly.

The two modes of manufacture are coupled with a social distinction. Hand-modeling is usually woman's work, a domestic product for home use. But men are the potters where the wheel is employed. The change may have come originally from the prior association of men with wheels, as wheelwrights and carters, reinforced by the possibilities of quantity production for livelihood.

The most common method of manufacture of hand-shaped wares is by coiling: adding strips of clay to the growing edge of the vessel, smoothing them down until they adhere firmly. A variant involves the use of a stone or clay 'anvil' held inside while the clay is compacted by beating the exterior with a paddle—a method invented at least twice: in North America and in the regions of southeast Asia. Molding over a form is less common and often no more than a rude substitute method in imitation of coil-made pottery.

The introduction of the potter's wheel or disc in the Bronze Age was the earliest adaptation to other mechanical purposes of the wheel, by origin a cart wheel. It serves as no more than a horizontal fly-wheel for the lump of clay set spinning at its hub. A complete invention in itself, more recent changes have been simply the use of a treadle, later power machinery, to turn it in place of the hand.

The potter's wheel is an Old World device of considerable antiquity whose point of origin is unknown. It was in use in Egypt and Mesopotamia by early Bronze Age (at least by 3000 B.C.), in Crete by 2500 B.C., in Troy before 2000 B.C. It spread slowly from this general region: northward to Britain in the Iron Age (where hand-shaped pottery persisted until Anglo-Saxon days), eastward to southern Siberia and China 2000 years ago. Three subsidiary focal points figured in this spread: (a) Egypt to the Mediterranean, northward through Europe, (b) China to its cultural dependencies Korea and Japan, (c) India to Sumatra and Java.

Decoration of the two classes of wares differs little, though there is more incising and stamping of lines and added modeled ornament on hand-shaped wares. Both varieties bear painted designs, usually on a base coat of colored clay applied to the outer surface. It is noteworthy that both incised and painted designs are more commonly geometric forms than realistic floral or human figures: these were geometric designs developed in basketry and weaving, transferred to quite another field, the vessel surface. The finest examples of native pottery—all hand-shaped—both in quality and decoration are those of the western Americas, where the modeled portrait jars of ancient Trujillo (Peru) are unexcelled.

The preparation of a surface coat led to the invention of glazes, coatings which when baked (fired) are glossy and render the vessels watertight. Glass-like coatings were known in ancient Babylonia and Egypt. An opaque glaze (tin enamel) was also known in Mesopotamia: brought to Spain by Moorish conquerors about A.D. 1000 it was copied throughout western Europe. A special derivative of this was majolica ware of Italy (sixteenth century), from which Delft ware of Holland and England was further derived to imitate porcelain. An independent origin of a glaze took place in southwestern United States some 600-700 years ago; but its use for designs alone, not as a surface coat, shows only partial parallel to the Old World development.

Porcelain, the highest type of pottery, is a Chinese invention. Its essential quality is given by a special glaze which fuses to a transparent coat adhering closely to a fine-grained core of clay. The old Mesopotamian glazing practices began to affect China, via the Iranian (Persian) lands, about 2000 years ago. By the third century of the Christian era these were being transformed; full-fledged porcelains appeared by the sixth and seventh centuries; and the art reached its pinnacle in the eighteenth, at which time European potters began to imitate it.

The sequence of developments in pottery shows that the normal course of invention is that of budding-off of specialized forms, recombination of bits of older knowledge and experience, and the spread of the arts by imitation rather than the re-invention of solutions to the common problems.

Weaving and the Loom

Woven fabrics have probably been repeatedly invented, unlike the few beginnings of pottery. Interlacing of cords occurs among all peoples and probably dates from remotest antiquity. Certainly by Neolithic times men were well equipped with specialized forms of nets, mats, baskets, and cloth to serve varied purposes.

Inventiveness in this field rests on skillful and accurate movements of the fingers. Fingering dexterity is a learned skill: the smooth sequence of thumb and finger movements, when automatic and habitual, becomes a basis for variant manipulations. All this rests on two fundamental and peculiarly human traits: the ability to move thumb and fingers in varying co-ordination and the tendency to vary the uses of acquired habits, largely in the spirit of play and discovery.

From this point of view distinctions between baskets, bags, nets, and cloth are somewhat fictitious—distinctions based rather on shape, use, or flexibility. It is reasonably clear that the several types were not outright new inventions but flowed one from another as new manipulations and new materials were tried.

Baskets serve as containers for storage, carrying, or cooking and especially in the last capacity substitute for pottery or wood or stone vessels. Even poorly constructed baskets are effective for holding liquids as the strands soon swell tightly closed.

Baskets occur in all parts of the world, but not among all peoples. The extent of use and craftsmanship varies. For example, among Indians in North America baskets were extensively made west of the Rockies only and were almost wholly lacking in the north; within the western area, their maximum development in use, perfection, decoration, and variety of form was in north central California. Here baskets served every domestic purpose from cooking to women's caps to cradles. These are the world's finest baskets. Outwardly from this center these features appear in progressively diminishing degree—a characteristic of culture traits in general.

Three fundamentally different techniques are employed in basket construction: (a) simple checkerboard weave, where semi-rigid split canes are interwoven at right angles; (b) twining, by twisting together two flexible strands (wefts) around a series of parallel warp rods (c) coiling, where a flexible strand is sewn over and over a coiled rod which forms the foundation in bottom and sides of the basket. The three have separate areas of occurrence as a rule: Philippine basketry is almost all checkerboard, central Californian coiled, on the Alaskan-west Canadian coast twined, for example. Their mutual exclusiveness derives from the circumstance that skills developed in each distinctive technique tend to inhibit the origin or imitation of the others.

Twining is akin to true weaving. Where very flexible warps are used, baskets are woven upside down with the warps hanging free, as in the Aleutian Islands. Immediately south of this, on the southern Alaskan coast, cloaks are woven in precisely this fashion using mountain goat wool. Incipient looms of this suspended warp type are known from various parts of the world.

True weaving of cloth involves four primary elements: fine spun yarns, a frame (loom) on which to stretch the limber warp yarns, a device (heddle) for separating and lifting alternate warps at one time for the insertion of the weft, the interlacing of weft yarns directly across the warps without twining.

Yarns for cloth are both more flexible and longer than basket strands. Where short cotton and wool fibers are used, they are spun into continuous cord. The age-old method for cordage, used throughout the world, is to roll the fibers together on the bare thigh under the palm. But wherever cloth is made, a spindle is employed for speed and quantity production—a slim stick set spinning by the fingers so that an attached bundle of fibers is twisted together at its tip. Spinning in this fashion, like the loom, dates from Neolithic times and is still used by outlying peoples over the world. The spinning wheel is simply a spindle turned by a belt from a large wheel flipped by hand. It is an Old World contrivance of restricted distribution which appeared in Europe about the fourteenth century, probably derived from India or adjacent territory. A smaller ('Saxon') wheel, invented in Europe in the sixteenth century, works with a treadle, performs spinning and reeling-in operations simultaneously, and thus permits continuous operation. Power-spinners (nineteenth century) are merely motor-driven forms of this.

Loom weaving was invented and used only in two well-defined areas: in the New World from Chile to southwestern United States, in the Old in the area from the Far East through southern Asia to Europe and

North Africa. The American loom represents the simpler older form of both areas. In this two sticks serve as heddles; to one are attached loops to lift every other warp, the other (without loops) shoved behind the remaining warps raises them in turn for the passing of the weft yarn. On such looms the unrivaled fabrics of ancient Peru, ancient Egypt, and India were woven. An improvement for speed and convenience was the frame heddle, but it involved no new principle. This is a frame carrying cords or wires with a loop or eye at the middle of each through which alternate warps pass; set vertically across the horizontally placed warps of the loom, they are raised by treadles. The loom with frame heddles was in use throughout the area from Europe (where it appeared by sixteenth century) to eastern Asia, but was unknown in the New World. A further improvement was the flying-shuttle (invented in 1733) by which the bobbin of weft yarn was mechanically thrown from side to side. The weaving of more complex designs calls for more numerous heddles, each holding its appropriate group of warps. Where too many heddles would have been awkward, groups of warps are linked by cords which are pulled by an assistant in memorized sequence, a European practice alone which prevailed for several centuries until replaced by the Jacquard loom in which a mechanical selector operates. But even the most complicated power-driven looms of today are basically little more than the primitive loom where the dividing of the warps in groups and the passing of the weft yarn between them is carried on by finger play.

An accidental outgrowth of interlacing warp and weft at right angles was the development in all weaving areas of straight line geometric designs. The difficulty of producing curves—which must proceed by minute steps diagonally across the rectangular web—inhibited decoration with floral or other curved figures unless fine threads were used. It is clear that the early development of geometric forms in cloth and basketry fixed the decorative style of many regions, where it was transferred bodily to other media, such as pottery, whose techniques and surfaces would have permitted free use of other designs.

Basketmaking, spinning, and loom-weaving are most commonly women's occupations—stay-at-home activities—among primitive peoples and, by inference, in ancient communities. Only where weaving became a gainful pursuit, as in the 'cottage-industry' of eighteenth-century Europe, were spinning and weaving taken over by men.

PLOW, WHEEL, AND POWER-PRODUCING DEVICES

The wheel, plow, and potter's wheel form a group of fundamentally important inventions which, with identical cultivated grains, shows the linkage of the early civilizations of the Old World from the Mediterranean and Europe to China. From this common basis, established in the Bronze Age of 5000 to 3000 years ago, divergent specialization produced the distinctive features of the historic civilizations: Egypt differentiated from Greece, China from India, Mesopotamia and Iran from both west and east. This whole area was set off by the sharing of these fundamental traits from the outer Old World (northern Asia, the Oceanic islands, Africa south of its Mediterranean fringe) and from the New, where they were wholly absent. All these inventions produced great changes in social life and habits from those of preceding Neolithic times.

In the Neolithic Period and among outlying primitive peoples of our day cultivation of the soil was small scale, hardly more than garden cultivation, carried on by laborious hand digging and hoeing. As a more or less incidental occupation close to home it was normally woman's work, while men were engaged in more arduous food quests by hunting and fishing. With the introduction of the plow, harnessed to draft animals, the scene changed: cultivation on a broad scale (agriculture) as a means of livelihood became a man's occupation. And with this came a shift in the products from emphasis on root crops and vegetables to broadcast cereals: wheat, barley, millet primarily.

The point of invention of the plow is unknown, save that it was somewhere in this area of Old World higher civilizations. The plow itself is no more than a digging stick, set crosswise as a plowshare to furrow the soil on a shaft to which oxen were harnessed. It is probable that men as handlers of the unruly beasts now substituted for women in cultivation—a somewhat accidental cause of a gross social change, but one furthered by the new possibilities for making a living. Except for substituting a metal share, and much later adding a mold-board to turn the furrow, the plow retained its form unchanged for centuries. Mechanical improvements, with the use of power devices, and the addition of mechanical drills and harvesters are developments of the nineteenth century.

The origin of the wheel—in the same region—is quite as obscure. It is by far the most significant of the early inventions, for the wheel lies at the basis of all our mechanical development and without it power-producing devices would probably never have come into existence.

It is clear, however, that the wheel was first devised for vehicles, for moving heavy loads other than by sheer muscular power. While there is some speculation that vehicles had their origin in certain wheeled toys and the discs of spindles known in antiquity, it is likely that these provided no more than some familiarity with wheel-like forms. The evidence favors, rather, the use of rollers under the dragging ends of poles which were attached to the shoulders of ox or horse, or even man. This 'dragcart' or 'travois' (which had even until recently a distribution over a vast area from peasant Europe eastward to the Plains of America) was often furnished with sledge runners where the load came on the dragging ends of the poles. When logs were pinned under the runners, so that they moved along with the vehicle, a cart was formed. Cutting away the unneeded central part of the roller or providing two solid discs fastened on a moveable axle were refinements. There were other problems involved—mounting moveable wheels on fixed axles, a pivoted front axle or separately pivoted front wheels to steer a four-wheeled wagon—which were, in fact, solved only well along in the historic period. This sequence in development is far from conjectural; there are many evidences supporting it in survivals of the rudimentary forms in backward communities.

The oldest form was clearly a two-wheeled cart, originally for farm use. Transport of goods in trade for any distance long awaited the building of roads. (Even as late as the eighteenth century in England rural transport by cart was suspended during winter and pack train substituted, because roads became impassable.) There is reason to think that the cart had its origin in interior Asia, spreading to southern Asia, thence, via the Mediterranean, into Europe. The earliest wheeled vehicle yet unearthed is from ancient Kish in Sumeria. The two-wheeled conveyance (a chariot) was derived by the Egyptians from the Asiatic Hyksos in the seventeenth century B.C. but only later spread through the Mediterranean world. By the Hallstatt Period (earlier Iron Age, 900-500 B.C.) ox-carts with solid wooden wheels were in use in central Europe, but did not reach distant Scandinavia until much later. In China the device was copied some time in the Bronze Age, certainly before the ninth century B.C.

The four-wheeled wagon was a development of the Near East in later Bronze Age, confined for a long time to Mediterranean lands as a vehicle for state occasions. It made no progress northward through Europe until the Middle Ages and was never in common use there until recent centuries. It is far more dependent on good roadways than the cart.

The earliest mechanical adaptation of the wheel seems to have been the potter's wheel. Cog-wheels (intermeshing forms of toothed wheels) are known from the Classical Period, as were pulleys and belted drive wheels. But there was little application of wheels to machinery until the advent of steam power made machine appliances possible on a large scale.

Most power-producing devices are relatively late in the world's history. Water-driven wheels for lifting irrigating water from low canals are very ancient in the arid lands of the Near East. Wind mills, a power substitute where flowing streams were lacking, were invented only in the Middle Ages (by twelfth century) in western Europe. While the Romans knew the expansive power of steam, their devices served merely as toys and curiosities. The effective use of this source of power came only with the invention of the steam engine in England toward the close of the eighteenth century. Applied first to pumping collieries and hauling out the mined coal, the inter-stimulus of the engine on the coal industry with the increased quantity of coal available to produce steam brought mechanical appliances in ever increasing number through the nineteenth century. Devices for generating electric power, inventions of the second half of the nineteenth century, provided a further source of power less fettered to locality than water, wind, and even steam. It has the obvious advantage of providing energy for power and light in convenient form at great distances from the source of supply. The invention of internal combustion engines (gasoline and diesel) in our own day offered compact mobile power units for ship, automobile, and plane, quite changing our social and economic life. The latest power-producing inventions, rockets and atom-smashing mechanisms, hold vast possibilities of further social change.

In the long range view the most noteworthy characteristics of these inventions have been: first, the accumulation of experiences; second, the acceleration in their appearance—few at first, at long intervals; coming with a rush in recent centuries, generations, years; third, the marked social changes they wrought in the societies that utilized them.

TIME-RECKONING AND THE CALENDAR

Time is man-made; nature knows only change. We are so much the victims of time in our culture, subject to self-imposed and unconscious routing by the hour and the day, the 'pressure of time,' 'the need for speed,' that we blindly assume the inevitability and naturalness of time-reckoning. Man is aware of changes in his body and in the outer world—changes through day and night, the succession of the seasons, and their recurrent nature. But the reckoning of periods of change, by hour, day, or year, is a human concept, projected on the world, and known to no other animal.

The reckoning of time in some fashion is universal among all peoples and probably has great antiquity. This is warranted by its unconscious and automatic character, and as such has been ingrained in all languages. In no known language is it possible to form a sentence without indicating time (tense) though the speakers are unaware of this requirement. The system of tense employed, however, often differs appreciably from a simple past, present, and future.

At the outset it must be explained that some of our units of time are based on the recurrence of changes in the outer world, others are wholly artificial. Changes through the day, the succession of days, the apparent movement of sun, moon, and stars, the phases of the moon, the cyclic change of the seasons, the succession of the years, all are easily recognized natural events. But there are no natural counterparts to the division of time by hour, minute, or second, to the grouping of days by weeks or by calendar (as opposed to lunar) months.

A number of quite different calendric systems have been invented; common to all is a count by years and lunar months, less frequently by seasons. The 'year,' however, may not be a solar year, a full circuit of the earth around the sun. Indians of southern Arizona, for example, reckon doubly: a record of events runs by solar years, but the 'year' that controls everyday life is six months long, with six named months repeated—this because there are two complete cycles of planting and harvesting in a solar year. The point at which a year begins must be arbitrary unless it be one of the solstices, which is quite rare as an initial point. The same Indians reckon their new solar year from the first appearance of cottonwood leaves, early February. The arbitrary initial point of our own calendar shows a chain of cultural inheritance: our calendar is that of the Romans who had adopted the Egyptian system with a solar year fixed by the rising of the star Sirius.

The month is ordinarily a more important grouping of days. This is almost universally the lunar month, the period of waxing and waning of the moon. To refer to particular periods—that is, to reckon time—the months must be named: the pattern of naming varies, but most commonly has reference to natural phenomena of the period (snow falls, corn ripens, et cetera). Types of name show systematic occurrence; while in general North American Indians used such descriptive designations, in the coastal strip from Alaska to northern California the pattern was one of numbering the months.

Unless something of great social significance hangs on it, primitive people are little concerned with the exact duration of these periods and the relation of one to another. The dark phase of the moon may be ignored in the reckoning. As there are twelve and a fraction lunar months in a solar year, a count by months can never agree with the year. Primitive peoples are little concerned with this discrepancy; continuing the count of month names with seasonal reference over the years, the name soon becomes inappropriate to the season, so, while they argue over it, they make a practical adjustment, beginning anew. The problem of adjusting the lunar month (29 days) and the solar year, which does not end evenly with a completed day (365 days, 6 hours, 48 minutes, 46 seconds), awaited more precise astronomical knowledge and in every case represented an intellectual achievement.

The origin of more precise reckoning lay in priestly observation of the solstices and the movements of the stars, coupled with month and day counts, for the purpose of regulating rituals. The time for a certain ceremony (of Pueblo Indians, for example) was fixed by one of the solstices (the moment of most northern or southern position of the sun); other rites followed by day count. The 'moveable' and 'fixed feasts' of our ecclesiastical calendars are such because they depend, one on astronomical events, the other on day and month count. Where it was assumed that the stars affected man's fate, as in the ancient Near East, very accurate reckoning was made of the movements of the planets among the fixed stars.

European peoples all use a twelve-month calendar derived from the Romans (as indicated by our Latin-based month names). Its history shows both the artificial nature of any calendar and the adjustments made as astronomical knowledge grew. Prior to Julius Caesar the Romans had attempted to fix ceremonials simultaneously by lunar and solar counts, which cannot be reconciled. In 46 B.C. Caesar (on the advice of a Greek astronomer, Sosigenes) ended the confusion by imperial decree, establishing arbitrary months of 30 and 31 days alternately, a short month to fill the gap, and decreed each fourth year should be reckoned with an extra day to absorb the accumulated quarter-days of the solar round. The extra 48 minutes 46 seconds was unknown to the Romans; its accumulation through the centuries again brought confusion. Since the Roman Catholic Church had an interest in keeping its ceremonials in proper relation to the sun's progress, Pope Gregory XIII, on the advice of his astronomers, in 1582 ordered 10 days dropped to restore the relation and directed that the added leap-day be omitted in all years beginning a century except those divisable by 400. (Actually the Gregorian year, which we now use, leaves a very small error between the reckoning by completed days and the completed earth's circuit around the sun.) As the principal international organization of the time, the Church's edict established the system throughout Europe.

Any day is designated in our calendar by assigning the proper one of 7 day names, 30, 31, 28 (or 29) number names in the month, and the year count from the birth of Christ. The Chinese calendar count is on a basis of a cycle of 60 days (without reference to beginning and end of the solar year) and one of 60 moons; thus reference is by naming the day of its cycle, the moon, and the year of the emperor's reign. The Maya of Yucatan devised a calendar based on a 'month' of 20 days, eighteen of which, with five days inserted, made a 365 day year; and a second cycle comprising thirteen groups of these 20 days which yielded another period, 260 days, the 'Sacred Year.' These two cycles, running concurrently, brought together the same named day in both cycles after 52 years had elapsed; hence a dating also in terms of 52 year periods. Their sequence of years was also reckoned in units of 20 years and units of 400 years. In addition, their long continued observations showed them that five apparent revolutions of the planet Venus equaled eight solar years, and 65 Venus 'years' the span of two 52 year periods.

The week is a short group of days on which intimate social activities are patterned (church, wash day, business, and domestic pursuits). Having no counterpart in nature, weeks can vary from two days (the minimum) to our seven, or more. West Africa, for example, has weeks of three, four, and five days, each with appropriate rites and activities. The origin of the week was in recurrent marketdays or ceremonial rites at fixed intervals. The many bases for weeks show the repeated invention of this reckoning. It is noteworthy that the week is Old World in occurrence, such short clusters of days hardly appearing in native America.

Like the patterning by the week, our activities through the day are regimented by its divisions. The day has no such natural units as hours, minutes, seconds: our '24' and '60' divisions are artificialities derived ultimately from Babylonia. They remain characteristic of the higher civilizations that have use and feel need for minor divisions of time, never having spread to the simpler societies of the outlying parts of the Old World. Our own civilization, with its insistence on routing activities by the clock and crowding each minute, has developed as one of its outstanding characteristics an almost hysterical attitude with respect to time.

GEORGE PETER MURDOCK

XI

How Culture Changes

IT IS A FUNDAMENTAL CHARACTERISTIC of culture that, despite its essentially conservative nature, it does change over time and from place to place. Herein it differs strikingly from the social behavior of animals other than man. Among ants, for example, colonies of the same species differ little in behavior from one another and even, so far as we can judge from specimens embedded in amber, from their ancestors of fifty million years ago. In less than one million years man, by contrast, has advanced from the rawest savagery to civilization and has proliferated at least three thousand distinctive cultures.

The processes by which culture changes are by now reasonably well known to science. They cannot be understood, however, without a clear comprehension of the nature of culture, and this must be summarized here even at the risk of some repetition of material in earlier chapters.

Culture is the product of learning, rather than of heredity. The cultures of the world are systems of collective habits. The differences observable among them are the cumulative product of mass learning under diverse geographic and social conditions. Race and other biological factors influence culture only in so far as they affect the conditions under which learning occurs, as when the presence of people of markedly different physique operates as a factor in the development of race prejudice.

Culture is learned through precisely the same mechanism as that involved in all habit formation. Hunger, sex, fear, and other basic drives, as well as acquired motivations, impel human beings to act. Actions encounter either success or failure. With failure, especially when accompanied by pain or punishment, an action tends to be replaced by other behavior, and its probability of recurring under similar conditions is

247

diminished. Success, on the other hand, increases the tendency of responses to occur when the same drive is again aroused in a like situation. With repeated success, responses are established as habits, and are progressively adapted to the situations in which they are appropriate.

A culture consists of habits that are shared by members of a society, whether this be a primitive tribe or a civilized nation. The sharing may be general throughout the society, as is normally the case with language habits. Often, however, it is limited to particular categories of people within the soceity. Thus persons of the same sex or age group, members of the same social class, association, or occupational group, and persons interacting with others in similar relationships commonly resemble one another in their social habits, though diverging behaviorally from persons in other categories.

The social sharing of habits has several causes. The fact that the situations under which behavior is acquired are similar for many individuals conduces in itself to parallel learning. Even more important is the fact that each generation inculcates on the next, through education, the cultural habits which it has found satisfying and adaptive. Finally, the members of any society exercise pressure upon one another, through formal and informal means of social control, to conform to standards of behavior which are considered right and appropriate. This is particularly true of behavior in interpersonal relationships, where the success or failure of an action depends upon the reaction of another person to it, rather than, for example, upon its adaptiveness to the innate qualities of natural objects. Once one has acquired a limited number of stereotyped patterns of social behavior one is equipped to cope successfully with widely diversified social situations, and one is also provided with a body of reliable expectations regarding the probable responses of others to one's own behavior. This gives confidence and spares the individual an immense amount of individualized learning, which is ever a painful process. It is with good reason, therefore, that every society lays great stress on social conformity.

The habits that are variously shared within a society, and which constitute its culture, fall into two major classes, namely, habits of action and habits of thought. These may be termed, respectively, 'customs' and 'collective ideas.' Customs include such readily observable modes of behavior as etiquette, ceremonial, and the techniques of manipulating material objects. Collective ideas are not directly observable but must be inferred from their expression in language and other overt behavior.

They include such things as practical knowledge, religious beliefs, and social values. Moreover, they embrace a mass of rules or definitions, which specify for each custom the persons who may and may not observe it, the circumstances in which it is and is not appropriate, and the limits and permissible variations of the behavior itself. Collective ideas also include a body of social expectations—anticipations of how others will respond to one's own behavior, especially of the sanctions, i.e. social rewards and punishments that can be expected from conformity and deviation. With every custom and with every organized cluster of customs, such as a 'culture complex' or 'institution,' there is ordinarily associated a mass of collective ideas.

Actual social behavior, as it is observed in real life, must be carefully distinguished from culture, which consists of habits or tendencies to act and not of actions themselves. Though largely determined by habits, actual behavior is also affected by the physiological and emotional state of the individual, the intensity of his drives, and the particular external circumstances. Since no two situations are ever exactly alike, actual behavior fluctuates considerably, even when springing from the same habit. A description of a culture is consequently never an account of actual social behavior but is rather a reconstruction of the collective habits which underlie it.

From the point of view of cultural change, however, actual or observable behavior is of primary importance. Whenever social behavior persistently deviates from established cultural habits in any direction, it results in modifications first in social expectations, and then in customs, beliefs, and rules. Gradually, in this way, collective habits are altered and the culture comes to accord better with the new norms of actual behavior.

Changes in social behavior, and hence in culture, normally have their origin in some significant alteration in the life conditions of a society. Any event which changes the situations under which collective behavior occurs, so that habitual actions are discouraged and new responses are favored, may lead to cultural innovations. Among the classes of events that are known to be especially influential in producing cultural change are increases or decreases in population, changes in the geographical environment, migrations into new environments, contacts with peoples of differing culture, natural and social catastrophes such as floods, crop failures, epidemics, wars, and economic depressions, accidental discoveries, and even such biographical events as the death or rise to power of a strong political leader.

The events which produce cultural change by altering the conditions under which social behavior proves adaptive, i.e. is or is not rewarded, are invariably historical, i.e. specific with respect to time and place. Events occurring at different places and times may resemble one another, however, and exert parallel influences upon different cultures. It is thus possible to view changes in culture either in relation to their spatial and temporal setting or in relation to comparable events wherever and whenever they have occurred. The former or 'historical' approach answers such questions as what? when? and where? The latter or 'scientific' approach, by illuminating the processes by which change occurs, answers the question how? Both approaches are valid and completely complementary.

Historical anthropologists commonly discuss particular traits of culture, such as the use of tobacco, the wheel, the domesticated horse, the alphabet, or money, treating of their 'invention' at specific times and places and of their 'diffusion' from the points of origin to other parts of the world. Since our problem is to describe *how* culture changes, we must abandon the bird's-eye view of the historian and examine the processes within societies by which all changes, and not merely particular ones, take place. These processes may be conveniently grouped under the terms 'innovation,' 'social acceptance,' 'selective elimination,' and 'integration.'

Cultural change begins with the process of *innovation*, the formation of a new habit by a single individual which is subsequently accepted or learned by other members of his society. An innovation originates through the ordinary psychological mechanism of learning, and differs from purely individual habits only in the fact that it comes to be socially shared. It is nevertheless useful to distinguish several important variants of the process.

An innovation may be called a *variation* when it represents a slight modification of pre-existing habitual behavior under the pressure of gradually changing circumstances. The slow evolution in the forms of manufactured objects over time usually represents an accumulation of variations. In the same manner, tattooing can be extended over a wider area of the body, additional barbs may be added to a harpoon, skirts may be lengthened or shortened, folk tales may grow by accretion, or ceremonial may become increasingly elaborate and formalized. Variation occurs in all cultures at all times. The individual increments of change are often so slight as to be almost imperceptible, but their cumulative effect over long periods may be immense.

When innovation involves the transfer of elements of habitual behavior from one situational context to another, or their combination into new syntheses, it is called *invention*. At least some degree of creativeness is always present. Most of the important technological innovations are of this type. Thus the invention of the airplane involved the synthesis of such elements as the wings of a glider, an internal-combustion engine from an automobile, and an adaptation of a ship's propeller. Though less well known, inventions are equally common in the non-material aspects of culture. The city-manager plan, for example, represents an obvious transfer of techniques of business management to the sphere of local government, and most forms of religious worship are modeled on behavior toward persons of high social status, e.g. sacrifice upon bribery, prayer upon petitions, laudation upon flattery, ritual upon etiquette.

Since invention always involves a new synthesis of old habits, it is dependent upon the existing content of the culture. A synthesis cannot occur if the elements which it combines are not present in the culture. It is for this reason that parallel inventions so rarely occur among unconnected peoples of differing culture. With the exception of such simple and obvious combinations as the hafting of tools, anthropologists know of only a handful of genuine inventions that have been arrived at independently by historically unrelated peoples. Among them perhaps the most famous are the fire piston, invented by the Malays and a French physicist, and the dome, developed by the ancient Romans from the arch and independently invented by the Eskimos for their snow igloos.

Among peoples of the same or related cultures, on the other hand, parallel inventions are extraordinarily common. The culture provides the same constituent elements to many people, and if one person does not achieve the synthesis others are likely to do so. The Patent Office furnishes thousands of examples. In one famous instance, the telephone, applications for a patent were received on the same day from two independent inventors, Bell and Gray. Another noted case is the independent formulation of the theory of natural selection by Darwin and Wallace. So common is this phenomenon that scientists often live in dread of the anticipation of their discoveries by rivals. Parallel invention thus appears to be frequent and almost inevitable among peoples of similar culture, though so rare as to be almost non-existent among peoples of different culture.

A third type of innovation may be called *tentation*. Unlike the previous types, which merely modify or recombine elements of habit already in existence, tentation may give rise to elements that show little or no continuity with the past. The mechanism by which these are acquired is that which psychologists call 'trial-and-error learning.' Tentation may occur in any situation in which established habits prove ineffective and individuals are so strongly motivated that they try out other modes of behavior in a search for an adequate solution to their problems. They will ordinarily try out first a number of variations and recombinations of existing habitual responses, but if all of these fail they will resort to 'random behavior,' in the course of which they may accidentally hit upon some novel response which solves the problem and thereby becomes established as a new cultural element.

Crises are particularly conducive to tentation. In a famine, for instance, people try out all sorts of things that they have never eaten before, and if some of them prove nutritious and tasty they may be added to the normal diet. An epidemic similarly leads to a search for new medicines, and both primitive and civilized peoples have discovered useful remedies in this way. War also leads to improvisation, as do economic crises. The New Deal in the recent history of the United States, for example, reveals numerous instances of tentation. Scientific experimentation, it should be pointed out, is often a form of controlled tentation, as when a new series of chemical compounds are systematically put to test. The saying that 'necessity is the mother of invention' applies more forcefully to tentation than to invention proper.

When accidental discoveries lead to cultural innovations, the process is commonly that of tentation. The origin of the boomerang in aboriginal Australia will serve as an example. Over much of that continent the natives used curved throwing sticks to kill or stun small animals, and in a limited part of the area the true boomerang was used for this purpose. Almost certainly the first boomerang was produced by sheer accident in the attempt to fashion an ordinary throwing stick. Observing the unique behavior of the particular stick in flight, the maker and his fellows doubtless attempted to duplicate it. They must have resorted to tentation, or trial-and-error behavior, until they eventually succeeded, and thereby established boomerang manufacture as a habit. The history of modern

'inventions' is full of such instances, the discovery of the photographic
plate by Daguerre being one of the most familiar examples.

Tentation also accounts for a type of cultural parallel which is distinct from genuine independent invention. There are certain universal
problems which every people must solve and for which there are a limited number of easy and obvious solutions, so that peoples in different
parts of the world have often hit upon the same solution quite independently. Rules of descent provide a good illustration. In all societies, each
individual must be affiliated with a group of relatives to whom he regards himself as most closely akin and to whom he can turn for aid in
time of need. There are only three possibilities: patrilineal descent,
which relates an individual to kinsmen in the male line; matrilineal
descent, which affiliates him with relatives through females; and bilateral
descent, which associates him with a group of his closest relatives irrespective of their line of descent. Every society must choose one of these
alternatives or some combination thereof, and, since the possibilities are
limited to three, many peoples have, of necessity, arrived independently
at the same cultural solution. Funeral customs present another example,
since there are only a limited number of feasible ways of disposing of
a dead body. In all such instances, if a society is compelled for any
reason to abandon its previous custom it will inevitably, through tentation, arrive at an alternative solution which other peoples have independently adopted.

The fourth and last type of innovation is *cultural borrowing,* which is
what the historical anthropologist, with his bird's-eye view, calls 'diffusion.' In this case the innovator is not the originator of a new habit, but
its introducer. The habit has previously been part of the culture of
another society; the innovator is merely the first member of his social
group to adopt it. From the point of view of psychology, cultural borrowing is merely a special case of the learning process known as
'imitation.' The innovator, faced with a situation in which the shared
habits of his own society are not fully satisfactory, copies behavior which
he has observed in members of another society, instead of resorting to
variation, invention, or tentation to solve his problem.

Of all forms of innovation, cultural borrowing is by far the most common and important. The overwhelming majority of the elements in any
culture are the result of borrowing. Modern American culture provides
a good illustration, as can be shown by a few random examples. Our
language comes from England, our alphabet from the Phoenicians, our

numerical system from India, and paper and printing from China. Our family organization and system of real property derive from medieval Europe. Our religion is a composite of elements largely assembled from the ancient Hebrews, Egyptians, Babylonians, and Persians. Metal coinage comes from Lydia, paper money from China, checks from Persia. Our system of banking, credit, loans, discounts, mortgages, et cetera, is derived in its essentials from ancient Babylonia, with modern elaborations from Italy and England. Our architecture is still largely Greek, Gothic, Georgian, et cetera. Our favorite flavors in ice creams, vanilla and chocolate, are both borrowed from the Aztecs of Mexico and were unknown to Europeans before the conquest by Cortez. Tea comes from China, coffee from Ethiopia, tobacco from the American Indians. Our domesticated animals and plants, virtually without exception, are borrowed. If the reader were to make a list of absolutely everything he eats during the next week, analysis would probably show that one third are products that were already cultivated in Neolithic times and that at least two thirds were being raised at the time of Christ, and it would be surprising if the list contained any item that was not cultivated for food somewhere in the world when Columbus sailed for America.

Our own culture is not unique in this respect, for it is doubtful whether there is a single culture known to history or anthropology that has not owed at least ninety per cent of its constituent elements to cultural borrowing. The reason is not far to seek. Any habit that has become established in a culture has been tried out by many people and found satisfactory. When a society finds itself in a dilemma, therefore, the chances that an element already present in the culture of another people will turn out to be an adequate solution to its own problem are vastly greater than those of any random and untested innovation of another type. Cultural borrowing is thus highly economical, and most peoples tend to ransack the cultural resources of their neighbors for adaptive practices before they resort to invention or tentation.

Cultural borrowing depends upon contact. Obviously the opportunity for borrowing is lacking in the case of a completely isolated society. Other factors being equal, the extent to which one culture will borrow from another is proportionate to the intensity and duration of the social intercourse between their bearers. Contact need not always be face-to-face, however, for there are numerous instances of cultural borrowing at a distance through the medium of written language or through copying of articles received by trade. By and large, however, societies borrow mainly from their immediate neighbors, with the result that the products of diffusion are ordinarily clustered in geographically contiguous areas.

Trade, missionary enterprise, and political conquest create conditions conducive to cultural borrowing. Peculiarly important, however, is inter-marriage, for this brings individuals of differing culture together within the family, where children can learn from both parents. Diffusion then proceeds through the socialization process, which produces far more per-fect copying than does cultural borrowing on the adult level. The American 'melting pot' operates largely through this mechanism. Primi-tive peoples practicing local exogamy, i.e. requiring individuals to ob-tain spouses from another village or band, commonly reveal considerable cultural uniformity over wide areas, as in aboriginal Australia and among the Indians of the Northwest Coast. By contrast, in areas like Melanesia and Central California where marriage normally takes place within the community, even villages a few miles apart may differ strikingly in dia-lect and customs. In the one case culture is diffused through the same process by which it is transmitted; in the other, even adult contacts tend to be restricted to a minimum.

Incentive—a need or drive—is as essential in cultural borrowing as in other types of innovation. A people rarely borrows an alien cultural ele-ment when they already possess a trait which satisfactorily fills the same need. Thus the blubber lamp of the Eskimos was not borrowed by the Indians to the south, who had plenty of wood for fires to heat and light their dwellings. On the other hand, the extraordinarily rapid diffusion of tobacco over the earth after the discovery of America reflected the gen-eral absence of competing traits. It has been observed that the first indi-viduals in a society to borrow alien customs are likely to be the discon-tented, underprivileged, and maladjusted. Thus in India Christian mis-sionaries have made many more converts among the 'untouchables' than in the higher strata of society, and in our own country fascism and com-munism attract an unduly high proportion of unsuccessful and neurotic people.

The presence in a receiving society of some of the habit elements in-volved in a new trait greatly facilitates borrowing. It is for this reason that diffusion occurs most readily among peoples of similar culture, who already share many elements of habit. Thus Englishmen and Americans borrow more frequently and easily from each other than from Russians, Chinese, or Hottentots. Conversely, aboriginal peoples are greatly handi-capped in taking over the complex technology of modern civilization.

They cannot, for example, begin to manufacture the steel products which they want without also taking over such things as blast furnaces and rolling mills.

Cultural borrowing will occur only if the new habit is demonstrably rewarding. The native quickly adopts steel knives and axes from the white man because their superiority to his former stone implements becomes immediately apparent. On the other hand, Europeans were slow to borrow paper manufacture from the Chinese because the advantages of paper over parchment appeared very slight at first. The Chinese and Japanese have not yet adopted the alphabet from western civilization because, however great its ultimate advantages, it would impose heavy burdens and discomforts upon all literate persons during the necessary period of readjustment. Geographic and climatic factors may prevent diffusion by withholding or reducing the possibilities of reward, and social prejudices such as ingrained conservatism may counterbalance potential advantages by inflicting disapprobation upon innovators.

Borrowing need not be exact. Oftentimes, indeed, all that is borrowed is the external 'form' of a custom and not its 'meaning,' i.e. the collective ideas associated with it. The familiar caricature of the cannibal chief wearing a silk hat provides a good illustration. Frequently an imperfect copy is quite adequate. Thus when the Plains Indians took over horses and riding equipment from the Spaniards they omitted the horseshoe, which was quite unnecessary on the prairie. Sometimes changes are imposed by the conditions of the geographical environment. When the Iroquois Indians adopted the birchbark canoe from their Algonkian neighbors, for example, they altered the material to elm bark because of the scarcity of birch trees in their habitat. Frequently cultural factors favor a modification. The original Phoenician alphabet lacked characters for vowels, the nature of their language being such that consonant signs sufficed for the identification of words. Since this was not true of the Greek language, when the Greeks borrowed the Phoenician alphabet they converted characters for which they had no need into symbols for vowels.

Modifications are so common in cultural borrowing that authorities like Malinowski have regarded the process as scarcely less creative than other forms of innovation. Often, indeed, it is inextricably blended with invention or tentation. This is well illustrated in instances of 'stimulus diffusion,' in which only the general idea of an alien cultural trait is borrowed, the specific form being supplied by improvisation. Thus a famous Cherokee chief named Sequoyah, though an illiterate man, had noticed that white men could somehow understand messages from pieces of paper on which peculiar marks were inscribed, and he came to the conclusion that this would be a useful skill for his own people to acquire. He therefore set himself the task of devising a system of marks by which

Courtesy of Mr. Tom B. Underwood,
Museum of The Cherokee Indian, and The Stephens Press.

Fig. 1. Sequoyah, the famous Cherokee Indian chief, invented this syllabary for recording his native language by giving syllabic values to alphabetic letters and typographical signs arbitrarily chosen and arranged from English and German type.

the Cherokee language could be written. Inventing some signs of his own and copying some from pieces of printed matter—numbers and punctuation marks as well as letters, upside down or on their sides as often as upright—he produced a novel form of writing, a syllabary rather than an alphabet, which his tribesmen learned and still use to this day. (See Fig. 1.)

The second major process in cultural change is *social acceptance*. So long as an innovation, whether original or borrowed, is practiced by the innovator alone in his society, it is an individual habit and not an element of culture. To become the latter it must be accepted by others; it must be socially shared. Social acceptance begins with the adoption of a new habit by a small number of individuals. From this point it may spread until it becomes part of the sub-culture of a family, clan, local community, or other sub-group, or until it becomes a 'specialty' characteristic of persons belonging to a particular occupational, kinship, age-graded, or other status category, or until it becomes an 'alternative' widely but optionally practiced. Eventually it may even become a 'universal,' shared by all members of the society. The term 'degrees of cultural saturation' has been proposed for the various steps in social acceptance.

The learning mechanism involved in social acceptance is imitation, as in the case of cultural borrowing, but the model whose behavior is copied is a member of one's own rather than another society. So similar are the two processes that the term 'diffusion' is often applied to both; social acceptance is called 'internal' or 'vertical' diffusion to differentiate it from cultural borrowing, which is termed 'external' or 'horizontal' diffusion. With minor exceptions, most of what has previously been stated about the latter process applies equally to the former. Since close contact and similarity of culture can be taken for granted, however, copying is usually far more exact, and this is accentuated by social control.

A factor of considerable importance in social acceptance is the prestige of the innovator and of the group who are first to imitate him. Changes advocated by an admired political or religious leader are readily adopted, whereas few will follow an unpopular or despised innovator. Clothing styles accepted by 'the four hundred' quickly diffuse throughout the masses, but the 'zoot suit' does not spread from the taxi dance hall to the ballroom. Women imitate men more readily than *vice versa*. In our own society, for example, many women have adopted masculine garments, smoking and drinking habits, and occupations, but there appears to be no concerted movement among men to wear skirts, use cosmetics, or apply for positions as nurses, governesses, or baby-sitters.

Selective elimination constitutes a third major process of cultural change. Every innovation that has been socially accepted enters, as it were, into a competition for survival. So long as it proves more rewarding than its alternatives a cultural habit will endure, but when it ceases to bring comparable satisfactions it dwindles and eventually disappears. The process superficially resembles that of natural selection in organic evolution. It should be noted, however, that cultural traits do not compete directly with one another but are competitively tested in the experience of those who practice them. Oftentimes the competition is carried on between organized groups of people with contrasting customs and beliefs, as between nations, political parties, religious sects, or social and economic classes, and the issue is decided indirectly by the victory of one group over the other. By and large, the cultural elements that are eliminated through trial and error or social competition are the less adaptive ones, so that the process is as definitely one of the survival of the fittest as is that of natural selection.

Few of the genuine gains of culture history—the achievements of technology, of science, of man's control over nature—have ever been lost. The so-called 'lost arts of antiquity' are largely mythical. To be sure, particular peoples have declined in civilization, but not until they have passed on their contributions to others. What man has lost, in the main, is a mass of maladaptive and barbarous practices, inefficient techniques, and outworn superstitions. New errors arise, of course, in each generation, but it is comforting to realize that the mortality of error is vastly greater than that of truth.

It is the genuine achievements of man that anthropologists have in mind when they say that culture is cumulative, comparing culture history to the growth of a snowball as it is rolled down a hill. Even achievements that are superseded rarely disappear. Today the electric light has proved superior to earlier methods of lighting, but the gas mantle, the kerosene lamp, and the tallow candle still survive in out-of-the-way places or under special conditions. Survival is often assured through a change in function. The use of outmoded weapons has been preserved, for example, in athletic sports like fencing and archery and in boyhood toys such as the sling and the peashooter. Other ancient usages survive in legal, religious, and academic ceremonial. Written records, of course, preserve much of the culture of the past from oblivion. Our libraries bulge with the puerilities as well as the achievements of history.

The fourth and last important process of cultural change is that of *integration*. The shared habits that constitute a culture not only fluctuate in their degree of social acceptance, and compete for survival, but they also become progressively adapted to one another so that they tend to form an integrated whole. They exhibit what Sumner has called 'a strain toward consistency.' Every innovation alters in some respect the situations under which certain other forms of habitual behavior occur, and leads to adaptive changes in the latter. Similarly it must, in its turn, be adjusted to modifications elsewhere in the culture. While each such change is in itself, of course, an innovation, their reciprocal interaction and cumulative effect deserve special recognition as an integrative process.

The history of the automobile during the present century in our own culture provides an excellent example. The changes brought about by this technological invention are described by Professor Leslie Spier in Chapter X. A similar story could be told for other modern innovations such as the telephone, the airplane, the radio, and electrical household gadgets, and all of them pale before the potentialities of atomic energy.

Certain anthropologists have erroneously assumed that the elements of any culture are in a state of nearly perfect integration, or equilibrium, at all times. Actually, however, perfect equilibrium is never achieved or even approached. The adjustment of other elements of culture to an innovation, and of it to them, requires time—often years or even generations. In the meantime other innovations have appeared and set in motion new processes of integration. At any given time, therefore, a culture exhibits numerous instances of uncompleted integrative processes as well as examples of others which have been carried through to relatively satisfactory completion. What we always encounter is a strain toward internal adaptation, never its full realization.

The period of time which must elapse between the acceptance of an innovation and the completion of the integrative readjustments which follow in its train Ogburn has aptly called 'cultural lag.' During such a period of lag people attempt, through variation, invention, tentation, and cultural borrowing, to modify old customs and ideas to accord with the new, and to adjust the new to the old, so as to eliminate inconsistencies and sources of friction and irritation. In a modern democratic society, politics is a major scene of such efforts.

The net effect of the various processes of cultural change is to adapt the collective habits of human societies progressively over time to the changing conditions of existence. Change is always uncomfortable and often painful, and people frequently become discouraged with its slowness or even despair of achieving any genuine improvement. Neither history nor anthropology, however, gives grounds for pessimism. However halting or harsh it may appear to participants, cultural change is always adaptive and usually progressive. It is also inevitable, and will endure as long as the earth can support human life. Nothing—not even an atomic war—can destroy civilization.

CLAUDE LÉVI-STRAUSS

XII

The Family

THE WORD FAMILY is so plain, the kind of reality to which it refers is so close to daily experience that one may expect to be confronted in this chapter with a simple situation. Anthropologists, however, are a strange breed; they like to make even the 'familiar' look mysterious and complicated. As a matter of fact, the comparative study of the family among many different peoples has given rise to some of the most bitter arguments in the whole history of anthropological thought and probably to its more spectacular reversal.

During the second half of the nineteenth century and the beginning of the twentieth, anthropologists were working under the influence of biological evolutionism. They were trying to organize their data so that the institutions of the simpler people would correspond to an early stage of the evolution of mankind, while our own institutions were related to the more advanced or developed forms. And since, among ourselves, the family founded on monogamic marriage was considered as the most praiseworthy and cherished institution, it was immediately inferred that savage societies—equated for the purpose with the societies of man at the beginning of its existence—could only have something of a different type. Therefore, facts were distorted and misinterpreted; even more, fanciful 'early' stages of evolution were invented, such as 'group marriage' and 'promiscuity' to account for the period when man was still so barbarous that he could not possibly conceive of the niceties of the social life it is the privilege of civilized man to enjoy. Every custom different from our own was carefully selected as a vestige of an older type of social organization.

This way of approaching the problem became obsolete when the ac-

261

cumulation of data made obvious the following fact: the kind of family featured in modern civilization by monogamous marriage, independent establishment of the young couple, warm relationship between parents and offspring, et cetera, while not always easy to recognize behind the complicated network of strange customs and institutions of savage peoples, is at least conspicuous among those which seem to have remained on—or returned to—the simplest cultural level. Tribes like the Andamanese of the Indian Ocean Andaman Islands, the Fuegians of the southernmost tip of South America, the Nambikwara of central Brazil, and the Bushmen of South Africa—to quote only a few examples—live in small, semi-nomadic bands; they have little or no political organization and their technological level is very low since, in some of them at least, there is no knowledge of weaving, pot-making, and even sometimes hut-building. Thus, the only social structure worth speaking of among them is the family, mostly monogamous. The observer working in the field has no trouble identifying the married couples, closely associated by sentimental bonds and economic co-operation as well as by the rearing of children born from their union.

There are two ways of interpreting this pre-eminence of the family at both ends of the scale of development of human societies. Some writers have claimed that the simpler peoples may be considered as a remnant of what can be looked at as a 'golden age,' prior to the submission of mankind to the hardships and perversities of civilization; thus, man would have known in that early stage the bliss of monogamic family only to forego it later until its more recent Christian rediscovery. The general trend, however, except for the so-called Vienna school, has been that more and more anthropologists have become convinced that familial life is present practically everywhere in human societies, even in those with sexual and educational customs very remote from our own. Thus, after they had claimed for about fifty years that the family, as modern societies know it, could only be a recent development and the outcome of a slow and long-lasting evolution, anthropologists now lean toward the opposite conviction, i.e. that the family, consisting of a more or less durable union, socially approved, of a man, a woman, and their children, is a universal phenomenon, present in each and every type of society.

These extreme positions, however, suffer equally from over-simplification. It is well known that, in very rare cases, family bonds cannot be claimed to exist. A telling example comes from the Nayar, a very large group living on the Malabar coast of India. In former times, the warlike type of life of the Nayar men did not allow them to found a family. Marriage was a purely symbolical ceremony which did not result in a permanent tie between a man and a woman. As a matter of fact, married women were permitted to have as many lovers as they wished. Children belonged exclusively to the mother line, and familial as well as land authority was exercised, not by the ephemeral husband but by the wife's brothers. Since land was cultivated by an inferior caste, subservient to the Nayar, a woman's brothers were as completely free as their sister's temporary husband or lovers to devote themselves to military activities.

Now, the case of the Nayar has been frequently misunderstood. In the first place, they cannot be considered as a vestige of a primitive kind of social organization which could have been very general, in the past, among mankind. Quite to the contrary: the Nayar exhibit an extremely specialized and elaborate type of social structure and, from that point of view, they do not prove very much.

On the other hand, there is little doubt that the Nayar represent an extreme form of a tendency which is far more frequent in human societies than is generally acknowledged.

There are a large number of human societies which, although they did not go quite as far as the Nayar in denying recognition to the family as a social unit, have nevertheless limited this recognition by their simultaneous admission of patterns of a different type. For instance, the Masai and the Chagga, both of them African tribes, did recognize the family as a social unit. However, and for the same reason as among the Nayar, this was not true for the younger class of adult men who were dedicated to warlike activities and consequently were not allowed to marry and found a family. They used to live in regimental organizations and were permitted, during that period, to have promiscuous relations with the younger class of adult girls. Thus, among these peoples, the family did exist side by side with a promiscuous, non-familial type of relations between the sexes.

For different reasons, the same type of dual pattern prevailed among the Bororo and several other tribes of central Brazil, the Muria, and other tribes of India and Assam, et cetera. All the known instances could be arranged in such a way as to make the Nayar appear only as the more consistent, systematic and logically extreme case of a situation which may eventually reappear, at least in embryonic form, in modern society.

This was well shown in the case of Nazi Germany, where a similar cleavage was beginning to appear in the family unit: on the one hand,

the men dedicated to political and warlike activities, with a great deal
of freedom resulting from their exalted position; and on the other hand,
women with their '3K' functional assignment: *Küche, Kirche, Kinder,*
i.e. kitchen, church and children. One might very well conceive that, had
the same trend been maintained for several centuries, this clear-cut division of functions between men and women, together with the accompanying differentiation of their respective status, could very well have
led to a type of social organization where the family unit would receive
as little recognition as among the Nayar.

During recent years anthropologists have taken great pains to show
that, even among people who practice wife-lending, either periodically
in religious ceremonies or on a statutory basis (as where men are permitted to enter into a kind of institutional friendship entailing wife-
lending among members), these customs should not be interpreted as
survivals of 'group marriage' since they exist side by side, and even
imply, recognition of the family. It is true enough that, in order to be
allowed to lend one's wife, one should first get one. However, if we consider the case of some Australian tribes as the Wunambal of the northwestern part of the continent, a man who would not lend his wife to her
other potential husbands during ceremonies would be considered as 'very
greedy,' i.e. trying to keep for himself a privilege intended by the social
group to be shared between numerous persons equally entitled to it. And
since that attitude toward sexual access to a woman existed along with
the official dogma that men have no part in physiological procreation
(therefore doubly denying any kind of bond between the husband and
his wife's children), the family becomes an economic grouping where
man brings the products of his hunt and the woman those of her collecting and gathering. Anthropologists, who claim that this economic unit
built up on a 'give and take' principle is a proof of the existence of the
family even among the lowest savages, are certainly on no sounder basis
than those who maintain that such a kind of family has little else in
common than the word used to designate it with the family as it has
been observed elsewhere.

The same relativistic approach is advisable in respect to the polygamous family. The word polygamy, it should be recalled, refers to polygyny, that is, a system where a man is entitled to several wives, as well
as to polyandry, which is the complementary system where several husbands share one wife.

Now it is true that in many observed cases, polygamous families are nothing else than a combination of several monogamous families, although the same person plays the part of several spouses. For instance, in some tribes of Bantu Africa, each wife lives in a separate hut with her children, and the only difference with the monogamous family results from the fact that the same man plays the part of husband to all his wives. There are other instances, however, where the situation is not so clear. Among the Tupi-Kawahib of central Brazil, a chief may marry several women who may be sisters, or even a mother and her daughters by former marriage; the children are raised together by the women who do not seem to mind very much whether they nurse their own children or not; also, the chief willingly lends his wives to his younger brothers, his court officers, or to visitors. Here we have not only a combination of polygyny and polyandry, but the mix-up is increased even more by the fact that the co-wives may be united by close consanguineous ties prior to their marrying the same man. In a case which this writer witnessed, a mother and daughter, married to one man, were together taking care of children who were, at the same time, stepchildren to one woman and, according to case, either grandchild or stepbrother to the other.

As to polyandry proper, it may sometimes take extreme forms, as among the Toda where several men, usually brothers, share one wife, the legitimate father of the children being the one who has performed a special ceremony and who remains legal father of all the children to be born until another husband decides to assume the right of fathership by the same process. In Tibet and Nepal, polyandry seems to be explained by occupational factors of the same type as those already stated for the Nayar: for men living a semi-nomadic existence as guides and bearers, polyandry provides a good chance that there will be, at all times, at least one husband at hand to take care of the homestead.

If the legal, economic, and sentimental identity of the family can be maintained even in a polygynous or a polyandrous set-up, it is not sure that the same would be true when polyandry exists side by side with polygamy. As we have already seen, this was to some extent the case among the Tupi-Kawahib since polygynous marriages existed, at least as a chief's privilege, in combination with an elaborate system of wife-lending to younger brothers, helpers, and visitors from different tribes. Here one might argue that the bond between a woman and her legal husband was more different in degree than in kind from a gamut of other bonds which could be arranged in order of decreasing strength: from rightful, semi-permanent lovers to occasional ones. However, even in that case, the children's status was defined by the legal marriage, not by the other types of unions.

We come closer to the so-called 'group marriage' when we consider the modern evolution of the Toda during the nineteenth century. They had originally a polyandrous system, which was made possible through the custom of female infanticide. When this was prohibited by the British administration, thus restoring the natural sex-ratio, the Toda continued to practice polyandry; but now instead of several brothers sharing one wife, it became possible for them to marry several. As in the case of the Nayar, the types of organization which seem remotest to the conjugal family do not occur in the more savage and archaic societies but in the relatively recent and extremely sophisticated forms of social development.

Therefore, it becomes apparent why the problem of the family should not be approached in a dogmatic way. As a matter of fact, this is one of the more elusive questions in the whole field of social organization. Of the type of organization which prevailed in the early stages of mankind, we know very little, since the remnants of man during the Upper Paleolithic Period of about 50,000 years ago consist principally of skeletal fragments and stone implements which provide only a minimum of information on social customs and laws. On the other hand, when we consider the wide diversity of human societies which have been observed since, let us say, Herodotus' time until present days, the only thing which can be said is as follows: monogamic, conjugal family is fairly frequent. Wherever it seems to be superseded by different types of organizations, this generally happens in very specialized and sophisticated societies and not, as was previously expected, in the crudest and simplest types. Moreover, the few instances of non-conjugal family (even in its polygamous form) establish beyond doubt that the high frequency of the conjugal type of social grouping does not derive from a universal necessity. It is at least conceivable that a perfectly stable and durable society could exist without it. Hence the difficult problem: if there is no natural law making the family universal, how can we explain why it is found practically everywhere?

In order to try to solve the problem, let us try first to define the family, not by integrating the numerous factual observations made in different societies nor even by limiting ourselves to the prevailing situation among us, but by building up an ideal model of what we have in mind when we use the word family. It would then seem that this word serves to designate a social group offering at least three characteristics: (1) it finds its origin in marriage; (2) it consists in husband, wife, and children born out of their wedlock, though it can be conceived that other relatives may find their place close to that nuclear group; and (3) the family members are united together by a) legal bonds, b) economic, religious, and other kinds of rights and obligations, c) a precise network of sexual rights and prohibitions, and a varying and diversified amount of psychological feelings such as love, affection, respect, awe, et cetera. We will now proceed to a close examination of these several aspects in the light of the available data.

MARRIAGE AND THE FAMILY

As we have already noticed, marriage may be monogamous or polygamous. It should be pointed out immediately that the first kind is not only more frequently found than the second, but even much more than a cursory inventory of human societies would lead to believe. Among the so-called polygamous societies, there are undoubtedly a substantial number which are authentically so; but many others make a strong difference between the 'first' wife who is the only true one, endowed with the full rights attached to the marital status, while the other ones are sometimes little more than official concubines. Besides, in all polygamous societies, the privilege of having several wives is actually enjoyed by a small minority only. This is easily understandable since the number of men and women in any random grouping is approximately the same with a normal balance of about 110 to 100 to the advantage of either sex. In order to make polygamy possible, there are definite conditions which have to be met: either children of a given sex are voluntarily destroyed (a custom known to exist in a few rare cases, such as female infanticide among the Toda already referred to), or special circumstances account for a different life expectancy for members of both sexes, as among the Eskimo and some Australian tribes where many men used to die young because their occupations—whale-hunting in one case, warfare in the other—were especially dangerous. Or else we have to look for a strongly hierarchical social system, where a given class: ancients, priests and sorcerers, rich men, et cetera is powerful enough to monopolize with impunity more than their share of the womenfolk at the expense of the younger or the poorer people. As a matter of fact, we know of societies—mostly in Africa—where one has to be rich to get many wives (since there is a bride-price to pay), but where at the same time the increase in wives is a means to increase wealth, since female work has a definite economic value. However, it is clear that the systematic practice of polygamy is automatically limited by the change of structure it is likely to bring up in the society.

Therefore, it is not necessary to wonder a great deal about the predominance of monogamic marriage in human societies. That monogamy is not inscribed in the nature of man is sufficiently evidenced by the fact that polygamy exists in widely different forms and in many types of societies; on the other hand, the prevalence of monogamy results from the fact that, unless special conditions are voluntarily or involuntarily brought about, there is normally, about just one woman available for each man. In modern societies, moral, religious, and economic reasons have officialized monogamous marriage (a rule which is in actual practice breached by such different means as premarital freedom, prostitution, and adultery). But in societies which are on a much lower cultural level and where there is no prejudice against polygamy, and even where polygamy may be actually permitted or desired, the same result can be brought about by the lack of social or economic differentiation, so that each man has neither the means, nor the power, to obtain more than one wife and where, consequently, everybody is obliged to make a virtue of necessity.

If there are many different types of marriage to be observed in human societies—whether monogamous or polygamous, and in the last case, polygynous, polyandrous, or both; and whether by exchange, purchase, free-choice or imposed by the family, et cetera—the striking fact is that everywhere a distinction exists between marriage, i.e. a legal, group-sanctioned bond between a man and a woman, and the type of permanent or temporary union resulting either from violence or consent alone. This group intervention may be a notable or a slight one, it does not matter. The important thing is that every society has some way to operate a distinction between free unions and legitimate ones. There are several levels at which that distinction is made.

In the first place, nearly all societies grant a very high rating to the married status. Wherever age-grades exist, either in an institutional way or as non-crystallized forms of grouping, some connection is established between the younger adolescent group and bachelorhood, less young and married without children, and adulthood with full rights, the latter going usually on par with the birth of the first child. This threefold distinction was recognized not only among many primitive tribes but also in peasant western Europe, if only for the purpose of feasts and ceremonies, as late as the early twentieth century.

What is even more striking is the true feeling of repulsion which most societies have toward bachelorhood. Generally speaking it can be said that, among the so-called primitive tribes, there are no bachelors, simply for the reason that they could not survive. One of the strongest field recollections of this writer was his meeting, among the Boróro of central Brazil, of a man about thirty years old: unclean, ill-fed, sad, and lonesome. When asked if the man were seriously ill, the natives' answer came as a shock: what was wrong with him?—nothing at all, he was just a bachelor. And true enough, in a society where labor is systematically shared between man and woman and where only the married status permits the man to benefit from the fruits of woman's work, including delousing, body painting, and hair-plucking as well as vegetable food and cooked food (since the Boróro woman tills the soil and makes pots), a bachelor is really only half a human being.

This is true of the bachelor and also, to a lesser extent, of a couple without children. Indeed they can make a living, but there are many societies where a childless man (or woman) never reaches full status within the group, or else, beyond the group, in this all important society which is made up of dead relatives and where one can only expect recognition as ancestor through the cult, rendered to him or her by one's descendants. Conversely, an orphan finds himself in the same dejected condition as a bachelor. As a matter of fact, both terms provide sometimes the strongest insults existing in the native vocabulary. Bachelors and orphans can even be merged together with cripples and witches, as if their conditions were the outcome of some kind of supernatural malediction.

The interest shown by the group in the marriage of its members can be directly expressed, as it is the case among us where prospective spouses, if they are of marriageable age, have first to get a license and then to secure the services of an acknowledged representative of the group to celebrate their union. Although this direct relationship between the individuals, on the one hand, and the group as a whole, on the other, is known at least sporadically in other societies, it is by no means a frequent case. It is almost a universal feature of marriage that it is originated, not by the individuals but by the groups concerned (families, lineages, clans, et cetera), and that it binds the groups before and above the individuals. Two kinds of reasons bring about this result: on the one hand, the paramount importance of being married tends to make parents, even in very simple societies, start early to worry about obtaining a suitable mate for their offspring and this, accordingly, may lead to children being promised to each other from infancy. But above all, we are confronted here with that strange paradox to which we shall have to return later on, namely, that although marriage gives birth to the family, it is the family, or rather families, which produce marriage as the main legal device at their disposal to establish an alliance between themselves. As New Guinea natives put it, the real purpose of getting married is not so much to obtain a wife but to secure brothers-in-law. If marriage takes place between groups rather than individuals, a large number of strange customs become immediately clearer. For instance, we understand why in some parts of Africa, where descent follows the father's line, marriage becomes only final when the woman has given birth to a male child, thus fulfilling its function of maintaining her husband's lineage. The so-called *levirate* and *sororate* should be explained in the light of the same principle: if marriage is binding between two groups to which the spouses belong there can be without contradiction a replacement of one spouse by his brothers or by her sisters. When the husband dies, the levirate provides that his unmarried brothers have a preferential claim on his widow (or, as it is sometimes differently put, share in their deceased brother's duty to support his wife and children), while the sororate permits a man to marry preferentially in polygamous marriage his wife's sisters, or—when marriage is monogamous—to get a sister to replace the wife in case the latter remains childless, has to be divorced on account of bad conduct, or dies. But whatever the way in which the collectivity expresses its interest in the marriage of its members, whether through the authority vested in strong consanguineous groups, or more directly, through the intervention of the State, it remains true that marriage is not, is never, and cannot be a private business.

FORMS OF FAMILY

We have to look for cases as extreme as the Nayar, already described, to find societies where there is not, at least, a temporary *de facto* union of the husband, wife, and their children. But we should be careful to note that, while such a group among us constitutes the family and is given legal recognition, this is by no means the case in a large number of human societies. Indeed, there is a maternal instinct which compels the mother to care for her children and makes her find a deep satisfaction in exercising those activities, and there are also psychological drives which explain that a man may feel warmly toward the offspring of a woman with whom he is living, and the development of which he is witnessing step by step, even if he does not believe (as is the case among the tribes who are said to disclaim physiological paternity) that he had any actual part in their procreation. Some societies strive to reinforce these convergent feelings: the famous *couvade*, the custom according to which a man is made to share in the inabilities (either natural or socially imposed) of the woman in confinement, has been explained by some as an attempt to build up a welded unit out of these otherwise not too homogeneous materials.

The great majority of societies, however, do not show a very active interest in a kind of grouping which, to some of them at least (including our own), appears so important. Here too, it is the groups which are important, not the temporary aggregate of the individual representatives of the group. For instance, many societies are interested in clearly establishing the relations of the offspring with the father's group on the one hand, and with the mother's group on the other, but they do it by differentiating strongly the two kinds of relationships. Territorial rights may be inherited through one line, and religious privileges and obligations through the other. Or else, status from one side, magical techniques from the other. Innumerable examples could be given from Africa, Australia, America, et cetera. To limit oneself to just one, it is striking to compare the minute care with which the Hopi Indians of Arizona traced different types of legal and religious rights to the father's and to the mother's lines, while the frequency of divorce made the family so unstable that many fathers did not actually share the same house as their children, since houses were women's properties and, from the legal point of view, children followed the mother's line.

This brittleness of the conjugal family, which is so common among the so-called primitive peoples, does not prevent them from giving some value to conjugal faithfulness and parental attachment. However, these are moral norms and they should be contrasted strongly with the legal rules which in many cases only acknowledge formally the relationship of the children with either the father's or the mother's lines or, when both lines are formally recognized, do so for wholly different types of rights and/or obligations. Extreme cases have been recorded such as the Emerillon, a small tribe of French Guiana now reduced to about 50 persons. Here, according to recent informants, marriage is so unstable that, during a lifetime, everybody has a good chance to get married to everybody of the opposite sex and the tribe is said to use special names for children, showing from which one of at least 8 consecutive marriages they may be the offspring. This is probably a recent development which should be explained on the one hand by the smallness of the tribe and, on the other, by the unstable conditions under which it has lived for the past century. However, it shows that conditions may exist where the conjugal family is hardly recognizable.

Instability accounts for the above examples; but some others may stem from quite opposite considerations. In most of contemporary India and in many parts of western and eastern Europe, sometimes as late as the nineteenth century, the basic social unit was constituted by a type of family which should be described as *domestic* rather than *conjugal:* ownership of the land and of the homestead, parental authority and economic leadership were vested in the eldest living ascendant, or in the community of brothers issued from the same ascendant. In the Russian *bratsvo,* the south-Slavic *zadruga,* the French *maisnie,* the family actually consisted of the elder or the surviving brothers, together with their wives, married sons with their wives and unmarried daughters, and so on down to the great grandchildren. Such large groups, which could sometimes include several dozen persons living and working under a common authority, have been designated as *joint families* or *extended families.* Both terms are useful but misleading since they imply that these large units are made up of small conjugal families. As we have already seen, while it is true that the conjugal family limited to mother and children is practically universal since it is based on the physiological and psychological dependency which exists between them at least for a certain time, and that the conjugal family consisting of husband, wife, and children is almost as frequent for psychological and economical reasons which should be added to those previously mentioned, the historical process which has led among ourselves to the legal recognition of the conjugal family is a very complex one: it has been brought about only in part through an increasing awareness of a natural situation. But there is little doubt that, to a very large extent, it has resulted from the narrowing down to a group, as small as can be, the legal standing of which, in the past of our institutions, was vested for centuries on very large groups. In the last instance, one would not be wrong in disallowing the terms joint family and extended family. Indeed, it is rather the conjugal family which deserves the name of: *restricted family*.

We have just seen that, when the family is given a small functional value, it tends to disappear even below the level of the conjugal type. On the contrary, when the family has a great functional value, it becomes actualized much above that level. Our would-be universal conjugal family, then, corresponds more to an unstable equilibrium between extremes than to a permanent and everlasting need coming from the deepest requirements of human nature.

To complete the picture, we have finally to consider cases where the conjugal family differs from our own, not so much on account of a different amount of functional value, but rather because its functional value is conceived in a way qualitatively different from our own conceptions.

As will be seen later on, there are many peoples for whom the kind of spouse one should marry is much more important than the kind of match they will make together. These people are ready to accept unions which to us would seem not only unbelievable, but in direct contradiction with the aims and purposes of setting up a family. For instance, the Siberian Chukchee were not in the least abhorrent to the marriage of a mature girl of let us say about twenty, with a baby-husband two or three years old. Then, the young woman, herself a mother by an authorized lover, would nurse together her own child and her little husband. Like the North American Mohave, who had the opposite custom of a man marrying a baby girl and caring for her until she became old enough to fulfill her conjugal duties, such marriages were thought of as very strong ones, since the natural feelings between husband and wife would be reinforced by the recollection of the parental care bestowed by one of the spouses on the other. These are by no means exceptional cases to be explained by extraordinary mental abnormalities. Examples could be brought together from other parts of the world: South America, both highland and tropical, New Guinea, et cetera.

As a matter of fact, the examples just given still respect, to some extent, the duality of sexes which we feel is a requirement of marriage and raising a family. But in several parts of Africa, women of high rank were allowed to marry other women and have them bear children through the services of unacknowledged male lovers, the noble woman being then entitled to become the 'father' of her children and to transmit to them, according to the prevalent father's right, her own name, status, and wealth. Finally, there are the cases, certainly less striking, where the conjugal family was considered necessary to procreate the children but not to raise them, since each family did endeavor to retain somebody else's children (if possible of a higher status) to raise them while their own children were similarly retained (sometimes before they were born) by another family. This happened in some parts of Polynesia, while 'fosterage,' i.e. the custom whereby a son was sent to be raised by his mother's brother, was a common practice on the Northwest Coast of America as well as in European feudal society.

THE FAMILY BONDS

During the course of centuries we have become accustomed to Christian morality which considers marriage and setting up a family as the only way to prevent sexual gratification from being sinful. That connection has been shown to exist elsewhere in a few scattered instances; but it is by no means frequent. Among most people, marriage has very little to do with the satisfaction of the sexual urge, since the social set-up provides for many opportunities which can be not only external to marriage, but even contradictory to it. For instance, among the Muria of Bastar, in central India, when puberty comes, boys and girls are sent to live together in communal huts where they enjoy a great deal of sexual freedom, but after a few years of such leeway they get married according to the rule that no former adolescent lovers should be permitted to unite. Then, in a rather small village, each man is married to a wife whom he has known during his younger years as his present neighbor's (or neighbors') lover.

On the other hand, and if sexual considerations are not paramount for marriage purposes, economic necessities are found everywhere in the first place. We have already shown that what makes marriage a fundamental need in tribal societies is the division of labor between the sexes.

Like the form of the family, the division of labor stems more from social and cultural considerations than from natural ones. Truly, in every human group, women give birth to children and take care of them, and men rather have as their specialty hunting and warlike activities. Even there, though, we have ambiguous cases: of course men never give birth to babies, but in many societies, as we have seen with the couvade, they are made to act as if they did. And there is a great deal of difference between the Nambikwara father nursing his baby and cleaning it when it soils itself, and the European nobleman of not long ago to whom his children were formally presented from time to time, being otherwise confined to the women's quarters until the boys were old enough to be taught riding and fencing. Conversely, the young concubines of the Nambikwara chieftain disdain domestic activities and prefer to share in their husband's adventurous expeditions. It is by no means unlikely that a similar custom, prevailing among other South American tribes, where a special class of women, half wantons and half helpers, did not marry, but accompanied the men on the warpath, is at the origin of the famous legend of the Amazons.

When we turn to activities less basic than child-rearing and war-making, it becomes still more difficult to discern rules governing the division of labor between the sexes. The Boróro women till the soil while among the Zuñi this is a man's work; according to tribe, hut building, pot making, weaving, may be incumbent upon either sex. Therefore, we should be careful to distinguish the *fact* of the division of labor between the sexes which is practically universal, from the *way* according to which different tasks are attributed to one or the other sex, where we should recognize the same paramount influence of cultural factors, let us say the same *artificiality* which presides over the organization of the family itself.

Here, again, we are confronted with the same question we have already met with: if the natural reasons which could explain the division of labor between the sexes do not seem to play a decisive part, as soon as we leave the solid ground of women's biological specialization in the production of children, why does it exist at all? The very fact that it varies endlessly according to the society selected for consideration shows that, as for the family itself, it is the mere fact of its existence which is mysteriously required, the form under which it comes to exist being utterly irrelevant, at least from the point of view of any natural necessity. However, after having considered the different aspects of the problem, we are now in a position to perceive some common features which may bring us nearer to an answer than we were at the beginning of this chapter. Since family appears to us as a positive social reality, perhaps the only positive social reality, we are prone to define it exclusively by its positive characteristics. Now it should be pointed out that whenever we have tried to show what the family is, at the same time we were implying what it is not, and the negative aspects may be as important as the others. To return to the division of labor we were just discussing, when it is stated that one sex must perform certain tasks, this also means

that the other sex is forbidden to do them. In that light, the sexual division of labor is nothing else than a device to institute a reciprocal state
of dependency between the sexes.

The same thing may be said of the sexual side of the family life. Even
if it is not true, as we have shown, that the family can be explained on
sexual grounds, since for many tribes, sexual life and the family are by
no means as closely connected as our moral norms would make them,
there is a negative aspect which is much more important: the structure
of the family, always and everywhere, makes certain types of sexual connections impossible, or at least wrong.

Indeed, the limitations may vary to a great extent according to the
culture under consideration. In ancient Russia, there was a custom known
as *snokatchestvo* whereby a father was entitled to a sexual privilege
over his son's young wife; a symmetrical custom has been mentioned in
some part of southeastern Asia where the persons implied are the sister's
son and his mother's brother's wife. We ourselves do not object to a man
marrying his wife's sister, a practice which English law still considered
incestuous in the mid-nineteenth century. What remains true is that
every known society, past or present, proclaims that if the husband-wife
relationship, to which, as just seen, some others may eventually be added,
implies sexual rights, there are other relationships equally derived from
the familial structure, which make sexual connections inconceivable, sinful, or legally punishable. The universal prohibition of incest specifies,
as a general rule, that people considered as parents and children, or
brother and sister, even if only by name, cannot have sexual relations
and even less marry each other. In some recorded instances—such as
ancient Egypt, pre-Columbian Peru, also some African, southeast Asian,
and Polynesian kingdoms—incest was defined far less strictly than elsewhere. Even there, however, the rule existed since incest was limited to
a minority group, the ruling class (with the exception of perhaps, ancient
Egypt where it may have been more common); on the other hand, not
every kind of close relatives were permitted as spouse: for instance it
was the half-sister, the full-one being excluded; or, if the full-sister was
allowed, then it should be the elder sister, the younger one remaining
incestuous.

The space at our disposal is too short to demonstrate that, in this case
as previously, there is no natural ground for the custom. Geneticists have
shown that while consanguineous marriages are likely to bring ill effects
in a society which has consistently avoided them in the past, the danger

would be much smaller if the prohibition had never existed, since this would have given ample opportunity for the harmful hereditary characters to become apparent and be automatically eliminated through selection: as a matter of fact this is the way breeders improve the quality of their subjects. Therefore, the dangers of consanguineous marriages are the outcome of the incest prohibition rather than actually explaining it. Furthermore, since very many primitive peoples do not share our belief in biological harm resulting from consanguineous marriages, but have entirely different theories, the reason should be sought elsewhere, in a way more consistent with the opinions generally held by mankind as a whole.

The true explanation should be looked for in a completely opposite direction, and what has been said concerning the sexual division of labor may help us to grasp it. This has been explained as a device to make the sexes mutually dependent on social and economic grounds, thus establishing clearly that marriage is better than celibacy. Now, exactly in the same way that the principle of sexual division of labor establishes a mutual dependency between the sexes, compelling them thereby to perpetuate themselves and to found a family, the prohibition of incest establishes a mutual dependency between families, compelling them, in order to perpetuate themselves, to give rise to new families. It is through a strange oversight that the similarity of the two processes is generally overlooked on account of the use of terms as dissimilar as *division*, on the one hand, and *prohibition* on the other. We could easily have emphasized only the negative aspect of the division of labor by calling it a prohibition of tasks; and conversely, outlined the positive aspect of incest-prohibition by calling it the principle of division of marriageable rights between families. For incest-prohibition simply states that families (however they should be defined) can only marry between each other and that they cannot marry inside themselves.

We now understand why it is so wrong to try to explain the family on the purely natural grounds of procreation, motherly instinct, and psychological feelings between man and woman and between father and children. None of these would be sufficient to give rise to a family, and for a reason simple enough: for the whole of mankind, the absolute requirement for the creation of a family is the previous existence of two other families, one ready to provide a man, the other one a woman, who will through their marriage start a third one, and so on indefinitely. To put it in other words: what makes man really different from the animal is that, in mankind, a family could not exist if there were no society: i.e. a plurality of families ready to acknowledge that there are other links than consanguineous ones, and that the natural process of filiation can only be carried on through the social process of affinity.

How this interdependency of families has become recognized is another problem which we are in no position to solve because there is no reason to believe that man, since he emerged from his animal state, has not enjoyed a basic form of social organization, which, as regards the fundamental principles, could not be essentially different from our own. Indeed, it will never be sufficiently emphasized that, if social organization had a beginning, this could only have consisted in the incest prohibition since, as we have just shown, the incest prohibition is, in fact, a kind of remodeling of the biological conditions of mating and procreation (which know no rule, as can be seen from observing animal life) compelling them to become perpetuated only in an artificial framework of taboos and obligations. It is there, and only there, that we find a passage from nature to culture, from animal to human life, and that we are in a position to understand the very essence of their articulation.

As Tylor has shown almost a century ago, the ultimate explanation is probably that mankind has understood very early that, in order to free itself from a wild struggle for existence, it was confronted with the very simple choice of 'either marrying-out or being killed-out.' The alternative was between biological families living in juxtaposition and endeavoring to remain closed, self-perpetuating units, over-ridden by their fears, hatreds, and ignorances, and the systematic establishment, through the incest prohibition, of links of intermarriage between them, thus succeeding to build, out of the artificial bonds of affinity, a true human society, despite, and even in contradiction with, the isolating influence of consanguinity. Therefore we may better understand how it came to be that, while we still do not know exactly what the family is, we are well aware of the prerequisites and the practical rules which define its conditions of perpetuation.

The so-called primitive peoples have, for that purpose, very simple and clever rules which the tremendous increase in size and fluidity of modern society makes it sometimes difficult for us to understand.

In order to insure that families will not become closed and that they will not constitute progressively as many self-sufficient units, we satisfy ourselves with forbidding marriage between near relatives. The amount of social contacts which any given individual is likely to maintain outside his or her own restricted family is great enough to afford a good probability that, on the average, the hundreds of thousands of families constituting at any given moment a modern society will not be permitted to 'freeze' if one may say so. On the contrary, the greatest possible freedom for the choice of a mate (submitted to the only condition that the choice has to be made outside the restricted family) insures that these families will be kept in a continuous flow and that a satisfactory process of continuous 'mix-up' through intermarriage will prevail among them, thus making for a homogeneous and well-blended social fabric.

Conditions are quite different in the so-called primitive societies: there, the global figure of the population is a small one, although it may vary from a few dozen up to several thousands. Besides, social fluidity is low and it is not likely that many people will have a chance to get acquainted with others, during their lifetime, except within the limits of the village, hunting territory, et cetera, though it is true that many tribes have tried to organize occasions for wider contacts, for instance during feasts, tribal ceremonies, et cetera. Even in such cases, however, the chances are limited to the tribal group since most primitive peoples consider that the tribe is a kind of wide family, and that the frontiers of mankind stop together with the tribal bonds themselves.

Given such conditions, it is still possible to insure the blending of families into a well-united society by using procedures similar to our own, i.e. a mere prohibition of marriage between relatives without any kind of positive prescriptions as to where and whom one should correctly marry. Experience shows, however, that this is only possible in small societies under the condition that the diminutive size of the group and the lack of social mobility be compensated by widening to a considerable extent the range of prohibited degrees. It is not only one's own sister or daughter that, under such circumstances, one should not marry, but any women with whom blood relationship may be traced, even in the remotest possible way. Very small groups with a low cultural level and a loose political and social organization, such as some desert tribes of North and South America, provide us with examples of that solution.

However, the great majority of primitive peoples have devised another method to solve the problem. Instead of confining themselves to a statistical process, relying on the probability that certain interdictions being set up, a satisfactory equilibrium of exchanges between the biological families will spontaneously result, they have preferred to invent rules which every individual and family should follow carefully, and from which a given form of blending, experimentally conceived of as satisfactory, is bound to arise.

Whenever this takes place, the entire field of kinship becomes a kind of complicated game, the kinship terminology being used to distribute all the members of the group into different categories, the rule being that the category of the parents defines either directly or indirectly the category of the children, and that, according to the categories in which they are placed, the members of the group may or may not get married. The study of these rules of kinship and marriage has provided modern anthropology with one of its more difficult and complicated chapters. Apparently ignorant and savage peoples have been able to devise fantastically clever codes which sometimes request, in order to understand their workings and effects, some of the best logical and even mathematical minds available in modern civilization. Therefore, we will limit ourselves to explaining the crudest principles which are the more frequently met with.

One of these is, undoubtedly, the so-called rule of cross-cousin marriage, which has been taken up by innumerable tribes all over the world. This is a complex system according to which collateral relatives are divided into two basic categories: 'parallel' collaterals, when the relationship can be traced through two siblings of the same sex, and 'cross' collaterals, when the relationship is traced through two siblings of opposite sex. For instance, my paternal uncle is a parallel relative and so is my maternal aunt; while the maternal uncle on the one hand, the paternal aunt on the other, are cross-relatives. In the same way, cousins who trace their relationship through two brothers or two sisters, are parallel-cousins; and those who are connected through a brother and a sister are cross-cousins. In the generation of the nephews, if I am a man, my brother's children will be my parallel-nephews while my sister's children are my cross-nephews.

Now, the startling fact about this distinction is that practically all the tribes which make it claim that parallel relatives are the same thing as the closest ones on the same generation level: my father's brother is a 'father,' my mother's sister a 'mother'; my parallel-cousins are like brothers and sisters to me; and my parallel-nephews like children. Marriage with any of these would be incestuous and is consequently forbidden. On the other hand, cross-relatives are designated by special terms of their own, and it is among them that one should preferably find a mate. This is true to the extent that quite frequently, there is only one word to mean both 'cross-cousin' and 'spouse.' What can be the reason for this claim, exactly similar among hundreds of different tribes in Africa, America, Asia, Oceania, that one should not marry, under any pretence, a father's brother's daughter, since that would amount to marrying one's sister, while the best conceivable spouse consists of a mother's brother's daughter, namely a relative, who on purely biological grounds, is exactly as close as the former?

There are even tribes which go a step further in these refinements. Some think that it is not cross-cousins who should marry, but only cross-cousins once removed (i.e. children of cross-cousins); others, and this is by far the most frequent case, are not satisfied with the simple distinction between cross- and parallel-cousins; they subdivide the cross-cousins themselves into marriageable and non-marriageable ones. For instance, although a mother's brother's daughter is, according to the above definitions, a cross-cousin in the same sense as a father's sister's daughter, there are in India, living side by side, tribes which believe that one of them, only different according to case, make a suitable spouse, death being preferable to the sin of marrying the other.

All these distinctions (to which others could be added) are fantastic at first sight because they cannot be explained on biological or psychological grounds. But, if we keep in mind what has been explained in the preceding section, i.e. that all the marriage prohibitions have as their only purpose to establish a mutual dependency between the biological families, or, to put it in stronger terms, that marriage rules express the refusal, on the part of society, to admit the exclusive existence of the biological family, then everything becomes clear. For all these complicated sets of rules and distinctions are nothing but the outcome of the processes according to which, in a given society, families are set up against each other for the purpose of playing the game of matrimony.

Let us consider briefly the rules of the game. Since societies try to maintain their identity in the course of time, there should be first a rule fixing the status of the children in respect to that of their parents. The simplest possible rule to that end, and by far the most frequently adopted, is the generally called rule of *unilineal descent*, namely that children get the same status of either their father (patrilineal descent) or their mother (matrilineal descent). It can also be decided that the status of both the father and the mother are taken into consideration, and that they should be combined to define a third category in which the children will be put. For instance, a child of a father belonging to the status A and of a mother belonging to the status B, would himself belong to a status C; and the status will be D if it is the father who is B and the mother who is A. Then, C and D will marry together and procreate children either A or B according to the sex orientation, and so on indefinitely. Everybody with some leisure time may devise rules of this kind, and it will be surprising indeed if some tribe, at least, cannot be found where each rule is actually being applied.

The rule of descent being defined, the second question is to know in how many exogamous groups the society in consideration is being divided. An exogamous group is one inside of which intermarriage is forbidden and which, consequently, requires at least another exogamous group with whom it may exchange its sons and/or daughters for marriage purposes. Among ourselves, there are as many exogamous groups as restricted families, that is an extremely high number, and it is this high number which allows us to rely on probability. In primitive societies, however, the figure is usually much smaller, on the one hand because the group itself is a small one, and on the other hand because the familial ties go much further than it is the case among us.

Our first hypothesis will be the simpler one: that of unilineal descent and of two exogamous groups, A and B. Then, the only solution will be that men of A marry women of B, and men of B marry women of A. A typical case will be that of two men, respectively A and B, exchanging their sisters so that each one may get a wife. The reader has just to take a pencil and a sheet of paper to build up the theoretical genealogy which will be the outcome of such a set-up. Whatever the rule of descent, siblings and parallel-cousins will always fall in the same category, while cross-cousins of whatever kind will fall in opposite categories. Therefore, only cross-cousins (if we are playing the game with 2 to 4 groups) or children of cross-cousins (if we are playing with 8 groups, for 6 provide an intermediary case) will meet the initial rule that spouses should belong to opposite groups.

So far, we have considered groups tied up in pairs: 2, 4, 6, 8. They can only come in even numbers. What, now, if the society is made up of an odd number of exchanging groups? With the preceding rule, there will be a group which will remain alone by itself, without a partner with whom to set up an exchange relationship. Hence, the need for additional rules which can be of use whatever the number of elements, either even or odd.

There are two ways to meet the difficulty. Exchange can either remain simultaneous and become indirect, or remain direct at the expense of becoming consecutive. The first type will be when group A gives its daughters as wives to group B, B to C, C to D, D to n · · · and finally n to A. When the cycle is completed, every group has given a woman and has received one, though it has not given to the same group as that from which it has received. In that case, pencil and paper will show that parallel-cousins always fall in one's own group, same as brothers and sisters, and cannot consequently be married according to rule. As to cross-cousins, a new distinction will appear: the female cross-cousin on the mother's side (i.e. the mother's brother's daughter) will always fall in the marriageable group (A to B, B to C, et cetera) while that on the father's side (father's sister's daughter) will fall in the opposite group (that is, the one to which my group gives wives, but from which it does not receive any: B to A, C to B, etc.).

The alternative would be to keep the exchange direct, though in consecutive generations: for instance, A receives a wife from B, and returns to A the daughter born from that marriage to become the spouse of a man A of the following generation. If we keep our groups arranged in a series: A, B, C, D, n · · · , the general set-up will be, then, that any group, let us say C, at one generation gives to D and receives from B; at the following generation, C repays B and gets its own return from D, and so on indefinitely. Here again the patient reader will find out that cross-cousins are being distinguished in two categories, but this time in a reverse way: for a man, the correct mate will always be the father's sister's daughter, the mother's brother's daughter being always in the 'wrong' category.

These are the simplest cases. All over the world there are still kinship systems and marriage rules for which no satisfactory interpretation has as yet been brought forward; such are the Ambrym system in the New Hebrides, the Murngin of northwestern Australia, and the whole North American complex known as the Crow-Omaha kinship system. It is fairly certain that to explain these and other sets of rules, however, one will have to proceed as we have shown here, namely to interpret kinship systems and marriage rules as embodying the rule of that very special kind of game which consists, for consanguineous groups of men, in exchanging women among themselves, that is building up new families with the pieces of earlier ones, which should be shattered for that purpose.

The female reader, who may be shocked to see womankind treated as a commodity submitted to transactions between male operators, can easily find comfort in the assurance that the rules of the game would remain unchanged should it be decided to consider the men as being exchanged by women's groups. As a matter of fact, some very few societies, of a highly developed matrilineal type, have to a limited extent attempted to express things that way. And both sexes can be comforted from a still different (but in that case slightly more complicated) formulation of the game, whereby it would be said that consanguineous groups consisting of both men and women are engaged in exchanging together bonds of relationships.

The important conclusion to be kept in mind is that the restricted family can neither be said to be the element of the social group, nor can it be claimed to result from it. Rather, the social group can only become established in contradistinction, and to some extent in compliance, with the family, since in order to maintain the society through time, women should procreate children, benefit from male protection while they are engaged in confinement and nursing, and, since precise sets of rules are needed, to perpetuate throughout the generations the basic pattern of the social fabric. However, the primary social concern regarding the family is not to protect or enhance it: it is rather an attitude of diffidence, a denial of its right to exist either in isolation or permanently; restricted families are only permitted to live for a limited period of time, either long or short according to case, but under the strict condition that their component parts be ceaselessly displaced, loaned, borrowed, given away, or returned, so that new restricted families may be endlessly created or made to vanish. Thus, the relation between the social group as a whole and the restricted families which seem to constitute it is not a static one, like that of a wall to the bricks it is built with. It is rather a dynamic process of tension and opposition with an equilibrium point extremely difficult to find, its exact position being submitted to endless variations from time to time and from society to society. But the word of the Scriptures: 'You will leave your father and mother' provides the iron rule for the establishment and functioning of any society.

Society belongs to the realm of culture while the family is the emanation, on the social level, of those natural requirements without which there could be no society, and indeed no mankind. As a philosopher of the sixteenth century has said, man can only overcome nature by complying with its laws. Therefore, society has to give the family some amount of recognition. And it is not so surprising that, as geographers have also noticed with respect to the use of natural land resources, the greatest amount of compliance with the natural laws is likely to be found at both extremes of the cultural scale: among the simpler peoples as well as among the more highly civilized. Indeed, the first ones are not in a position to afford paying the price of too great a departure, while the second have already suffered from enough mistakes to understand that compliance is the best policy. This explains why, as we have already noticed, the small, relatively stable, monogamic restricted family seems to be given greater recognition, both among the more primitive peoples and in modern societies, than in what may be called (for the sake of the argument), the intermediate levels. However, this is nothing more than a slight shift of the equilibrium point between nature and culture, and does not affect the general picture given in this chapter. When one travels slowly and with great effort, halts should be long and frequent. And when one is given the possibility to travel often and fast, he or she should also, though for different reasons, expect to stop and rest frequently. The more roads there are, the more crossings there are likely to be. Social life imposes on the consanguineous stocks of mankind an incessant traveling back and forth, and family life is little else than the expression of the need to slacken the pace at the crossroads and to take a chance to rest. But the orders are to keep on marching. And society can no more be said to consist of families than a journey is made up of the stopovers which break it down into discontinuous stages. They are at the same time its condition and its negation.

DAVID G. MANDELBAUM

XIII

Social Groupings

THERE ARE MANY WAYS in which people get themselves organized to live and work together. Every one of us belongs to a number of different social groups. Each group consists of a set of people who co-operate for some purpose. Sometimes the membership of the group is small and its purpose is very specific, as in the case of a baseball club or the workers in the corner market. Sometimes the membership of the group is very large and its purpose more general, as in the case of a large school or the national government.

For the most part, the groups to which a person belongs were there before he participated in them and will continue to exist after he leaves them. These established units of society are, in a way, like a college football team; individual players join the squad and then leave it, but the team goes on.

The nature of the groups to which an individual will normally belong varies among the different peoples of the world. An Australian tribesman, one of the aboriginal inhabitants of that island-continent, is concerned about the grouping and subgrouping of the fellow tribesmen he considers to be his relatives. His own place in these intricate groups of relatives determines whom he can marry and what ceremonies he may perform. A villager in south India is aware, from his childhood days, of his membership in a group called a caste. His hereditary membership in that group not only determines whom he may marry, but also regulates such diverse matters as the trade or profession he may follow, the kinds of food he may take, and in whose company he may eat.

Everyone Belongs to a Family and to a Community

Whatever diversity there may be among social groupings the world over, there are at least two types which are found in every human society. The family is one of them, as has been noted in the preceding chapter. In every land, among every people, the child is ordinarily raised and nurtured within a family. And the family is the first social group that the child comes to know.

The other type of group which is universal to humanity—and frequently enough the second group which the child begins to recognize—is the local community. Just as no person normally lives all his life alone, devoid of any family, so does no family normally live entirely alone, apart from any local group. All of us, you and I and the Australian tribesman and the villager of India, have neighbors.

We behave toward these neighbors according to the rules and notions of proper neighborly behavior of our respective societies. And our neighbors have similar, reciprocal behavior toward us. These rules and notions, patterns of behavior they may be called, are almost never consciously recognized or written out. It is only the anthropologist and other students of society who attempt to analyze and catalogue the patterns of local group behavior. Nevertheless, the patterns are fixed and effective, even though they are not neatly listed in a rule book. In parts of Australia, each Bushman is expected to, and does, defend the hunting territory he shares with his neighbors against any trespassers who do not belong to his local group. In many sections of India, a villager is obligated to help his neighbors on the occasions when offerings are made to the local deity and when celebrations are staged in its honor. In India, as indeed is true in the farming communities of western countries, a villager often helps his neighbors at harvest time and in turn receives help from them in ways which are regularly repeated every year.

Horde, Village, and Neighborhood

The local group is known by various names. It is called a *horde* in the descriptions of the social organization of the Australian tribesmen. The term *band* is frequently used to denote the local group, especially in books about American Indians. Among the old civilizations of Europe and the Orient, the local community is best known as the *village*. In our own country, we often speak of the local community as a *neighborhood.*

The essential idea, no matter which particular term is used, is that of a group of people, all of whom live within a limited area and co-operate to some extent. The area may be a valley or the shores of a lake or a city block, but the families within the area usually know each other, or at least recognize enough common interests so that they can act together in certain ways to meet mutual problems. This mutual action to meet common problems accomplishes more than just the attainment of some specific goals. It renews the solidarity of the people of the group, preparing them for more action together. Because in acting together they feel rewarded for so doing, they are ready and willing to work together in the future.

Each family within the local group will have some different customs from those of its neighbors, but all will have certain common ways, especially in relation to each other. Similarly in a set of local groups, any one group will have some peculiarities of its own but all in the set will act alike in some important ways, particularly in those ways which govern the relations among the local groups. The size of the local group and the extent of the area it occupies depend in large part on how the community makes its living. A band of Plains Cree Indians in western Canada needed a large territory in which to pursue the migratory buffalo. A village in the more fertile tracts of India will need only a few square miles in which to grow enough rice to support its population.

How New Communities Are Founded

New local groups usually come into being when some families feel that they can make a better living by moving to some richer and more promising territory. But this is not the only way in which new communities may arise. When I lived among the Plains Cree I found that one of the eight bands of the tribe, the group called the 'Parklands People,' had had a curious history. Its story began in 1790 when one George Sutherland arrived in Saskatchewan from Scotland as a trader in the employ of the Hudson's Bay Company. He was evidently a restless kind of person who did not take kindly to the restricted life of a storekeeper. So he took a Cree wife and left the Hudson's Bay Company to live on the prairie in the native style. Subsequently he took two more Indian wives and begot twenty-seven children who grew to adulthood. All the children married with the neighboring Cree but always returned to live with the old man. So George Sutherland came to be the first chief of a band which he had himself engendered and the band became one of the recognized communities of the tribe.

Another way in which new communities may be founded stems from the factions within a local group. It is extremely common to find two factions within a local group in any society. The differences of opinion between the factions may be centered on religious matters or political ideas or claims to land and property. In any one culture, the causes of these quarrels and the means of settling them tend to be alike in all the local groups. Usually these arguments do not prevent the families of each faction from co-operating in matters of general community concern. But occasionally the rifts become so bitter that one faction may just up and leave the local area to settle in another place.

One such incident occurred not many years ago in a village of the Hopi Indians, the agricultural tribe of Arizona which is widely known for its Snake Dance ceremony. For many years there had been antagonism in the village between the faction which believed in taking over a few of the ways of the white man, especially in the matter of sending the village children to the government school, and the more conservative faction which wanted to have nothing whatever to do with the whites or any of their ways. At last matters came to a head and it was decided to settle the argument once and for all. The men of the two factions met in a field facing each other. A line was drawn at each end of the field and the two sides began pushing, one against the other. After much heaving and straining, the conservative side slowly began to give ground, and with a final shove the pro-school side pushed them back across the line. That was the Hopi way of settling a dispute that had become too bitter to be borne any longer. The losing side packed up and went off to found a new village where they still live.

All these reasons for the founding of new local communities have been at the root of great historic movements in the past and are still operating today. In the history of the United States, religious reasons led to the founding of the Pilgrim communities in New England; later, political reasons led some Tory groups to move to Canada after the Revolutionary War and to establish new settlements there; still later, economic motives made for the westward migration and the founding of new communities in the western states; more recently, the operation of wartime industries, such as the atomic energy establishments, have attracted thousands of workers to sites where new communities have come into being.

Home Is Where Your Neighbors Live

The local group is so important to men the world over not only because it marks off the area within which the family lives and works, but because it is home for every one of its members. Within the territory of his local community a person knows the lay of the land, he knows the hills and the paths, he is familiar with the plants and animals and can recognize which are useful and which are dangerous. In urban life, the member of the local group knows the streets and stores of his home neighborhood and is familiar with the good places and with those that are to be avoided. Moreover, he knows the people and knows their ways. In his relations with neighbors whom he does not like, he knows in what manner they are apt to be disagreeable. His friends are there and he knows their gestures and speech; in central Australia, he can even recognize their footprints. It is there that he is usually most comfortable, most secure. There he is at home.

This feeling is shared by tribes which have been called wild savages. Even the people with the simplest and crudest ways of life do not wander aimlessly through the forest or across the plain. The Australian tribesmen have as little in the way of tools and possessions as any primitive folk. Yet they have strong and clear notions about the territory of a local group and the families which rightfully belong to it. For the Australian natives, as for most of humanity, the local community contains practically all of his society and his culture. Most of the people he knows and cherishes, all the customs, beliefs, and manners which he follows, exist within his local community.

As a matter of fact, it is only in the great new cities of our civilization that the local group has lost some of its importance. A city dweller may not know who lives in the next house or apartment and so can have little feeling for, or participation in, a neighborhood. Perhaps for that very reason there are many efforts, in the form of community centers, local clubs, regional associations, to re-establish the friendly neighborly spirit that was lost in the course of the swift growth of a large city. Many people who now live in cities grew up in congenial, long established neighborhoods, and they miss the loyalties of the local group. Often they transfer their loyalty to the next larger group, the city itself. And they tend to be great boosters for the city and fanatically devoted to such a symbol of the city as, for example, a baseball team like the Brooklyn Dodgers.

RELATIVES OF THE CLAN

In many parts of the world there is yet another way in which people group themselves. A person will consider himself related by bonds of kinship to certain people within the local group and often to certain people in other local communities as well. All the individuals with whom he has this special relationship form his clan.

Some of these individuals are really his blood relatives whom we would call by such terms as uncle and cousin. Others have no kinship that would be considered close in our society except that they belong to a clan of the same name and so must treat each other as though they all actually were blood relatives. It is as though all the people with the same last name in our society, say MacDonald, considered themselves to be relatives, treated each other as relatives, and were considered by their fellow citizens to be a distinct group of relatives.

Indeed it was not so many centuries ago that the MacDonalds did form a clan in Scotland. And the men of the clan MacDonald worked together and fought together. The Scottish clans were defeated in 1746 and their clan solidarity was dispersed forever. But on that battlefield is the last evidence of the old clan unity. The slain Scottish soldiers were not placed in individual graves; all the dead of one clan were buried in a common grave and on the tombstones which now mark each place can still be read 'the MacDonalds,' 'the Mackintoshes,' and so on down the roster of Scottish clans whose members and whose very existence as functioning social units were wiped out on that field. For after that day in 1746 the clans were not even permitted the symbols of clan membership, such as the distinctive kilts. It was not until later, when the unity and the pride of each clan had been thoroughly broken, that the wearing of the MacDonald tartan and the piping of clan tunes were again allowed. That clan pride had something to do with the defeat, because the MacDonalds had been placed to the left of the line of battle, not in the place of honor at the right which they believed was their due. And so historians tell us that the clan MacDonald did not fight as well that day as they might have done if they had not been angry about this affront to the honor of their group.

CLAN MEMBERSHIP THROUGH THE FATHER . . . AND THROUGH THE MOTHER

The Scottish clans traced descent through the father, and so were of the type called patrilineal clans. That is, all the children of the family, both boys and girls, were members of the MacDonald clan if their father was a MacDonald. If a MacDonald girl married a man of the clan Gordon, she still was accounted a MacDonald, although her children were Gordons and stood by the Gordons in time of clan need.

In some areas, the clans are matrilineal, and the children of a family belong only to the clan of their mother. That is the case in the former native state of Travancore at the southernmost tip of India. The ruler of the state, the Maharaja, must come from the royal clan. Here, as among every people who have clans, a man must not marry a woman of his own clan. Hence the Maharaja's wife is not of the royal clan and his children, who belong to the clan of their mother, are therefore not of the royal lineage. When a Maharaja dies, not his own son, but his sister's son—who does belong to the royal clan—succeeds to the throne.

CLAN FUNCTIONS: SOCIAL INSURANCE AND REGULATION OF MARRIAGE

The clan, whether matrilineal or patrilineal, is in many ways simply an expansion of the family. It frequently happens that all clan members who are about the same age call each other brother and sister. And a fellow clansman of one's father's age, in a patrilineal clan society, will often be called 'father'; a clanswoman of that generation will be called by the term for father's sister. Of course, a person always knows the difference between his real brother and a clan-mate whom he calls 'brother.' But he will share with the clan-mate something of the pattern of mutual helpfulness that he has with his real brother. Thus the individual is strengthened by his relationship with a group much larger than the immediate family.

Just as a person's family helps him and stands by him in case of need, so does his clan support him when he needs its aid. This support may range from helping him collect the price of a bride to protecting his life should he incur the wrath of other clansmen bent on blood-vengeance. This very collective responsibility of the clan for the deeds and demeanor of its individual members makes it a strong force for social order. Since all the clansmen know that they will bear a share of the trouble if one of their clan-mates goes astray, they try to see to it that a potentially erring member is kept within socially approved limits.

Both the clan and the family are important in regulating the choice of a partner in marriage. Apart from a very few, highly exceptional instances, marriage within the family, of brother and sister, is everywhere prohibited and regarded as incest. Similarly, marriage within the clan is prohibited. As we have noted in regard to the marriage of the Maharaja of Travancore, a man can never marry a woman of his own clan. This clan exogamy, as the rule of marrying outside the clan is called, occurs wherever there are clan groupings.

There is this important difference between the functioning of a family and that of a clan. In every form of the family, the relationship of the children to both the father and the mother is recognized. But a clan stresses the relationships through one side of the family only. In a matrilineal clan, only your mother's kinsmen and her mother's kinsmen are considered close relatives, while your father's uncles and cousins may hardly be considered as related to you at all. In one matrilineal society, among those Nayar of south India who still carry on the traditional ways, the matrilineal principle is developed to such a degree that the father comes to the house of his wife and his children only as a visitor; his real home and his place is with the household of his mother and her brothers. However, the bonds of the family, the emotional ties among father and mother and children, are universally present, and so the emotional and social relationship between father and children are not completely obliterated even by extreme emphasis of the mother's kin.

PUBLIC SERVICE BY THE CLAN

Another difference between the family and the clan is that the simple family of parents and children has a relatively short duration in time. When the children grow up, they may found families of their own and the former family group breaks up. The clan is more stable through the passage of years. It is a corporation which outlasts any of the individuals in it. True, a clan may die out, or may amalgamate with other clans, or may split into several different clans, but generally a clan exists through many generations. For that reason, it is often the responsibility of the clan to perform certain services for the public good, services which the clan can always perform since it is a social unit which continues to exist beyond the lifetime of any individual in it.

One such function of a clan has already been mentioned, that of providing the chiefs of a state, as has been the case in Travancore. Among the Hopi Indians, certain clans provide priests for the performance of religious ceremonies. Among some of the Australian tribes, each clan is responsible for the religious propitiation of an animal or plant which is useful to the tribe. The members of the Kangaroo clan, for example, must perform the ceremonies which are believed to be necssary for the continued appearance of kangaroo in the tribal territory. Usually clan members may not eat the animal with which they have a special relationship. So the Kangaroo clan gets no economic benefit from performing the rituals, but assures the supply of that animal for the rest of the tribe.

TOTEMISM AND SOME TECHNICAL TERMS

This special relationship between a clan and some animal or object, is known as *totemism*. Sometimes, as in Australia, clan totemism is important in many aspects of the tribal culture. In other cases, clan totemism amounts to no more than the animal name by which a clan is known. It must be noted that clans always have distinctive names; these are labels by which all the members of a clan can be referred to and by which co-membership can easily be recognized. Frequently the members of a clan will wear a special symbol or have similar dress as was true of the Scottish clans.

In some societies, two or more clans may be grouped together in a section which is technically known as a *phratry*. The members of each clan in the phratry consider themselves more closely related to the other clans in their phratry than to the rest of the clans in the tribe. Where the whole tribe is divided into two divisions, whether matrilineal or patrilineal, each division is called, in anthropological terminology, a *moiety*. A few more technical terms may be noted for those who will want to read further on the subject of social organization. The term *sib* is used in the same sense as we have used the more popular term, clan. A patrilineal clan may be referred to as a *gens* or a *father-sib*. A matrilineal clan is also known as a *mother-sib*, or simply as a clan.

STRENGTH AND IMPORTANCE OF THE CLAN

Clans are found at various levels of human life, from relatively crude hunting and gathering cultures, such as those of the Australian tribes, to high civilizations of ancient tradition, such as those of India and China. Conversely, peoples who do not have clans are found at all social and economic levels, from the hunting Eskimo to ourselves.

Generally the clan is most important in those societies where the clan

members live together in the same local community. When I first visited
the Kota of South India, I noticed that each tribal village was arranged
in three rows of houses, or streets. The houses of each street were inhabited by men of a single patrilineal clan. When the girls of a clan
grow up, they marry and move to another village or to another street
in the same village. But the men of the clan stay together and live together all their lives and their clan solidarity is strong. The sense of
unity and the mutual co-operation of any social group, whether clan,
club, or army company, is strengthened by common residence. If its
members live together, they inevitably come to know each other better,
and come to rely on each other more than if the group is scattered and
its members rarely meet.

This consideration has much to do with the weakening of clans in
many parts of the world. When people stay put for most of their lives,
co-operation within a clan is feasible and advantageous. Even in the
great populations of north China, clans have been, until recently, live
social groupings. Although a clan might have hundreds of thousands of
members, it did have its home territory where a great many clansmen
lived together, it had its ancestral temple, and there were lands owned as
clan property. The poorer members were helped by funds donated by
the richer families. To this day, no intermarriage is permitted within
the clan. In India, also, the clan remains effective as a means of regulating marriages.

However, when economic and social conditions change rapidly, and
when there is much shifting of population, clan members become scattered, they lose touch with each other, and forget their consciousness
of clan. Clan functions are apt to be taken over by other social groupings. In the villages of India and China, where conditions of life have
remained fairly stable, the clan still functions, at least in regulating marriages. But among the people of the large cities in both countries, the
function of the clans and their very memory is fast passing away.

What Makes a Tribe

The families of a local community, both in societies that have clans
and in those that do not, almost always have a sense of belonging to a
social unit larger than the local group, one that includes a number of
different communities. Among most primitive people, this larger unit of
society is the tribe.

The communities that make up a tribe usually occupy the same general territory, commonly speak the same language, and follow the same way of life. But neither mutual territory, common language, nor similar culture can alone account for the existence of any tribe. Often enough two primitive groups have occupied adjoining country and have been mortal enemies. Some peoples who speak the same language consider themselves to belong to utterly different social groups. In fact, sharing the same manners and customs may only increase the frequency of disagreements between two tribes.

The important basis for the existence of a tribe is not any one of those factors, but the combination of them that gives every person in the tribe a feeling of belonging with the other men and women of the tribe. The real bonds which hold any group together, whether it be tribe, clan, or state, are the attitudes which the individuals in that group have toward each other, and the behavior patterns of reciprocal help, of co-operation, which are the tangible demonstrations of those attitudes. Formal patterns of organization, like tribal councils or annual conventions, contribute much to the feeling of unity and to the united action of a group, but they are not absolutely essential for its functioning.

As the children of the tribe grow up, they learn the formal patterns of organization—how to take part in a tribal council—and the informal ways of co-operating with fellow tribesmen—how to recognize them, what to expect of and from them, when to give them hospitality and support. Thus the tribe perpetuates itself from generation to generation. In modern times, many tribes have been shattered and scattered because alien peoples and cultures disrupted the tribal way of life. In much of Africa, this has been so recent and so unnerving a process that the very term 'detribalized' native has come to mean a person who represents great social and personal problems. He has lost the traditional standards by which his forefathers guided their lives and he has not been able to adopt other patterns adequate for the new conditions in which he must live. In the face of the disrupting influences, many tribesmen, in various continents and conditions of life, try to keep their tribal identity and to build a new way of existence which will preserve something of their traditional tribal identity.

THE MEANING OF TRIBAL MEMBERSHIP AMONG THE PLAINS CREE

The tribal grouping of the Plains Cree Indians of western Canada will illustrate these ideas about the nature of a tribe. The eight bands of the Plains Cree, as they existed just before the buffalo vanished from the Canadian prairies, ranged over a vast territory that was some six hundred miles from one end to the other, from the Qu'Appelle valley near the present Manitoba-Saskatchewan line to the region where Edmonton now stands. Several of the bands would come together once a year to participate in the Sun Dance, the great ceremonial event of this and of other Plains tribes. But there was never any occasion on which all of the bands met together. And there was no tribal council or any meeting of representatives from all the sections of the tribe.

Nonetheless there never was any doubt as to who was a member of the tribe and who was not. When a young man of the tribe reached an age when he began to feel restless and wanted to see a bit of the world beyond the terrain of his own band, he would commonly go to visit the other Plains Cree bands. If he was from one of the easternmost communities, he would travel westward, staying a while with one encampment of the tribe and then going on to another, until he reached the westernmost bands, those whose territory adjoined the habitat of the Blackfoot Indians, the constant enemies of the Plains Cree.

As he came into a new band encampment, he would seek out those who were related to his family (the Plains Cree did not have clans) or were relatives of relatives of his. Some kinship connection could always be found because there was frequent intermarriage among the various bands. In one of the tipis of his relatives he would first be fed, and then he would be asked to tell the news and gossip of his own community.

The young man might be a total stranger to the band he was visiting, in that no one there had ever seen him before or perhaps had ever heard of him, but he was never a stranger socially. He always could be placed as a member of a group that was known to the host, and as such, he was accorded the same hospitality that his host would receive were he visiting a family in the young man's community. Gossip about people known to both the host and the visitor always helped establish the social relationship between the two on a firm footing. Though gossip may sometimes seem to be mean and unnecessary, it is, in all human societies, one of the best ways of reaffirming friendly relations—between the gossipers at least.

It not infrequently happened that the young man would take a fancy to one of the girls of the community he was visiting, and when he returned to the encampment of his parents, he would come with a bride. Plains Cree parents generally preferred that their sons marry girls from their own community, girls whom they knew and whose family they knew. But the young men themselves often found the girls of distant bands of the tribe more attractive than the girls they had seen and known since childhood. This, of course, is not a kind of happening restricted to the Plains Cree; among the young men of any people, the young women of other communities tend to seem more glamorous than those from the home group.

Occasionally visitors from other tribes would come to an encampment, usually for purposes of trade. But there was a great difference between the attitude toward a fellow tribesman, even if he were a young fellow whose name was unknown, and the attitude toward a familiar and respected man from another tribe. Both would be given food and shelter, but there could not be the intimacy and the exchange of greetings and gossip with a member of another tribe that there was with a fellow tribesman. This was true even with the northern neighbors of the tribe, the Wood Cree, who spoke the same language, and from whom the Plains Cree had descended. But the Wood Cree lived in the forests, they were not buffalo hunters and warriors, and their whole way of life and their world view was different from that of the Plains Cree. Despite the bond of language the disparities of culture were so great that the Plains Cree did not like to have much to do with the forest dwellers.

With the tribe's southern neighbors, the Assiniboine, there were more close and cordial relations, even though the two languages were completely different. There was even some intermarriage between Plains Cree and Assiniboine. But even the best known Assiniboine was felt to be more of a stranger, in some ways, than a fresh young tribesman newly arrived from a distant band. There was always something of an unknown quantity about a person from another tribe, while one knew pretty much what to expect of a fellow tribesman, just as one knew what to expect of one's neighbor in the band.

Blackfoot Indians sometimes came on trading missions, but their visits had to be well prepared and announced, because they came much more often to raid the encampments and steal the horses. A party of Blackfoot seen lurking about the camp would be liable to be shot on sight. The Plains Cree did their share of raiding in return, usually in small war parties recruited within a single band. If a young man from another band should be visiting at the time a raiding party was setting out, he would be quite likely to join the raiders and attempt to make a name for himself. Such mutual participation in arms would further strengthen the bonds of tribal unity among the bands of the tribe.

Indeed the main occasion on which the members of several, perhaps all, of the bands of the tribe would deliberately come together for a common purpose, was related to warfare. Sometimes when a dearly loved son or daughter had been killed in an enemy raid, the parents would make the circuit of the various bands, bewailing their child and asking the warriors to join a vengeance party. They usually would have no trouble in recruiting young men from every band they visited, and when the party was complete, it would penetrate enemy territory until an encampment of the enemy tribe was found and wiped out.

Tribal War and Peace

It is in making war that a tribe most commonly functions as a unified social group. Because the tribesmen feel themselves to be related, they react to an attack against one part of the tribe as though it were an attack on all, and they quickly rally to concerted defense and counter-attack. Moreover, outsiders are usually not considered to be human beings in the same sense that fellow tribesmen are human. Hence it is no crime or sin to treat outsiders as hunted animals. A tribesman who is always kind and considerate toward persons in his own group, can therefore be completely cruel and callous when dealing with those outside his tribe. There is a feeling, even among the most advanced nations, that the consideration and proper behavior shown toward a person of one's own kind need not be used when dealing with a person of another race, or belief, or country. The Plains Cree, like most tribesmen of the primitive world, felt that theirs was the only way of life fit for real men, that the manners and customs of other people were somehow degraded just because they were different. This tribal attitude, too, is not unknown among the citizens of modern states.

Making peace and keeping the peace are much more difficult for a tribe to accomplish than is making war. Matters of social control, of education, of the punishment of transgressions are usually carried out by the family and the local community in a tribal society. It often happened in the history of the Plains Cree that a famous and respected Plains Cree chief would agree to a peace, smoke the pipe of peace, and even while he was so doing, a party of warriors from one of the bands of his tribe would be out raiding an encampment of the other group. Tribes usually have only meager means of preventing the individuals of the separate bands from behaving in this fashion.

FROM TRIBE TO STATE

The state is the grouping which does have the means of controlling such behavior. Basically a state consists of a set of local communities which are so organized that certain men of the group have the power to act for all in making the people of the several communities do certain things and seeing to it that they refrain from doing other things. Among all the communities of a state there is general agreement as to who shall act for them and according to what patterns such action should be taken. It must be noted that this agreement does not always spring up voluntarily, because many of the states that have grown to be great arose when a tribe went on a military rampage, subdued other peoples, and kept them in subjugation for long periods. In that case, the agreement among the communities of the subjugated people was an enforced agreement, just as the Anglo-Saxon groups agreed to pay tribute and to be ruled by the Norman overlords after the Norman conquest of Britain.

A good many tribal societies show the beginnings of the functions of a state. Among the Plains Cree, for example, each band had a kind of club to which most of the warriors belonged. This club, though it is usually called the Warrior Society, did no military duties. Its main task was to regulate the buffalo hunt.

When the tribesmen were gathered in a large encampment, individual hunting could not be tolerated because all the game would be driven away from the vicinity in a short time, and the encampment then would have to break up. So when a buffalo herd was sighted, the Warrior Society members stood guard to see that no one disturbed the buffalo before proper preparations had been made. When all the hunters were ready, a signal was given and the tribesmen charged into the herd.

If any man tried to make a kill before that signal was given, or scared off the herd because he could not control his horse, the Warriors immediately rode up to that man's tipi. They slashed it to ribbons, broke his bows and guns, destroyed all that he possessed, as punishment for his offense. Ordinarily a man's relatives would immediately come to his support to prevent such harm from befalling him. But in this case, no one would try to stop the Warriors; one of the Society members who was busily tearing up the guilty man's blankets might be his own brother.

In this latter instance the obligations of kinship that the Warrior would normally act upon, were subordinated to his obligations to all the people of the encampment. In like manner, a Warrior carried out his obligations to the group as a whole, rather than to the narrow circle of his own kin, when the family of a murdered man was seeking blood vengeance. Then a Warrior related to that family, instead of joining them in the hunt for the murderer, would forcibly take them into a meeting with the relatives of the murderer. He would help restrain them from violence until some payment was arranged which would settle the feud. Here again, the welfare of the whole community was the guide to a Warrior's action, rather than the usual demands of kinship.

But among the Plains Cree, as in other tribal societies, the occasions on which certain men had the right and the duty to act for the several communities were few and infrequent. Those few occasions did form the beginnings of true government but never went beyond these mere beginnings. The obligations to one's relatives, and the action patterns based on blood relationships were much more important than any obligation to a set of local groups, from which develop the patterns essential to the existence of a state.

CONFEDERATION AND CONQUEST IN THE MAKING OF A STATE

There have been times when a number of tribes would get together to fight off a common enemy and, in order to do so effectively, would adopt patterns of mutual aid and follow leaders who would act in the interests of the whole confederation of tribes. The League of the Iroquois, in what is now upstate New York, was an example of such a confederation which developed in the direction of becoming a state. These confederations worked very well as long as the common danger was great. But as soon as the common enemy was defeated, each tribe and the local communities within a tribe would forget about co-operating and drift back to the condition in which each local group followed its own sweet way without consideration of the interests of the former confederation as a whole.

States more often have come into being through conquest rather than through confederation. The members of a conquering tribe sometimes discover that they can get a good steady income from keeping the conquered people under their rule, that it is more profitable to turn a beaten enemy into a subject than into a corpse. Then the victorious group has to develop some kind of system whereby certain of the tribesmen have the job of acting for all of the overlords in keeping the subjects subdued and the income from them flowing to the victorious tribesmen. This process has frequently led to the rise of a new state.

When tribesmen overrun an established state, they usually take over much of the established system of government. This happened when the Mongol tribes conquered the Chinese kingdoms and when the Vandals and other tribes defeated Rome. But in the modern world, subject peoples have a way of remembering their old independence and of overthrowing the conquerors sooner or later. Hence some nations have pretty much given up the idea of keeping other nations permanently under their rule. Defeated peoples are dealt with so that they supposedly will never be a threat to the victors again, and independent government, real or presumed, is returned to a conquered nation.

FROM NATION TO CONFEDERATION OF NATIONS

The very term nation implies a group of people who not only are organized into a state, but also have a common way of life. Thus the French state includes under its authority such diverse peoples as North African Arabs and the folk of tropical Madagascar. But when we speak of the French nation we mean those peoples mainly of France proper who (despite all political differences) have certain manners and customs and linguistic habits in common.

Those men who are now trying to set up an effective confederation of nations are faced with problems that were familiar to those who tried to bring about a permanent confederation of tribes. After the common danger is over, each group tends to go its own way and to place its own interests above the mutual welfare of the whole set of communities. Because a lasting confederation of nations has never been set up effectively before, the task is difficult. But it is not at all impossible. In fact, the development of human social organization toward a real confederation of nations promises to be faster and possibly smoother than the earlier development from tribe to state.

AGE GROUPS

Local community, tribe, state—all are groupings which arise from the universal situation that people who live in the same locality have similar interests and problems. There are also other types of social groups based on mutual interests and problems. Among the most common of such types are those based on age.

Persons of the same age, in any community, tend to congregate and co-operate. In some societies, groupings according to age are very important. Among the Masai tribe of east Africa, for example, there is an initiation ceremony held once every four years for the boys who have reached puberty since the previous ceremony was given. In the course of the ceremony the boys are circumcised and thereafter may live in the bachelors' dormitory and assume the duties and privileges of a warrior. Each initiation class becomes an age-class, and the youths of the age-class live together in the same dormitory, earn a distinctive name for their class, and get a distinctive design for their shields.

The exact groupings according to age vary among different peoples, but all societies recognize at least three divisions in the life of the individual as a basis for social organization. The distinctions always made are: children, adults, and aged. Though children often have their own social groupings, such as the Cub Scouts in our society, these units are not usually of any great influence on the community as a whole.

However, children may occupy a very important place in a society. Dr. Ralph Linton tells the story of visiting the chief of a tribe on one of the Marquesan islands in the South Seas. The chief's wife was of royal blood and so the chief's son was even more royal than his father. Since the son, then aged nine, was so full of the supernatural power called *mana* because of his extremely royal blood, any attempt to discipline him would have been sacrilege. The boy had had an argument with his father a few days before Dr. Linton's visit, and had made the house taboo for the others by naming it after his own head. So the family had to move out and could not use the house again until the boy lifted the taboo. The nine-year-old was getting along very well because he could use the house himself and could eat anywhere in the village. He was enjoying the situation thoroughly.

RITES OF PASSAGE

The passage of an individual from the social status of a child to that of an adult does not always coincide with his physical maturation. Thus a person is legally a child in our society for a number of years after he has become an adult physically. Among many primitive peoples, as among the Masai, an individual's transfer from childhood to adulthood is marked by the celebration of a ceremony. Such ceremonies, and others which similarly mark a person's change of status, are called rites of passage. These rites of passage occur not only in relation to entering adulthood, but also in relation to birth, marriage, and death. Our own society observes a number of such rites of passage, baptisms, weddings, and, among the wealthier classes, coming-out parties for debutantes.

The passage of an individual from the adult group to that of the aged is hardly ever marked by one of the rites of passage. This is partly because it is difficult to tell just when a man enters old age, and even more because men rarely like to think of themselves as old. It is true that in many regions, the aged are given a great deal of respect and are highly honored. This was true in China; among some Australian tribes, the old men were so important that these societies are characterized by the term *gerontocracy*, the rule of the aged. This is in marked contrast with the situation in our culture, especially for women. In certain parts of our society, it is very difficult for a woman to admit that she is more than relatively few years beyond puberty. At least, it is difficult for her to do so until she is far enough beyond puberty to be a grandmother.

STATUS AND ROLE

The importance of social status becomes especially apparent when we see a person changing from one status position to another. In the everyday behavior of people, status is no less important. Within every social group, from the smallest to the largest, there are different status positions. The individuals do not have the same parts to play in the functioning of the group; they perform and are expected to perform different parts. Each status position requires the individual who holds it to perform certain obligations in respect to others in the group and it entitles him to receive certain rights from the others.

Thus in a family of our society, or of any society, there are such status positions as husband, wife, father, mother, daughter, brother, sister. The husband and father in your family is the same person, but he has different rights and obligations when he is acting in the status of *father* in regard to his children than when he is acting as *husband* in regard to—perhaps it is better put, in respect to—his wife. In the family in which he was born (his family of 'orientation') he had other status positions, that of son and perhaps that of brother. These required still different kinds of behavior than the kinds he is expected to follow in his statuses of husband and father in his later family (of 'procreation').

In a large, highly formalized social organization such as an army, the rights and obligations of each status position are carefully spelled out in numbered paragraphs. The requirements of the status of private or colonel are defined in the manuals and regulations. Even more, the specific rights and duties of such a particular status as captain of the

chemical warfare company in an armored division are meticulously detailed in the army's regulations.

In such large formal establishments, there are usually informal status
positions as well, which are not part of the official table of organization.
Usually a soldier is not only a member of his platoon but he is also one of
an informal group of buddies (a 'primary group') with whom he spends
his leisure hours and whose members help each other in many ways.
Within this informal group, there often are status positions of leaders
and followers, and these positions may not be in accord with the official
rank, since a corporal may be the leader there and his sergeant one of
the followers.

The corporal who is a leader among his buddies although of lower official rank than some of them exemplifies another aspect of status. Within
the requirements of a status position, its duties and prerogatives will be
differently enacted by different kinds of persons. One captain may be
content merely to carry out the minimal requirements of his status while
another may spend long hours in looking after the welfare of the men
of his company and perfecting himself and them in the skills expected
of the unit. Or one may concentrate on perfecting the internal, technical,
spit-and-polish details while another may concern himself mainly with
the relations of his unit to the others in the outfit and to the larger tasks
of the division.

Role is the manner in which different personalities carry out the status
requirements. It refers to the fact that some captains are diligent and
others are dilatory in the fulfillment of the expectations of their status,
yet both fulfill the requirements of the position. Some are usually temperate and others are usually short-tempered in their relations with the
men of their command; both kinds of captain have the same status but
perform different roles within the status.

Role also refers to the fact that a person tends to show similar behavior in his several status positions. The intemperate captain may also
be a short-tempered husband, an impatient father, an impulsive partner
at bridge. He plays a similar role in these statuses. Lest this example
seem too invidious, it is well to add that the very quality which may
make him an uncomfortable bridge partner may qualify him as a superb
combat leader. Moreover, most people do not show a patently consistent
role in their various statuses. The overbearing boss may come home to
act as a tender and thoughtful father. It is one of the intriguing prob-

lems for future research to ascertain whatever personal and social consistencies underlie such apparently inconsistent roles.

Certain roles are approved by the group, others are disapproved or indifferently regarded, yet in every society there is a range of role enactment. Esteem is a term used to describe the fact of group approval of a certain kind of role. A well-behaved but not too docile child is esteemed. Prestige refers to the group-approval power of status: in fulfilling the patterns of a prestige status a person generally affects the behavior of others, usually subordinate to him in some degree, while in playing an esteemed role a person need not influence the reciprocal action of his fellows nor is subordination necessarily involved.

The subordination involved in prestige status need not be more than that of following the lead of those in prestige positions in certain particular activities. The leading fashion designers of Paris and New York have widespread prestige, but only in the realm of women's dress and not in, say, religion or politics. At the other extreme of prestige status may be the authoritarian father in a society which expects fathers to be sternly authoritarian. Within his family circle, his word is law on everything.

There are broadly two ways in which a person gets his status positions. Some are ascribed to him: these are assigned without much reference to his personal qualities. The status of male or female, of child or adult, of daughter or sister are ascribed statuses. Others he achieves by his own efforts. In our society, the status position of mayor, doctor, varsity fullback are achieved statuses. Among most peoples of India, the status of wife is ascribed rather than achieved because marriages are arranged by parents without much consultation of the prospective spouses. In American society there is a bit more achievement involved. Some status positions are partly ascribed and partly achieved, others are mostly ascribed or mostly achieved.

RANKED GROUPINGS: CASTE AND CLASS

More often among the nations we call civilized than among the tribes of primitive folk, there are social groupings according to caste and class. These are groups within a community which are graded so that one is considered to be higher in prestige and power than another. Each person has a class or caste status position which governs his behavior toward the other individuals. A person of the highest caste in an Indian village, because of his caste status, may not eat in the company of fellow villagers of lower caste rank, or associate with them freely, or take a wife of different caste status than his own.

There is no sharp distinction between a caste and a class. The term caste is used when a person's membership in the ranked group is ascribed and is so important that it affects every part of his life, his religion, his occupation, the life prospects of his children. A class is also a ranked group but one in which status may be achieved and whose members have social functions apart from their class status.

Caste groupings have been most highly developed in India where, as we have mentioned before, a villager is born into a caste, may marry only a woman of his caste, and often follows the occupation traditional for his caste. In the parts of India where the caste system is still important, a member of the highest caste, the Brahmins, may not even eat food that has been prepared by one of low caste. The Brahmins of a local community will often be the priests, or at least will be more educated in the sacred Sanskrit scriptures than their neighbors of other castes. A Brahmin boy who has undergone the rite of passage which initiates him into the status of a scholar will wear the sacred thread over his shoulder, the symbol of the higher castes. And a boy who has been born into a family of the blacksmith or musician caste—these occupations are among those lower in esteem—will generally be given little formal education and will probably follow the trade of his father.

Social classes are similar to castes in that one class is higher in the social scale than the others, as was true for the classes of nobles, commoners, and serfs in Europe of the Middle Ages. In modern societies, social classes are less definite and there is much more mobility by families and individuals between classes than there was. Wealth, family history, personal interests, and other factors enter into the determination of the class structure which can be found in present-day social organization.

In the United States, the class hierarchy is particularly fluid and most Americans think of themselves as belonging to a middle class. But class rankings do exist widely in America, although the gradations between classes may not be sharp and class distinctions may be fuzzy. In some sections of the American population, class status is relatively unimportant, in others it counts for a great deal throughout the life span of the individuals involved.

The social organization of the Deep South in the United States has sometimes been called a caste system. In some respects it certainly has been such. Intermarriage and interdining between the groups are forbidden; members of one group may not associate freely and openly with members of the other; mobility of individuals or families from one side of the community to the other is tabooed except where a few Negroes are able clandestinely to 'pass' into the other group; the status positions entailed in the respective groupings affect a large part of the individual's life. All this as in the classic caste system of India.

There are certain important differences. There was not the high religious sanction for caste in the South that there has been in India. Members of the lower caste in the South have increasingly rejected the assumptions necessary for caste differentiation. It is well to note that this occurred in India also, but in earlier centuries the rejection took the form of a new religion, as Buddhism. In India also, the caste system was not the rigid strait-jacket it sometimes is made out to be. There was mobility both for social groups and for individuals, although the opportunity to change one's caste status was much smaller than in a more open-class society such as that of the north or west of the United States. And the classic caste system of India has been undergoing change just as the traditional social system of the Deep South is changing.

Caste and class stratifications may exist together in the same community. In the South, there are quite clear class distinctions within the white group and within the Negro group. The criteria for, say, upper class status in the two groups are similar but there is little communication and informal association by members of the respective upper classes across the color—or if you like, the caste—line.

In Indian villages, the castes may be grouped into classes. There may be three castes which are called the lowest, 'untouchable' castes. The members of one of these castes may acquire some wealth, give up such degrading practices as beef eating, take on high caste customs and thus succeed in raising the position of their whole caste in that village to the next class of 'middle' castes. Each caste member retains his caste status, but the status of all members of their caste has been raised in the local hierarchy.

SOCIAL ORGANIZATION IN OUR SOCIETY

In western societies, there are many other types of social groupings, ranging from trade unions and medical associations to bridge clubs and parent-teacher associations. Each of these groupings is held together by a common interest, an interest arising from mutual participation in the same trades, the mutual enjoyment of a game, or mutual problems in relation to a set of children.

The primary social group, the family, remains basic in our social system. The local community, in the sense of a small set of people who know each other personally, is also essential in spite of the temporary weakening of this unit in large cities. The clan has probably disappeared from our social tradition for good, but its place has been taken partly by the social units which are extensions of the local group—the various state agencies within the nation—and partly by voluntary associations based on common interests.

The outline of social organization which has been sketched in this chapter, rudimentary though it is, nevertheless provides a basis for further questions of considerable theoretical and practical importance. For example, the subject of voluntary associations in our society has been relatively little studied. What kinds of voluntary associations are there in your community? What do they do for their members? Under what circumstances and for what people is one such association more important than another? How are voluntary associations related to age groupings, to class stratifications, to economic interests?

The study of these questions will necessarily lead to enquiry about other elements of social organization in the local and in the larger society because the various social units are interrelated and interdependent, because each person has various status positions. Therefore research on voluntary associations must take into account the factors of family and kinship, of age and social stratification, of community and state.

The political aspects of social organization are of special concern in our times. Great interest is devoted to setting up various kinds of new international organizations and in perfecting those we now have. Underlying all the detailed and technical discussions there are some broad problems which have been mentioned above. What makes a unified, co-operating political entity? Is a tribe only a collection of local bands? Is a state only a confederation of local communities? How can a union of sovereign states stay united? Much illuminating knowledge on such questions has been developed in the studies of social scientists. Much remains to be developed in future studies.

R. GODFREY LIENHARDT

XIV

Religion

LESS THAN A HUNDRED YEARS AGO, scholars discussed with interest such questions as how men could have come to conceive of gods, whether there might be tribes so primitive as to have no religion, and how far the faiths and superstitions of savages could properly be related to the great universal religions.

No one who studies tribal religions today is interested in trying to answer such questions, nor even thinks that satisfying answers to them could be found. There is no evidence for any theory of an origin of religion in time or place; and most anthropologists have ceased to take their bearings in the study of religion from any religion practiced in their own society.

The publication of well-authenticated works of travel, and the growth of speculation about human nature at large, led in the eighteenth century to an increase in curiosity about tribal religions. In Boswell's *Life of Samuel Johnson* for example, we find Johnson—that firm churchman—rebuking a gentleman for wishing to spend three years living with the natives of New Zealand to find out what sort of a religion people denied a special revelation might have. 'And what account of their religion can you suppose to be learnt from savages?' asks Dr. Johnson. 'Only consider, sir, our own state. Our religion is in a book: we have an order of men whose duty it is to teach: we have one day in the week set apart for it, and this in general pretty well-observed; Yet ask the first ten gross men you meet, and hear what they can tell of their religion.'

Johnson thought that the fullness of religion lay in the presence of a theology and a church, a large measure of intellectual formulation and social formalization. For him, to learn about a religion was to find out what people knew of its doctrines. 'Gross men' and savages could not know enough for their knowledge to form the basis of serious study.

This has not been the view of anthropologists. It is true that some of the main differences between the tribal religions of non-literate peoples, and those religions with literate traditions, are as Johnson stated; but a religion is something more than that part of it which appears in its sacred scriptures and in written commentaries upon them. These represent what people know and are prepared to say about their religion when they reflect upon it; we need also to understand how their religion figures in the ordinary conduct of their lives. To learn what a people say about their religion is not always the same thing as to know how they practice it.

Most tribes lack any formal theology, and in most of them there is no distinct religious organization, like a church, which can be studied in isolation from other forms of social organization. Faced with such difficulties, Professor Lowie suggested in his general work *Primitive Religion* (1925) that in the last resort religion could only be defined by reference to 'the subjective condition of believers and worshippers.' This view is strongly marked by the influence of William James's popular work, *The Varieties of Religious Experience,* published early in this century. James there dismissed some of the dogmatic features of religious thought and practice as 'phenomena of mere tribal or corporate psychology,' not to be confused, he said, with 'those manifestations of the purely interior life' in which he was then exclusively interested. In that study, he sought the grounds of religious phenomena in special conditions of the individual conscience, and understood religion as a matter of useful aspirations, rather than as an inevitable and formal duty.

This view has influenced many students of tribal religions. It is natural that it should have done so, for most tribes are without those very doctrinal and dogmatic elements of religion which James preferred to disregard, and an investigation of a tribal religion must therefore ultimately be based upon what individuals say and appear to think and feel. By regarding religion as grounded in features of a common human psychology, some students have thought themselves able to account for specific religious beliefs and practices by referring them to sentiments which they have recognized in themselves. They have thus tried to get over, in one way, a difficulty which is perhaps peculiar to the study of religion and magic in tribal societies, and which must be considered if we wish to understand the balance between fact and interpretation in most anthropological accounts of religion.

The difficulty may be thus explained. It is easy for a visitor to share the political sentiments or the economic interests of members of a tribal society, for he readily understands the nature of the reality upon which those sentiments and interests are based. If a tribesman says that his people have been attacked by an enemy, or that birds have spoilt the crops, our understanding of the situation is not fundamentally different from his own, for we do not doubt the reality of enemies or birds. The case is different if a man says that his people are being killed by a spirit, or that the birds which spoilt the crops were sent by witchcraft. Spirits, or witchcraft, are not directly known to us as are enemies or birds, and though we see the effects of course—the sick people, the spoilt grain— we do not attribute them to the same causes as does the tribesman. It is then that we come to ask ourselves what the spirits or witchcraft can be said to represent *for us,* as well as for the tribesmen who believe in them.

The most important differences in approach and interpretation arise between students of tribal religion at this point. St. Augustine (and perhaps also some missionaries today) answer this question in their own way by being able to regard foreign gods and spirits as daemons, powers other than the true God, but nevertheless conceivably real powers operating independently in the world, acting from without upon the human imagination and will and not merely created by those human faculties. This, at least, is not to deny to foreign gods some sort of real existence; and tribal peoples do indeed represent their gods to themselves as real powers existing apart from men, not as figments of human thought and feeling.

Most anthropologists, however, do not believe in daemons any more than they believe in the foreign gods, the spirits or the witchcraft they are trying to account for. Yet, they wish to bring the tribesman's thought and experience ultimately into one world with their own. If we cannot believe in the gods which other peoples accept as the basis of their religions, we seek for the basis in something other than those gods—in something we ourselves believe in. What is that something?

The answers which have been given to this question may be divided into three main groups, the theological, the psychological, and the philosophical or sociological.

St. Augustine's answer above was one example of a theological answer, but there are others, given from less well-defined theological standpoints and nearer to our present studies of religion. F. Max Müller, the scholar of comparative religious studies at the end of the last century, answered the question from the point of view of a liberal theology. 'However imperfect and however childish the conception of God may be,' he wrote, 'it always represents the highest ideal of perfection which the human soul for the time-being can reach and grasp . . .' So he fitted the pagan gods into his own theology, not by regarding them as daemons, but by regarding them merely as 'false or imperfect names for God'—for a God, that is, in which he himself believed.

Max Müller was praised by a missionary for having shown that heathen religions were not the work of the devil. In doing so, however, he also made them appear other than they seem to the tribal peoples themselves. Max Müller's conception of God was of an abstract ideal of primarily ethical perfection. There can now be no doubt that the gods of many tribal peoples are of a very different nature, and are thought of as active powers, willful, intelligent, capricious, jealous, and even, at times, greedy. Since for Max Müller God was an idea rather than an active power, he was surprised by a characteristic of primitive religion which he nevertheless intelligently noted—its preference for the concrete, its attachment to material symbols. He noted that there were

two distinct tendencies to be observed in the growth of ancient religion . . . on the one side, the struggle of the mind against the material character of language, a constant attempt to strip words of their coarse covering, and fit them, by main force, for the purposes of abstract thought. But . . . on the other side a constant relapse from the spiritual into the material, and, strange to say, a predilection for the material sense instead of the spiritual.

It is true that in primitive religions we find a preference for the local and specific understanding of divinity rather than for the general, abstract, and theoretical. Since Max Müller took his own abstract God to be the real basis of all religion, other conceptions of gods were interpreted as lowly conceptions of that God. He explained many gods as personifications of natural phenomena, such as the sky; what those who worshipped such gods thought to be personal agents, Max Müller explained as having originally been impersonal and general forces in which he also could believe.

The most famous examples of a psychological interpretation of tribal religions are those of what is sometimes called the 'English' school of anthropologists, and particularly those of the two great figures of nineteenth-century anthropology, Sir Edward Tylor and Sir James Frazer. To these we may add also the name of Malinowski, one of the first anthropologists to study a native people through their own language in the intimate way which is considered essential today.

Tylor put forward a theory of primitive religion which was widely accepted in his day, and which has had a great influence on the study of the subject until the present time. He claimed that what underlay tribal religions was a belief in spiritual beings, personal spirits which were thought to animate nature. This primitive faith Tylor called *animism*.

Tylor suggested that primitive man, reflecting upon his experiences in dreams and visions, and upon the differences between living men and corpses, concluded that man had a soul, which was a sort of spiritual counterpart of the body. The conception of a human soul then according to Tylor seemed to have 'served as a type or model on which primitive man framed not only his ideas of other souls of lower grade, but also his ideas of spiritual beings in general, from the tiniest elf that sports in the long grass up to the heavenly Creator and Ruler of the world, the Great Spirit.'

In so far as such theories pretend to be historically based, we know that they are not capable of proof. In so far as they pretend to describe the way in which all tribal peoples think today, they are misleading, thought not without a hint at truth. Let us consider the element of truth in them first.

It is well known that in many tribes material objects, such as bundles of sticks and roots or carved representations of beings, are treated with special reverence and are believed to have religious virtue. Such objects of religious and magical value are usually classed together as *fetishes*. They are treated as sacred because they are objects in which deities are located or manifested. They *could* be regarded, however, as implying nothing more than the material of which they are composed, as when it is said in the hymn that

> "The heathen in his blindness
> Bows down to wood and stone. . ."

Tylor saw that this was a misunderstanding, and that no people worshipped material objects simply *as* the material objects which we see them to be. In this he took the view which every serious student has taken, and encouraged an interest in the distinction between material symbols and the divine beings they symbolized.

His theory had another virtue too. At a time when public opinion often represented savages as moved by almost subhuman instincts, unreasoning and perhaps incapable of reason, Tylor imputed reasoning to them as the very basis of their religion. It is true that there is an element of reason in tribal religions. They involve argument from effect to cause in some cases, such as the treatment of sickness, when a diviner may be called in to use his special insight to discover the spiritual reason for the complaint. The causes and treatment thus decided upon are not such as we should accept; but the conception of a cause which can be discovered by special investigation is certainly present. Tylor's error was not that he imputed the possibility of logical inference to primitive peoples, but that he assumed that they arrived at their religious beliefs by means of it. A little reflection upon the religion of his own society would have persuaded him that though reason and argument by analogy may support a faith, they do not found one. To show a religion to be reasonable, and to suggest that it is the result of reasoning from faulty premises, as Tylor and Frazer did, are not the same thing.

It is certainly wrong also to suggest that tribal gods and spirits are thought of as having personality analogous, in all important ways, to human personality, or that all spiritual beings are thought to resemble in kind the human soul. Some gods may be thought of in man's image, or may be deified men. Often, however, it would be truer to say that the force of tribal gods depends upon their being quite other than human in nature, and that it is this difference which is the basis of religious service offered to them. The Book of Job, with its emphasis upon God's transcendence of human knowledge and argument, indeed of the human scale altogether, is often nearer to the kind of understanding of the divine we find among primitive peoples than is the kind of crude anthropomorphism ascribed to them by some scholars of the last century.

Tylor's account of what *we* can regard as the basis of primitive religion thus grounds religion in processes of reasoning, found equally among savages and among ourselves. For the gods of the primitives, he substitutes something he can himself take for granted—logical processes, combined with primitive error and ignorance. The gods of the tribes need not then be supposed to correspond to any other-than-human reality, as Max Müller and St. Augustine both in their different ways thought possible; they may be seen to correspond to certain human mental processes.

This is one kind of psychological interpretation, based upon an intellectualist psychology. There are others more influential today; but before considering them we must take into account some attempts to modify Tylor's theory. Objections were raised to his notions of a primitive world filled with *personal* spiritual beings. These objections were based upon reports, from Melanesia, Polynesia, North America, and elsewhere, of native conceptions of an *impersonal* power active in the world. Tylor's theory of personal spiritual beings did not allow for this conception, which Tylor's successor Marrett was one of the first to investigate.

The Polynesian and Melanesian word for the conception is *mana;* that word has become almost as familiar a part of our vocabulary for the discussion of primitive religions as the North American Indian word, *totem,* and another Polynesian word, *taboo.* Each of these native terms sums up in a word a complex range of conceptions which many books have been written to explain.

The study of *mana* has produced so many general theories about religion and magic that it is interesting to see how it was described in the early accounts of those who studied it in its context of native life. The word became known primarily through R. H. Codrington's work *The Melanesians* (1891); but I quote an account of the meaning of *mana* in Polynesia from a slightly older source, *Old New Zealand* by a Paheka Maori. There the writer, a European who lived for long with the Maori, says of *mana* that:

Virtus, prestige, authority, good fortune, influence, sanctity, luck, are all words which, under certain conditions, give something near the meaning . . . *mana* sometimes means a more than natural virtue or power attaching to some person or thing, different from and independent of the ordinary natural conditions of either. . . I once had a tame pig which, before heavy rain, would always cut extraordinary capers and squeak and run like mad . . . all the Maori said that it was . . . a pig possessed of *mana:* it had more than natural powers and could foretell rain.

Many further examples of the situations in which *mana* is thought to operate are given:

The *mana* of a priest . . . is proved by the truth of his predictions . . . *mana* in another sense is the accompaniment of power but not the power itself . . . this is the chief's *mana* . . . the warrior's *mana* is just a little something more than mere good fortune . . ."

and so on.

It is clear that this is a conception for which no simple equivalent exists in our language. One way of giving an account of it is by giving lengthy descriptions of the contexts in which it is used. General theories of religion based upon the concept of *mana*, however, may omit much that is specific in the meanings of the term in its native context and try to give a general account of what it is. Goldenweiser, for example, explains *mana* as

a projection or objectivation of what, on the subjective side, is the religious thrill; *mana* is what causes the religious thrill. Now if the religious thrill is accepted as the basic emotional root of religion, then *mana*, a psychologically basic *mana* underlying its historic forms, becomes the fundamental idea of religion. *Mana* is but a term for an emotion, projected as 'something into the supernatural realm'. . .

This is a very clear example of the emotional kind of psychological interpretation of religious phenomena. The *mana* which the Polynesians and Melanesians conceive of as an objective reality is represented as being really certain special feelings or emotions which we are assumed to accept as being characteristically religious. Many anthropologists would doubt whether anything so undefinable as a 'thrill' should be regarded as forming the basis of religion; though we cannot ignore the work of Rudolf Otto, who in his book *The Idea of the Holy*, made out a case for the direct sensory and emotional apprehension of God by men. Otto, however, wrote as one who predicated the existence of a God. He was not content to allow religious 'feelings' to remain *mere* features of human psychology, but regarded them as a manner of apprehending divinity. The divine, and not the human mind, was for Otto the ground of religion and the final object of his study, and he wrote as a theologian, not a psychologist.

Other attempts to give an account of the grounds of religious phenomena emphasize the psychological *functions* of religious belief and practice. This approach is best seen in the writings of Malinowski, who built partly upon the theories of his English predecessors Tylor and Frazer, but much augmented their views through his own deep and first-hand understanding of some Melanesian peoples. Malinowski seemed to think that religion had its most important functions in the crises of life, and particularly in the situation of death, in which, he wrote:

the call to religion arises out of an individual crisis, the death which threatens man or woman. Never does an individual need the comfort of belief and ritual so much as in the sacrament of the viaticum, in the last comforts given to him at the final stage of his life's journey—acts which are well-nigh universal in all primitive religions. These acts are directed against the over-whelming fear, against the corroding doubt, from which the savage is no more free than the civilized man. These acts confirm his hope that there is a hereafter, that it is not worse than the present life; indeed better.

Anthropologists today would question such a broad generalization; it is by no means certain that anything corresponding to a sacrament for the dying is 'well-nigh universal,' and many primitive people neither seem acutely afraid of death, nor have any hope for or interest in a future life. It was Malinowski rather than tribal peoples who saw religion as a force for social and psychological integration, and it was in a human need for comfort and peace that he sought the grounds of primitive religions. So, after a death, the bereaved are, according to Malinowski

thrown into a dangerous mental chaos . . . torn between fear and piety, reverence and horror, love and disgust, they are in a state of mind which might lead to mental disintegration. Out of this, religion lifts the individual. . .

In such passages, Malinowski makes it clear that he regards the basis of religion, for the purposes of study, as the emotional needs of individuals, and the need for social integration. If the gods or ancestors of tribal peoples cannot have any real existence for us, we can recognize a universal validity in the human desire for individual peace of mind and social order; it is this which we are invited to substitute for the gods and the ancestors, as the grounds of primitive religion.

Malinowski stands between a psychological interpretation of religious phenomena, and the philosophical or sociological interpretation to which I now turn. While Malinowski sought the basis of religion in the emotional integration of the individual, and saw the integration of society as a function of the integration of its individual members, those who adopted a philosophical approach tended to reverse the argument. They sought the grounds of religion in the integration of the society, from which individual religious beliefs and practices were seen to derive.

Philosophical and sociological interpretations of religion are associated primarily with a group of French writers of the turn of the century. The best known of these are Emile Durkheim, H. Hubert, Marcel Mauss, and Lucien Lévy-Bruhl. They rejected the theories of the English anthropologists Tylor and Frazer because such theories assumed that all peoples had the same categories and processes of thought. Lévy-Bruhl attempted to show that this was not so. He maintained that there was a difference in kind between the experience of the world which characterized primitive peoples and that characteristic of the civilization of his own time. In his view, the thought of primitive peoples was what he called 'mystical'—

it proceeded less by logical inference and empirical verification than by imaginative and metaphorical associations of ideas and experience, in a way which we might regard as poetic. Their thought was not analytic, but synthetic, in intention.

Further, individuals accepted the very categories in which they thought, including the categories of religious thought and experience, from the societies in which they were reared. They did not choose their religious belief and practice; it was a product of social life, not of individual reasoning. Durkheim similarly maintained that just as a society must be regarded as something other than a mere collection of individuals living together, so its religion must be studied as something other than a feature of the psychology of individuals. A religion then imposed itself on individuals from without, from the society in which they were brought up and in which religious beliefs and practices were taken for granted.

What is the main difference between this philosophical approach and the psychological approach already mentioned? The psychological interpretation of religion requires the abstraction of such sentiments as those of fear, guilt, desire, awe, helplessness, or of certain reasoning processes, from the individual consciousness. It then relates these in a more or less systematic way to each other, and to religious beliefs and situations. Philosophical interpretation, on the other hand, requires the abstraction from our own thought of certain religious conceptions. Such conceptions are those of sacredness, divinity, cult, sacrifice, sin, truth, and many others. They are terms of our own thought, not words for sentiments or feelings, and whatever sentiments may be supposed to accompany them, the conceptions remain the same. So, for example, sacrifice may be studied in several societies irrespective of the feelings which may be supposed to precede and follow the act. Again, conceptions of sacredness—such as *mana*—may be studied in social and moral contexts, without assuming any special sensations or emotional experiences as their basis.

Much of the work done by those who have attempted philosophical interpretations of primitive religions has been in the study of congruences between particular forms of religion and the structures and values of the societies in which they are found. Durkheim's work on the religion and society of the Australian aborigines, *The Elementary Forms of the Religious Life,* is the most ambitious study on these lines. There he maintained that religion was characteristically a social and not an individual

matter, and that Australian aborigines' totemic animals were revered because they symbolized the unity of their social groups, their clans. In
regarding their totems as sacred, they were thus regarding the groupings
of their society as sacred, and in respecting their totemic animals and
objects, they were in fact expressing the relationship of individual members of society to the society itself, as a source of their moral traditions
and their very sustenance. The gods of the tribes might then represent,
for us, the order of tribal society itself. Other directions taken by philosophical enquiry have resulted in studies of the place of religious conceptions in wider contexts of primitive philosophy and symbolism. Two
very different examples are Professor Radcliffe-Brown's study of the
social significance of the beliefs and rites of the Andaman Islanders, and
a more recent book by Professor Henri Frankfort, *Kingship and the
Gods*, an interpretation of religion, philosophy, and art in ancient Egypt
and Mesopotamia.

In deriving religion ultimately from a God *we* believe in, or from psychological needs, or from society itself, we are substituting for tribesmen's beliefs in their gods something which we can take for granted—
whether our God, or psychology, or society—as sufficient grounds for
religion. Each general theory of religion is thus, in a way, a substitute
for any particular religion, an alternative way of giving an account of
those situations which different tribal religions give accounts of.

We may now see to what extent the kinds of theory discussed above
help us in understanding a specific situation. Livingstone, in his *Missionary Travels*, gives an account of a typical conversation between a
medical doctor and an African rain-doctor or rain-maker. Parts of the
conversation are as follows:

Medical Doctor: So you really believe you can command the clouds? I think
   that can be done by God alone.
Rain-Doctor: We both believe the very same thing. It is God that make the
   rain, but I pray to him by means of these medicines, and, the rain coming,
   of course it is then mine. . . If we had no rain, the cattle would have
   no pastures, the cows give no milk, our children become lean and die,
   our wives run away to other tribes who do make rain . . . and the whole
   tribe become dispersed and lost; our fire would go out.
Medical Doctor: . . . you cannot charm the clouds by medicines. You wait
   till you see the clouds come, then use your medicines, and take the credit
   which belongs to God only.
Rain-Doctor: I use my medicines, and you employ yours; we are both doctors,
   and doctors are not deceivers. You give a patient medicine. Sometimes
   God is pleased to heal him by means of your medicine; sometimes not—
   he dies. When he is cured, you take the credit of what God does. I do

the same. Sometimes God grants us rain, sometimes not. When he does, we take the credit of the charm. When a patient dies you don't give up trust in your medicine, neither do I when rain fails. If you wish me to leave off my medicines, why continue your own?

Medical Doctor: I give medicine to living creatures within my reach, and can see the effect though no cure follows. . . God alone can command the clouds. Only try and wait patiently; God will give us rain without your medicines.

Rain-Doctor: Mahala-ma-kapa-a-a! Well, I always thought white men were wise until this morning. Whoever thought of making a trial of starvation? Is death pleasant then?

Almost all theories of primitive religion derive some support from this conversation, as we should expect if all had elements of truth in them. Theological interpretations receive support, since both Livingstone and the rain-maker are able to accept that they are referring to a single God, though thought of in different ways. A theory of Frazer, that the characteristic attitude of religion is that of supplication for benefits beyond human-beings' power and knowledge to achieve for themselves, is supported by the rain-maker's attitude. Interpreted psychologically, the conversation might permit us to say that in using his medicines and rituals the rain-maker is expressing a desire for rain and anxiety lest it should not come, and that the use of medicines and prayers releases the tension built up by desire and anxiety. Those who follow the interpretations of an intellectualist psychology may see in the argument a form of reasoning about the causes of rain, and an attempt at a rational justification of the use of medicines by one who is ignorant of 'natural' causation. The sacred medicines are also obviously used in situations which vitally affect the well-being of the whole society, and even the rain-maker has the theory that the tribe would disintegrate without them. Every interpretation—theological, psychological, or philosophical and sociological—may thus be placed upon the rain-maker's conversation: yet, none quite takes into account the whole of what he says.

The rain-maker's attitude is a blend of faith and skepticism, even cynicism, about his own medicines and about those of the medical doctor. It shows a grasp of the difference between what men can *know* and what they have been brought up to believe, and of the relations between experience and belief. It recognizes that experience sometimes contradicts belief, and it attempts to resolve that contradiction. The rain-maker is clearly not entirely 'mystical,' as Lévy-Bruhl would have us believe; nor, however, is he the logic-chopping savage of Tylor. It is left for modern students of primitive religion to show how beliefs are not simply the result of ignoring blandly the experience which contradicts them at times; nor are they arrived at by a kind of reasoning, though they may be defended by a kind of reasoning; nor are they just taken over, quite unthinkingly, from social tradition. They are supported by all three of these—by the will, by the reason, and by traditional teaching. We see also in the conversation other features of primitive religions: a respect for the seriousness of the concerns which religion, in its way, deals with, which excludes deliberate experiment to put faith to the test; and a concern for truth, though that truth may not be established by scientific methods of verification.

Two very recent works on the subject, *Nupe Religion* by Professor Nadel and studies of Nuer religion by Professor Evans-Pritchard, not yet published in book form, show how much nearer we have now come to understanding the complexities of tribal religions than did many of our predecessors. This is partly because those who study primitive religions today are required to have a good knowledge of the languages of the tribes they study, and can no longer mistake metaphorical or symbolic statements for literal assertions. Once the difficulty of full and subtle translation is overcome, a religion can be made to appear to us much as it does to those who practice it. We do not then have to substitute our picture, or 'explanation,' of it, for theirs. That stage—of giving our own explanation—comes later, when we have understood in their context what sacrifices, for example, or prayers, mean for the people themselves; then, by comparing their conceptions with our own and with those of other peoples, we can deepen our understanding of our own conceptions of sacrifice, or prayer, or whatever we choose to abstract for special comparative study.

Sacrifice is a good example. In many tribes blood-sacrifice is the central religious act; and sacrifice has been studied comparatively by two of the most able exponents of philosophical interpretation, Hubert and Mauss.

Hubert and Mauss, like Durkheim, thought that the two basic categories for our thought about religion were those of the sacred and the non-sacred or profane. All religions depend, in some way, upon the setting apart of certain objects, persons, and situations, as standing in a special relationship to the divine; these together compose the category of the sacred, as distinct from the profane objects, persons, or situations which are without any religious significance. I have mentioned earlier that these French sociologists equated this category of the sacred with the social world, but I do not further consider this wider implication of their theory here.

By examining several situations of sacrifice, Hubert and Mauss concluded that what sacrificial ceremonies had in common was the attempt to establish communication between the sacred and the non-sacred, through a victim which was consecrated and then destroyed for this purpose. The victim was killed and offered to the gods, who were thought to accept it perhaps as food, perhaps in other ways. By means of the gift of the victim, communication was established with the sacred, and those who offered sacrifice received in return spiritual, moral, and physical benefits which they could obtain in no other way.

Such an analysis clearly fits the facts of blood-sacrifice as it is known among many peoples of the world. If, however, we compare the blood-sacrifice of the peoples of Africa with what is found in the very striking and well-described religion of the American Crow Indians, we see no immediate resemblance. In his chapter on Crow religion in his book on that people, Professor Lowie writes:

> In a crisis an African Negro calls a diviner, who casts his sacred dice and by occult lore interprets the throw; such and such a one of his client's ancestors is angry, and so many head of cattle must be slaughtered to appease his wrath. The Crow had no system of divination, never worshipped their ancestors and made no bloody sacrifices. When hard put to it, the Indian tried to meet divinity face to face.

To do this, the Crow set out to mortify himself in various ways, in order to try to receive a vision or a revelation from a spirit guardian who would guide him and help him to prosper. One of the commonest forms of self-mortification was the cutting off of a finger-joint:

> Most probably he would set out for a lonely mountain peak and fast, thirst and wail there. . . Rising at daybreak he sat down towards the east. As soon as the sun rose, he laid his left forefinger on a stick and chopped off a joint. This he put on a buffalo chip and held it towards the Sun, whom he addressed as follows 'Uncle (i.e. father's clansman) you see me, I am pitiable. Here is a part of my body, I give it to you, eat it. Give me something good. . .'

Later, when the man has suffered enough, the helping vision comes in his sleep and strengthens and guides him for his life.

Thus, although the Crow offer no animal victims, like many African peoples, yet they give over to the gods a part of themselves; this giving of the self in sacrifice is consistent with the analysis by Hubert and Mauss of the central feature of the sacrificial act. To observe a similarity between this act of the Crow Indians and some animal sacrifices is not to minimize the great differences which exist between the religion of the Crow Indians and those of many African tribes. It is merely to observe that from one point of view we are dealing with one situation, not two, when the Crow offers his finger-joint as a victim while the African offers a sheep or ox. Further, recent investigations of animal sacrifice in Africa have made it clear that underlying the offering of a victim to the gods is the theme of offering a part of the self, for the victim is identified with the person for whom the offering is made. The two cases may thus be viewed in the light of single interpretation of the sacrificial act, though the search for individual visions which is such a marked feature of Crow religion is less prominent in much of Africa.

Even in this respect, however, there are some similarities which suggest further lines of investigation. Recent studies in Africa indicate that since tribal societies began to disintegrate under foreign rule, there has been a multiplication of individual 'spirits' and of individual religious leaders, outside the traditional religious order, at least on such a scale. Modern changes in Africa have resulted in a type of individual self-sufficiency not previously possible, and it seems consistent with this trend that private religious revelations and experiences should have increased. A book by a Lutheran missionary, B. Sundkler, called *Bantu Prophets in South Africa,* gives an account of the way in which even the original Christian churches have now splintered into hundreds of semi-pagan sects, each with its own leaders; and among the Nilotic peoples of the Sudan, whose tribal integrity has begun to be undermined in comparatively recent times, many 'spirits,' thought to be also of recent origin, have possessed individuals and through them become known in the society. These spirits are not spirit-guardians, as are those of the Crow Indian; but they do represent a growth of a kind of individual and eccentric religious experience which the people themselves think to be on the increase. Among the Crow Indians, whose cult of individual revelations is now so marked as to seem to represent a distinct class of tribal religion, it is also suggested that at one time the emphasis was different. Professor Lowie writes that:

. . . the hypertrophy of the individual vision represents an overlay that has pushed other beliefs into the background, encroaching even on the widespread American worship of the Sun. Visions themselves are doubtless very old, but the one-sided stressing of individual visions as a source of power is a comparatively late development that largely remolded the rationale of Crow religion.

Only further research might establish whether there is a general correspondence between the dislocation of tribal life owing to an overwhelming conquest and an increased emphasis on individual self-sufficiency both in the religious and in the moral and economic situations of life. Such are some of the types of questions which a student of tribal religions today might ask himself.

I mentioned earlier that the anthropological study of tribal religions requires a different approach from that adopted by students of comparative religion who rely upon sacred writings for their knowledge. We study religious beliefs and practices in relation to particular social situations; and what people do in particular situations is not always consistent with what they are prepared, on reflection, to say they believe.

A little example of this occurs in an account by a missionary, John Roscoe, of the Kingdom of the Bakitara, or Banyoro, in Uganda. Roscoe wrote several valuable ethnographic accounts of peoples of Uganda, without attempting any elaborate theoretical interpretation of the facts, which he was content to report as he knew them. The honesty of his reporting makes it possible for us to note in his account an example of the discrepancy between theory and practice of religion which he seems himself to have overlooked.

Roscoe obtained native statements about the gods of the Banyoro, among which is an account of a god named *Ruhanga*. The Banyoro told Roscoe that *Ruhanga* was

. . . the creator of things . . . people did not call upon him for assistance because he had done his work and there was no need to ask further favours of him. Other gods could assist in multiplying men, cattle, crops. . .

Such statements about a creator who, having finished his creation, takes little further interest in it, are common in other tribes. The Anuak of the Sudan, for example, say that when man was created, the creator gave instructions that he should at once be thrown away. These statements seem to depict a creator very different from, say, the Christian God; in writings on African religion, such gods who no longer have apparent functions in the world have been described as otiose.

But this statement about *Ruhanga* seems to represent only a part of the truth. A very few pages after Roscoe has reported the statement, he describes a rain-making ceremony, and there he writes

A vessel of water was next brought from a spring near, and the rain-maker raised his hands and prayed thus to *Ruhanga*: 'Ruhanga, bless us. Thou king of all the earth, hear us. The people are dying with hunger.'

Reports of such differences between professed notions and actual practice are obviously of importance for our understanding of tribal religions. When we see that sometimes, in practice, the creator of the Banyoro is asked for help and blessing, we see that their religion in practice is not always so very different from our own as the difference of doctrines might suggest. The behavior of people has often more in common than have their conceptions of gods.

Studies of tribal religions have so far had to treat the subject in very crude abstractions. It is as though we had not yet glimpsed what might be the elements which, in different combinations, would be seen to re-appear wherever we recognized 'religion.' We write of 'ancestor wor-ship,' 'sky-religion,' 'totemism,' and so on, though we well know that these words may be applied to religions which differ in very important ways, and that each is a crude compound term. This is true also of such terms as 'polytheism' and 'monotheism,' which are too general to take a proper account of what is actually found in any religion.

Again, the definitions we use tend to be ambiguous even in our own language. When we consider, for example, Tylor's minimal definition of religion as 'a belief in spiritual beings' we realize that we ourselves have no very clear idea of what such beings are; if we say that religion is the service of the gods, we are again faced with the difficulty of knowing what the gods are, for tribal peoples can often tell us nothing of their nature in themselves. They can only name them and indicate effects which they attribute to them. Durkheim seems to have recognized this difficulty when he wrote that

. . . a god . . . is a power of producing certain manifestations . . . which are related to a particular, determined subject. . . it does not matter whether this power be imagined as pure spirit, or whether it is attached to a material substratum; the essential thing is that it should be individualized. . .

A definition of this kind is useful in that it saves us from asking ques-tions about the nature, in themselves, of tribal gods, questions to which tribesmen often have no answers. Such questions as 'is God good?' for example often cannot have the same meaning, in a tribal language, as it has in our own; for the gods are 'good' when they produce effects which human beings find good; in other situations, when suffering or sickness or death are attributed to them, they may just as easily be said to be bad. These are not comments on their nature, but upon the ways in which they are affecting human beings.

We talk also of religious 'belief'; and for us, the word has come to have the sense of an assertion about something which is admitted to be ultimately uncertain. But for tribal peoples, the *existence* of the gods is not a matter of uncertainty; they cannot be doubtful whether the gods exist, when they see everywhere effects which they attribute to them. Their faith is a matter of certainty about the operation of powers whose ways and nature are ultimately incomprehensible, not a matter of knowledgeable opinion about beings whose existence can ultimately be called into doubt. We often conceal this when we speak of religious 'belief'; in many cases it might be better to speak of religious knowledge. For, as I shall finally suggest, religion is a way of knowing about, and dealing with, certain situations of human life. Religious knowledge and practice are ways in which men apprehend some truths, and adjust themselves to their condition in the light of that apprehension.

A concern with knowledge of truth is an element we find among all tribal peoples, and one which is present in many religions. Let us consider a common feature of African religions, a sacrifice for a man who is sick. The man's relatives call in a diviner to attempt to diagnose the true ground of the illness, which the diviner's greater insight qualifies him to do. He may attribute the sickness to a particular spirit, or to a particular sin of the man or of his ancestors. To cure the illness, a beast must be offered in propitiation. Perhaps a priest is called to pray for the man's recovery and to offer the sacrifice. The prayer may be simply a statement of what *will* happen. Here is an example from the Dinka tribe:

And you, ox, it is not for nothing that we have tethered you in the mid-day sun, but because of sickness, to exchange your life for the life of the sick man. You, God, hear my words, and you, my totemic spirit, hear my words, and you, spirit of illness, I have separated you from the man. I have spoken thus: You leave the man alone. . . You, totemic spirit of my father, do not let me speak a lie. . .

The implication is that the words of the priest *must* be true and so they create the situation which they state. The true cause of illness has thus been diagnosed; the priest who speaks truth prays as though that which is desired is already accomplished, in the manner of a Hebrew prophet; and sacrifice is made in the light of this representation of the truth of the whole situation.

It was reported of the spiritual power *mana* that the *mana* of a priest was shown in the truth of his predictions; and from other parts of the world also it is clear that a divination and representation of truth, as a guide to action, is a part of the task of religion. Among the Crow Indians, who lack any of the African forms of divination, individuals search for visions of a truth which it is necessary and profitable for them to know. That truth often contains trivial and arbitrary elements, from our point of view—'capricious taboos of a dietary or ritualistic character' are what spirits often reveal to the Crow, according to Professor Lowie. It might be claimed, however, that it is in their very triviality and arbitrariness that they carry conviction, as being really revealed to a man and not merely thought out by him. Their peculiar and unlikely nature guarantees their divine origin. The relation of primitive religious practice to knowledge of truth is well conveyed by this charm spoken by a Maori diviner wishing to know the grounds of a sickness:

> A seeking a searching,
> To seek whither?
> To search the land, to seek the origin,
> To seek the base, to search the unknown,
> To seek out the *atua* [spirit]
> May it be effectual.

And we may think of other cases of the relation between religious practice and the definition of truth, such as oaths and oracles, in the first of which the divine is called in to guarantee the truth of men's words, and in the second of which men have truth revealed to them by operations over which, they suppose, they have no control.

Tribal religions then involve on the one hand a sense of human ignorance and weakness and on the other a means of guaranteeing the assumptions upon which are based a people's only means of dealing with the disabilities which follow from human ignorance and weakness. If there were no guarantee, for example, that a diviner was permitted an insight into the true grounds of an illness, there would be no means of dealing with that illness. As we know in our own civilization, it is not only in religion that a guarantee of such a measure of certitude may be sought, and what, for primitive peoples, is truth often seems to us to be a fallacy based upon ignorance. But it is a concern for truth, as they see it, which often prevents them from accepting assumptions upon which our own notions of truth are based, just as it is a concern for truth which prevents us from accepting what we see as their errors.

I do not suggest that tribal peoples see the world and their life in it as a puzzle, to which they anxiously seek an answer. But like ourselves, they sense that human life is lived within circumscribing conditions which they can discover but cannot alter; their religions are in part theories of what those conditions, moral and physical, really are, and means of adapting themselves as best they can to them. And if, from our point of view, their theories of the conditions are sometimes false and misleading, they share with us a concern for the truth of them.

DARYLL FORDE
in collaboration with
Mary Douglas

XV

Primitive Economics

THE ECONOMIES of primitive peoples differ widely. The Australian aborigines, for example, or the Californian Indians live solely by hunting and foraging, without any knowledge of plant-cultivation or stock-raising. The Fula of the west Sudan or the Bedouin Arabs are herders and depend on cultivation only to a minor degree, or may themselves not grow any crops at all. There are hand-cultivators with no large livestock as in tse-tse infested districts in central Africa. There are stockraisers who grow cereals and supplement their larders by hunting, as do the Southern Bantu of Africa.

Agriculture appeared late in human history, and afforded a means of greatly increased production. But the food-gatherers do not necessarily all live at a lower level of subsistence than the cultivators. Some non-agricultural peoples developed elaborate techniques for exploiting the wild products of their environment. The fishing and hunting tribes of the northwest coast of North America not only made huge catches; they knew how to split trees into planks for their solidly built loghouses, how to construct ingenious dams and fishtraps, and even how to organize successful whaling expeditions. Technically they were more advanced than many cultivating peoples. Pastoral nomadism which is popularly believed to have preceded the development of agriculture actually appeared at a later stage in the Old World on the fringes of settled populations used to cultivation with the rearing of livestock.

The distinguishing features of a primitive economy are not to be found in any particular mode of securing a livelihood. The basic condition is

330

a low degree of technical knowledge. However favorable the climate, and rich the natural vegetation and animal life, peoples equipped with only simple techniques are limited in their exploitation of their country's resources.

The level of production of food supplies and the tools by which they are secured is everywhere vitally dependent on the amount of energy that can be harnessed for productive tasks, and it is important to realize the limited capacity for production of peoples lacking power-driven machines. An adult human being can directly exert energy equivalent to only about one tenth of a unit of horsepower and many primitive peoples have lacked any other prime source of power, apart from a limited use of fire. Without animal or water power for lifting and traction, their productive capacity is severely limited by their restriction to hand-tools such as the bow, the hoe, and the fishnet. These must remain mechanically simple and accordingly require little specialization in their manufacture and use. At the same time the level of output per man that they make possible is not great enough to release any significant proportion of the population from the common task of food-production, so that there is little scope for any considerable division of labor.

Advanced civilizations have tended to spread into the most favorable lands, so that there is also a tendency for the least well-equipped peoples to be found living in the most harsh and intractable regions.[1] To these they have adapted themselves as best they can—the Eskimos to snow and ice, the marsh-dwellers of the Euphrates to swamplands and flood, Bushmen and Bedouin Arabs to drought and desert. In many tropical lands, rapid exhaustion of the soil sets a basic limitation on cultivation by primitive methods.

Natural conditions restrict certain kinds of development and permit others, but they do not dictate in any precise way the lines on which an economy shall develop. Man by his skill and labor produces a kind of secondary environment, which is a function of techniques as well as of resources. This ecological framework, product of man's skill and his environment, varies widely from one people and region to the next, according to the different materials at hand and the individual bent of their interests and skills.

Preoccupation with the daily or seasonal food supply, the frequency

[1] On the other hand, some of the richest lands, the western forest and central plains of North America, were still occupied by primitives until the opening of the nineteenth century.

of hardship, and the risks of hunger are obvious characteristics of a primitive economy. So also are the limitations of transport, though this applies, of course, with less force to the livestock breeders such as the horse and camel nomads. Less obvious, but just as fundamental, are the difficulties of storage, which restrict the accumulation of food and other goods. Heat, damp, and the white ant effectively destroy any possessions which the Bemba of North Rhodesia or the Nambikwara of the South American Mato Grosso may succeed in amassing. In Polynesia the people of Tikopia did not know how to cure fish, and only one of their crops had good keeping properties. The Eskimo, admittedly, can freeze his meat, and keep it for indefinite periods, but the ice which makes food-storage possible for him causes other shortages, of vegetable foods, of wood for fuel and shelter. Pastoralists are better off in this respect, as herds provide a natural store of wealth, but cattle are vulnerable to disease, the onset of which may disrupt the whole economy.

Productive equipment is relatively simple and few durable goods of any kind are made. In short, the productive effort of a primitive economy is capable of anticipating its future needs only for a very brief span. Accumulation is difficult, long-term planning impossible.

Insecurity, then, is frequently the mark of a primitive economy. But on this score there is considerable variation from one primitive economy to another. Some food-gathering peoples, for example, the acorn-eating Yokuts of California, and the Kwakiutl fishers of British Columbia, were blessed with a natural abundance of basic resources.

Another common characteristic of a primitive economy, though also not a universal one, is a lack of diversity in the major resources. Some peoples are heavily dependent on a few products, which are processed so as to provide food, shelter, weapons, tools, and nearly all the main needs of the people. This tendency is particularly noticeable among hunters and herders. The Eskimo takes from the seals he kills meat to eat, fat for fuel and for lighting, fat for anointing himself, skins for covering, sinews for thongs, bones for harpoons and arrow heads. There is an economy of effort, but the risks are high. If, during a stormy winter, seals are absent from a usually sheltered bay, starvation and death for the whole community may result. The cattle-keeping Nuer of the southern Sudan turn the products of their cattle to meet most of their essential requirements: blood, milk, cheese, and meat for sustenance; horn and bone for weapons; dried dung for fuel; hides for covering and thongs and bags. But during the rinderpest epidemic at the end of the last century, when their cattle died wholesale, they were in desperate straits. Among such peoples enormous stress is placed on the value of their main resource, which tends to become the focus of their religious symbolism. For the Nuer, cattle play a central role in their religious life, being used for every ceremonial and sacrifice. Such a tendency to place exceptionally high value on a few vital resources may distort the development of an economy. Nuer country abounds in game and wild birds, yet they seldom exploit them, despising wild-game as food if they can get milk and beef. Conversely hunting peoples often disdain the meat of domesticated animals. One effect is that the full range of resources actually available with existing techniques are not exploited. Another is to inhibit internal and external exchanges. Thus the Nuer were averse to dealing with Arab traders, as these had no cattle and cattle were the only form of wealth which interested the Nuer.

We may sum up the basic characteristics of primitive economies as follows: preoccupation with the daily and seasonal food supply, limitation of transport, difficulties of storage, overdependence on one or two major resources. These restrictions derive mainly from a low level of technical knowledge, which severely limits productive capacity. Wherever these characteristics are found, certain consequences flow from them. The economic unit is small and, save for occasionally bartered specialities, does not transcend the population of a small village. Social relations are of the personal, face-to-face kind. Everyone has known everyone else from childhood, everyone is related to everyone else. The sick and unfortunate are able to depend on the kindliness of immediate neighbors. The sharing of tools and of supplies to meet individual shortages are matters of moral obligation between kinsfolk and neighbors. Impersonal commercial relations hardly exist. The group which lives and works together has strong feelings of solidarity, partly because they are isolated from other groups by poor communications.

The small size of the social group within which production is organized and exchange effected also reduces the opportunity for specialization. Such skills as are practiced are known to everyone of the appropriate age and sex [2] in the community. Certain kinds of work are traditionally assigned to men, others to women, but fulltime specialists are very rare. The work of the potter, boatbuilder, smith, or magician is a voluntary spare-time task.

[2] See Redfield's paragraphs on the sexual division of labor, p. 346.

In such a setting economic relations have not been separated out from other social relations. There is no question of one man working for another whom he knows only as an employer. Men work together because they are related to each other, or have other social obligations to one another. Important economic processes are thus embedded in wider social needs, and are inextricably mixed with politics, ceremonial, and general festivity. When the Blackfoot Indians of the Plains used to congregate in the summer for tribal buffalo drives, which were their main economic activity, a short period of intensive hunting was followed by feasts and dances, and the social life of the tribe reached its peak. The great annual ceremony of the Sun Dance brought not only the economic, but also the political and religious activities of the year to a grand climax.

In an economy for which these general conditions hold true, economic exchange is necessarily limited. Markets remain undeveloped because the advantages of internal exchange are slight. The household provides for its daily needs from its own production. Surpluses cannot speedily be sent to areas of scarcity because of the difficulties of transport. On the other hand, if the surplus is to be used at all, it must somehow be distributed at once, because of the technical difficulty of storage. As everyone produces much the same range of articles as everyone else, there will be little demand locally for any excess production. Often the only way an individual can dispose of a surplus is by holding a lavish feast or simply by giving it to kinsmen and neighbors who will feel bound to repay one day.

But primitive economics are not, as a rule, completely closed. Some external trade, however sporadic, is usually possible. Hunters may be in contact with cultivators and exchange meat for cereals, as did the Congo forest pygmies with their Negro neighbors in a silent trade in which the two parties to the exchange never came face to face. Shore-dwelling people may exchange fish for crops with inland cultivators. One community may produce a surplus of one speciality, a local delicacy, a raw material, or a prized ornament, and trade it with another speciality of another tribe. Among the Kalahari Bushmen there was a system of trade relations, both with their Bantu neighbors and between the different tribes. Centrally placed groups played the part of intermediaries, obtaining from their northern neighbors supplies which they bartered further south, and vice versa. In this trade eggshell beads and tobacco, because there was always a steady demand for them, had a fixed value according to which other goods could be 'priced.'

Internal exchange is also possible, as when four or five little communities meet regularly in a local market and cancel out small inequalities of output by exchanges. The difference between this kind of market and the markets of developed economies is that goods which are offered for exchange have not been produced primarily for sale, but are the fortuitous surplus of subsistence production. This is an essential difference between production in the primitive and in the developed economy. For these economies, instead of 'primitive,' the word 'subsistence' is often used, to emphasize the contrast with complex modern exchange economies.

The production unit does not necessarily correspond to the unit of consumption; the size of the former is generally determined by technical considerations, while the size of the consumption unit may vary from a group of households to include the whole of the local community.

For production people co-operate in different groups at different seasons, according to the nature of the work. For some tasks the most efficient unit may be only one man: the Eskimo hunter waiting at his seal hole is better alone. The success of Bushman hunting often depends on fleetness of foot; in the wet season the sodden ground impedes the animals and even in the dry season the young buck can often be chased and run down, as the hot sand causes their hoofs to come off. For this kind of hunting, one man and a dog is the best team. At other times the whole male force of a large band may set barricades and pitfalls across a valley, and then drive a herd of wild animals into the great trap.

Other kinds of production can be broken up into a number of tasks performed by separate individuals. Only one man at a time can operate a Congolese handloom for weaving raffia. But the various processes for preparing raffia and the loom can be farmed out to different individuals to do in their own time: an old man may be the most suitable person for the intricate sorting of the strands, and a young man for the heavy work of actual weaving.

In agricultural work the pressure of the changing seasons may make it urgent for each farmer to get help in clearing the fields. In bush clearing a team is more efficient than a series of separate workers. According to local custom, a man may be able to call out a labor gang composed of his age-mates, his kinsmen, or all the able-bodied men of the district. The nature of the work tends to determine the size of the working unit, but because most tasks are not very complex, and because those few that do involve large-scale collaboration are of short duration, large working units are rare.

As to the reward of labor, there is little attempt to calculate the contribution of each unit, and to give it a corresponding share of the product. Among Bushmen, whether the game brought to the camp has been run down by an individual hunter, or killed in a communal battle, the rules for distributing the meat are still the same: all members of the camp are entitled to their share. A man who has killed a buck on his own, still has to hand it in to be divided by the camp leader according to fixed rules which set aside certain parts for the married men, others for the young men, others for women, according to their several status. The women of the band who collect the vegetables daily keep for their families the product of their own foraging, but meat represents an irregular supply of an important food, and the system of even distribution of game insures a share for all families of the community.

Where labor gangs are formed to clear land, each member in turn gets the benefit of the work of the whole group. In some cases a feast is offered as inducement to the workers, but the ultimate incentive is the maintenance of good will, which insures to each worker similar help in his need. In a primitive economy there are no wages (except for specialists' fees to healers, magicians, and smiths). A man does not normally earn his right to a particular share of output by contributing a particular piece of work. His claim to a share is based on his membership and on his status in the social group, household, camp, club, et cetera for which the work is being done. He works in order to fulfill his social obligations, to maintain his prestige and the status to which his sex, age, rank et cetera may entitle him.[3]

It is as difficult to distinguish a regular unit of consumption as a regular unit of production. Rights to enjoy certain things may be vested in individuals, in families, or in the community as a whole. Different kinds of sharing-situations may be set in the framework of different social groups, so that it is impossible to consider the society as divided into a fixed series of units of consumption such as the family. Food may be cooked by wives at their domestic hearths, but part of it is carried out to contribute to a general supply which the men share among themselves.

Among the Nuer, for example, the extended family is the cattle-holding unit, and each family's rights to cattle in payment of fines or at mar-

[3] See the analogy drawn by Professor Redfield with work and consumption within the family, Chapter 16.

riages are jealously guarded. But where the food-products of cattle are concerned, men habitually eat in each other's homes to such an extent that the whole village seems to draw on a common stock. In agricultural communities, the land-rights of individuals are generally restricted by overriding rights vested in the village as a whole. A Bemba village, under its headman, owns its land by right of occupation; each male member has rights in the land he has cleared, by virtue of accepted residence. Each wife has her granary for storing the crop she has raised on the fields provided by her husband. But the whole village, with its fields, and granaries, is at the same time a kind of joint housekeeping concern, for the rules of hospitality and the habit of food-sharing distribute the product of the year's work over the whole village.

Such customs are common in most primitive economies, and tend to even out the inequalities of income that result from primitive techniques. Public opinion forces a household whose harvest has prospered more than those of the neighbors to share its advantages with them. Equality of distribution, then, according to status rather than reward allocated according to work, is another characteristic feature of a primitive economy. This does not mean that some economic privilege is not accorded to those who have high status.

The obligation to distribute income is supported by two factors. One, which brings home to all the importance of generosity, is the constant menace of want. Everyone is aware of his own insecurity and consequent dependence on his neighbors. The second, as we have already seen, is the technical difficulty of conserving goods for future consumption. Perishable goods constitute a major part of the wealth of these economies, and enjoyment cannot be postponed to an indefinite future. The man who distributes his surplus to his neighbors has the satisfaction of gaining prestige. And since the obligation to repay gift for gift is fully recognized, he is even laying up some security for himself for the future. By giving away his own surplus he is making a number of people beholden to him. This is an elementary form of credit. The recipients of his gifts will be expected to treat him likewise when occasion arises. They also accept his influence, and help to build up his standing in the community.

In a primitive economy political power is not related to economic control in the same way as in a highly developed economy. Since, as we have seen, the system of production is based on small independent units, it does not offer means for concentrating power through control of resources or productive equipment. A man can best satisfy the drive

for power and prestige by attaching to himself a group of adherents:
to them he affords protection and a lavish board; they give him status
and authority. Competition, in a primitive economy, is not specifically
economic, but social. On the other hand, economic advantages do often
follow from high social status. Only a chief or a shaman among the
Nambikwara can have more than one wife, and this is regarded as a
reward for his responsibility. The chief of a district among the Bemba
needs many wives, simply in order to organize the catering for councilors
and visitors to the court. The payment of tribute to the chief, and the
distribution by him of hospitality and largess are complementary aspects
of his status. He needs the contributions of his subjects in order to fulfill his obligation to give lavishly to them. Thereby he also maintains
his position. Although loyal villages send teams to cultivate his fields,
and so ensure a grain supply commensurate with his responsibilities,
the Bemba chief does not try to organize maximum production. He
prefers to fill his granaries from windfall payments of tribute in kind.
This illustrates a bias in the relation between economic and political
organization in a primitive economy. It is not through control of production that political advantages and privileges in consumption can be acquired; rather it is that distribution can be controlled only by building
up social status and gaining political authority.

The dominant institutions in a primitive economy, while predominantly
political or religious, are nevertheless important channels for the redistribution of wealth. Where there is powerful chieftainship, what is brought
in as tribute is quickly given out again as rewards and gifts: local inequalities of production over the chiefdom are thus evened out. It is
usual for those who have met with disaster to ask for help from the chief,
and he can call on his prosperous subjects to provide emergency supplies.
In some societies one important channel of economic redistribution may
be through associations of leading men, in the so-called 'secret societies.'
As entrance to them is gained by payment of fees, which are shared by
all members, the accumulated wealth transferred in fees receives wide
redistribution.

Marriage, too, often has a prominent economic function as a distributing agency. Where descent is patrilineal, marriage transfers rights over
a woman and her children from her father to her husband. As in many
societies this transfer is secured by substantial gifts to the bride's kinsfolk, so through the constant succession of marriages redistribution of
wealth takes place. A man may build up his herd of cattle until he has

enough to acquire a new wife, for himself or for one of his sons. Negotiations are opened, and shortly his herd is reduced again to a few beasts.

Since all regular social obligations are channels of economic distribution in these ways, it is not exaggerating to say that social ties perform the function of rudimentary credit institutions in primitive economies. One tribe in South Africa has recognized this in their saying: 'A man is the bank of his father-in-law.'

Although labor is given for the sake of fulfilling social obligations, and although distribution similarly follows the same lines, this is not to say that there is not a keen sense of *quid pro quo* in particular transactions. A meanness is well-remembered and paid off at an early opportunity. A man who consistently fails to turn up at working parties is forfeiting his title to membership in the group in question, and losing any right to a share in its product. The idea of equivalence in giving and receiving is clearly recognized. There is no such thing as a free gift. Every act of generosity is expected to be repaid by an equivalent deed at some later date. Under this convention of strict reciprocity, what may seem at first sight to be reckless squandering can often be a prudent outlay of resources.

The crucial difference between gift and sale is that the first object of gift exchange is the building up of a social relationship, whereas in buying and selling, any continuous social relation between the parties is merely incidental. Even in a modern economy, a significant part of the distribution of wealth is by gift-exchange, although the main part is by trade. In a primitive economy there may be no trade, or it may account for very few of the transactions which take place, but there will certainly be a well-developed system of exchange through gifts, which distribute supplies at the same time as they cement social relations.

Most of the concepts devised for analysis in economic science, such as capital, investment, saving, interest, et cetera have been developed for the study of complex exchange economies. Entities and processes corresponding to these basic categories can be recognized in embryonic form in a primitive economy. But they are not necessarily significant for describing the economy of peoples who have few durable goods, no money, and few commercial exchanges. How, for example, should the distinction between liquid and fixed resources be applied to an economy where nearly all goods can be used in all kinds of transactions? Should cows be classified as producer or as consumption goods? Is any insight gained by describing a polygamist's wives in one context as capital investment for him, as his labor force in another, as the principal consumers in another? Conditions in these simple undifferentiated economies seem to make nonsense of fine distinctions elaborated for highly specialized modern economies. On the other hand, these fine distinctions apply to economic realities which have developed out of the less specialized economic relations of the primitive societies. In the latter one can, as it were, trace them back to their more generalized roots.

The simplest definition of capital, and one which is significant for any primitive economy, concentrates on the tools and equipment for production. A man, or a group, who gives up time and energy to make a special tool for a special task, be it a digging stick, or a fish weir, or canoe, expects to be able to use it for a considerable period. In a wider sense, not only tools, but any of the things which are produced in order to yield future services over a stretch of time such as houses, bridges, or granaries, are capital.

Primitive economies are, by definition, poor in capital equipment. The quantity, effectiveness, and variety of their tools and weapons, the durability of their houses, the serviceability of their roads and paths, are strictly limited by the low level of technical knowledge. Cultivators have their hoes and granaries, knives and baskets; hunters have their spear-throwers, harpoons, bows, hunting poisons, implements for curing hides and skins. Some fishing communities, and especially ocean-going peoples, maintain a greater amount of capital equipment for their exploitation of the sea. They have different kinds of canoes, elaborate fishtraps, nets, and lines, which all represent considerable outlay of labor in their manufacture, and which give valuable services over many years.

The fact that fishing communities invest in more capital equipment than cultivators, herders, or hunters, might be expected to put them in a class apart from other primitive economies, were it not for two things. First, all their equipment is directed to one kind of production only, the harvest of the sea. An economy which is heavily dependent on one main resource cannot develop the complexity and high degree of internal differentiation of the modern economy. For another, this main resource of a fishing economy is essentially perishable. Drying or smoking only preserves fish for a very limited period in all but the coolest climates. A community is incapable of developing a complex exchange economy so long as the greater part of its production is devoted to perishable goods. Only by mastering the technical difficulties of storage, and so being able to accumulate a variety of goods, can a community save. Saving is abstaining from consuming in the present, in order to consume in the future. If its wealth is in the form of perishable goods, a community cannot save. Thus low capacity to postpone consumption is the mark of a primitive economy.

In such an economy there can be little specialization of production and correspondingly little exchange. From this follows the absence or very limited development of money, which is essentially a medium of exchange. But primitive economies are not necessarily entirely without money. Some kind of currency, accepted for certain exchanges, was long in use in Melanesia, western North America, and parts of tropical Africa.

Almost anything, from pigs, cowries, iron rods to strings of shells or tobacco, can be used as a standard for measuring relative values and as a medium of exchange. When some such object is used as money in a primitive economy, it is usually employed only for a restricted range of transactions. We find that by convention only certain kinds of goods or services can be bought and sold, or that only between certain categories of persons can there be a buying and selling relationship. Between other persons, or where other essential commodities are concerned, there are conventions of giving or sharing, not of buying and selling.

The existence of a monetary system, however rudimentary, gives the individual member of the economy an opportunity of saving. He accepts money in exchange for his products because it gives him a title to buy something else, at once, or in the future. So it enables him to postpone consumption to a time of his own choosing. It provides him with a link between the present and the future, extending the period during which his present wealth can be enjoyed. If an individual puts a store of money aside, he builds up a right to spend it in the future. Even if the borrower spends it all, the lender is still saving, so long, of course, as the borrower can be trusted to repay. When the debt is later repaid, the lender can enjoy the benefit of having refrained earlier from consuming his wealth. He will have saved for his own future, but as far as the economy as a whole is concerned there will have been no saving at all. The saving of one individual has been canceled by the spending of the other. Monetary savings of individuals do not imply that the total community will necessarily be saving anything. In a modern economy, savings correspond in this way to one type of spending, investment, or spending on durable goods. But where the economy is capable only of producing perishable goods, this cannot be so. Even if it has some kind of monetary system, the money saved by all the individuals is equivalent only to so much chalking up of claims against each other. Where the goods which can be acquired with the money are of a perishable kind, the people would, for all their individual saving of money, be no more secure against death or famine than if, without any monetary system, the rotting away of food were anticipated by great feasts. Money of itself does not give a closed economy any link between the present and the future. It does not enable the community to save, even though it makes individual saving possible. As saving simply means laying by wealth which is not immediately consumed, a community can only be said to save to the extent that durable goods are produced, houses, carved cups and bowls, well-tilled fields, canoes, fishing nets, spears, knives, et cetera. Such production in primitive economies is restricted in amount by the limited techniques available.

In a primitive economy the character of the distributive system can have adverse effects on the incentives to labor, and so on production. The incentive to work is derived not only from the simple need to provide subsistence, but largely from the drive for prestige, the satisfactions of working together, the pleasures of conviviality, and the common interest in the product of the work. The sum of these incentives may not necessarily secure maximum production. The obligation to share with neighbors any private windfall or surplus may have a deterrent effect on production. In the rural economy of Java, if a man wishes to become rich, it may be necessary for him to leave his home and settle in another village, as a stranger on whom the usual obligations of village membership do not fall. Otherwise every improvement in his own condition must be shared with all the village. A rank system may have a similar deterrent effect if a certain standard of living is considered suitable for a chief and another lower one right for a commoner. An ordinary man may be afraid of amassing riches for fear of seeming to aspire beyond his station, or be deterred by knowing that he will have to hand over a great part of his gains to the chief.

Many economies today lie at an intermediate stage between primitive and developed. There are still in Europe rural communities of farmers who mainly produce for their own needs, but send their surplus products to markets which link them with the world markets of modern capitalism. Through this link they are able to acquire tools, machinery, clothing, which they do not produce for themselves. Such dependent economies are found, for example, in rural Ireland, in Poland, and in the Balkans.

Other economies of an intermediate type are those which, though characterized by a simple technical knowledge, are only partly self-subsistent as a result of their access to the world market. They are able to produce some crop or offer their labor for sale in a modern market, and can satisfy many of their wants from that market. The fishing villages on the coast of Malaya are linked by Chinese middlemen with markets in Singapore or Indonesia. Cocoa farmers in the Gold Coast, or cotton growers in Uganda, are intimately affected by changes in world prices for their produce. These are economies that combine an important element of subsistence production with an important element of external exchange. They are not a new development. Coastal West Africa, for example, has had cash-crop economies of this type for over three hundred years.

The essential difference between the way affairs are run in a primitive economy and the working of a developed economy cannot be summed up by the absence or presence of the profit motive. Primitive peoples are as alive to the furthering of their own advantage as anyone in a capitalist economy. It is not true that they are devoid of economic sense. The most striking difference is the personal nature of all relations in a primitive economy, compared with the impersonal nature of most economic relations in modern society.

In the intermediate dependent economies, as in the truly primitive economies, all social relations are of the personal kind, but the people will also have some impersonal relationships with traders, moneylenders, and middlemen from the external economy. Such contacts give them access to valuables and capital goods produced by techniques that are far beyond their capacity. The technical difficulty of storing wealth may be overcome, partly by importing durable goods, partly by financial means. A banking system, or the mere circulation of money which has value in a nearby advanced economy, creates possibilities of postponing consumption, not only for the individual, but for the community as a whole. In these cases money put by can mean real saving, because at any time it can be used to import goods into the community.

Every contact which a primitive economy comes to have with a complex economy modifies its primitive characteristics. The feelings of village solidarity, the obligations of mutual aid and hospitality, will be present, but diluted. Family ties will still regulate production and distribution to a considerable extent, but the subsistence unit which shares a common board and common purse will be relatively smaller than in the primitive economy. It will be possible to distinguish within the total residential group regular units of consumption corresponding to family units. The social pressure forcing a man to share his gains with the whole community will still be there, but less pronounced, and the conflict between his economic ambitions and his responsibilities to the community will generate social friction. Inequalities of wealth will be tolerated. Some equivalence between the unit of labor and the amount of its reward will be increasingly aimed at. Wages will begin to be paid as one of the incentives to labor. These intermediate economies are not to be classed with modern capitalist economies, but they owe to their contact with them those features which distinguish them from the truly primitive.

ROBERT REDFIELD

XVI

How Human Society Operates

WHAT IS A SOCIETY?

A SOCIETY IS PEOPLE with common ends getting along with one another. A brawl in a barroom is not a society, nor is there yet a society when ten exhausted shipwrecked sailors clamber up on a lonely beach—at least there is none until they begin to work out their common problems of getting a living and of living together. A society has, then, organization. It is people doing things with and to and for each other to the interests of each and all in ways that those people have come to accept.

In this sense a group of boys organized to play baseball or to exchange postage stamps is a society, but here we have in mind those societies in which people are organized not for some special purpose or interest, but for all the business and pleasure of living. The societies that are the subject of this chapter are composed of men and women and children living together, generation after generation, according to traditional ways of life. Such societies are whole societies, in that they exist for all human needs and interests. They are enduring societies in that children are born and raised to become adults with ways of life much like those of their parents and grandparents. A nation is such a society, and so is an Indian tribe. So, too, is a town or village, and even a single family in so far as its members have traditions that are transmitted to each succeeding generation and make that family, through time, distinguishable from other families. On the other hand groups of nations taken together are great societies; one speaks of Western society in contrast to Oriental society. In some sense all the people of the world taken together constitute a single society. But it is of the separate tribes and nations that

345

we are chiefly thinking here. Because there have been and still are so
many and so various primitive societies, one learns a good deal about
society in general by referring, as will be done in this chapter, to one
or another of these simple societies.

A society is easily seen as people doing work. It has other aspects,
too. A society is also people sharing common convictions as to the good
life. This is to say that it is not merely a system of production and of
services—an anthill is that—but that a human society exists in the fact
that its members feel that certain conduct is right and other conduct
wrong, and act more or less accordingly. And a third aspect of human
society is to be recognized in the sentiment its members have of belonging together as against other people who do not belong. A society is
people feeling solidarity with one another.

A SOCIETY AS PEOPLE DOING WORK

In every society the work is divided. Everyone takes advantage from
work done by others of a kind which he does not do and in exchange
serves those others by doing useful things that are not done by them.
The division of labor between men and women is universal, in that
everywhere what women do is on the whole different from what men
do; on the other hand what each sex does varies with the society: in
Polynesia the men did the cooking; among the Hidatsa Indians the
women did the farming. Equally obvious is the division of labor that
goes with differences in age. Beyond these bases for the organization of
work, there are those which depend on differences in temperament, or
on training, or on the accidents of opportunity, or on the variations in
demand.

In some small, isolated, primitive societies there is almost no division
of labor except between the sexes and the age-groups, and except some
individuals who act as magicians or as leaders of ceremonies. Every adult
man does about what every other does, and so it is with women. With
the development of tools and techniques, with increase in population,
and with the advancement of communication and transportation, the division of labor has become far more complete and complex. In the
Guatemalan village of San Pedro de la Laguna, fifty-nine different kinds
of specialists are to be recognized in a population of less than two
thousand. A classified telephone directory suggests but by no means
completely lists the thousands and thousands of kinds of specialists that
make up a modern city.

An obvious result of this increasing division of labor is the increasing ease in the number and kinds of commodities and services which people can enjoy. But another effect is to limit the view which any one individual has of the operations and goals of his society to a very small segment of the whole, with corresponding difficulties for industrial management, for democratic government, and for personal happiness. Another result is greatly to extend the number and distribution of people who divide labor with one another. Millions of people, from China to the Congo to Akron, come to depend upon one another for services and products exchanged, and yet these people have no common purposes and understandings; they hardly know that one another exist. The organization of work tends to become worldwide while national and other local groups distrust, dislike, or fear one another. So men come to depend upon one another while yet without common sentiments and values.

A SOCIETY AS PEOPLE SHARING CONVICTIONS ABOUT THE GOOD LIFE

The organization of work takes place in ways other than the mere division of labor. Slavery is a way of organizing work. The market, to be discussed below, is another way. And a third, perhaps the basic form of the organization of work, arises from the fact that in a society people share common sentiments and beliefs as to what it is good to do. People work, not only because in most cases they are uncomfortable or even starve if they do not, but because work is a part of the meaning of life. To the primitive agricultural Indian, farming is a necessary part of decent and appropriate human existence, an essential way of maintaining relationship with the supernaturals, a test and duty of honorable manhood. In such a society one prays as one works, and work is, in part, religion. In aristocratic societies of recent times on the other hand, work was appropriate only to the underprivileged masses; while in modern Western society work is again a general positive value, and men work for wealth and power and to excel their neighbors.

The more general statement to make about society is that it consists of a plan of life. Society operates because its members have around them a universe which to them makes sense. Moreover, this plan is not merely a pattern without moral meaning: it is a plan for right conduct, an organization of conceptions as to the good, the true, and indeed the beautiful. The body of conventional meanings that are made known to us through acts and artifacts is by anthropologists called 'the culture' of a community. In the primitive societies the 'wholeness' of these meanings is more easily seen than in the case of large, complex, and rapidly changing societies. The customs and institutions fit together to make a single moral representation of the universe. The Papago Indians, for example, carry on warfare not as an opportunity for exploit separate from their other interests. The Apache scalp taken in a foray is the symbol of the supernatural power brought to the Papago camp by the warrior who killed, a source of spiritual strength, a form of divine power, solemnly to be welcomed into the camp, into the home of the killer. When the men are away on the expedition, the women and children, by abstaining from noisy or indecorous conduct, in effect share in the making of war, just as, in some primitive societies, men share in the importance and responsibilities of childbirth by 'lying in'—by restricting their behavior for the welfare of the newborn child. Labor is divided, but all members of the society act in terms of common conceptions and ideals. Commonly the myths of such a society are narrative representations of its moral values, as its ceremonies are dramatic expressions that correspond. So every culture is a provider of a course of action for the individual, a source of his motives, and validater of his convictions.

This is the way a simple and isolated society operates. But as societies have become larger and rapidly changing, with many different kinds of people in them, the customs and institutions no longer preserve this unity and harmony. There is then no single culture for all, even in one nation or town, but rather a great many incomplete cultures, so that what a man does at his office or in his factory is not always closely related to what he does when he plays or goes to church or visits the neighbors—if he does visit them. And what his children do and believe may be notably different from what he himself was brought up to do and believe. Then the sense of the meaning of life tends to be lost; men experience uncertainty, insecurity, and confusion. On the other hand as this happens men more and more come to think rationally and critically about the life around them and to act intentionally to change and to guide it. Science develops, along with rational administration and planning. The basis for the operation of society thus tends to shift, over the course of human history, from tradition to deliberate social invention and thoughtful choice.

A SOCIETY AS PEOPLE FEELING SOLIDARITY WITH ONE ANOTHER

A society also operates by virtue of the confidence its members feel in one another and of the loyalty they have to their own group. It is said that the dangers of a great war between the present great powers of this earth would be quickly averted if Mars would attack this planet. Perhaps it would be sufficient for us earth-dwellers merely to know that there were Martians. We would feel a new sense of solidarity for all fellow earth-beings as contrasted with those inferior or iniquitous Martians. At any rate it appears that the members of every society, small or great, think very well of themselves as contrasted with the members of comparable societies. What is seen on a small scale in gangs, appears again in nations. Every tribe and nationality, in some parts of the world every valley or cluster of hamlets, refers to itself in favorable terms and to others unfavorably. Many primitive tribes reserve the term for 'people' or 'human beings' to themselves alone, while everywhere the terms used to refer to neighboring peoples are contemptuous, derogatory. It would seem, indeed, that the resentment and scorn shown toward other peoples are strongest with regard to neighboring people, as though, as though, as Sigmund Freud remarked, one could least well bear to see what is so much like oneself and yet so different.

In cases where one society is divided into subgroups, each with its own loyalty, but yet a loyalty subordinated to that of the entire tribe or nation, this fact of appreciation of the lesser in-group and depreciation of the out-group contributes to the effective operation of the society. There is a special kind of strength in a tribe divided into clans, for each clan is a warm and supporting intimate group for every individual within it; its limited solidarity is intensified by the contrast and competition with other clans. A similar effect is brought about by the grouping of colleges within a university, and perhaps was realized among the nations of Europe in the nineteenth century, when all the nations were held together by a degree of common tradition and by common commercial and banking interests, so that national pride flourished while wars were limited to moderate destructiveness.

This sense of common membership, pleasant in itself and often referred to as *esprit de corps,* increases the effective operation of the society by making it possible for its members to withstand difficulty and defeat and to act together powerfully for the common good. Then we know it as morale. The sentiments are unifying when they attach to the same single society, or are qualified by limited attachments to balanced component units, as just indicated. The sentiments may, however, attach to groupings which cut across societal lines, and then may have a divisive effect. In-group sentiments may attach to religious groupings, or to racial groupings. When Christendom was a political and regional community as well as a religious community, the loyalties to the brotherhood of Christians as contrasted with infidels, however unchristian these loyalties were, may have served the solidarity of that part of the world that was Christian, as corresponding sentiments united the Islamic world, but the prejudice and conflict between Jew and Christian within a modern nation is disruptive of that nation. The disposition of a society or part-society to seek a basis for a revived solidarity in an intensification of hatred of some other group than itself is illustrated by the anti-semitism, anti-Catholicism, or anti-foreignism of groups threatened or insecure in many a land in modern times. As a technique of waging war on an enemy, thus to be weakened by intensifying the ethnic and religious hostilities within it, the general principle was well understood by Hitler and Goebbels, as it is also employed for special advantage by occasional rousers of the masses everywhere. In peacetime also a nation may suffer when the in-group sentiment excludes some of a man's fellow citizens and neighbors, as appears in the racial prejudices of modern times, and especially in the prejudice and intolerance directed by white Americans or South Africans to Negroes. In these cases a large minority or even majority of fellow citizens are excluded in great measure from both the privileges of citizenship and from the sense of group solidarity corresponding to the nation. The result is a loss in man power, material and spiritual, for the dominating group is itself weakened by the unresolved inconsistency between its professed ideals and its evident practices. In these cases, then, the restriction of group-sentiments to only those racially qualified is to be recognized, in appraising the working of the society, as unfavorable to the effective operation of the nation.

WARFARE

Of many forms of organized violence, warfare is that one which has political consequences. The rivalry between closely related groups that is an aspect of the in-group sentiments just referred to, often leads, obviously enough, to organized violence. The brawls between gangs of boys in the city characteristically are regulated by custom and form; and this formal aspect of violence between closely related groups is marked in the primitive societies. Usually such violence, which is not war, follows upon the commission by some individual of an act which in a modern society would be called a crime. Among Australian aborigines the offender is required to stand and receive spears thrown at him. Among the Eskimo the quarrelers publicly sing insulting songs at one another. All these cases of limited and regulated fighting are ways to adjust differences between constituent groups of a larger unit; they are more closely related to law than to war. Distinguished also are the very common instances, in primitive society, of armed raids upon unfriendly groups to take heads, scalps, or other trophies, or to bring back human sacrifices. This resembles war, in that the groups engaged are persistingly hostile, and the military enterprises are organized and lethal. Yet in many of these cases there is a strong element of sport: such organized conflict is a dangerous game, in which glory may be won and lives lost. This element persisted in the warfare of western societies until very recently. Other cases of this general group involve a religious motive: the head or the scalp is taken to bring supernatural power to the taker's group, or the captive is brought home as an offering to the deities.

In none of these cases is warfare an instrument of tribal or national policy. True warfare is probably to be recognized in those military activities in which political power is extended to include culturally related peoples, and in those in which the rivalries of two culturally different groups are put to the test of armed conflict. In the operation of societies such warfare plays a double role. It both destroys and constructs societies. In ancient Mexico the Aztecs entered upon warfare with neighboring peoples; the object was in large part the obtaining of captives for sacrifice, but a result was the subordination of many neighboring peoples of similar culture to the Aztec military power. In ancient Peru warfare led to a much stronger political and administrative organization: a state over a thousand miles in extent was the result. Similar political consequences followed from warfare among the Maori of New Zealand and among several African tribes. With this political motive an economic motive enters in, not among the most primitive people, but where there is enough property and wealth to attract the military marauder. And mixed also, as causes, are the personal ambitions of military leaders. So fused into a well-established practice, warfare became an instrument of social development, an extension of political activity. In East Africa, especially, one can see how military conquest was culturally constructive. Hamitic cattle-breeders invaded this part of the primitive world and subjected to their domination the agricultural Bantus. There resulted a complex state, with a ruling class on top of the farmers below, and there resulted also an exchange and multiplication of inventions and ideas. The society that resulted after conquest was a society of classes, a society in which there was division of labor between ethnic groups, and a society in which the political institutions had developed far to provide for the regulation of these complexities. Under the impact of conquest and of cultures now included in a single polity, native custom is codified as law, and religious and scientific ideas are exchanged. One thinks of the history of Rome. How many new inventions, how many critical thinkers, arose in the mixing of peoples which followed upon warfare! At the same time, of course, the waging of war consumes immense quantities of goods and lives, destroys whole societies, and, with the accelerated destructiveness of weapons, threatens the very extinction of civilization.

THE ORGANIZATION OF PRODUCTION, DISTRIBUTION, AND CONSUMPTION

In the first part of this chapter the division of labor was emphasized as a universal method for organizing work. This aspect of the operation of society may now be examined more fully. The division of labor does bring it about that the whole society realizes the advantages of having some people do some things well through their freedom from necessity to do other things. But this is not all there is to the social organization of economic activity. In every society it is also necessary to determine, somehow, what resources shall be used in producing what products. How shall products and consumable commodities be distributed, and to whom? Who shall consume what commodities? The organized ways of accomplishing these ends may be called the economy of that society. The technology is the tools and techniques for producing and making useful things; the economy is the institutions and customs that get raw materials into products and that get both distributed and consumed.

It is easy for us, who read these words, to think of factories, markets, and money as principal social machinery for getting these things done. But looking at primitive and ancient societies shows that these three are recent and special devices for bringing about production and distribution. In most societies raw materials and manufactured goods get around to producers and consumers without markets and money. The ancient and the basic form of economy is one in which goods are made and goods are distributed not by buying and selling at all, but by virtue of the traditional rights and obligations that custom recognizes to exist between one individual and another in that society, or between one group in that society and another. This kind of economy is easily seen in most families. The product of the father's labor, whether it be meat from the hunt or a pay-check brought home from office or factory, is shared with his wife and children not because he sells something to them which they buy, but because it is recognized to be part of his role as father to share his produce with his wife and children. The allocation of the father's labor to daily work, of the mother's labor to cooking and sewing, and perhaps of the small son's labor to fetching firewood or going to the store for lemons and soap, is a matter which requires no competitive bidding to determine and in most cases no payment of money to compensate. It is fixed by the very relationships of the members of the family to one another. The word 'status' is conveniently used for all the rights and obligations which attach to an individual or a group, according to the customs of the society. The father's status, in our society, includes his right to choose the place to live, according to his need and ability to get work, and his duty to provide for his family, as well as to share in the practical and moral guidance of his children. The work he does and the sharing of what he earns are parts of his status, too. So we may speak of this kind of economy as a status economy.

The basic form of economy in human societies is a status economy. In primitive societies most of the production—whether by hunting or by farming or by raising cattle or by handicraft manufacture—is brought about not because somebody sees a chance to make a profit in some market, but because it is part of the traditional status of that man or woman to hunt or farm or make baskets. And what is made is shared with others according to status. In many South Pacific societies a man works, not to feed his own children, but to feed his sister's children; his own children will be fed by his wife's brother. In certain hunting tribes it is usual for the hunter to give certain parts of the slain animal to just certain relatives—perhaps eight or nine different parts go, respectively, to eight or nine different relatives. So goods are distributed and consumed. These are reciprocal exchanges according to status: what a woman's brother gives to his sister's son is balanced by what that same man, as sister's son, gets from his own mother's brother, in the long run, and on the average. It is also common for goods to be distributed in status economies by the gathering of these goods in one place and by their distribution to all from this center. In a certain Melanesian community every gardener brings some of his best yams and puts them into the chief's yam house. They are 'given' to the chief. As the large and beautiful yams pile up, the villagers take satisfaction in the richness and industry of their own community; the abundance of the chief's yams redounds to the credit and glory of all. At a certain festival, the chief distributes these yams, some to visitors, and some to the villagers themselves. So everyone participates, in both the pride and the eating. In many simple societies there is neither money nor market. The whole society is, in respect to this matter of the economy, like a family; the status relationships determine production and distribution. The medieval manor had an economy which was largely a matter of status.

In contrast with this is that economy which depends upon the market. For the beginnings of the market economy in primitive societies we must look outside of the local society to its relations with other societies. The beginnings of human social living must be thought of as taking the form of small groups scattered over a territory and pretty much isolated from one another. In the section above on warfare it might have been made clear that the relation between such groups is not ordinarily one of warfare. Organized aggressive violence against a neighboring society is not characteristic of the very simplest societies. Many such societies get along with one another in a more or less friendly way: both societies recognize customary visits, without hostile intention, from one to another. An occasional invader from the outside may be killed, but the formal visit is expected and is received without violence. Many such visits are the occasion of the exchange of goods.

More commonly, in primitive societies, people from one community pay a visit to another community, taking with them goods produced by the visitors and wanted by those visited. Then goods are exchanged, partly by barter, and partly by exchange of gifts. Something is given in the expectation that something will be given to the giver by the one to whom he gives. It is an equivalence of good will, rather than of precise market value, that determines the transaction. So in such a market personal relations, and the status of guest and host, affect the exchange. In larger communities, where people do not know each other personally, and more goods and more kinds of goods appear, the market may be more fully a matter of an effort to sell at the highest price and to buy at the lowest; then buyer and seller alike 'shop around,' and who the man is who buys or sells does not matter as compared with the opportunity to get the best price. Such a market can to some degree operate by the exchange of one sort of good for another, but money, as a universal measure of value, is an enormous help in facilitation of market exchanges. In some societies incomplete money appears: in some Melanesian communities certain strings of shell beads are used only in payment for pigs or wives. But in other places metal hoes or copper axes or coined metal or engraved certificates of promises to pay both serve as tokens of value that measure the value of one article against all others in the market, and also provide a way of temporarily holding buying power from one market or opportunity to buy to another.

In most societies of the world, and through most of human history, the production and distribution of goods has taken place chiefly as an aspect of the status relationships of the society: the market has been not the central mechanism for making society work, but a special or peripheral part of it. In modern times, and especially in the western world, the market became much more important. In our society the effort of the laborer is to a considerable extent bid for and offered to the highest bidder, and the use of land, paid for as rent, also enters into market competition. Now markets are very wide; for some goods, like wheat and rubber and tin, the market is worldwide; and, with rapid and universal communication, and with the machinery of banking and credit, what goes into production where and what goes where to what consumer are matters that the market 'decides,' rather than status and moral custom. So, in our society, the operations of the market have a principal and even determining influence on all sorts of affairs. Many a worker must live where the opportunity to get a job determines, and if suddenly the produce he makes ceases to be wanted, he may have no livelihood at all, and perhaps cannot keep his family together; in parts of the world men starve because the market no longer needs their labor. Where a family goes to live, perhaps its own solidarity, perhaps even whether its members live at all, follow from what happens in an immense impersonal market, and the actions of a nation, from its form of government to its remaining at peace or its going to war, may be shaped by what happens in markets.

The operation of the economy may also be regarded from the point of view of the organization and regulation of productive effort. Even in the simplest societies there is more to this than the mere separate work of single individuals. The household economy is in many cases under the leadership or direction of someone: the husband of several wives, as among the Hidatsa Indians, an older woman in a large matrilineal family of the Iroquois. When the Chukchee of Siberia go to hunt seal or walrus, the builder of the boat is master: he gives the orders and he receives the largest share of the meat. In modern societies with highly developed markets, the enterpriser may be one or a group that brings together a

very great amount of money and credit, labor and raw materials, in order
that automobiles or steel plate may be made. Furthermore, with the development of the state as formal government, its own efforts enter largely
into production and distribution. The state may itself be the principal
producer, as in Russia, or it may supplement private production, or it
may impose regulations upon the conduct of private enterprise, either
to limit the operations of a free market, as in granting a monopoly to a
single telegraph company, or in helping a freer market to operate, as in
legislation against trusts.

PROPERTY

Among the common understandings which constitute the ultimate basis
of society are those which attach to things that may be used, enjoyed,
or disposed of. Where the understandings limit or otherwise define such
rights and obligations of one individual or one group as to others, we
speak of 'property.' Property operates to keep use and enjoyment and disposal in expected channels; it contributes to the working of society in
wide and far-reaching ways: to confer and to limit power and the basis
for getting more power; to serve as a criterion for status; to provide motives for effort. Wanting to own things, men may work, steal, or go to
war. Owning things, men may enter social groups otherwise barred to
them, exercise influence over political decisions, or assume correspondingly great responsibility for serving the common good.

Property is thought of most immediately in connection with such tangible goods as tools, automobiles, houses, and land. It exists also, with
respect to such intangibles as magical spells, power-inducing songs addressed to supernaturals, hunting and fishing rights, patents and copy-
rights. In some societies personal names are owned in that they may be
disposed of by sale or gift; in our society, a trade name may be registered
and so owned. On the whole, the conceptions of ownership have become
more complex with the developing complexity of society. Land, in particular, has become subject to private and exclusive ownership, with
rights of sale and disposition by will; in most primitive societies such
precise and exclusive rights to land are not recognized; nevertheless,
individual or familial rights over hunting and fishing territories may be
sanctioned in custom in some very simple societies.

In primitive societies, and to an extent in modern society that is not
always recognized, property does not consist of a single all-embracing
bundle of rights held by one man as against all the world. On the other

hand, thoroughly communal ownership of important goods, in the sense that every individual has the same right in most goods as has every other, is not to be found. What is usual, rather, is that every species of ownership turns out to be the exercise of certain rights as to the thing owned subject to other rights in that thing held by others, at least in possibility. The Melanesian canoe-maker does not completely 'own' his canoe: he is expected to share it with certain others, and to share the catch it helps to bring about. The owner of land on Main Street may own it subject to zoning regulations, and to the right of the state to take it from him for certain public uses. Beyond this, furthermore, are the claims on property which are made outside of the law, but through expectations resting on custom. The primitive fisherman may share his catch with the whole settlement, as a matter of course. The rich American is expected to do something useful and generous with his riches; and everywhere the claims of the nearest of kin constitute a real limitation on ownership of many kinds of goods. And still further it is to be recognized that property rights are deeply associated with attachments that are sentimental and outside of the rights of control and disposal. It is not so much that the aborigine, long established on the desert or in the forest, owns the desert or the forest; he is attached to it, is a part of it, almost 'is owned' by it. And the reader of these pages may feel similarly about his home, if he happens to live in a home and not simply in a house, or about an heirloom of tender memories, or about a familiar old garment.

STATUS, PRESTIGE, AND RANK

Society operates through the division of labor and the social organization of production and consumption. Society operates through understandings as to proper conduct which have become traditional. Society operates through the guidance provided by conventional rights and obligations connected with the individuals and the groups making up the society. These, as already indicated, constitute the 'status' of the individual or the group. What is expected of any particular person, or group of them, or of the occupier of any particular role or office, is known in advance, and this foreknowledge enables the people of the society to do what is expected and what is consistent, more or less, with the ideals that the people have in common. In this way, too, society operates.

Society may thus be seen as a system of status relationships. Many of these take the form of relationships of kinship, and are described in Chapter XII. Also mentioned already is the status of the members of the in-group as contrasted with that of the out-group. And easily added are the differences in status of a man as contrasted with a woman, or a priest, policeman, or potentate as contrasted with a man who is none of these things. Conduct is expected of the one, and is due to him, different from that expected of or due to the other. In every society there are status-groups connected with differences in age. Any school reveals them, where they are connected with the grades through which the child passes. In many primitive societies this sort of classification in terms of status is made without schools; boys and men pass through a series of ranked groups, each perhaps with its name, its rights and duties, its growing prestige. In many cases certain of these age-groups enjoy a special clubhouse, or have special secrets or ceremonies. Such a ladder of attainment defines what is expected of everyone according to successive categories, from birth to death.

The attitudes that make up the status of any one individual, or group, in a society include, it will be noticed, authorization of various degrees of approach and intimacy. If someone has the status of 'best friend' I may go close to him and claim his sympathies as he may claim mine. They also include attitudes of superiority and inferiority. A cat—or a commoner—may look at a king, but he must look up when he looks at him. The 'place' in which an American Negro is thought by most white men to be 'all right' is a place that is down, not up, with reference to the white man. These differences of ranked status, of 'vertical' social position, are apparent as one individual is compared with another. In any gang or small school group the individuals with superior prestige are well known as such, and it may be possible even to rank all the members in an order of 'up-or-down.' There is no society in which the relative vertical status of the individual does not depend in some degree on himself—on his own conduct and personal chances. On the other hand in many societies the vertical position of any one individual is that of a great many others who are associated with each other more than they are associated with contrasting groups that are 'above' or 'below' their own. Such social classes make of the society a sort of column of layers: the vertical status of every individual is in large part determined by his birth. He takes the degree of prestige associated with his class, and as he works, plays, and probably marries within it, the classes remain distinguishable. On the other hand, the exceptional son of a nineteenth-century English workingman might 'become a gentleman,' and in societies nearer the frontier movement between classes is much less 'sticky'

and the classes may be hard to see at all. Where the classes are very
rigid, so that there is no possibility of escape to a superior class, they are,
after the East Indian example, described in an earlier chapter, known
as castes. All these organizations of society into persisting layered groups
are ways of defining the rights and obligations of people with regard to
one another, and so contribute to its operation. In most cases, there are
special kinds of occupations appropriate to each of the classes in a society
so organized; thus classes constitute an aspect of the division of labor.
In India the correspondence between inherited social position and the
kind of work or useful function performed is very close. In America it
has been the immigrant or latest arrival who has done the most unpleasant work. And also social classes are ways of maintaining an unequal
distribution of wealth and power that is to the advantage of the dominant classes. The upper layers get more than their share of prestige,
social influence, and wealth. At the same time, in societies where class
or caste is well established, the glories of the privileged provide a certain second-hand satisfaction to the less privileged. In many societies
that include conspicuously different racial groups, relative vertical social
positions correspond with the racial groupings, and as the skin color or
other racial mark is permanent, the racial classes become caste-like, with
the taboos against contact and the ceremonial separation of the racial
groups which are characteristic of castes.

Custom and Law

The simplest answer that can be made to the question, how does society operate, is that it operates because on the whole people do what is
expected of them. But why do people do what is expected of them? To
this question there are many true answers. It is easier to do what one has
done before than to do something else; a habit that everyone in a society
has we call a custom. Further, the things that one has done, and that
one's father's father has done, as well as some things that have been
thought over and struggled for, have come to be so rooted in sentiments
and in explanations and justifications that they have the force of what
we speak of as conscience: they are felt to be right, ultimately and
necessarily right. And still further, one does what is expected of one
because it is often extremely inconvenient, even dangerous, if one does
not. That is why I do not start out tomorrow to drive on the left-hand
side of an American road. There is an efficiency, an ease, about doing
what is expected of one. In a more special form, the expediency of doing

what other people expect appears in the exchanges of services and benefits which help us all to get along. I do a thing helpful to another
knowing that he is then more apt to do something helpful to me. If I
pay my bills, lend my lawnmower, keep out of those of my neighbor's
affairs which correspond to those of mine that I want him to keep out of,
and yet listen to enough of his troubles so that I may tell him mine, we
all get along pretty well. It is, however, to be emphasized that it is the
nature of human society to regard these considerations of expediency,
important as they are, as less worthy than those which are rooted in
conscience and the sense of duty. Society is not, basically, so much a
body of traffic rules and favors exchanged as it is a system of moral
convictions.

At a more obvious level society operates because conduct is sanctioned. A sanction is a consequence, pleasant or unpleasant, that follows
the doing of something and is known to follow it. Some such consequences are internal—the pangs of conscience—but others fall upon the
transgressor from without. Of those that so fall, many are imposed by
almost anybody in a diffuse and generalized way, as is illustrated by the
looks I receive from the people who know me if I do something of
which they disapprove. Perhaps what I do is not otherwise punishable.
If a specific consequence follows through the exercise of some centralized authority, we begin to think of the transgression and its consequence as an affair of the law. Legal sanctions have a quality of precise-
ness about them: the misconduct is defined in advance in clear terms,
and the consequence is also precisely known. Commonly the procedure
for matching the transgression to its appropriate consequence—complaint
or arrest, charge, hearing, trial, judgment—is specific and formal. Also,
for the matter to be one of law and not just custom, the consequence
that is the sanction is carried out not entirely if at all by the particular
person that suffered from the transgression, but by someone or some body
that stands for the society as a whole and acts for it. Law is the whole
society settling a local dispute or punishing or redressing a wrong in the
interests of the whole society and according to its common conscience.
When in a Plains Indian tribe a society of warriors finds a wrongfully
wounded man and sees to it that the wrongdoer heals the wound and
pays horses as a fine, law has begun. One may recognize law-making
and law-administering in groups smaller than the whole society: there is
something like law in some families; and there is certainly law in many
gangs. But there is a tendency for that group which is the principal

in-group, the tribe or the nation, to insist on its chief or exclusive power and right to make and enforce law. So law appears more clearly in the centralized and monopolizing force of the state.

POLITICAL INSTITUTIONS

In the simplest societies there is nothing that is 'political' if we use that word for institutions to express or enforce the common will or the ruler's will formally and publicly. In the Andaman Islands the natives lived in small bands without chief, council, law, or administrative regulation. If a man lost his temper and smashed things, the rest of the people just let him alone till he got over it. No one exercised any general authority to rule or to decide or to negotiate on behalf of the community. In such a society there is no state, no political government. Political institutions do clearly appear, however, in many tribal societies; there is a chief who has power to decide issues or to lead in the making of decisions; there may be a council; there may be groups to police the people.

The dependence of modern complex societies upon political institutions for their operation is obvious. The making, enforcing, and interpreting of law is the manifold business of thousands of individuals and hundreds of bodies: from legislatures, courts, and executives to the citizens who vote or obey orders, bring law suits or defend them, pay taxes, and discuss public issues with their neighbors or write a letter to some newspaper. These political institutions keep people's behavior more or less within the rules. They also are a means to the reconsideration of the rules and for the changing of the rules. They operate in that frontier of rule-making and rule-observing where conflicts occur, or at least differences of opinion, and the enforcement and interpretation of the rules helps to keep at least some of the people conscious of them, and so pushing to change them. Formal political institutions not only keep societies going in the good old ways; they also provoke a challenge of those ways.

What is, then, not so obvious is that political and administrative acts have an effect upon moral custom. It is commonly said that the laws express the customs and grow out of them. This is true, but it is also true that the passage of a law or the making of an administrative decision has an impact upon the sentiments and convictions of the society. To punish a criminal is to make a solemn gesture renewing the collective moral judgment with regard to the conduct for which the criminal is punished. Sometimes the law stands for a sort of theoretical or ideal norm which the society does not really mean to have realized, at least without exception, as when a Southern jury of white men find confessed lynchers of a Negro not guilty. Then the decision expresses a moral judgment that is inconsistent with the letter of the law. At the same time such a decision sharpens the conflict between the general principles and the exception, and helps either to remove the exception, or to weaken the principle. The decision and act whereby American citizens of Japanese descent were locked up during the war had one effect in strengthening the prejudices of those who were prejudiced against Orientals, for by conspicuous and effective public action a discriminatory act was performed. On the other hand, it aroused or strengthened sentiments of condemnation of the act. It is true that the customs make the law. It is also true that legal and administrative acts help to change the moral judgments of the society.

RELIGION

Some of the sanctions that keep men doing what is expected of them are neither the exterior sanctions of the law or of public opinion, nor the wholly interior sanctions of conscience. The sentiments that arise within a man that prevent him from doing that of which he would be ashamed, or that condemn him for doing it, in certain situations seem to come from outside him, yet not to come from this earthly world. Then it is a religious sanction that affects him. The convictions about the good are associated with unseen powers; these powers *are* the good, or represent it. A man's relationships to them have a unique quality; they are supremely critical for his ultimate welfare; and before the powers or their symbols he feels awe. The consequence of his action that is the sanction in this case may be a punishment, a suffering here on earth or a suffering in some other life. It may be a hand withered, or a soul damned. The suffering—or the reward, should his conduct be right, not wrong—may be simply the sense that the unseen powers are satisfied or dissatisfied, the feeling that one is or is not in harmony with ultimate goodness, final and unearthly authority.

Religion has been briefly defined as the adoration of goodness. It is goodness that is its essence; religion is not concerned with the trivial, nor with the morally neutral. It is about what most matters. But though an aspect of the moral life, it is not the same as morals. There are peoples—and many of these are primitive, uncivilized—whose religions are the worship or propitiation of supernatural beings who do not enforce the rules of good conduct among men. In such religions it is the worship and the propitiation, the ritual and the relationship between man and god, that matter; earthly morality is supported by conscience and the interplay of reciprocal obligations among people. In other religions, of which Christianity, Islam, and some primitive ones are examples, what a man should do to or for another *is* a matter of divine concern. On the whole, the ethical aspects of religion have grown stronger in the course of human history.

Religion is, moreover, activity; it is something going on in mind and in overt act; it is belief and rite. The power that is beyond men and that holds the welfare of men, mundane and spiritual, is thought about, conceived in certain forms and powers, and approached in prayer and offering and sacrifice. Commonly the power is conceived with qualities that are personal; the god may be angered, appeased, gratified. But in some religions, as in forms of Buddhism, the rites and beliefs have to do with conduct and with spiritual qualities. A religion is yet a religion even though it does not center about a god or gods.

Religion thus contributes to the operation of society through the power and authority and sacred meaning which it provides to the support of man's conduct and to his understanding of his place in the universe. In the totemic societies of aboriginal Australia groups of men carry on rituals at water-holes in their arid land to bring about the multiplication of the wild animals which the natives hunt for food. These rituals act out events and evoke sacred beings that were there before man was, and that were man's ancestors and benefactors. So the life of today is, through religion, conceived as an outcome of powers mysteriously greater than men's powers; they are greater, and yet men today share in that power through the goodness of these beings and the effectiveness of the rites. Similarly, the heavenly hierarchy of Christian faith is a version, in religious thought, of the hierarchies of earthly power of medieval times. These divine beings provide help to the worshipper; and the rite of the Mass, solemnly commemorative of the great act of sacrifice of God become man, is effective in bringing to the worshipper a benefit and strength which only religion can give.

THE EXPRESSIVE LIFE: PLAY, ART, CEREMONY, MYTH

In many of the preceding pages of this chapter the operation of society has been described as a matter of work and discipline. It has been suggested how people become and continue as a society by virtue of the fact that they labor together for common ends, and how they are kept

at it by the convenience of co-operation and by the rewards and penal-
ties which are provided by law, the general opinion, or the conscience
of the individual. In this account the sober, the practical, and the con-
straining have perhaps been too strongly emphasized. Perhaps the impression has been given that society gets along wholly or chiefly because
people do what they are compelled to do, or that work is the sole or the
basic form of activity.

As a matter of fact, a very great part of human social behavior is
quite the opposite of work. In work one does what a particular end demands in just the way it demands it and when the end requires it. To
hoe corn effectively is usually work because one must move the hoe just
so, one must do the hoeing just when the weather and the weeds make
it necessary, and one may not stop when one would care to. But a very
great deal of human activity is simply expressive. It is activity which
responds to the impulse of the individual to be active; it is activity which
takes a form that shows what the individual is thinking and feeling; it
is a fruit of the human impulse to create. Some expressive activity takes
place when it occurs to the individual to express himself; much takes
place at times fixed by the expectations and rhythms of society, but even
then without having to meet the demands of practically useful effort.

Laughing, joking, improvising with language, storytelling, praying,
arranging flowers, painting pictures, enjoying or playing a ball game or
Beethoven, and dancing are all forms of expressive activity. The expressive forms of behavior in large part give each society its own special
character as they give special flavor to each personality. Different societies may have the same tools and the same work habits, but if their art
and storytelling are different, the societies are then different. 'What do
you dance?' is the first enquiry a man of a certain Bantu tribe puts to
a stranger. What a man dances in that part of Africa is the key to a
man's whole life, the way to ask about a foreign society.

The relations between expressive activity and work appear in considering magic. If a man has something immediate and practical to accomplish he may do a little work to get the thing done. If the pipe leaks, I
may unscrew the faucet and put in a new washer. If the pigs are eating
the Melanesian's yams, he may fence the yam patch to keep out the pigs.
What is done is done in just the way that the end requires. The putting
in the new washer and the building of the fence are technically 'correct'—
that is, in both cases what is done is responsive to the demands of the
situation outside of the state of mind of the worker. I may not express

my anxieties or my annoyance too vividly and originally in putting in the washer or building the fence; if I attempt to express my sentiments I may not do a good job with the washer or the fence. These are practical actions appropriate to the mechanical solutions of the problems.

But in some cases there is room for expressing the way one feels besides doing the appropriate practical acts, and in other cases no appropriate practical acts are known and one expresses the way one feels, believing that what is done is effective, instead of doing something really effective in getting the result desired. The Melanesian who wants his yams to grow may fence them and cultivate them; he may also recite little spells expressive of his desire for a good crop. Tom Sawyer knew how to get rid of warts by putting water from a decaying stump on them while reciting a charm imploring the warts to go away. We call these actions 'magical.' Magic is that activity directed toward accomplishing some special limited end and done in a form which is determined not by the real effectiveness of the act to bring about the result but by the desires and fears and general thinking and feeling of the man who performs them. Magic is practical action in that it is done for a certain limited end, like work; but it is expressive action, and work is not. Magic is characteristically colorful, even dramatic. Magical rites are little pictures of what one wants. One sticks pins into a figure of one's enemy. One sacrifices not just any hen; it must be a black hen. If a problem bothers a deliberating assembly it may appoint a committee; the result may be practically effective, or it may in part just express the concern and desire to do something about the problem; it is then not so different from many acts recognized as magical.

While magic is unusual among expressive forms of action in that it is directed to some limited practical end, like work, other forms of expressive activity are less closely directed to such an end. Play is a familiar case of those expressive acts which are carried on for their own sake. If what is done carries with it no satisfaction from the mere doing of it, it is not play. Play is doing what is fun, and what is done does not have to bring about some immediate useful result. The contributions of play to the operation of society are apart from the immediate goal, which in many cases is put there only as a stimulus to the carrying on of the activity. In 'playing house' and in playing 'cops and robbers' the housekeeping and the criminal-catching are of course only pretenses to provide form and zest to what is done, although the playing may help to develop in children qualities or capacities needed in their later life. In

competitive games the apparent end—the winning of the game—is not a
real accomplishment, as work is; it is there, again, in order to give zest
to what is done; it is there to make the doing important, not the result.
If all one cares about is winning, the play is no longer play.

Art is like play in that it has its justification in itself, not in getting
something done by its means. In art the limitations set around what is
done are not rules for contestants and make-believe goals, as in play; the
limitations that give art its character are the expectations and satisfactions of a technique mastered, a creation made or appreciated. There
are standards, as in play; but in art they are the standards of craftsmanship and the conceptions of the beautiful that prevail in that society and
as they are modified by the creative artist.

Until modern times artist and artisan were thought of as the same.
Art, in general, makes something. If a wall is built, a shoe made, or a
room set in order, in this generous sense of the word, there is a work
of art. Most works of personal making give the maker some scope to
express himself. The expression may be of no particular idea, and there
may be no conscious aesthetic judgment, but there is often expression in
the sense that the imagination shapes and varies and so creates. In so far
as a work made, whether a useful product or not, is ordered to beauty,
it is a work of art in a more limited sense. Where the work is ordered
first for beauty, as in sculpture, painting, or poetry, we nowadays speak
of it as belonging to the 'fine arts.' So far as a made thing is beautiful
it is self-sufficient; it is a delight in itself. As there is no tribe or nation
that has no way of making, as in every case there is some shaping, drawing, or speaking in forms that are for themselves enjoyed beyond the
usefulness of the thing done, so it must be that art makes apparent some
impulse or quality present in all societies of mankind. The relation of
artist to society includes, therefore, the expression he gives to the more
ultimate values and standards of that society. With the priest, and the
thinker, the artist makes known the collective character of a people, and
so unites and directs it by stating its nature and its ideals.

All these forms of expressive action help in the operation of society
by providing opportunities for carrying out the expectations which are
the basis of society and by depicting to its members the related conceptions and ideals. Games involve the ideas and ideals as to sportsmanship
which the society entertains; playing them disciplines player and audi-
ence toward these ideals and tests each player by them. In many primitive societies some games are representations of religious ideas. A game

played by the ancient Maya represented the movement of the divine sun through the heavens; yet the game was sport too. 'Pure art' is a relatively new and unusual conception; in most times and places art is or has been a form for the expression of the religious conceptions, or for the earthly ideas and ideals. The totem poles carved by Indians of the Northwest Coast proclaimed the social position and divine connections of the family connected with the pole.

In ceremony and in mythology the expressive side of life appears in forms plainly related to the persistence of society. A ceremony is a meaningful formal act that signalizes an occasion of special importance. It is a little drama to underline the significance of a person or a moment that is out of the ordinary and that the society wishes to recognize. Some ceremonies are in ancient forms of deep religious meaning, like the Mass; others are unconnected with the church but yet are public and solemn, like the pledge of allegiance before the national flag; still others are domestic matters and not solemn at all, like the merry little ceremonies of a birthday party. All of them are representations of beliefs that the people hold; they are ways in which people together show that they care about something. Although not every society has well-developed myths and also well-developed ceremonies, myths are the stories that correspond to the ceremonies. Myths are ways in which the institutions and expectations of the society are emphasized and made dramatic and persuasive in narrative form. Myths show that what a people has to enjoy or endure is right and true—true to the sentiments the people hold. It does not so much matter whether or not little George Washington really cut down the cherry tree and told his father about it; what matters is that the story expresses some ideas the tellers had about telling the truth when it goes against you. The religious myths are true to the moral and sacred ideas that inspire them; they need not be true as legal evidence must be true. Myths and ceremonies, like much of art and some of play, are collective and traditional forms in which the people of a society remind themselves of what matters to them and why it matters. They are gestures made by a people to itself. Work and sanctions alone do not suffice to keep a society in operation. It is also needful that the tendencies of people to leap, move, shape, and tell fall into representations that satisfy and intensify the conceptions which, held in common, make that people a society.

This chapter suggests some of the answers to the question expressed in its title: How does a human society operate? In its first pages the answer given was that a society is kept in operation by arrangements whereby a number of people can do the work that needs to be done to keep them going and whereby they can feel that they belong together and share a kind of life which they believe to be good. There is a world of necessity into which people are born; to survive they must live together; to live together they must have tacit agreements as to who does what, and is what. They must, in short, regulate their common life. The regulation is a matter of conventional understandings partly as to what each one should do, and partly as to what is, generally and for everybody, the good life. The plan of the good life finds expression, it was then added, in religion, myth, and art. We can think of the operation of society as machinery for social control and also as a sort of charter or drama of a scheme of all things.

But there is another way to think of the operation of society that is, probably, implicit in what has been written here. We may also think of society as operating so as to realize impulses and meet needs of human beings. Instead of asking, as we have, What operations keep this society going? we can ask, What is there about society that keeps human beings going? Any human being must have protection and food, and we can see society as providing for these necessities. Human beings have also sexual demands or needs, and every society provides some arrangement for meeting these. Moreover, beyond this, human beings have characteristics that are not shared with the animals but are peculiarly human. The foregoing discussion of the 'Expressive Life' rests on the assumption that there is an 'impulse of the individual to be active,' that it is the nature of human nature to use the imagination and to shape things that please themselves. While it is perhaps not possible very definitely to describe the human impulses and needs beyond those that are shared with animals, it is hardly possible to deny that there are some; and society may thus be seen as a way of providing for the development and expression in everyone of human nature. In this sense, society operates by doing for us what our natures, given society, demand.

LIST OF SUGGESTED READINGS

Benedict, Ruth
    Patterns of Culture. Houghton Mifflin Co., Boston, 1934.
        An outstanding exposition of the concept of patterns in culture, written with lucidity.

Bennett, Wendell C., and Junius B. Bird
    Andean Culture History. Handbook Series No. 15, American Museum of Natural History, New York, 1949.
        The most recent résumé now available for the civilizations of the Andean area.

Boas, Franz
    Primitive Art. Instituttet for Sammenlignende Kulturforskning Series B: Skrifter VIII. H. Aschehoug and Co., Oslo, 1927.
        One of the outstanding books on this subject. Especially valuable for its analytical treatment of the subject.

    The Mind of Primitive Man. Revised edition. The Macmillan Company, New York, 1938.
        Although the original edition appeared over a generation ago, this is a book that still has great vitality and in particular represents a landmark in the development of anthropology.

Childe, V. Gordon
    Man Makes Himself. Library of Science and Culture No. 5, Watts and Co., London, 1936 (also: New American Library, New York, 1951).

    What Happened in History. Penguin Books, New York, 1942. (Reprinted in 1943, 1946, 1948.)
        The author is a generally acknowledged authority on European prehistory and has in these books infused considerable life and vigor into the study of the remains of early cultures. Perhaps the best introductions for this complex subject.

Clark, W. E. LeGros
    History of the Primates. An introduction to the study of fossil man. 2nd edition. British Museum (Natural History), London, 1950.

An extremely useful, although brief, account of primate and human evolution. It includes the recent fossil discoveries.

The Fossil Evidence for Human Evolution. An introduction to the study of paleoanthropology. The Scientist's Library. Biology and Medicine. University of Chicago Press, Chicago, 1955.
An admirable exposition of the methods employed in studying human evolution.

Dobzhansky, Theodosius
Genetics and the Origin of Species. Third edition, revised. Columbia Biological Series, No. XI, Columbia University Press, New York, 1951.
Much of the modern orientation on race formation is based on biological processes developed in this book.

Forde, C. Daryll
Habitat, Economy and Society. A geographical introduction to ethnology. Methuen and Co., Ltd., London, 1934.
An excellent survey of the various types of primitive economy that relates their characteristics to physical environment and to levels of social organization.

Griffin, James B., editor
Archeology of Eastern United States. University of Chicago Press, Chicago, 1952.
A comprehensive survey of the archaeology of the major part of the United States, the various sections of which were written by well known authorities.

Herskovits, Melville J.
Economic Anthropology. A study in comparative economics. Alfred A. Knopf, New York, 1952.
A scholarly and erudite description of the economic life of primitive people.

Honigmann, John J.
Culture and Personality. Harper and Brothers, New York, 1954.
The complex interrelationship of personality and culture has become a subject of active research in anthropology. Honigmann has summarized in this book many of the aspects of the current research.

Howells, William W.
The Heathens. Primitive man and his religions. Doubleday and Co., Inc., Garden City, 1948.
A lively description of the religious life of primitive peoples. This is one of the few general books available.

Linton, Ralph
The Tree of Culture. Alfred A. Knopf, New York, 1955.
In this book the reader is presented on a broad canvas a picture of the way in which human culture has evolved. The erudition and skill of the author more than compensate for the few instances of debatable generalization.

Lowie, Robert H.
History of Ethnological Theory. Farrar and Rinehart, Inc., New York, 1937.
This résumé of ethnological theory is valuable for its clear presentation of the conceptual framework within which anthropologists have worked.

McGregor, John C.
> *Southwestern Archaeology.* John Wiley and Sons, Inc., New York, 1941.
> Southwestern archaeology is in many ways a classic example of what can be achieved by modern, scientific methods. This book provides an excellent coverage of the various aspects of the subject.

Murdock, George Peter
> *Our Primitive Contemporaries.* The Macmillan Company, New York, 1935.
> A book very useful for the brief portraits of the culture of a variety of people.

> *Social Structure.* The Macmillan Company, New York, 1949.
> An important contribution to our understanding of social structure.

Redfield, Robert
> *The Folk Culture of Yucatán.* University of Chicago Publications in Anthropology, Social Anthropology Series. University of Chicago Press, Chicago, 1941.
> The study of folk cultures by anthropologists is relatively recent and Redfield has been one of its principal exponents. This book provides an excellent introduction to that field.

Sayce, R. U.
> *Primitive Arts and Crafts.* An introduction to the study of material culture. The University Press, Cambridge, 1933.
> A succinct guide to the study of material culture.

Underhill, Ruth Murray
> *Red Man's America.* A history of Indians in the United States. University of Chicago Press, Chicago, 1953.
> A valuable successor to Wissler's earlier treatment of the same subject. Dr. Underhill deals with the cultures of the American Indians in the light of recent scholarship.

Vaillant, George C.
> *The Aztecs of Mexico.* Origin, rise and fall of the Aztec Nation. Penguin Books, Harmondsworth, 1950 (also: American Museum of Natural History Science Series, Vol. 2, Doubleday, Doran and Co., Inc., Garden City, 1941).
> As an example of one of the indigenous civilizations of the New World, the Aztecs are noteworthy and rich in documentation. Vaillant's account is the best general summary.

GALAXY BOOKS

HESPERIDES BOOKS